Continued from previous page

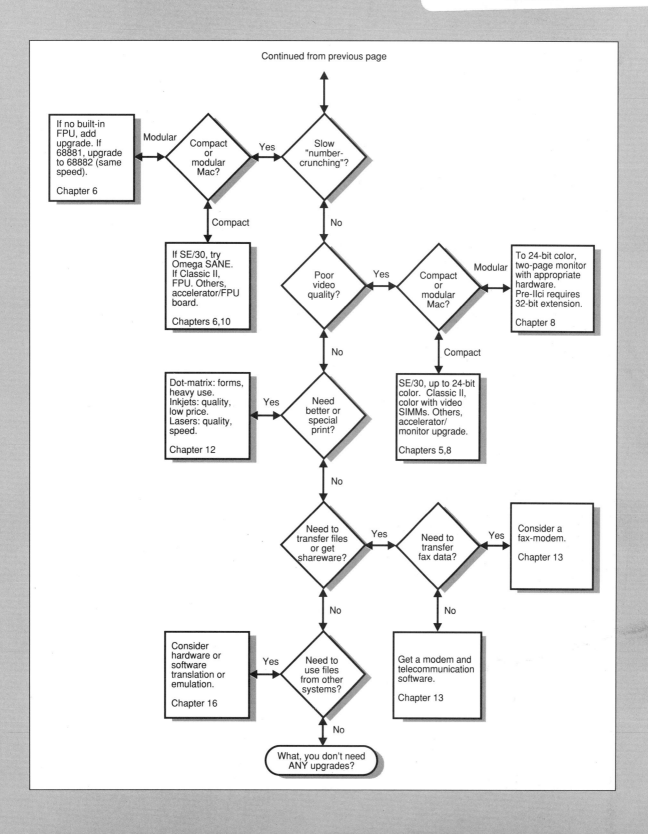

If no built-in FPU, add upgrade. If 68881, upgrade to 68882 (same speed).

Chapter 6

Modular ← **Compact or modular Mac?** → Yes → **Slow "number-crunching"?**

Compact ↓

If SE/30, try Omega SANE. If Classic II, FPU. Others, accelerator/FPU board.

Chapters 6,10

No ↓

Poor video quality? → Yes → **Compact or modular Mac?** → Modular → **To 24-bit color, two-page monitor with appropriate hardware. Pre-IIci requires 32-bit extension.**

Chapter 8

Compact ↓

SE/30, up to 24-bit color. Classic II, color with video SIMMs. Others, accelerator/ monitor upgrade.

Chapters 5,8

No ↓

Dot-matrix: forms, heavy use. Inkjets: quality, low price. Lasers: quality, speed.

Chapter 12

← Yes — **Need better or special print?**

No ↓

Need to transfer files or get shareware? → Yes → **Need to transfer fax data?** → Yes → **Consider a fax-modem.**

Chapter 13

No ↓

Consider hardware or software translation or emulation.

Chapter 16

← Yes — **Need to use files from other systems?**

No ↓

Get a modem and telecommunication software.

Chapter 13

What, you don't need ANY upgrades?

Books that Work Just Like Your Mac

As a Macintosh user, you enjoy unique advantages. You enjoy a dynamic user environment. You enjoy the successful integration of graphics, sound, and text. Above all, you enjoy a computer that's fun and easy to use.

When your computer gives you all this, why accept less in your computer books?

At SYBEX, we don't believe you should. That's why we've committed ourselves to publishing the highest quality computer books for Macintosh users. Externally, our books emulate the Mac "look and feel," with powerful, appealing illustrations and easy-to-read pages. Internally, our books stress "why" over "how," so you'll learn concepts, not sequences of steps. Philosophically, our books are designed to help you get work done, not to teach you about computers.

In short, our books are fun and easy to use—just like the Mac. We hope you find them just as enjoyable.

For a complete catalog of our publications:

SYBEX Inc.
2021 Challenger Drive, Alameda, CA 94501
Tel: (510) 523-8233/(800) 227-2346 Telex: 336311
Fax: (510) 523-2373

SYBEX

The Macintosh
Do-It-Yourself Upgrade Book

The Macintosh® Do-It-Yourself Upgrade Book

GARRY HOWARD

SYBEX ®

San Francisco • Paris • Düsseldorf • Soest

Acquisitions Editor: Dianne King
Developmental Editor: Kenyon Brown
Editor: Barnard David Sherman
Project Editor: Kathleen Lattinville
Technical Editor: Sheldon M. Dunn
Word Processors: Chris Meredith and Ann Dunn
Book Design and Chapter Art: Charlotte Carter
Technical Art: Rick van Genderen
Computer Graphics Artist: John Corrigan
Desktop Publishing Specialist: Thomas Goudie
Proofreader/Production Assistant: Elisabeth Dahl
Indexer: Matthew Spence
Cover Designer: Ingalls + Associates
Cover Illustrator: Max Seabaugh

Library of Congress Card Number: 92-82606
ISBN: 0-7821-1123-8

Manufactured in the United States of America
10 9 8 7 6 5 4 3 2 1

I'd like to dedicate this book to my wife, Lynne, and my daughters, Kristen, Diana, and Melanie.

Acknowledgments...

I would like to acknowledge the following for their contributions of hardware, information, and advice to this book:

Ken Brown and Kathleen Lattinville at SYBEX

David Sherman

Sheldon (Mac) Dunn

Steve O'Grady, Renzo Costa, Tim Shilson, and the good folks at the Calgary Apple Corps

Glen Boyd and Steve Hellyer at Apple Canada

Julie Rusciolelli at National Public Relations

Patrick Rouble at NewLife Computer Corporation

Tom Burke at Envisio Incorporated

David Methven at DayStar Digital

Linda Smith at Novy Systems/Systech

Rebecca Smith at SuperMac Technology

Marilyn Jordan at Supra Corporation

Kensington MicroWare

Aztech Micro Solutions, Incorporated

Outbound Systems, Incorporated

... at a Glance

Table of Contents

Chapter Eight

Monitors   202

Introduction

One of the most amazing aspects of the Mac is its upgradeability. Most Mac setups have dozens of different upgrade possibilities—and most of these upgrades are relatively easy to do.

This book spells out all your Mac upgrade options—including, I'd bet, at least a few you hadn't known about before. And if doing the upgrade yourself appeals to you, this book tries to make it as easy as possible.

I've noticed that too many do-it-yourself guides cover the key steps, but leave out a critical precaution here or a helpful detail there—information that when neglected can spell disaster for the project. I've tried to avoid that. I've covered every important point, no matter how seemingly minor, that you need to know.

I've included numerous pictures and schematics to help you as you do the upgrade. In many cases, you'll be able to refer to them while you're working on your machine. I've also summarized large bodies of information in tables.

A few sections, for example the early parts of Chapters 1 and 7, go into more technical background than most upgrade books do. Understanding in more detail how your Mac works will help you with your upgrade decisions. However, if you *don't* find these sections interesting, feel free to skip them and go to the more practical parts.

In fact, I've tried to keep this book as flexible as possible. You can identify your needs and go right to the section that interests you, or you can read the book from cover to cover. If you do read it straight through, you'll notice that I sometimes repeat information. That's to accommodate readers who read it "modularly."

HOW THIS BOOK IS ORGANIZED

Chapter 1 provides technical background about the Mac and an overview of the Macintosh line. Some readers may want to start with Chapter 2, which details a number of upgrade options.

Based on these chapters, you can check out vendors—be careful to consider quality and price. When you've compared products and settled on the perfect choice, the rest of the book shows you how to actually do the upgrade.

Chapter 3 shows you how to safely "crack the case" on your compact, modular, or portable Mac. The chapter will also help you build the simple toolkit necessary to do most upgrades.

Each of the chapters thereafter details a different type of upgrade and explains how to install it on your system. Chapter 4 describes how to configure your Mac and install different combinations of SIMMs (single inline memory modules), the memory expansion boards used by all Macs since the Plus.

Chapter 5 covers the addition of accelerators, hardware cards that increase the operating speed of your Mac. Chapter 6 goes through the addition of coprocessors—chips that take over certain functions from your Mac CPU—and cache cards, which speed up Macs by a technique known as hardware caching. Chapter 7 covers installation of internal and external floppy and hard drives, and the addition of CD-ROMs, cartridge hard drives, and "floptical" drives. I'll also describe how to "build-it-yourself" for those hardy souls who always wanted to build an external hard drive. Chapter 8 describes how to install large-screen external monochrome, grayscale, and color monitors. Chapter 9 evaluates different input devices—alternative keyboards, trackballs, mice, and graphics tablets. Chapter 10 provides some "software upgrade" ideas. Software upgrades let you enhance your system without going to the time and expense of a complete hardware upgrade. Chapter 11 covers "hardware packaging" of Macintosh logic boards ("the guts") and discusses Apple CPU upgrades.

Chapter 12 offers suggestions for upgrading or adding a printer. The Mac has outstanding graphics and publishing capabilities, but without the right output device, you'll never appreciate on paper what you see on screen. Telecommunications standards, modems, fax modems, and how to choose them are covered in Chapter 13. Chapter 14 covers networking, the hot topic of the 90s. The chapter gives some tips on how to set up a small or full-blown local area network.

Modern Macs are not just graphics machines, and the introduction of QuickTime makes the integration of animation and sound easier than ever. Chapter 15 covers Macintosh sound, music, and multimedia. Hardware and software emulators, discussed in Chapter 16, allow the Mac to use software written for other machines. In Chapter 17, I'll provide some troubleshooting aids, advice, help, and references.

Finally, I've included four appendices: vendor addresses, Mac error codes, a glossary, and a troubleshooting guide.

Once again, I've tried to design this book to give you a lot of flexibility. Have a look, decide what you want to do, and enjoy!

CHAPTER ONE

So You Want to Upgrade Your Mac...

When

you buy a Macintosh, it's hard not to be impressed with how easy the machine is to use and how smoothly applications work together. Eventually, though, you will want more. You'll find yourself longing for more memory, a faster processor, a bigger and faster hard drive, a larger screen, a CD-ROM player, and other goodies.

Whether you're a new user or a hardened hardware hacker, this book will show you a path to higher Mac performance. If you're comfortable with "cracking the case," you can supercharge your machine with high-powered hardware at a low-ball price. If you like the idea of a hardware upgrade but are squeamish about getting into your Mac, you can use the book as a source of hardware enhancement suggestions and let a good local technician do the installation. Finally, if the idea of adding internal hardware to your Mac gives you the shakes, you can use the book for ideas on software and external hardware enhancements, and on new and used Mac hardware purchases.

A Word about Words The classification I've used for various Macintosh models is based on industry usage wherever possible. This led me to select the term *modular Macintosh* for any Mac that consists of a separate system unit or *CPU* (central processing unit) and monitor. Macintoshes with a built-in monochrome monitor, such as the Plus, are called *compact Macs* throughout the book. I'll be referring to Apple's first portable Macintosh as the *original Portable* and the new portable machines as the *new Portables* or *PowerBooks*.

This chapter reviews the Mac family and takes you through some sample upgrade decisions. But first, I want to tell you about the core of your Mac, its CPU. The discussion is a bit technical, but it's important background for a serious upgrade job, and I think you'll find it interesting, too.

CENTRAL PROCESSING UNITS—THE BRAINS OF THE OUTFIT

Central processing units are chips that control the operation of all aspects of a computer. When the Macintosh was born, Apple decided to go with a CPU called the 68000, from Motorola Corporation. Apple has continued with the 680X0 series (68020, 68030, and 68040) to date, but will be using a new chip built by Motorola (under a license from IBM) called the *PowerPC* in future Macs.

How CPUs Are "Packaged"

The Motorola 68000 chip in pre-Classic Macs is called a *DIP*, or dual inline package. It is a long plastic chip with pins running down each side. The original 68000 has 64 pins and is "notched" on one end. The notch indicates the orientation of the pins on the chip.

All of the chips on your Mac's main circuit board (called the *logic board*) are marked to indicate the orientation. You should note the orientation if you remove and reinsert them, to prevent nasty occurrences like fried logic boards!

The pins on the DIP 68000 pass through the logic board and are soldered in, so orientation is not a problem here. The 68000 in the Mac Classic is a square chip and has "legs" around the edges. These legs are designed to be soldered to pads on the surface of the Classic logic board. This kind of chip is an *SMD*, or surface-mount device. Because the Mac Plus and earlier machines, as well as the newer Classic, have their CPUs soldered to the Mac logic board, easy removal and access to the chip socket is not an option. Therefore, upgrade devices are generally clipped to the CPU. Some folks call these *clip-on Macs*.

The Mac SE and SE/30 introduced the "SE slot," an internal expansion slot that's attached directly to the CPU bus, giving expansion boards a fast, powerful access route to the CPU without resorting to a clip. A similar slot on modular Macs is called a *PDS*, or processor direct slot.

More powerful 68020, 68030, and 68040 chips used in the SE/30, Classic II, and the modular Macs come in *PGA*, or pin grid array packages. These chips have multiple rows of pins around the edges, making them interesting (even challenging) to insert or remove. The more complex structure and data path of these chips necessitates the extra pins.

 Once again, if you remove these CPUs, please, please, PLEASE note the orientation markings on the chip. Make a sketch if necessary and *make sure* that you reinsert the chip the right way!

The Mac II has no PDS slot, but has a socketed CPU that can be removed to add devices like accelerator boards. Newer CPUs are surface mounted and have a PDS slot, which means you don't have to remove the CPU to add devices—you just use the PDS slot. This gives the PDS slot approach an advantage—you don't have to remove a large, potentially fragile CPU. (Either approach gives a solid connection, though, and should cause no problems.) The 68020 chip used in the Mac II is socketed and must be removed, while the 68020 in the LC is surface mounted. The 68030 in the IIx and IIcx is socketed, but in the IIci and later modular Macs, it is once again surface mounted.

The surface-mount 68030 chip in the Mac Classic II has no processor direct slot and the pins on the CPU are too close to allow a clip-on adapter to be attached. The Classic II has other expansion slots—maybe some enterprising hardware vendor will come up with a way to add an accelerator via one of these.

Chip Internal "Architecture"

The 68000 is a 16/32-bit chip. This means that while the CPU's internal bus is 32 bits "wide," its external bus is only 16 bits wide. A bus is a number of conductors simultaneously carrying electronic signals. The 68000 CPU has data and address buses, your machine's SCSI chain is a bus, and modular Macs accept expansion cards in slots connected by NuBus. Anyway, the difference between the 68000's 32 internal registers and 16 external data bus lines creates a bottleneck for data, insuring that the 68000 can't run as quickly as chips with a full 32-bit bus.

The internal *registers* store addresses where data is located in a computer's memory and receive instructions for execution by the CPU. While the 68000 has 32-bit address registers, it only uses 24 of them. Because computers operate under the binary system, 24 bit addresses can access up to $2^{24}/1,024,000=16MB$ of memory. Classics and pre-Classic Macs only take advantage of 4MB of this.

The 68020 chip in the Mac II and LC is a full 32-bit processor, making it substantially faster than the 68000. The full 32-bit addresses also allow the chip to access up to 4 gigabytes (4×10^9 bytes of memory), although the Mac II and LC hardware won't handle this kind of memory. The 68020 chip has an on-board 256-byte cache that stores often-used instructions. When this cached information is used by the processor, in what's called a "cache hit," the processor doesn't have to go out to the slow system memory and can operate much more quickly.

System 7 and Unix use something called *virtual memory*, where disk space is used as system memory. The 68020 chip can use virtual memory, but only if it's equipped with an external *PMMU*, or paged memory management unit. You can easily upgrade a Mac II by adding a PMMU, but the Mac LC doesn't have a socket for this chip.

All of the new Macs with the exception of Quadras use the Motorola 68030 chip, which has a 32-bit data bus, a built-in PMMU, 256-byte instruction, *and* 256-byte data caches. It operates significantly faster than the 68020.

The Mac IIci included a feature not copied by any other Macintosh—a cache memory slot. The cache slot allows you to accelerate the IIci to near Mac IIfx speeds by expanding the 68030 chip's internal cache memory. To do this, the cache memory board has to use ultra-fast, and ultra-expensive, *static RAM* chips.

The new Macintosh Quadras, and some accelerator boards, sport the new 68040 chip. The 68040 has 4K data and instruction caches, a built-in PMMU, a partially implemented *numeric coprocessor*, and a 32-bit data bus. It's optimized for fast processing speed through a technique called *pipelining*. The 68040 is the fastest Mac processor. Its only problem is that some existing applications are incompatible with its caches. To get around this, you can use software utilities that let you turn off the 68040's internal caches.

Number Crunchers—Numeric Co-Whats?

Macintosh models prior to the Quadras use a chip called a numeric coprocessor or floating point unit (FPU) to speed math calculations, especially complicated transcendental functions (trigonometric, logarithmic, and natural log calculations) and floating point math. The model number of the first Mac numeric coprocessor is 68881, and of the current coprocessor is 68882.

The effect of numeric coprocessors will be most obvious when using draw programs, rendering programs, complex spreadsheet models, and the like, where they can double or triple processing speed.

A number of Macs, including the SE/30 and IIci, have a numeric coprocessor built in. The Classic II has a dedicated slot where an FPU can be added. Quadras have numeric coprocessor operations built into their CPUs and ROMs.

What's Clock Speed Anyway?

For a 680X0 to follow an instruction, it must execute a number of well-timed actions. These actions are timed by an oscillator chip. The speed of the oscillator is measured in a unit called megaHertz (MHz), which means millions of *clock cycles* per second. The speed of a processor instruction is measured by how many clock cycles it requires. Simple instructions can take as little as two or three clock cycles, while complex instructions require five cycles or more. CPUs with faster oscillators can execute more instructions per second.

Some folks tend to interpret clock speed a little too literally. A 16MHz 68000 chip is *not* as fast as a 16MHz 68030 (not even close, as a matter of fact). The larger bus and internal caches in the '030 have a greater effect than processor speed. Both the SE/30 and Classic II have a 16MHz 68030 processor, but the Classic II CPU is forced to feed its instructions and data into a 16-bit bus, slowing it to about 30% below the SE/30's speed.

Accelerator boards work their magic by replacing a Mac's CPU with a chip clocked at a faster speed. The boards often add an FPU as well, providing a performance boost for applications with a lot of numeric processing.

CLASSES OF MACS

Apple has come a long way since Steve Jobs introduced the original Mac. The Classic, LC, IIsi shown in Figure 1.1, and most recently the Classic II and LC II have made Macintosh computing affordable. To date, there are three main classes and some 23 models of Macs (including the "Mac XL" or Lisa). The hardware features of most of these machines are summarized in Table 1.1.

FIGURE 1.1:   Three modern Macs: the Classic, LC, and IIsi (photo courtesy of Apple Computer)

The Compact Macs

First, there were the *compact Macs*, including the original 128K Mac and its descendents, the 512, 512KE, Mac Plus, SE, SE/30 and the newer Classic and Classic II. The 128 and 512 Macs were ground-breaking machines, with their built-in graphics toolbox, innovative graphic operating system, 3½" 400K floppy drives, and sharp "paper-white" built-in monitor. It's still possible to upgrade these now somewhat antiquated Macs to approach the performance of a modern machine, but the economics of the upgrade may be tight. 512KE Macs are the best bets for an upgrade because of their built-in 800K 3½" floppy drive.

The Mac Plus gave Apple instant credibility in the workplace because of its built-in *SCSI* (small computer systems interface) port and memory expansion of up to 4MB. The SCSI port finally gave the Mac access to up to seven hard drives or other peripherals *daisy-chained* to the SCSI bus. Unfortunately, the Plus is also showing its age. Large modern applications run slowly on the machine, and the SCSI port, with a maximum transfer rate of 600MB/sec, is slow by today's standards. The Plus introduced "mini-DIN 8" serial connectors to the Macintosh. The small, round 8-pin connectors were necessary to save space on the back of the crowded Mac case. Keyboards for the Mac Plus and earlier Macs use the RJ-11 (modular telephone jack) interface.

The Mac SE and SE/30 are high-performance computers, able to mount a hard drive and up to two 1.44MB floppy drives (with the high-density floppy upgrade) in the case. These machines introduced the first PDS slots, allowing easy, safe internal expansion. The machines have enough SIMM slots to mount up to 4MB of memory in the SE and 32MB or more in the SE/30 (with the Mode32 software patch). Both machines use the same mini-DIN 8 serial connectors that the Mac Plus uses. In addition, the SE and SE/30 both have a new feature, the Apple Desktop Bus (ADB). The ADB has a lot of similarities to the

Enclosed Macs

MODEL	PROCESSOR	MEMORY	VIDEO	SLOTS	SCSI	PORTS
Lisa/Mac XL	8MHz 68000	512K	Mono, 512 × 342	4 Sys.	No	Mouse, Keyboard, 2 Serial, Video
Mac 128	8MHz 68000	128K	Mono, 512 × 342	0	No	Serial, Disk, Mouse, Keyboard
Mac 512	8MHz 68000	512K	Mono, 512 × 342	0	No	Serial, Sound, Disk, Mouse, Keyboard
Mac 512KE	8MHz 68000	512K	Mono, 512 × 342	0	No	2 Serial, Sound, Disk, Mouse, Keyboard
Mac Plus	8MHz 68000	1MB (4MB max.)	Mono, 512 × 342	0	Yes	2 Serial, Sound, Disk, Mouse, Keyboard
Mac SE	8MHz 68000	1MB (4MB max.)	Mono, 512 × 342	1 PDS	Yes	2 Serial, Disk, 2 ADB, Sound
Mac SE/30	16MHz 68030	2MB (32MB max. with Mode 32)	Mono, 512 × 342	1 PDS (>1MB/sec)	Yes	2 Serial, Disk, 2 ADB, Stereo
Classic	8MHz 68000	1MB (4MB max.)	Mono, 512 × 342	1 Memory	Yes	2 Serial, Disk, ADB, Sound
Classic II	16MHz 68030	2MB (10MB max.)	Mono, 512 × 342	1 FPU	Yes (>1MB/sec)	2 Serial, Disk, ADB, Sound In/Out

TABLE 1.1: Macintosh Models

Modular Macs

MODEL	PROCESSOR	MEMORY	VIDEO	SLOTS	SCSI	PORTS
Mac LC	16MHz 68020	2MB (10MB max.)	Built-in 8/16-bit color/gray.	1 PDS	Yes (>1MB/sec)	2 Serial, Video, ADB, Sound In/Out
Mac LC II	16MHz 68030	4MB (10MB max.)	Built-in 8/16-bit color/gray.	1 PDS	Yes (>1MB/sec)	2 Serial, Video, ADB, Sound In/Out
Mac II	16MHz 68020	1MB (32MB+ max. with Mode32)	To 24-bit color (with exp. card)	6 NuBus	Yes (>1MB/sec)	2 Serial, 2 ADB, Stereo
Mac IIx	16MHz 68030	4MB (32MB+ max. with Mode32)	To 24-bit color (with exp. card)	6 NuBus	Yes (>1MB/sec)	2 Serial, 2 ADB, Stereo
Mac IIcx	16MHz 68030	1MB+ (32MB+ max. with Mode32)	To 24-bit color (with exp. card)	3 NuBus	Yes (>1MB/sec)	2 Serial, Disk, 2 ADB, Stereo
Mac IIci	25MHz 68030	5MB+ (32MB+ max)	Built-in 8-bit color	3 NuBus, Cache	Yes (2MB/sec)	2 Serial, Disk, 2 ADB, Stereo
Mac IIsi	20MHz 68030	2MB (32MB+ max.)	Built-in 4/8-bit color	PDS or NuBus	Yes (2MB/sec)	2 Serial, Disk, ADB, Sound In, Stereo
Mac IIfx	40MHz 68030	4MB (32MB+ max.)	To 24-bit color (with exp. card)	6 NuBus, 1 PDS	Yes (>1MB/sec)	2 Serial, 2 ADB, Stereo
Quadra 700	25MHz 68040	4MB (20MB+ max.)	Built-in—to 24-bit	1 PDS, Up to 2 NuBus	Yes (5MB/sec)	2 Serial, Ethernet, 1 ADB, Video, Stereo

TABLE 1.1:   Macintosh Models (continued)

MODEL	PROCESSOR	MEMORY	VIDEO	SLOTS	SCSI	PORTS
Quadra 900	25MHz 68040	4MB (64MB+ max.)	Built-in—to 24-bit	1 PDS, Up to 5 NuBus	Yes (>5MB/sec)	2 Serial, Ethernet, 1 ADB, Video, Stereo
Quadra 950	33MHz 68040	4MB (64MB+ max.)	Built-in to 16-bit on 21" monitor	1 PDS, Up to 5 NuBus	Yes (>5MB/sec)	2 Serial, EtherNet, 1 ADB, Video, Stereo
Mac Portables						
Original Mac Portable	16MHz 68000	2MB (9MB max.)	Active Matrix, 640 × 400	PDS, RAM, ROM, Modem	Yes	2 Serial, Disk, ADB, Sound
PowerBook100	16MHz 68000	2MB (8MB max.)	LCD, 640 × 400	Modem, RAM	Yes (<1MB/sec)	Serial, Disk, ADB, Sound
PowerBook140	16MHz 68030	2MB (8MB max.)	LCD, 640 × 400	Modem, RAM	Yes (>1MB/sec)	2 Serial, ADB, Sound In/Out
PowerBook170	25MHz 68030	4MB (8MB Max.)	LCD, 640 × 400	Modem, RAM	Yes (>1MB/sec)	2 Serial, ADB, Sound In/Out, Telecom.

TABLE 1.1: Macintosh Models (continued)

Macintosh's SCSI port—there's a dedicated ADB controller, and a number of different devices can be connected on an ADB chain. Unlike SCSI, however, ADB is a parallel interface. There are two ADB connectors on the back of the SE and SE/30. The SE/30 comes with a 16MHz 68030 processor on a full 32-bit bus, as well as a 68882 numeric coprocessor. Both machines are *outstanding* secondhand purchase or upgrade candidates.

Apple's newest compact Macs, the Classic and Classic II, are throwbacks to the Plus and earlier Macs. Built for easy assembly and low price, these machines lack the quality and expandability of the SE and SE/30. The Classic is as fast as an SE and normally comes with 2MB of memory, a 40MB hard drive, and a keyboard. It has 1MB of memory on the logic board, and a memory expansion slot that lets you add up to 3MB of additional memory. It has no internal PDS slot and can be enhanced only by a clip-on adapter over the CPU or a special card for the memory slot.

The Classic II has a 16MHz 68030 processor, but it's on a 16-bit bus, so it lacks the speed of the SE/30. The II has no FPU but does have an FPU/RAM slot. It also has SIMM slots, and will support memory expansion up to 10MB. The II has Mac LC ROMs, so it's capable of driving a color display.

Upgrading Your Compact Mac

Steve Job's concept of an "information appliance" didn't involve opening the compact Mac case for internal expansion. As a result, any internal expansion of compact Macs involves "cracking the case."

While opening a compact Mac requires some care, it's not a difficult job. And the newer models' internal expansion slots make upgrading easier. Logic board upgrades are available to take an SE to an SE/30 and a Classic to a Classic II.

One tip: older Macs with an upgrade should be well-ventilated or have an internal fan installed.

Mac upgrades that use a Killy clip over the CPU (central processing unit) chip should be treated gently to prevent the clip from loosening up.

Aside from these and other normal cautions, expansion of a compact Mac does not pose undue risk to the machine and can be done by any reasonably handy hobbyist.

Modular Macs

The next step up on the Macintosh evolutionary ladder is occupied by modular Macs. These consist of a CPU with expansion slots and a separate external monitor. Apple's modular line includes the LC, Mac II, IIx, IIsi, IIcx, IIci, IIfx, and the Quadra 700, 900, and 950 (Figure 1.2).

The Mac II was the first modular, slotted Macintosh. It is equipped with six slots that use the NuBus standard supported by Apple and has a 16MHz Motorola 68020 CPU and a 68881 FPU. The machine supports a 5¼" hard drive and up to two 800K floppy drives.

Apple's other six-slot Macs are the IIx and IIfx. The IIx added a 16MHz 68030 CPU, a 68882 FPU, and a 1.44MB floppy drive. The IIfx, the latest six-slot modular Macintosh II, comes with a 40MHz 68030 processor, a 68882 FPU, a PDS slot, and what was meant to be a high-speed DMA (direct memory access) SCSI chip, though the SCSI controller chip in the IIfx never achieved its full potential.

The Macintosh IIcx was the first of the "small-footprint" three-slot modular Macs and came with the same features as the IIx in a cheaper, more compact machine. The IIci adds a fast 25MHz 68030, built-in 8-bit video, and a cache slot.

The IIci is one of *the* most popular modular Macs ever built and offers the best dollar value of any model.

The Quadra 700 is a three-slot modular Mac with a 68040 25MHz CPU and on board video expansion to 24 bits using *VRAM* (video memory). A Mac IIci-to-Quadra 700 upgrade should be available by the time you read this.

In a drive to reduce Macintosh prices while maintaining performance, Apple introduced the Mac LC, LC II, and IIsi. These are all one-slot modular Macs and are somewhat limited in their potential. The single slot in all three machines is a PDS. None of the three machines offers an FPU but one can be added, often as part of a multifunction slot adapter card. The LC and LC II have 16MHz 68020 and 68030 processors, respectively, feeding into a 16-bit bus. This limits 68030 performance—there is virtually no difference in performance between the two machines. The LCs are limited to 10MB of memory expansion, and can be upgraded from 8-bit to 16-bit video with the addition of VRAM. The Mac IIsi has a 20MHz 68030 chip, a fast SCSI controller, and memory expansion potential up to 17MB. This package makes the IIsi a decent, if not spectacular, performer.

FIGURE 1.2:   The Quadra 900, one of the most powerful Macintoshes (photo courtesy of Apple Computer)

As I write this, the modular Macintoshes at the performance pinnacle are the Quadra 900 and 950. Apple has finally done it right and produced machines with 25MHz (900) and 33MHz (950) 68040 processors, a PDS slot, up to five NuBus slots if the PDS slot is not used, up to 256 megabytes of memory expansion, and dual SCSI buses supporting the SCSI-2 standard and true DMA for up to 14 devices. The Quadra's SCSI bus, properly used, is capable of transferring data at up to 8MB/sec.

Upgrading Your Modular Mac

Modular Macs are easy to upgrade. The case lid is designed to be removed, so installing an expansion board, chip, or *SIMMs* (single inline memory modules) in existing slots or sockets is straightforward. Logic board swaps are available for the Mac II to the IIx and IIfx, the IIcx to the IIci, the IIci to the Quadra 700, and the Quadra 900 to the 950.

Apple Portables

The final members of the Macintosh family spearhead Apple's entry into the hot portable and notebook market. These Macs include the original Mac Portable and the PowerBook 100, 140, and 170 (Figure 1.3). Like all recent Macs, Apple's portables have expansion slots to make enhancements easier.

Apple's original Portable was a superbly engineered machine that unfortunately weighed in a little too heavy to be truly portable. The original Portable has a 16MHz 68000 CPU, PDS, ROM, RAM, and modem slots, and supports up to 9MB of memory expansion. The case is easy to open and the slots are easy to get to.

Apple's PowerBook 100, 140, and 170 are true lightweight portables. The 100 has a 16MHz 68000 CPU, internal slots for up to 8MB of memory expansion and a modem, a backlit supertwist LCD screen, and external 1.44MB floppy and internal 20MB hard disk drives. A system adapter allows the 100 to act as an external hard drive for data transfer to and from other machines.

Like the 100, the PowerBook 140 and 170 can be expanded to 8MB of memory. The 140 and 170 use a 16MHz and 25MHz 68030 CPU, respectively. Both machines have internal 1.44MB floppy and 20 or 40MB hard disk drives. They can handle color if you add adapters. The 170 has a 68882 FPU and an active-matrix LCD screen like the original Mac Portable.

FIGURE 1.3:   Apple's PowerBooks—finally, Macs to go (photo courtesy of Apple Computer)

DECISIONS, DECISIONS

When you've made the decision to enhance your compact, modular, or portable Macintosh, you'll want to decide just how to go about it. Chapter 2 provides details on different types of Macintosh upgrades to aid you in this choice.

Before you start your enhancement project, consider your requirements. What do you do with your Mac and where does it have trouble meeting your needs? Do you do a lot of desktop publishing and find that the slow speed and small screen of a compact machine irritate you? Do you have trouble running more than one application under System 7 and constantly run out of disk space? Do CAD, mapping, or multimedia projects run slowly on your modular machine?

Once you've identified what portions of your system need upgrading, you'll want to find the most cost-effective ways of doing the upgrades. First decide on a budget, then evaluate the options that will solve your Mac upgrade problems within this budget.

For instance, I like my Mac Classic (which has 4MB of memory and an 80MB hard drive) but find it somewhat slow. I'm a little annoyed by the small screen and I'm running out of hard disk space. I've identified three possible upgrade options:

- Upgrade my Classic to a Classic II for $700. This will give me increased speed, but I'll still have to upgrade my hard drive to 150MB and my system memory to 4MB. I'll also have to add a large screen video adapter.

- Sell my current system and buy a Classic II equipped the way I want it. I'll still have to buy a video adapter separately.

- Add an accelerator/video board/fast memory combination and a large hard drive to my existing system.

My Evaluation:

To choose between the three options, I'd first total the costs of each one.

OPTION 1: Classic II Logic Board Swap

Upgrade cost	$700
Hard drive	$500

Memory	$300
Video adapter	$600
Less memory, hard drive resale	−$300
TOTAL	**$1800**

OPTION 2: Classic II Purchase, Sale of Classic

Purchase Classic II 4/80	$2400
Upgrade to 150MB hard drive	$300
Video adapter	$600
Less sale of current system	−$1300
TOTAL	**$2000**

OPTION 3: Classic Upgrade with Accelerator Board

Purchase accelerator board (video, fast memory)	$570
Purchase 150MB hard drive	$500
Less sale of old hard drive	−$200
TOTAL	**$870**

It appears that the third option, the purchase and installation of an accelerator board, may be my best choice. A couple of other factors favor this decision. My accelerated Mac will be considerably faster than a Classic II, and I'll be able to run older software that's not System 7 compatible. (The Classic II *must* run System 7.02. See Table 1.2, an operating system compatibility chart.) However, if I wanted sound and color capability built in, the Classic II might be a better choice.

I haven't included installation costs in any of these upgrade options. If I had decided to have installation done, I would have had to add this to my price comparison. All three options add the ability to use a large-screen monitor. I haven't added this cost as it would be the same for all three machines.

System

Machine	3.2	6.05	6.07	6.08	7.0	7.01	A/UX 2.01	A/UX 3.0
512	•							
Plus		•	•	•	•	•		
Classic		•	•	•	•	•		
Classic II					•	•		
SE		•	•	•	•	•		
SE/30		•	•	•	•	•	•	•
LC			•	•	•	•		
LCII					•	•		
IIsi			•	•	•	•	•	•
II		•	•	•	•	•	PMMU	PMMU
IIx		•	•	•	•	•	•	•
IIcx		•	•	•	•	•	•	•
IIci		•	•	•	•	•	•	•
IIfx		•	•	•	•	•	•	•
Quadras						•		•
Portable		•	•	•	•	•		
PowerBook 100						•		
PowerBook 140						•		
PowerBook 170						•		

TABLE 1.2:   Mac Operating System Compatibility

There's a fourth option I could consider—purchasing an older machine. The Mac SE/30 is faster than the Classic II and has an expansion slot, stereo capability, and a numeric coprocessor (a chip for speeding numeric calculations) built in. With a large screen display card, 4MB, and 150MB hard drive, a used SE/30 should cost about $2700. While this is more than any of my upgrade options, it is more machine than any of the options. Used SE/30s are a hot property.

The Price Is Right

The popularity of the Macintosh ensures that vendors will continually provide new products to enhance its performance and ease of use. Even Apple has indicated that it will release new products every year, so the price of older software and hardware will continue to decrease. This is a good deal for you. But any prices I quote in this book will change rapidly. Figures 1.4, 1.5, and 1.6

Computer Price Histories

	Mac Plus	Mac SE/30	Mac Classic
1989	$1,900	$6,500	
1990	$1,799	$4,100	$1,500
1991	$800	$2,800	$1,300
1992	$600	$2,000	$1,100
1993	$400	$1,200	$800
1994	$200	$800	$500

FIGURE 1.4:   Compact Macintosh price history

Computer Price Histories

	Mac II	Mac IIci	Mac LC
1989	$3,600	$7,000	
1990	$2,500	$5,700	$2,800
1991	$200	$4,200	$2,400
1992	$1,400	$2,725	$1,550
1993	$800	$2,000	$900
1994	$500	$1,200	$500

FIGURE 1.5:   Modular Macintosh price history

document the decrease in hardware prices over time and provide a tool for comparing the current and projected cost of different upgrades.

It's important to realize that with the rapidly changing computer market, the most successful and economic solution to your computer upgrade needs will change too. You should try to choose a solution that will fill your requirements well into the future. This might mean buying or building more machine than you need today. But if your budget permits, that machine will be around a lot longer tomorrow.

A HORSETRADER'S GUIDE TO MAC UPGRADES

Getting the lowest possible price on computer hardware will require a little thought and more than a little strategy. If you're looking for new Mac hardware, you'll have to decide whether to go with a local (or mail-order) discounter, or

Computer Price Histories

	80 Mb HD	030 Accel.	1 Mb SIMM
1989	$900	$5,000	$150
1990	$700	$2,000	$90
1991	$380	$1,200	$50
1992	$300	$800	$30
1993	$200	$500	$20
1994	$100	$300	$15

FIGURE 1.6:   Macintosh hardware price history

to stick with your local Apple dealer. Buying from discounters will get you the best price, but you'll need a good idea of what you're buying. Don't expect a great deal of product knowledge and troubleshooting assistance from discounters, unless they've been in the Mac business for some time. Obtaining warranty service or replacements can be awkward.

Your Apple dealer should be a ready source of product aid and service, although his or her prices are apt to be somewhat less competitive. However, Apple, like every other major computer reseller, has good and bad dealerships so that even buying from a registered dealer doesn't guarantee good service. If you go this route, choose your dealer well. When you find a local dealer you can trust, haggle him or her by comparing prices available elsewhere to ensure that you get the lowest possible price.

If you're buying used Mac hardware, you'll have to be aware of the normal discounted selling price of the hardware you're looking for and how much you'll have to pay to bring the used equipment up to your requirements. Use these numbers when you're negotiating a price. Used equipment comes with *no* guarantee and *no* support. If the equipment is no longer in production, repairs may not be available. Still, if you choose carefully, you can find outstanding bargains in used Mac equipment.

Price may be your first Mac upgrade consideration, but the quality of the equipment you're buying is a close second. When you purchase new equipment, consider the manufacturer, along with its reputation, source(s) of components, and warranty. If you get a chance to look at the equipment firsthand, evaluate the quality of workmanship, as this may give you a little more comfort about the overall quality of the product. Circuit boards should be clean, well designed, and well finished. Wiring should be neatly done. Any mechanical parts should work smoothly without undue noise or vibration.

New Mac equipment should be "burned in," that is, left on for at least 24 hours (with the possible exception of monitors) to test for any heat-sensitive components that might tend to fail. Better to get this stuff replaced or repaired while it is still under warranty.

The quality of used Mac equipment is even more important. If electronic components have made it to the used equipment stage, the odds are good that they are fairly reliable (the burn-in has already been done). However, mechanical components are another story. The more mileage hard and floppy drives have on them, the more probable that failure is just around the corner. Apple's Sony floppy drives wear like iron, but they will give up the ghost eventually. Secondhand hard drives, floppy drives, and other mass storage devices should be in *very good* condition. If you have any doubt, give them a pass and spend your money elsewhere. A good choice for a secondhand hard drive is one owned by someone whose computing habits you're really familiar with.

Your final consideration when evaluating new and used equipment should be the future of the equipment—choose your Mac hardware with an eye to its "staying power" and upgradability. Try to buy the most power that you can afford, as the hardware will be usable for a longer period of time. An example of hardware with limited life is any Mac with a 68000 or 68020 CPU. While Apple has just introduced the Classic and PowerBook 100, based on the 68000, and the LC, based on the 68020, the company has made it clear that the 32-bit 68030 chip is the way of the future. The introduction of the Classic II and LC II indicates that Apple is gradually replacing its "bottom line." However, the widespread use of 68000-based machines and widely available upgrades should keep existing machines usable for some time. Upgradability will allow you to keep hardware current with new ROM chips or expansion boards.

Try to keep your expansion options open, where possible, by selecting hardware upgrades that can be removed and easily reused on other machines. Good examples are external modems, CD-ROMS, VGA and MultiSync monitors, and printers. Some hardware can be used with several different computer families. This hardware versatility greatly increases your chances of getting good resale value some time down the road when you decide to upgrade again. This type of hardware doesn't have to be a poor second choice to dedicated Macintosh hardware, as the manufacturers often include major brand names.

LET'S GO!

Now that you've thought about how to plan Macintosh upgrades and compare costs, it's time to get on with it. We'll start by finding out just what you'll need to do to produce the power system that you want.

CHAPTER TWO

What Do I Want... and What Do I Need?

The most important step in your Mac system upgrade is choosing what sort of upgrade you want, need, and can afford. First, decide what you want your system to do and where it's falling short of your requirements. Then consider how you work and whether an upgrade will fit your style or just make using your system more of a chore. High-priced hardware doesn't guarantee satisfaction. It does, unfortunately, guarantee a dent in your bank account, so think carefully when you're coming up with an upgrade plan.

MACS AT HOME

Some time ago, John Sculley told Apple users that he didn't believe in home computers, preferring to think that most computers are used in business, science, and engineering. Macs used in the business market probably still outnumber those at home, but these days the home market is becoming *very* significant.

A home system has to be low in cost, have reasonable performance, and be very flexible. Compact Macs, new or used, fit these requirements. The cheapest printers for a compact Mac are ImageWriter substitutes, like those by Olympia or Seikosha. If you want higher print quality, consider the Hewlett-Packard DeskWriter or Apple's StyleWriter.

The DeskWriter is reasonably quick; the StyleWriter is about half its speed. BetterWriters has faster drivers for the StyleWriter, which is quite slow on a 68000 Mac with Apple drivers.

The Mac Plus, SE, or Classic are good choices for a basic home system. A used SE is the best deal if you can get it for a good price. If you need higher performance, consider adding more memory and/or an accelerator board to your basic machine. Combination boards are even available to bring a Mac 512KE into the 1990s. With a logic board upgrade, you can convert a 512KE into a Plus, but you'll have to do this one yourself, as it is no longer available from Apple. The economics of this conversion requires a careful look, however.

For a higher performance system, a Mac LC, LC II, Classic II, or SE/30 is not a bad choice. Both the Mac Classic and LC can be upgraded to the equivalent version II with Apple's upgrade packages. Apple is still offering the Mac SE to SE/30 upgrade.

With the correct video cable, the Mac LC can use relatively inexpensive VGA monitors.

You can add large screen monitors to compact Macs by using internal or external video adaptors. The large screen is a boon to anyone doing desktop publishing or creating graphics.

Print options for an LC system include the HP DeskWriter, Apple StyleWriter, and a variety of relatively low-cost HP LaserJet-compatible laser printers. These can be made to work with Macs by using special LaserJet drivers.

Most home systems can get a performance and storage boost from the addition of a high-density disk drive, a larger hard drive, or a removable hard disk cartridge drive. Home systems with a CD-ROM player get the benefit of having entire encyclopedias, atlases, or world histories on disk.

Mac Home System Prices

In order to give you an idea of prices for Mac home system upgrades, I've included some estimates below. As prices are continually changing you may have to use these estimates as a guideline to prepare your own more up-to-date price estimates. Keep in mind that you'll often be able to recover a portion of the cost by selling your old equipment.

Memory Upgrades

Mac Classic, Plus, or SE with 1MB on the logic board to 4MB memory expansion	$180
Classic II or SE/30 with 2MB on the logic board to 4MB memory expansion	$90

Advantages of the Upgrade   By adding memory to a home system, you gain the ability to run System 7 and larger applications, run and multitask multiple applications, reduce the problems with a "loaded" system file, or set up printer buffer (print spooler) or RAM disk. A memory upgrade is the cheapest and most effective upgrade performance booster for your Mac.

Where You'll Find the Information   The following chapters will show you how to add memory and how to use it.

- How to add memory to a compact Mac—Chapter 3, *Starting Out* and Chapter 4, *Memory Upgrades.*

- System 7, RAM disks, and print spoolers—Chapter 10, *"Software Upgrades."*

Multifunction/Accelerator/Logic Board Upgrades

Add an accelerated 68000/FPU combination board	$250
Add a 68030 accelerator/expansion/multifunction board to a 512KE, Plus, or Classic	$600–900
Take advantage of Apple's logic board exchange programs for the Classic, SE/30, and LC	approximately $800, $900, $1000 respectively

Advantages of the Board Upgrade   Upgrading an existing Mac with a third-party or Apple board can boost speed, memory capacity, calculating capability (with an FPU), video capability, and can add a SCSI port. This type of upgrade is expensive and involves a fair bit of work, but gives a Mac a massive performance increase.

Where You'll Find the Information   When adding memory is just not enough, these chapters will provide information on adding higher performance with an accelerator or logic board upgrade.

- Adding accelerators and multifunction boards—Chapter 5, *Accelerators*.
- Adding an FPU—Chapter 6, *Coprocessors and Cache Cards*.
- Logic board swaps—Chapter 11, *Repacking Your Mac*.

Printer Upgrades

Add a StyleWriter printer, BetterWriters (GDT Toolworks) printer driver package, and ParaLink cable to a compact system	$450
Add an HP DeskWriter printer to your system	$400
Add an HP DeskWriter C to your system	$750
HP DeskJet C (color) upgrade with GDT or similar printer driver package	$450–550
HP LaserJet-compatible printer and GDT Toolworks PowerPrint or similar printer driver package	$1100

Advantages of the Upgrade   This upgrade adds better print quality and color capability to a home system at a reasonable speed and price. Some lasers are now low enough in price to bring laser printing home. (Even some PostScripts are getting relatively cheap.)

Where You'll Find the Information　Printing at home demand a printers with a great deal of longevity and reliability.

- Adding a non-Apple printer to your system and speeding up Apple printers with a faster drivers—Chapter 12, *Printers and Plotters*.

MACS AT SCHOOL

The basic requirement for a school computer lab, especially these days, is maximum power at a minimum price. Moderately priced color systems that run common educational programs and commercial software are the ideal.

A good basic classroom or school computer lab workstation is a Mac Classic 2/40, with basic educational software, and an integrated program such as BeagleWorks, ClarisWorks, or GreatWorks. An ImageWriter II (or equivalent) is a good basic printer for this setup.

If a classroom is already well equipped with Apple II and/or IIgs computers, then a Mac LC II with an Apple IIe emulator board will let a teacher prepare lesson plans and tests, as well as help students who use AppleWorks and Bank Street Writer on the IIe. An LC II equipped with a CD-ROM drive and software such as Grolier's Illustrated Encyclopedia or the Software Toolworks World Atlas can act as a class color workstation, with a teacher scheduling times among students.

To set up an inexpensive school computer lab, you'll need a roll of phone wire, some RJ-11 modular phone jacks, and a connector tool. Individual computers can be connected with Farallon's PhoneNet connectors. This costs considerably less than Apple's LocalTalk connectors and cabling.

You can use a Mac IIsi for a file server and connect a dot-matrix or laser printer to the network depending on who'll be using it. A Mac Classic, Apple IIe with an Apple II workstation card, and Apple IIgs can all use the network. The Apple II and IIgs can even boot from the network server.

You can run a school multimedia lab with a Mac LC II or IIsi running HyperCard or dedicated laser disk access software. You can even use QuickTime presentations to enhance some classes. A Mac system in the classroom provides a lot of potential at a minimal price.

Upgrading Your School's Macs

Some economical Mac upgrades can enhance a classroom workstation or network server without eating a school's computer budget. A few are listed below.

Memory Upgrades

Take a Mac LC or LC II workstation to 6MB using 2×2MB SIMMs (2MB on the system board)	$160
Take a Mac IIsi server to 9MB using 4×2MB SIMMs (1MB on the system board)	$320

Advantages of the Upgrade   Adding memory will increase the performance of a classroom workstation and the speed and performance of a network server.

Where You'll Find the Information   You'll need some specifics on how to upgrade memory.

■   Adding memory to an LC or IIsi—Chapter 4, *Memory Upgrades*.

Video Upgrades

Add a 13" color monitor to a Mac LC with a grayscale monitor	$700

Advantages of the Upgrade   Allows a classroom lab to take better advantage of educational and graphics applications using color.

Where You'll Find the Information   It's easy to upgrade the monitor on a modular Mac. This chapter will give you some selection and installation details.

■   Adding higher resolution and color to a Mac system— Chapter 8, *Monitors*.

CD-ROM and Multimedia Upgrades

Add a NEC CD player and five CDs	$500+

Educational HyperCard Stacks	$70
Add a MacRecorder or a sound editing package	$150 or $70

Advantages of the Upgrade   Multimedia software and hardware are *very* expensive—schools need to get the most impact for a reasonable price. This means using low-cost CD-ROM packages, and HyperCard drivers for the laser disk players often found in schools. You can build educational stacks using HyperCard and sound from a recording package such as Paracomp's Mac-Recorder (or sound recorded from the microphone contained in the IIs or LC).

Where You'll Find the Information   Multimedia in the classroom can be an effective teaching technique, and installation of a system doesn't have to be costly.

■　Add a low-cost multimedia upgrade—Chapter 15, *Graphics, Sound, and Multimedia.*

Adding Network Cabling, Connectors, and Software

100' of phone cable, modular phone jacks, and connector tool	$100
Farallon PhoneNet connectors and AppleShare server software	$40/connector, $800/AppleShare server

Advantages of the Upgrade   A low-cost network upgrade gives students more access to available information, and gives teachers more access to the students. With network-compatible software packages, students can all share the benefit of educational software. Tests or projects can be sent and stored on the network server.

Where You'll Find the Information   Setting up a network is not easy, but it can help a few pieces of expensive equipment go a long way.

■　Get the details on setting up a network, what hardware to use, and costs—Chapter 14, *Networking.*

SMALL BUSINESS

Small businesses run accounting, database, and spreadsheet software. Small printshops usually also run a page layout program such as Aldus Pagemaker or Quark Express. All of these normally require a system with more speed, power, and memory than a home system.

Depending on the workload it handles, a small business should consider a Mac Classic II, LC II, or IIsi. A grayscale monitor is more than adequate for the modular machines. Since an LC or LC II can use a VGA monitor with the appropriate cable, one of these may be a good choice for a moderate-priced business system. When color is required, the aforementioned machines can be upgraded to handle it. The modular machines are the only ones that are easy to upgrade to 24-bit color if required by, for instance, a small printshop.

Most small business printing requirements will be well served by an Apple StyleWriter, HP DeskWriter, or—if they need to print multipage carbon forms—a 24-pin Epson-compatible dot-matrix printer.

The Epson should be used with GDT PowerPrint and ParaLink cable or Orange Micro's Grappler cable and software drivers. With the StyleWriter, GDT's BetterWriters software considerably enhances print speed and versatility.

Printshops have stricter requirements and probably need low-priced PostScript laser printers.

Small business machines need more memory than home machines; 4MB is an absolute minimum, with 8MB more reasonable for a business system running System 7. A 100MB or larger hard drive is a good choice for a business system.

For data security, a large hard drive should be backed up regularly. If a small business can afford it, a good backup device, such as a SyQuest removable hard drive or a tape drive, is a worthwhile investment. Using a faster machine, a small business shouldn't need an accelerator, but an FPU might be a useful addition.

Small Business Upgrades

Small businesses can benefit from low-cost video upgrades, more mass storage, and low-cost, durable, high-quality printers.

Video Upgrades

Add a sharp grayscale monitor to a Mac LC, LC II, or IIsi	$450
Add a 24-bit card and high-resolution color monitor for a small publisher	$1300

Advantages of the Upgrade   Adding a sharp grayscale monitor to a business system will give the best possible resolution for long-term use without adding undue cost. A 24-bit color graphics system may be necessary for a small printshop doing advertising work or graphics layouts.

Where You'll Find the Information   If you'll spend a lot of time working on accounting and invoicing programs, it's critical to choose the right monitor to avoid eye strain and headaches.

- Add a sharp grayscale monitor to a small-business system, or a 24-bit color system to a small printshop—Chapter 12, *Printers and Plotters*.

Disk and Tape Drives

Add a 100MB hard drive	$400
Add a 44MB SyQuest cartridge hard drive for backups	$500
Add a tape drive and backup software	$700

Advantages of the Upgrade   An increase in disk space will give a small business more room for accounting, inventory, and if desired, point-of-sale software. Large hard drives with important data need to be backed up regularly. A tape drive or cartridge hard drive fulfills this requirement admirably.

Where You'll Find the Information   Disk space and adequate backup systems are vital to ensure data security for a small business. Running out of disk space or losing vital data at the wrong time can be catastrophic.

- Adding disk drives, tape drives, and backup software—Chapter 7, *Storage Options*.

Upgrading Printer Speed and Quality

StyleWriter and BetterWriters driver from GDT Toolworks	$450 (prices given here are street prices at press time)
HP DeskWriter	$400
HP DeskWriter C (Color)	$750
300 DPI (dots per inch) PostScript laser (for printshops or graphics professionals)	$1500(approximately)

Advantages of the Upgrade   These printer upgrades can add 300 DPI print quality and, potentially, color to a small business system for forms, menus, and other print jobs. A low-cost PostScript laser can give fast, high-quality printing to a small print shop or graphics professional.

Where You'll Find the Information   A wide selection of PostScript and QuickDraw printers can provide high-quality print or invoice printing capabilities to small businesses.

- What printers to use, how to choose one, and what drivers to use with them—Chapter 12, *Printers and Plotters*.

LARGE COMPANIES AND INSTITUTIONS

Large companies will probably want to network the Macs used by specific work groups and connect these *local area networks* (LANs) to each other through *gateways*.

Companies need the fastest and most reliable network available. These days, that probably means the Ethernet or Token Ring protocol.

For large workgroups, a fast server with lots of room for disk-drive expansion is imperative. A Mac IIci or IIfx with a fast SCSI controller, and possibly an accelerator, is a good choice. A Quadra 700, 900, or 950 is an excellent choice for a server, if budgets permit (Figure 2.1).

High-traffic LANs using large databases need fast, high-capacity hard drives. Once again, high-speed NuBus caching disk controllers can help. Controllers that take over the NuBus, or *bus masters*, are capable of very high data-transfer rates.

Downtime on LANs can be catastrophic. That's why many LANs now run *disk arrays*. These are groups of hard drives that simultaneously receive similar network data. If one, or even two, disk drives go down, the network runs from the remaining drives while the offending hard drives are repaired or replaced.

FIGURE 2.1:   The Quadra 700 and 900—good choices for network servers! (Photo courtesy of Apple Computer)

Large, high-capacity networks require fast, secure backups. DAT (digital audio tape) backup units or optical drives can do the job safely and relatively quickly. Where data integrity is vital, WORM (write once, read many) drives are even better. Data written to WORM drives cannot be altered or destroyed by normal processes. Large WORM drive arrays can hold hundreds of *gigabytes* (10^6 KB) of data.

Macs on a network should be chosen for the tasks they'll be performing. The Classic II and Mac LC are good secretarial workstations. A good quality grayscale monitor and at least 4MB of memory are a must for these machines. A fast, heavy-duty laser printer is good equipment for these secretarial stations. A Mac IIsi can be used for more demanding applications. These machines can be equipped with slot extenders, FPUs, and accelerators as needed. A Mac IIci can be used where speed, memory expandability, and additional NuBus card expansion are required.

Network printers should be fast, high-capacity, heavy-duty lasers. These can be upgraded with memory expansion or replacement RISC boards. Individual workstations can be equipped with StyleWriter or DeskWriter printers and fast drivers such as BetterWriters.

Adding Network Hardware and Software

Ethernet board	$200-$300/board
PhoneNet connectors	$30/connector
Routers, hubs, gateways	$500/unit
Cable, fasteners, jacks, tools	$150/100 ft
Server software	$700

Advantages of the Upgrade   Adding a high-speed, high-capacity network to an office increases data transfer, frees up printers, increases communication, and allows workgroups to prepare projects faster.

Where You'll Find the Information   Choosing the right network will make the difference between business computing being a joy or a chore.

■   Choosing a type of network, network software, and network configuration—Chapter 14, *Networking*.

Adding a Disk Array and DAT Tape Backup

Add a disk array, controller, and software	$2000
Add a DAT tape and backup software for backups	$1500
Add an optical drive and software for backups	$1500
Add a WORM drive "jukebox"	$25,000

Advantages of the Upgrade   A large, heavily used network needs fast, safe disk storage and equally fast and accurate backups. DAT tapes, optical drives, and WORM drives all do a good job of backing up network data, although DAT is probably the fastest.

Where You'll Find the Information   Fast, fail-safe storage and backup preserve vital corporate information.

■   For information on setting up disk arrays and backup devices—Chapter 7, *Storage Options*.

Adding Fast Network Printers

Add a fast 8–10 ppm network laser printer	$2500

Advantages of the Upgrade   Upgrading a high-traffic network printer will ensure that network printing speeds and quality are satisfactory.

Where You'll Find the Information   Network and heavy-use printers get an extreme workout and need to be fast and sturdy.

■   Adding a high-performance printer—Chapter 12, *Printers and Plotters*.

USING A MACINTOSH IN THE FIELD

Students, salespeople, field engineers, and wellsite geologists often need a lightweight portable they can carry to class or in the field (Figure 2.2). In the past, this has meant a laptop or notebook MS-DOS PC, because a truly portable Macintosh was not available. The original Macintosh Portable is a technical masterpiece but not a true portable because of its weight.

Enter the Apple-Sony alliance and the introduction of the Power-Books. The PowerBook 100, with its 16MHz 68000 processor, meets the needs

FIGURE 2.2:   The PowerBook takes power into the field (Photo courtesy of Apple Computer)

of students and field personnel who need a machine for relatively simple data entry. Students will want to add an external floppy drive to the PowerBook 100, which has no built-in floppy drive. Others may want to use the 100 as an external disk drive to transfer files to their desktop Mac. This aspect of the 100 makes it quite handy for data transfer.

Engineers and geologists with more advanced requirements will want to use the PowerBook 140 or 170 because of the 68030 CPU and the FPU in the 170.

Fieldwork often involves transferring data by modem. The PowerBooks are well equipped for mounting both internal and external modems. AppleTalk Remote Access software allows PowerBook users to access a network remotely via modem.

 Disk and memory space is at a premium in the PowerBooks and applications that make economical use of both are good choices to add to your hard disk. The integrated applications BeagleWorks, ClarisWorks, and GreatWorks are efficient and capable. Write Now! and the compact version of Nisus are small but efficient word processors.

Video boards such as Envisio's Notebook Display Adapter (Figure 2.3) and an external hard drive with a special cable turn a PowerBook into an office machine.

FIGURE 2.3:   A PowerBook with the Envisio large-screen monitor upgrade (Photo courtesy of Envisio Inc.)

Adding External Drives to a PowerBook

Add a PowerBook 100 external floppy drive	$200
Add an external 100MB hard drive	$400

Advantages of the Upgrade   Adding an external drive to a PowerBook 100 lets you spend less time with the notebook hooked by SCSI cable to another system. The external floppy allows you to exchange data disks when you're away from a base station to hook the PowerBook into. The external hard drive upgrade means less wear and tear on the PowerBook's internal hard drive, less drain on the battery, and more application space.

Where You'll Find the Information   Large capacity hard drives provide a large storage resource at your home or office "base station."

- Adding external drives to a PowerBook—Chapter 7, *Storage Options*.

Adding a Modem to a PowerBook

Internal fax/modem	$400
External 2400/9600 baud fax/modem	$300

Advantages of the Upgrade   A modem allows you to send data to, and receive data from, an office or university network or bulletin board system. AppleTalk Remote Access software makes it easy to access a network that has a dedicated external communication line. A fax board with modem capability allows you to send and receive documents via modem.

Where You'll Find the Information   In business, communication is critical and modems can be your window to the world. The chapter listed will help with modem selection and installation.

- Buying and installing modems and fax modems—Chapter 13, *Telecommunications*.

Adding a Video Upgrade to a PowerBook

Add a video expansion board and monitor to a Mac portable	$1600+

Advantages of the Upgrade   A number of manufacturers produce a variety of expansion products for Apple's PowerBooks. One of the most obvious areas for PowerBook expansion is the screen. While the PowerBook screen is reasonably sharp, working with the machine sitting on an office desk for longer period of time could result in serious neck and eye strain. Envisio Inc. is one of the first companies to produce a video expansion board for the PowerBooks. The company also makes a video card for the original Apple Portable. Putting a video board in a portable lets you connect a sharp, large-screen monochrome, grayscale, or color monitor in an office or at home, improving your portable's usability.

Where You'll Find the Information   The following chapter will aid you in selecting a monitor for your Mac Portable or PowerBook. The clarity and color of a large-screen monitor will reduce eye strain and may be crucial for the completion of presentations and projects.

■   Purchasing and installing a portable video upgrade—Chapter 8, *Monitors*.

MACS AS GRAPHICS WORKSTATIONS

The Macintosh, because of its built-in graphics tools, excels at graphical applications. However, the Mac's graphics routines have been in use without modification for some years now and are beginning to show their age. When used with some high-end graphics applications, even the Quadra can probably use some help. Hardware developers have produced a variety of graphics display and accelerator options to help the Mac shake off the cobwebs of its old graphics routines and perform like a high-end workstation. It appears that Apple itself may be looking to the future and is developing improvements for Macintosh QuickDraw.

For use as a graphics workstation, Macs can range from the IIsi or IIci for basic computer-aided design (CAD) and rendering (Figure 2.4) to the Quadra 900 for a 3D animation and/or multimedia. Basic color graphics (Figure 2.5) and CAD benefit from a sharp large-screen monitor running 8-bit color graphics. Mac systems requiring the photo-realism of 24-bit graphics benefit from large-screen monitors and graphics accelerators. Machines like the LC and Quadras receive a large performance boost from the addition of VRAM, or video memory SIMMs. Systems doing rendering or animation, where speed and number-crunching capability are vital, get enhanced performance from an accelerator board and an FPU, if one is not built into the machine.

FIGURE 2.4:   Macintosh—a natural CAD workstation

These days, many Macintosh workstations run digital color prepress (DCP) systems. The requirements discussed above apply to these systems as well. A DCP system probably needs to be able to rapidly create and output calibrated *RGB* (red-green-blue) or CMYK (cyan-magenta-yellow-black) files and drive high-resolution PostScript color printers. Color calibration devices and graphics coprocessor boards (which help create Macintosh color PostScript print files) are becoming very popular these days.

With the introduction of QuickTime, Apple has announced its intention to become a major player in the suddenly popular area of multimedia computing. Multimedia computing, as I understand it at least, involves the addition of animation and sound to computer presentations and applications. Compressing and decompressing large graphics files while displaying animation and playing sound take a lot of computer horsepower. A variety of hardware enhancements aid computers in the production and use of multimedia. Among the most prevalent enhancements you'll find accelerators and graphics coprocessors yet again, as well as video and audio capture and display hardware and utilities.

FIGURE 2.5:   Graphics on a Macintosh IIci

Adding Monitors, Video Accelerators, Calibration

14" monitor with 8-bit accelerated graphics card	$1000
Large screen 24-bit color system with accelerator	$3000+
Accelerated graphics board with built-in CMYK conversion and video color calibration	$2500

Advantages of the Upgrade   This upgrade allows a medium- or high-end system to give a realistic idea of what final graphics output will be. The acceleration allows a graphic artist or draftsperson to work reasonably quickly, without waiting for the system to catch up. The color conversion and calibrator boards speed the creation of accurate high-resolution magazine and advertising layouts and minimize problems with the final product.

Where You'll Find the Information   A top-notch monitor is the most important component of a high- or low-end graphics workstation and as you choose, so you shall work. The following chapter will help you choose carefully.

■   Adding high-resolution monitors, graphics accelerators, and color calibrators—Chapter 8, *Monitors*.

Adding a CPU Accelerator

Add a fast cache card to a Mac II or SE/30	$260–$1500
Add a fast 68030 or 030/FPU combination	$1000–$1200
Add a 68040 accelerator board	$1900–$2200

Advantages of the Upgrade   A CPU accelerator board lets your system keep up with the millions of calculations per second required for high-resolution rendering, CAD, or multimedia animation and sound, and run applications at a reasonable speed.

Where You'll Find the Information   You'll need a lot of speed and power on a Mac used as a graphics workstation. The following chapters will help you upgrade without breaking your budget.

■   Adding an accelerator board—Chapter 5, *Accelerators*.

TAKE THE MONEY AND RUN

Obviously, any Macintosh upgrade is going to chew gently at the edges of your pocketbook. Now that you've seen some real-world upgrade information (and know where to go for more), you can make the most cost-effective choices. It's almost a given that your upgrade plans won't exactly match everything I suggest—I want to give you a foundation, but you should feel free to refine the details.

CHAPTER THREE

Starting Out

This chapter explains safety precautions and toolkit assembly—information you need to safely open your Mac and insert or remove hardware.

Opening a Mac case, at least with compact machines, is not a trivial job. But neither is it a difficult one. If you're reasonably handy with a screwdriver, you should have no problem. Still, if the idea of playing around with the guts of your compact or modular Mac makes you nervous, you should consider an external upgrade such as adding a large external hard drive or CD-ROM, or upgrading performance with software.

As an alternative, you can get a good local shop to install a hardware upgrade for you. This is not a bad option, but can be expensive depending on the shop—so choose your upgrade technician carefully.

YOUR MACINTOSH UPGRADE—STARTING OUT

First, the disclaimer—I am not responsible for any damage done to your Mac, or to you, by poor or incorrect hardware upgrades. This is not an attempt to stop you from proceeding with your upgrade, but is a flagrant attempt to instill some caution!

Safety: Dangers and Cautions

These are some basic items to think about when you're upgrading your Macintosh. There's nothing hard or dangerous about an upgrade, as long as you keep these basics in mind.

The Warranty

Apple's warranty is voided when you open the case of your machine. This is especially true of compact Macs, but may be literally applied to modular machines as well. If this bothers you, and your machine is still under warranty, wait for the warranty to expire and do the upgrade then. Your alternative is to have the upgrade done by a certified Apple dealer.

Voltage

The only dangerous high-voltage areas in a Mac are the power supply and the monitor. You generally shouldn't have to mess with either and are strongly advised not to. This advice falls by the wayside when working in a compact Mac where both the power supply and monitor are in the area you'll be working in. You will, of course, have the power off, and that just leaves the residual charge in the CRT (cathode ray tube) monitor. This can be drained and I'll describe how.

The residual charge in the CRT is of the order of 12,000 volts, but the maximum current is in the order of microamperes. This shouldn't hurt you, but won't be a lot of fun either. On the other hand, if not drained properly, this charge can kill your motherboard—something to think about!

Static Electricity Static is a chip-killer and can quickly do serious damage to electronic equipment. Just consider that a static charge can have a potential of 50,000 volts—once again at very low amperage (current). Any time you're working inside the case of a compact, modular, or portable Mac, you should be grounded with an antistatic wrist strap. These are available from good electronics supply stores.

Mechanical Damage

Be careful opening Mac cases—they're well made but can be damaged if you're over-enthusiastic. The Classic in particular is "frameless." The contents are supported by the stiff external case, and the internal structure is quite light. The compact Mac monitor CRT is under high vacuum and any damage could result in an implosion. Safety glasses are advised! Floppy drives are not especially fragile, but they're not designed to withstand a lot of abuse, either. Hard drives have come a long way in durability, but they still require careful treatment. Avoid dropping or bumping them, and keep that antistatic strap on to avoid zapping the controller.

 When you place a bare drive on a hard surface, put something underneath! Even a sheet of paper can ease the shock of the hard drive touching a surface. (Thanks to Renzo Costa for the tip.)

If this seems like excessive caution, remember that the faster the hard drive, the smaller and lighter the read/write heads. It doesn't take much of a shock to bang them around. Don't overtighten or force any screws or fasteners—snug will do. Pulling or inserting chips, especially larger multipin packages, can result in bent pins—bad news. Bent pins can be straightened if you do it carefully, but it's better not to create the problem in the first place. Don't force clips or try to force-fit expansion boards. If you can't get the lid on a modular Mac or the back on a compact Mac case, check your installation. It's not likely that these boards were manufactured too large to fit.

Your Work Area

To do your upgrade, choose a well-lit area with lots of room and not too much traffic. When you're working, keep your work area clean, organized, and free of obstructions. Tie up long hair and remove watches and rings before you start.

This will prevent the nasty accidents and loss of parts that can turn your hair gray and reduce the warranty on your heart. Keep small parts such as screws in a container (preferably with a lid) where they can't get lost and will stay organized.

If you feel you'll get confused when reassembling any part of your project, draw yourself a well-labeled diagram for reference. This is an especially good idea when removing chips.

If your job will be extensive and involve a lot of time, choose a work area where you can leave your project safely unattended. Budget lots of time and never hurry. If you're not sure about a step in the assembly of your upgrade take your time and work through it to make sure you've got it right. Don't force *anything*—connectors, screws, or chips. Bent pins and stripped screws won't enhance the value of your project.

Power Off, Cord Unplugged!

When you begin, first and foremost unplug the Mac. Sure, with modular Macs you could leave the machine turned off and ground yourself out to the metal power supply case, but why take chances? (And again, be sure to wear an anti-static strap.)

As a matter of fact, don't just unplug the Mac—disconnect the power cord and set it off to one side. It's out of the way, out of trouble, and so are you. Just follow my basic rules and stay organized—remember where you put the power cord. (We all know it's impossible to lose a power cord, but why push it?)

The danger of working in a powered-up Mac is fairly high, especially in compact Macs like the Classic where a high-voltage cathode ray tube, power supply, and video analog board are all sitting there waiting to do you some damage.

Mac Cracking

Now that you've heard my safety sermon and have prepared a good work area, you can start thinking about "cracking" your Macintosh.

The Tools

Figure 3.1 shows a set of Mac cracking tools for a compact machine. These include from top to bottom:

■ A 1" spring clamp, used for "cracking" the compact Mac case. I bought this clamp at a local hardware store—it's a standard woodworking clamp and should be easy to find. If you can locate a good electronics store that stocks a lot of Mac parts, you should be able to get your hands on an official Macintosh "case-cracking" tool. This is 6 inches (15.24 cm) long and has two wide handgrips. This tool, if you can find one, makes the case-cracking process easy.

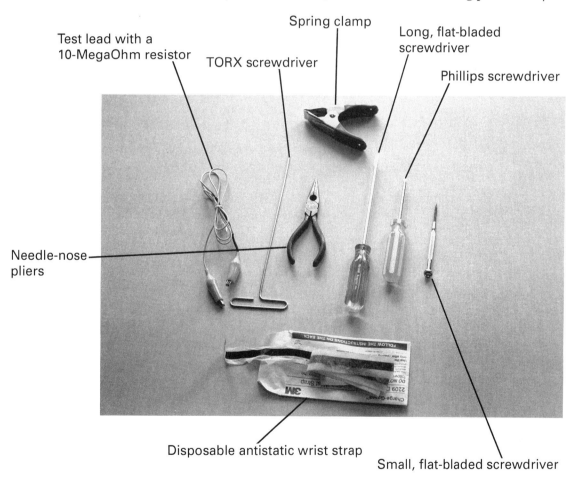

FIGURE 3.1:   The Mac cracker's toolkit

- A grounding wire. This one was made from a test lead, with alligator clips at both ends, bought at Radio Shack. I cut and stripped the test lead, soldered a 10-megohm resistor in, and covered the resistor with "heat-shrink" tubing. This cable is used to discharge a compact Mac CRT anode. I'll get to the "how" shortly.

- A Torx screwdriver, at least 9 inches (22.86 cm) long. A simple tool of the type shown will work fine, or you can go first class and get a proper Torx screwdriver from an auto parts dealer.

- A pair of needle-nose pliers. Handy for a variety of jobs, such as holding and inserting small screws.

- A long flat-bladed, insulated screwdriver (this one is 6 inches, or 15.24 cm, long). This is used with the grounding lead to drain residual charge from a compact Mac CRT.

- A medium-size Phillips-head screwdriver to be used when dismantling your Mac.

- A small electronic or jeweler's screwdriver. Useful for a variety of jobs, including *carefully* prying out chips, setting DIP switches on hard drives and printers, and installing SIMMs.

- A disposable antistatic strap. (You may want to get something a little more permanent than this.)

Not shown in the figure is a soft pad used when cracking compact Macs. The pad has to be *clean* and wide enough to easily accommodate a compact Mac. I use a stadium seat cushion and I'm sure you have your own ideas.

A Modular Mac Toolkit

Since modular Macs are designed to be opened, your toolkit is much simpler. Of the tools listed above, you'll only need:

- A grounding wrist strap

- A medium-size Phillips screwdriver

- A small flat-bladed screwdriver

A Toolkit for the Original Mac Portable

The original Apple portable was designed to be upgraded. To install an upgrade, you'll need:

- A grounding wrist strap

- A small flat-bladed screwdriver

The Basic PowerBook Toolkit

■ For the PowerBook 100, a Phillips screwdriver

■ For the PowerBook 140/170, a #8 and #10 Torx screwdriver

Some Additional Tools You May Want

■ A chip extractor/pin straightener tool. Chip extractors are available for chips with 40 pins and probably greater.

Some people prefer to use extractors to remove chips, while others feel that extractors increase the chances of damaging the chip when you remove it. The pin straightener tool will aid in straightening any chip pins bent during extraction. But it's better to be careful enough not to *need* a pin straightener.

■ Nut drivers. Some upgrade boards use additional fasteners. In this case, you may need a nut driver to secure the board and/or an additional power supply.

■ A hemostat. This is useful for holding small parts or screws (even better than needle-nose pliers; I'd use them if I weren't cheap!)

Opening and Dismantling Your Compact Mac

Gather up your tools, prepare your work area, put down a soft, *clean* pad, and place your Mac face down on the pad. Cleanliness insures that the monitor and the surface of the machine will not be scratched (see Figure 3.2). Some of the Mac cracking pictures that follow feature the talented pinkies of my daughter Kristen. I'm mentioning this for three reasons:

■ It's a shameless plug for my daughter.

■ I needed someone to help me with the photos.

■ To emphasize that cracking a compact Mac is perfectly safe *as long as you are careful*.

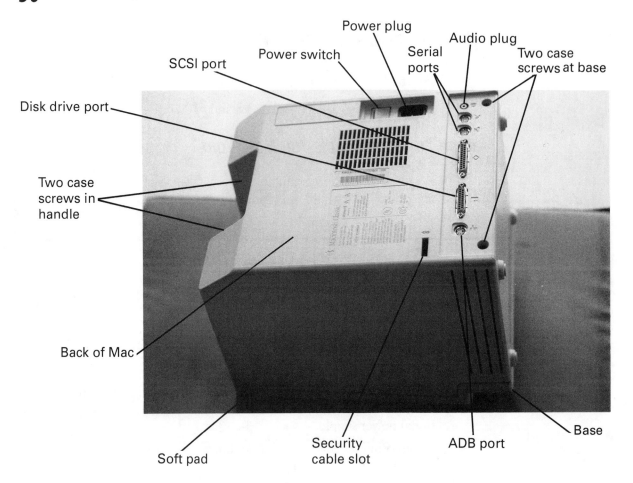

FIGURE 3.2:   Start with your compact Mac face down on a soft pad

For a pre-Classic Mac with a programmer's switch—a small plastic switch on the lower left side of the Mac case—*gently* remove the switch by prying it off. The programmer's switch was provided to give software developers a way out of nasty situations. Apparently, Steve Jobs felt that completed programs shouldn't crash and need to be reset (what a great concept!), so these Macs have the switch instead of a reset button.

Remove the Mac's case screws using a Torx screwdriver. Start with the screws inside the case handle (see Figure 3.3; now you know why you need a 9-inch Torx screwdriver). If you're working on a Mac Plus or earlier, open the battery door—just below handle level on the right rear side of the case—and remove the screw at the top. Now remove the two screws at the base of the Mac case (Figure 3.4).

Back

Removing
case screws
from inside the
handle with
a TORX
screwdriver

Top

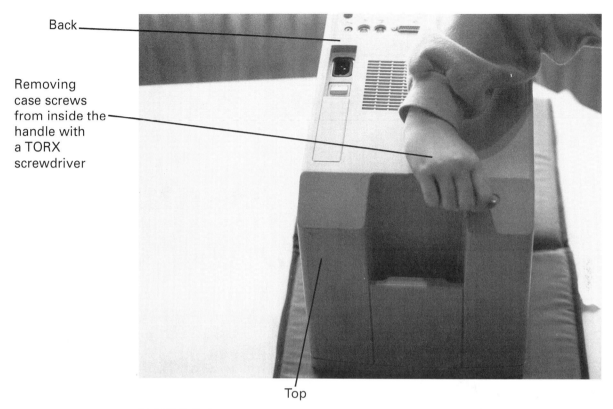

FIGURE 3.3:   Undoing the Torx screws in the Mac's handle

Start cracking the case by pressing down on the power plug connector while pulling up on the case (Figure 3.5). This should break the seal of the adhesive strip around the edge of the Mac case. You can now start working your case-cracking tool around the edge of the Mac (Figure 3.6). Don't put too much pressure on any one point, and keep the tool moving! This will keep the cracking tool from notching the edge of your Mac. A little patience here will prevent any damage to your case.

Once you've freed the back of the Macintosh, lift it off and set it to one side. If you haven't removed the case screws, you can leave them in the case back. I prefer to do this—it makes the screws a lot harder to misplace. If you're taking apart a Mac 128, 512, or Plus, remove the 9-inch long L-shaped piece of aluminum-colored material over the I/O plugs. This is the *RFI* shield and may fall off during disassembly.

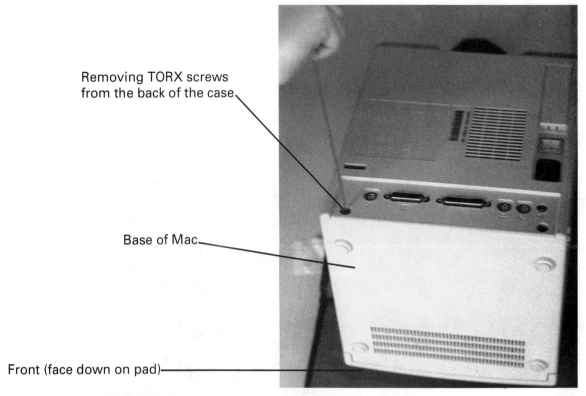

Removing TORX screws
from the back of the case

Base of Mac

Front (face down on pad)

FIGURE 3.4:   Undoing the screws in the base of the case

Figure 3.7 shows the Mac Classic "with the hood up." The Mac monitor CRT is in the lower left of the picture. The suction cup on the side of the CRT covers the anode. The wire across the top of the CRT connects to the grounding lug in the lower right of the picture. The CRT video card, on top of the CRT neck, is present in the Mac SE and later. The main logic board power cable is the bundle of wires that runs between the Mac CRT and the base of the Mac.

The board on the far side of the case, behind the CRT, is the analog board/power supply. The Mac SE and SE/30 have the power supply shielded in a metal enclosure. You can see the Mac external power plug at the base of the analog/power supply board, in the upper-left corner of the picture.

This Mac Classic has a memory card installed. This projects from the upper right corner of the chassis. The Classic is the only compact Mac to use a specialized memory expansion slot. The Mac Plus and later Macs, excluding the Classic, use SIMM slots mounted on the logic board to add system memory.

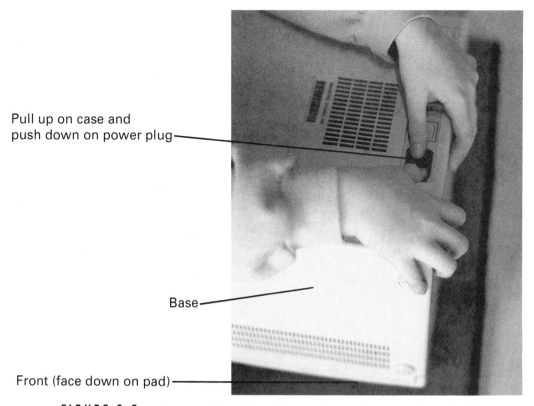

Pull up on case and
push down on power plug

Base

Front (face down on pad)

FIGURE 3.5:   Start cracking the case by pressing on the power plug and pulling up on the case

The FDHD (floppy disk high density) drive enclosure is in the middle of the picture, just to the right of the CRT, attached to the Classic's base chassis. You'll notice a ribbon cable connecting the floppy drive to the Mac's logic board (or motherboard, to us old-fashioned types). When a hard drive is installed, the bracket mounts on top of the floppy drive enclosure. The logic board in the Classic sits in rails at the base of the chassis, though the logic board is mounted slightly differently with each member of the compact Mac family.

Now that you have the Mac case open, it's time to take the safety precaution that I mentioned previously—grounding the compact Mac CRT. This works the same for all compact Macs (see Figure 3.8). Fasten one of the alligator clips on the grounding wire to the Mac's ground lug and the other to a long, insulated, flat-headed screwdriver. *Gently* insert the screwdriver tip under the cup that covers the Mac CRT anode and touch the anode to ground it out. Remember that the CRT is under high vacuum, so caution is advised!

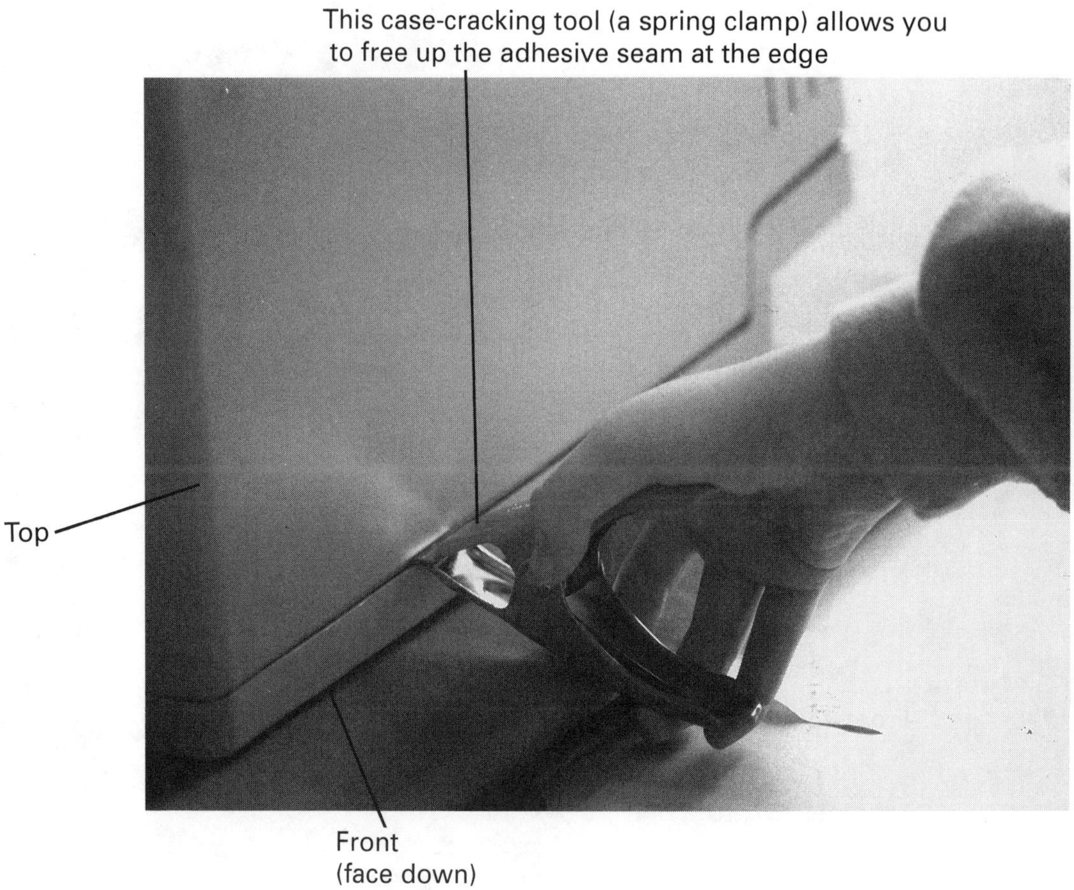

This case-cracking tool (a spring clamp) allows you
to free up the adhesive seam at the edge

Top

Front
(face down)

FIGURE 3.6: Using the "case-cracking" tool

The video card on the neck of a Mac SE or later CRT can break when you
work on the machine, so you should remove it before doing any further work (Figure 3.9). Remove the card by *carefully* lifting it straight up. You can wiggle it *very*
slightly. Set the card off to one side. To give you more room to maneuver inside a
Classic, remove the memory expansion board (see Figure 3.10).

Now, disconnect the logic board main power supply cable (Figure 3.11).
The clip at the top of the power connector should be unfastened. The cable can
be wiggled slightly to remove it. Take your time and *make sure* that your hand
does not fly back into the CRT.

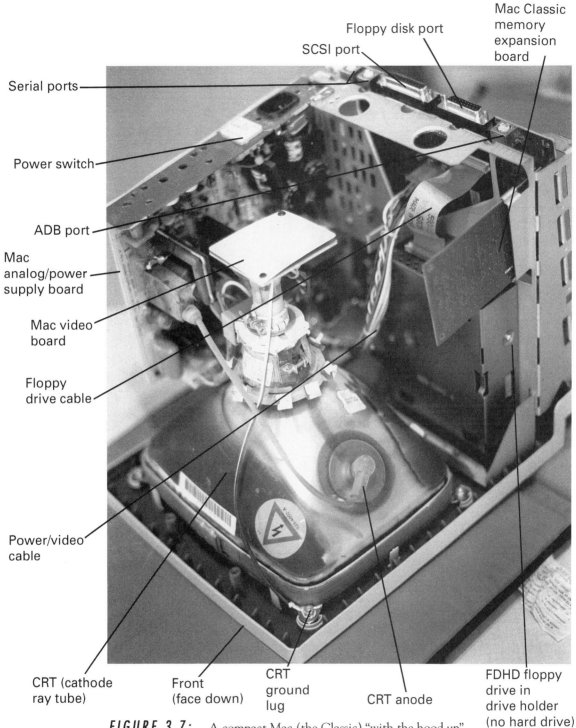

Serial ports

Power switch

ADB port

Mac analog/power supply board

Mac video board

Floppy drive cable

Power/video cable

Floppy disk port

SCSI port

Mac Classic memory expansion board

CRT (cathode ray tube)

Front (face down)

CRT ground lug

CRT anode

FDHD floppy drive in drive holder (no hard drive)

FIGURE 3.7: A compact Mac (the Classic) "with the hood up"

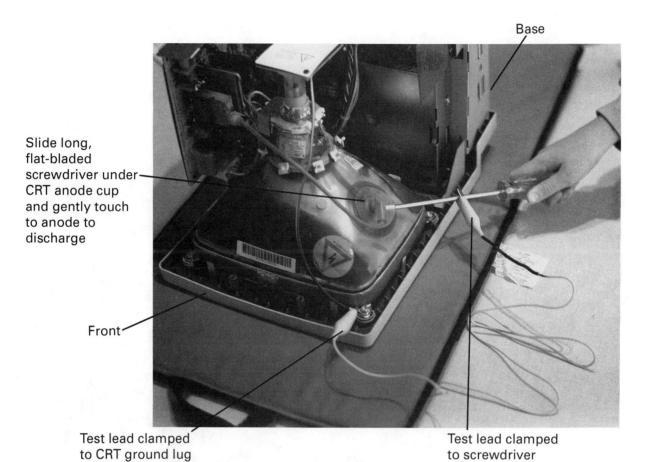

Base

Slide long, flat-bladed screwdriver under CRT anode cup and gently touch to anode to discharge

Front

Test lead clamped to CRT ground lug

Test lead clamped to screwdriver

FIGURE 3.8: Grounding the CRT anode

If you have a hard drive, the 50-conductor SCSI cable at the back of the drive should be unplugged from the logic board, and the hard drive power cable connector should be unplugged from the power supply/analog board. The floppy disk drive connector (or connectors in an SE or SE/30) can now be unplugged from the logic board (see Figure 3.12). As with the logic board power cable, *do not* let your hand fly back into the CRT.

Now you're ready to remove your Mac's logic board. Removing a logic board is slightly different for different compact Mac models.

With a Mac 128, 512, or Plus, you can just slide the logic board out at this point. The same is true of the Classic and Classic II (Figure 3.13). Once again—be careful with the Classic frame. It's light, not rigid like previous compact Macs.

Two metal tabs on either side of the SE or SE/30 frame hold the logic board in. Remove these and slide the board up a few inches. Match the notch

Removing the Mac
Classic video card

Antistatic strap

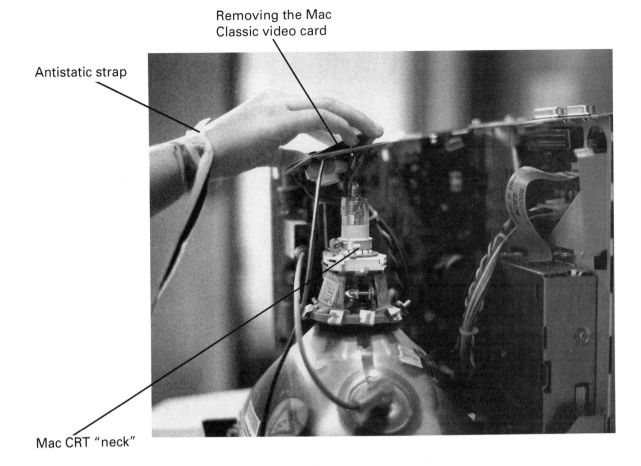

Mac CRT "neck"

FIGURE 3.9:   Removing the CRT video card on a Mac Classic

on the SE or SE/30 logic board to those in the chassis frame and tilt the board toward you. Remove the twisted pair speaker wire plugged into the logic board. Note its position, just to the left of the main logic board power connector.

With the logic board out, you'll see two screws in the metal platform that the floppy and hard drives sit on. Remove these screws (needle-nose pliers to hold the screws will help here), while *holding on to the hard drive* (see Figure 3.14). If you have no hard drive installed, hold on to the metal floppy drive enclosure.

 This is very important: do NOT let the hard and/or floppy drives fall forward on to the CRT tube!

Base

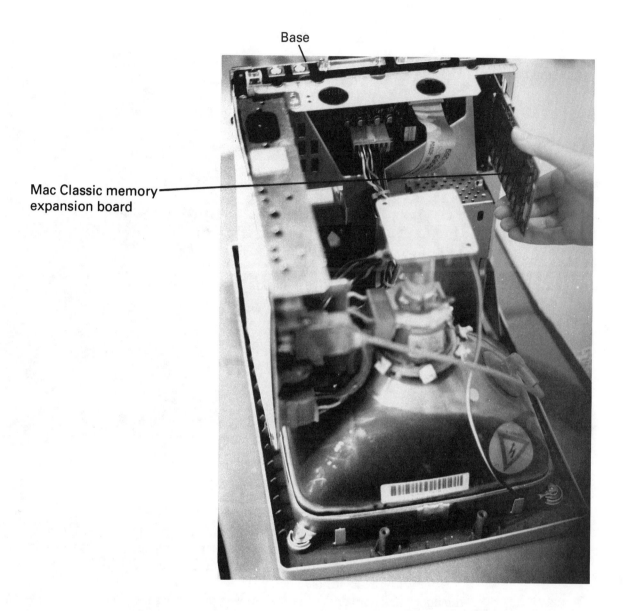

Mac Classic memory
expansion board

FIGURE 3.10: Removing a Mac Classic memory expansion board (the
surface-mount variety)

When the mounting screws are removed, lift out the hard and floppy
drives and undo the screws holding them together. Congratulations, you're done!
To reassemble the compact Mac, just reverse the process.

Base

Removing a
Compact Mac
video/power
cable—note
orientation of
plug locking
latch

Unlatch and
remove carefully

CRT neck

Mac Classic video board

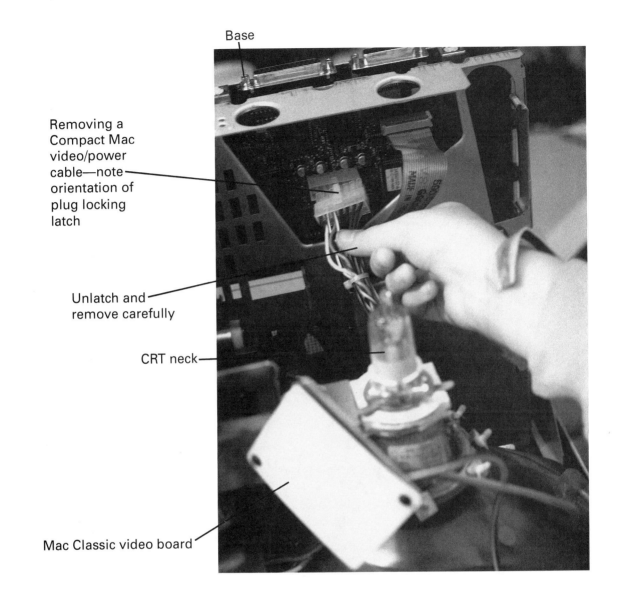

FIGURE 3.11:   Removing the logic board power plug

Compact Mac Slots

The early 128K and 512K Macs had no internal and few external upgrade options. When upgrading these machines, you have to attach an upgrade board to

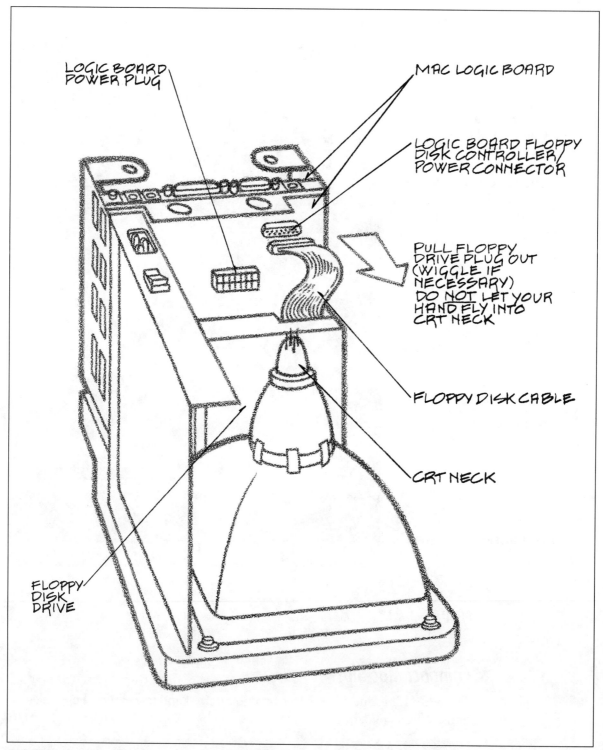

FIGURE 3.12: Removing the floppy disk drive cable

the CPU with a *Killy clip* (discussed in detail in Chapter 5). This has prompted many people to refer to these machines as "clip-on" Macs.

The Mac Plus added substantial external and internal upgrade potential to the Macintosh with a built-in SCSI port and internal SIMM memory expansion slots. However, the Plus is still a "clip-on Mac" because many expansion options have to be added via a Killy clip.

The SE and SE/30 were giant steps forward for compact Macs because they included a PDS (processor direct slot). This feature is becoming standard in all of Apple's high-end Macs. The processor direct slot allows expansion boards to connect firmly to the Mac logic board, preventing potential oxidation and loosening, which are always possibilities with a Killy clip. Expansion boards can communicate directly with the Macintosh CPU via the PDS, providing hardware developers with much more powerful design options. The SE 96-pin

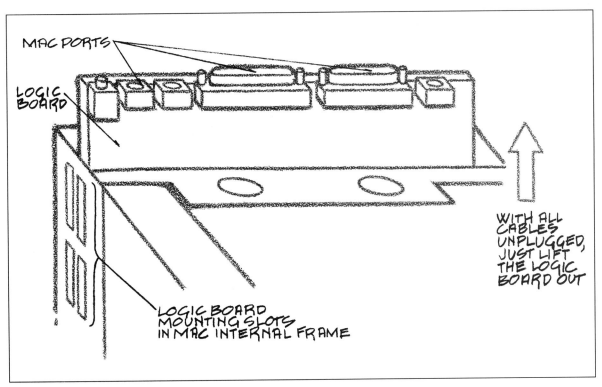

FIGURE 3.13:   Just slide the logic board out

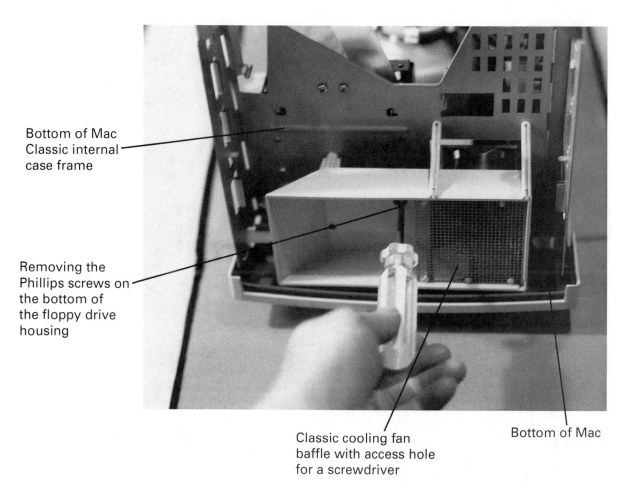

Bottom of Mac
Classic internal
case frame

Removing the
Phillips screws on
the bottom of
the floppy drive
housing

Classic cooling fan
baffle with access hole
for a screwdriver

Bottom of Mac

FIGURE 3.14: Removing the drive mounting screws

and SE/30 120-pin PDS slots are located on the right front edge of the Mac logic board. The SE and SE/30 also included additional SIMM space and internal connectors for up to one hard drive and two floppy drives.

Apple's two recent compact Macs are a step back. Neither includes a PDS slot, although they both have some internal expansion and plugs for one hard drive and one FDHD floppy drive. The Mac Classic has a 22-pin memory expansion slot which can be used to add SIMM slots to the machine. There are, unfortunately, no SIMM slots on the logic board. Some upgrades, notably video/SIMM combination boards, can be added via the memory slot, but many upgrades are throwbacks to the "clip-on Mac" days. The Classic II has two SIMM slots and a slot for a numeric coprocessor or expansion ROM.

Because the Classic II has Mac LC ROMs, it can be upgraded to color capability using video SIMMs.

There is one reason for the limited expansion potential of the Classic and Classic II, and it is cost. The machines are designed for quick, low-cost assembly. The up side to this is that you get a lot of features for a lot less money. Used Mac SE and SE/30 machines at a good price are an *excellent* buy.

Figures 3.15, 3.16, and 3.17 are schematic diagrams of the Mac 512/Plus, SE and SE/30, and Classic and Classic II logic boards. Figure 3.18 shows (top to bottom) a 3½" FDHD drive (high-density 1.44MB floppy drive) in its mounting bracket, a Classic surface-mount memory board, a small SCSI terminator board that plugs into the internal 50-pin SCSI hard drive connector in a single-floppy Classic, and a Classic logic board.

Getting into Your Modular Mac

"Never trust a computer without slots!"

Well, that viewpoint may be a tad extreme, but it is true that Apple's modular Macintoshes are easy to open and upgrade with expansion boards. The modular Macs also allow a lot of flexibility in the choice of mass storage devices, memory, and video displays. I'll cover the modular Macs in four parts: six-slot Macs, three-slot Macs, PDS Macs, and the Quadra 900.

The Mac II, IIx, and IIfx have large cases with six expansion slots (they're the six-slot Macs). The Mac IIcx, IIci, and Quadra 700 have compact cases (hence the "c" in IIcx and IIci) and three NuBus slots, hence the designation of three-slot Macs. The new, low-priced LC, LC II, and IIsi use a single PDS for expansion, so I've referred to them as PDS Macs. The Quadra 900 with its large tower case and five NuBus slots is in a class by itself, so I'm treating it separately. Figure 3.19 has schematics of the six-slot Mac logic boards, Figure 3.20 has the schematics for the three-slot Macs, Figure 3.21 shows the PDS Macs, and Figure 3.22 is a schematic of a Quadra 900 logic board.

Six-Slot Macs

As noted, opening any modular Mac is a breeze, and six-slot Macs are no exception. Choose a well-lit area with lots of elbow room and remove the monitor

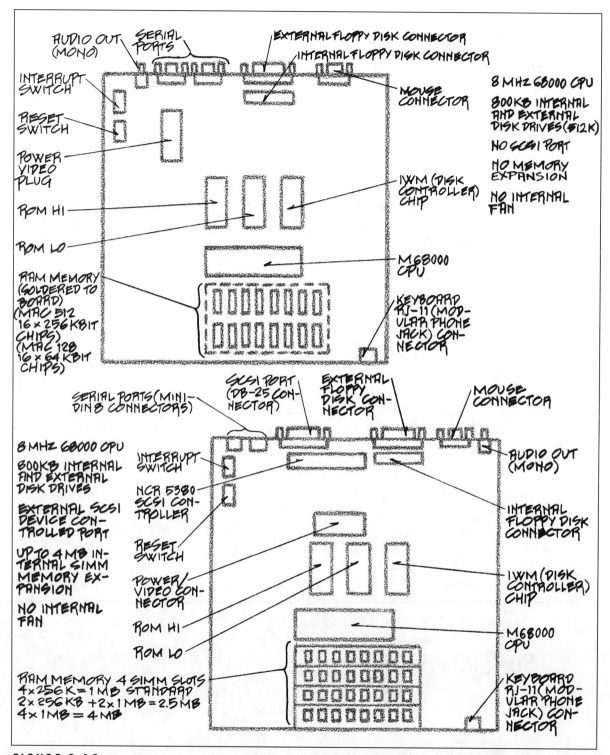

FIGURE 3.15: Schematic diagrams of the Mac 512 (top) and Plus (bottom) logic boards

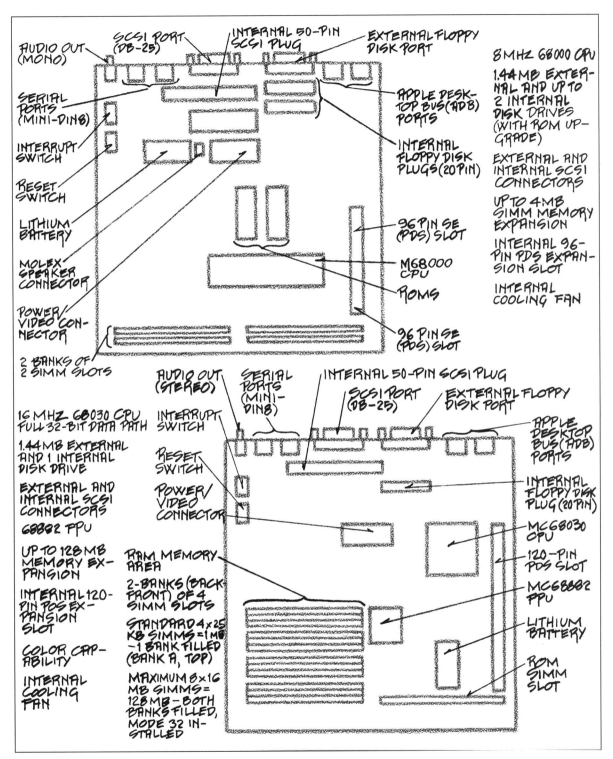

Labels (Mac SE, top):
AUDIO OUT (MONO) • SCSI PORT (DB-25) • INTERNAL 50-PIN SCSI PLUG • EXTERNAL FLOPPY DISK PORT • 8 MHz 68000 CPU • 1.44 MB EXTERNAL AND UP TO 2 INTERNAL DISK DRIVES (WITH ROM UPGRADE) • EXTERNAL AND INTERNAL SCSI CONNECTORS • UP TO 4 MB SIMM MEMORY EXPANSION • INTERNAL 96-PIN PDS EXPANSION SLOT • INTERNAL COOLING FAN • SERIAL PORTS (MINI-DIN8) • INTERRUPT SWITCH • RESET SWITCH • LITHIUM BATTERY • MOLEX SPEAKER CONNECTOR • POWER/VIDEO CONNECTOR • 2 BANKS OF 2 SIMM SLOTS • APPLE DESKTOP BUS (ADB) PORTS • INTERNAL FLOPPY DISK PLUGS (20 PIN) • 96 PIN SE (PDS) SLOT • M68000 CPU • ROMS • 96 PIN SE (PDS) SLOT

Labels (SE/30, bottom):
16 MHz 68030 CPU FULL 32-BIT DATA PATH • 1.44 MB EXTERNAL AND 1 INTERNAL DISK DRIVE • EXTERNAL AND INTERNAL SCSI CONNECTORS • 68882 FPU • UP TO 128 MB MEMORY EXPANSION • INTERNAL 120-PIN PDS EXPANSION SLOT • COLOR CAPABILITY • INTERNAL COOLING FAN • AUDIO OUT (STEREO) • SERIAL PORTS (MINI-DIN8) • INTERRUPT SWITCH • RESET SWITCH • POWER/VIDEO CONNECTOR • RAM MEMORY AREA • 2-BANKS (BACK FRONT) OF 4 SIMM SLOTS • STANDARD 4 x 256 KB SIMMS = 1 MB — 1 BANK FILLED (BANK A, TOP) • MAXIMUM 8 x 16 MB SIMMS = 128 MB — BOTH BANKS FILLED, MODE 32 INSTALLED • INTERNAL 50-PIN SCSI PLUG • SCSI PORT (DB-25) • EXTERNAL FLOPPY DISK PORT • APPLE DESKTOP BUS (ADB) PORTS • INTERNAL FLOPPY DISK PLUG (20 PIN) • MC68030 CPU • 120-PIN PDS SLOT • MC68882 FPU • LITHIUM BATTERY • ROM SIMM SLOT

FIGURE 3.16: Schematic diagrams of the Mac SE (top) and SE/30 (bottom) logic boards

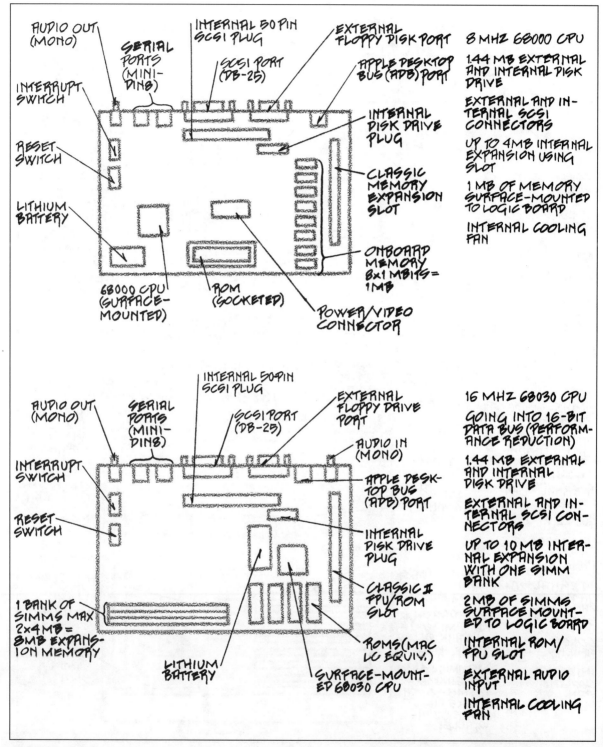

AUDIO OUT (MONO)

SERIAL PORTS (MINI-DIN8)

INTERNAL 50 PIN SCSI PLUG

SCSI PORT (DB-25)

EXTERNAL FLOPPY DISK PORT

APPLE DESKTOP BUS (ADB) PORT

INTERRUPT SWITCH

RESET SWITCH

LITHIUM BATTERY

INTERNAL DISK DRIVE PLUG

CLASSIC MEMORY EXPANSION SLOT

ONBOARD MEMORY 8x1 MBITS= 1MB

68000 CPU (SURFACE-MOUNTED)

ROM (SOCKETED)

POWER/VIDEO CONNECTOR

8 MHZ 68000 CPU

1.44 MB EXTERNAL AND INTERNAL DISK DRIVE

EXTERNAL AND INTERNAL SCSI CONNECTORS

UP TO 4MB INTERNAL EXPANSION USING SLOT

1 MB OF MEMORY SURFACE-MOUNTED TO LOGIC BOARD

INTERNAL COOLING FAN

AUDIO OUT (MONO)

SERIAL PORTS (MINI-DIN8)

INTERNAL 50-PIN SCSI PLUG

SCSI PORT (DB-25)

EXTERNAL FLOPPY DRIVE PORT

AUDIO IN (MONO)

INTERRUPT SWITCH

RESET SWITCH

1 BANK OF SIMMS MAX 2x4 MB = 8MB EXPANS-ION MEMORY

APPLE DESK-TOP BUS (ADB) PORT

INTERNAL DISK DRIVE PLUG

CLASSIC II FPU/ROM SLOT

ROMS (MAC LC EQUIV.)

SURFACE-MOUNT-ED 68030 CPU

LITHIUM BATTERY

16 MHZ 68030 CPU

GOING INTO 16-BIT DATA BUS (PERFORM-ANCE REDUCTION)

1.44 MB EXTERNAL AND INTERNAL DISK DRIVE

EXTERNAL AND INTERNAL SCSI CON-NECTORS

UP TO 10 MB INTER-NAL EXPANSION WITH ONE SIMM BANK

2 MB OF SIMMS SURFACE MOUNT-ED TO LOGIC BOARD

INTERNAL ROM/ FPU SLOT

EXTERNAL AUDIO INPUT

INTERNAL COOLING FAN

FIGURE 3.17:   Schematic diagrams of the Mac Classic (top) and Classic II (bottom) logic boards

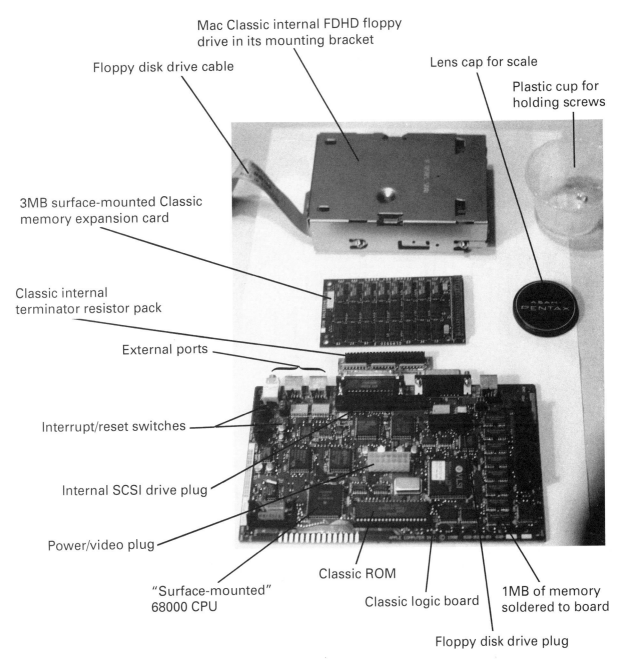

Mac Classic internal FDHD floppy drive in its mounting bracket

Floppy disk drive cable

Lens cap for scale

Plastic cup for holding screws

3MB surface-mounted Classic memory expansion card

Classic internal terminator resistor pack

External ports

Interrupt/reset switches

Internal SCSI drive plug

Power/video plug

"Surface-mounted" 68000 CPU

Classic ROM

Classic logic board

1MB of memory soldered to board

Floppy disk drive plug

FIGURE 3.18:   Top to bottom: an HD floppy, a Classic surface-mount memory board, SCSI terminator board (for the internal SCSI plug), and a Classic logic board

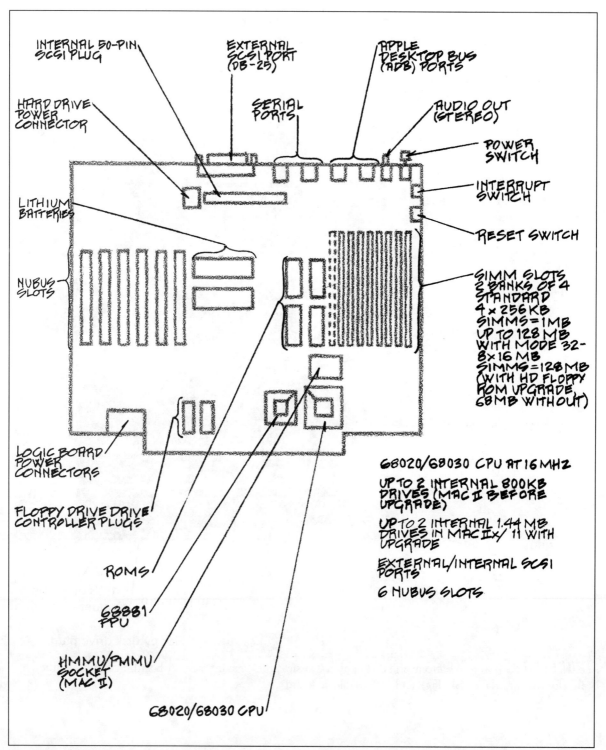

INTERNAL 50-PIN SCSI PLUG

EXTERNAL SCSI PORT (DB-25)

APPLE DESKTOP BUS (ADB) PORTS

HARD DRIVE POWER CONNECTOR

SERIAL PORTS

AUDIO OUT (STEREO)

POWER SWITCH

INTERRUPT SWITCH

RESET SWITCH

LITHIUM BATTERIES

SIMM SLOTS 2 BANKS OF 4 STANDARD 4 × 256KB SIMMS=1MB UP TO 128 MB WITH MODE 32- 8×16 MB SIMMS=128MB (WITH HD FLOPPY ROM UPGRADE, 68MB WITHOUT)

NUBUS SLOTS

LOGIC BOARD POWER CONNECTORS

FLOPPY DRIVE DRIVE CONTROLLER PLUGS

68020/68030 CPU AT 16 MHZ

UP TO 2 INTERNAL 800KB DRIVES (MAC II BEFORE UPGRADE)

UP TO 2 INTERNAL 1.44 MB DRIVES IN MAC IIx/ II WITH UPGRADE

EXTERNAL/INTERNAL SCSI PORTS

6 NUBUS SLOTS

ROMS

68881 FPU

HMMU/PMMU SOCKET (MAC II)

68020/68030 CPU

FIGURE 3.19: Schematics of the six-slot Mac logic boards (Mac II, IIx)

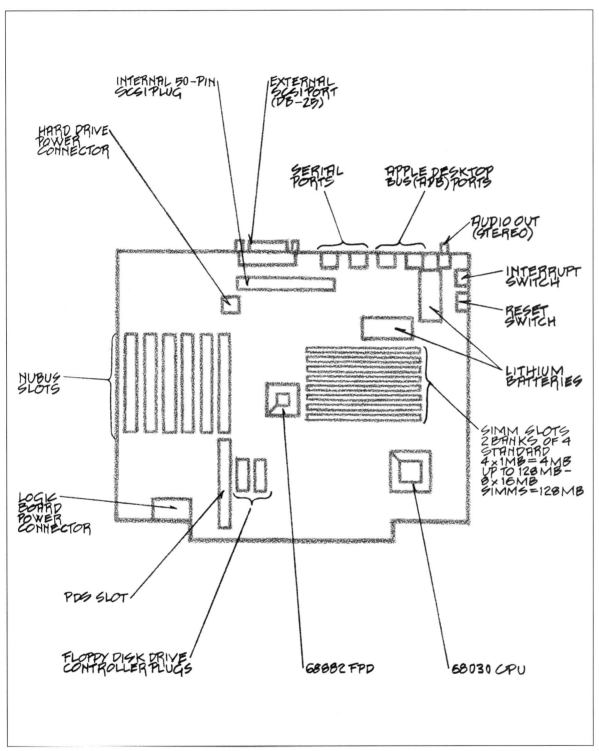

FIGURE 3.19:   Schematics of the six-slot Mac logic boards (Mac IIfx) (continued)

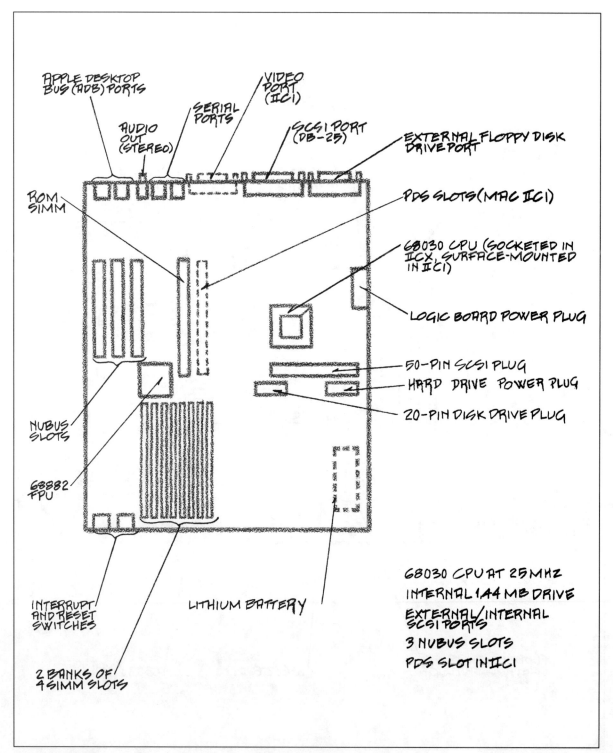

APPLE DESKTOP
BUS (ADB) PORTS

VIDEO
PORT
(IICI)

SERIAL
PORTS

AUDIO
OUT
(STEREO)

SCSI PORT
(DB-25)

EXTERNAL FLOPPY DISK
DRIVE PORT

ROM
SIMM

PDS SLOTS (MAC IICI)

68030 CPU (SOCKETED IN
IICX, SURFACE-MOUNTED
IN IICI)

LOGIC BOARD POWER PLUG

50-PIN SCSI PLUG
HARD DRIVE POWER PLUG
20-PIN DISK DRIVE PLUG

NUBUS
SLOTS

68882
FPU

INTERRUPT
AND RESET
SWITCHES

LITHIUM BATTERY

2 BANKS OF
4 SIMM SLOTS

68030 CPU AT 25 MHz
INTERNAL 1.44 MB DRIVE
EXTERNAL/INTERNAL
SCSI PORTS
3 NUBUS SLOTS
PDS SLOT IN IICI

FIGURE 3.20: Schematics of the three-slot Mac logic boards (Mac IIcx/IIci)

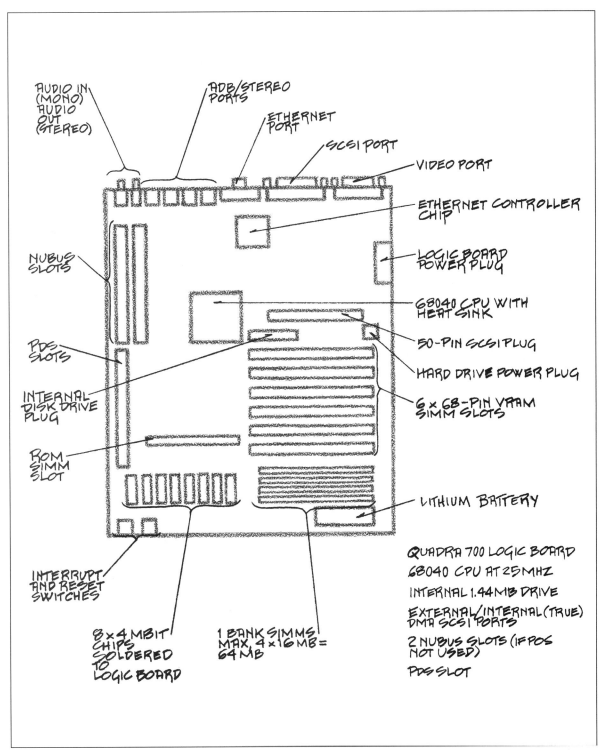

FIGURE 3.20:   Schematics of the three-slot Mac logic boards (Quadra 700) (continued)

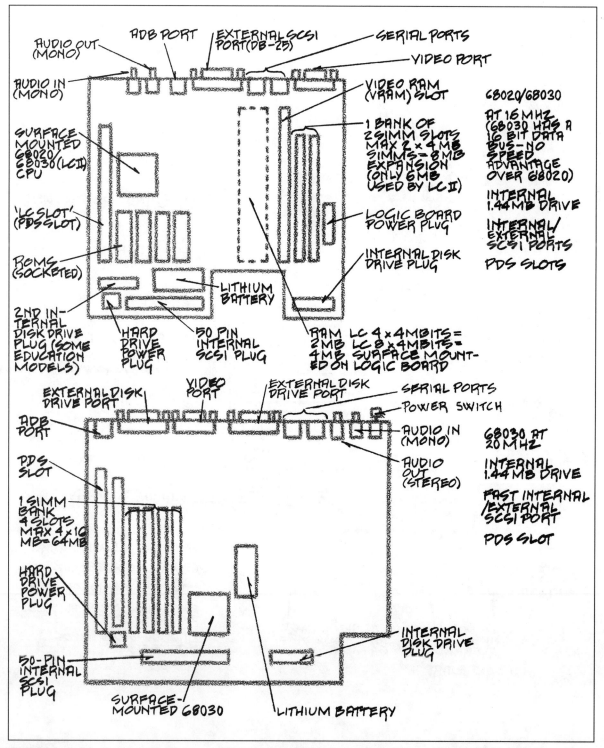

FIGURE 3.21: Schematics of the Mac LC/LCII (top) and Mac IIsi (bottom) PDS logic boards

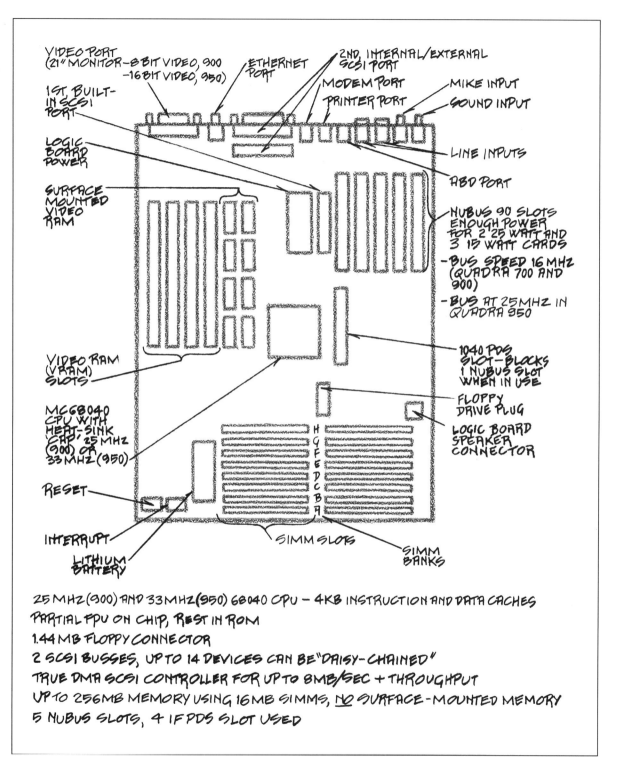

VIDEO PORT
(21" MONITOR-8 BIT VIDEO, 900
-16 BIT VIDEO, 950)

ETHERNET PORT

2ND. INTERNAL/EXTERNAL SCSI PORT

MODEM PORT
PRINTER PORT

MIKE INPUT
SOUND INPUT

1ST, BUILT-IN SCSI PORT

LOGIC BOARD POWER

SURFACE MOUNTED VIDEO RAM

LINE INPUTS

ABD PORT

NUBUS 90 SLOTS
ENOUGH POWER FOR 2 25 WATT AND 3 15 WATT CARDS
-BUS SPEED 16 MHZ (QUADRA 700 AND 900)
-BUS AT 25 MHZ IN QUADRA 950

VIDEO RAM (VRAM) SLOTS

1040 PDS SLOT-BLOCKS 1 NUBUS SLOT WHEN IN USE

FLOPPY DRIVE PLUG

MC68040 CPU WITH HEAT-SINK CAP. 25 MHZ (900) OR 33 MHZ (950)

LOGIC BOARD SPEAKER CONNECTOR

RESET

INTERRUPT

LITHIUM BATTERY

H
G
F
E
D
C
B
A

SIMM SLOTS

SIMM BANKS

25 MHZ (900) AND 33 MHZ (950) 68040 CPU — 4KB INSTRUCTION AND DATA CACHES
PARTIAL FPU ON CHIP, REST IN ROM
1.44 MB FLOPPY CONNECTOR
2 SCSI BUSSES, UP TO 14 DEVICES CAN BE "DAISY-CHAINED"
TRUE DMA SCSI CONTROLLER FOR UP TO 8MB/SEC + THROUGHPUT
UP TO 256MB MEMORY USING 16MB SIMMS, NO SURFACE-MOUNTED MEMORY
5 NUBUS SLOTS, 4 IF PDS SLOT USED

FIGURE 3.22:   Schematic of the Quadra 900 logic board

and all cables from your six-slot Mac. Now, undo the locking screw in the middle of the case back, just below the lid. Then "hug" the Mac, grab the two rear corners of the case, and push the locking tabs in. Lift the cover to about a 30° angle and move it back a small amount.

 Lifting the cover right up will break three plastic loops at the front of the case, something that will complicate matters no end and cause you to swear.

Six-slot Mac cases have a drive platform on the right-hand side of the case (see Figure 3.23). The platform is designed to support a 5¼" or smaller hard drive and up to two floppy disk drives. You can remove the drive platform without removing the drives. Simply remove the four screws with lock washers on the left and right corners of the platform and unplug the drive cables. Note that there are two 20-pin floppy drive connectors on the logic board, marked "Upper" and "Lower." The "Upper" connector is on the right side and is for the right floppy drive. The "Lower" connector is on the left side and is for the left floppy drive. Remember the connector's location for reinstallation of the floppy drive ribbon cable(s). Remove the 50-conductor SCSI cable from the 50-pin connector on the logic board, and lift the drive platform out.

The hard drive and floppy drives in a six-slot Mac are in drive-mounting brackets screwed on to the drive platform. To remove hard or floppy drives, just unscrew the bracket and lift them out. The hard drive or floppy drive mechanism can be removed from its bracket by simply undoing the mounting screws.

 Modern drives are in fairly light cases and are easily damaged if torqued. BE CAREFUL when mounting or removing hard or floppy drives. Do not overtighten mounting screws!

It's easy to add (or remove) a NuBus card with a modular Mac. To add a card, just remove the metal RFI shield from the inside, and the plastic cover from the outside, of the case "window." Slide the NuBus card into place, keeping the metal tab on the card in the metal guides on the back of the Mac case and gently seat the pins on the card into the NuBus slot.

To remove a NuBus card, just reverse the above process.

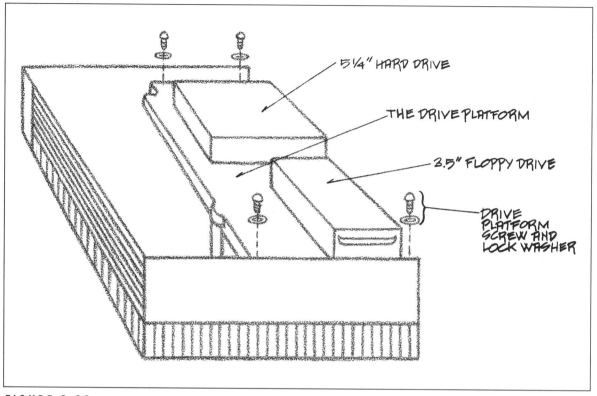

5¼" HARD DRIVE

THE DRIVE PLATFORM

3.5" FLOPPY DRIVE

DRIVE PLATFORM SCREW AND LOCK WASHER

FIGURE 3.23:   Drive platform in a six-slot Mac

The SIMM slots that contain Mac II memory chips are in two "banks" of four slots running front to back on the extreme right side of the case. They're just behind the logic board center line. "Bank A" refers to the four SIMM slots on the left, "bank B" to the four slots on the right. To remove the SIMMs, carefully move the small plastic tab on the left side of a SIMM, called a retainer, back and tip the SIMM forward enough to catch the retainer. It's easy to break these retainers, so don't force anything. A small, flat-bladed, nonmagnetic screwdriver is useful for moving SIMM retainers.

Now move back the retainer on the right side of the SIMM and tip the SIMM forward at a 45° angle. The SIMM should lift out easily. To reinsert SIMMs, just place them in the slot, chips up, at a 45° angle and tip the SIMM up until the retainers click into place.

With everything off of the logic board, the power supply plug can be removed. The plug is the large plastic connector on the left front side of the logic board with wires going to the big metal box on the left side of the case (the power supply). After you remove the power supply plug, the logic board is ready to remove—just take out the two Phillips-head screws at the back of the logic board and lift it out.

Three-Slot Macs and the Quadra 700

The three-slot Macs have a slightly different internal arrangement than the six-slot Macs (see Figure 3.24). The SIMMs in three-slot Macs are completely exposed and easy to add or remove, unlike the ones in six-slot Macs, which are covered by the drive platform. (The Quadra 700, unfortunately, is a throwback to the "bad old days" and the SIMMs are again covered by the plastic drive platform.)

The hard drive and floppy drive in three-slot Macs are in a plastic drive holder on the right side of the case (viewed from the front). The metal hard drive bracket has two locking tabs that hold it in place. Removing the drive is a simple matter of unplugging the 50-pin SCSI (see Figure 3.25) and hard drive power cables, squeezing the tabs on the hard drive bracket (Figure 3.26), and lifting the hard drive out of the plastic drive holder. The speaker at the front of the case can now be removed.

Remove the speaker wires from the logic board, tilt the speaker back, and lift it out. A plastic tab from the drive holder fastens the power supply in place. Place your hand under the power supply between it and the drive holder, then push the tab from the drive holder. This releases the power supply. Lift out the power supply and unplug the logic board power cable.

Now, remove the screw holding the plastic drive holder (Figure 3.27) and unplug the 20-pin floppy drive cable. Then, lift out the drive holder. If you haven't done it by now, remove any SIMMs or NuBus cards on the logic board.

Now, remove the reset and interrupt switch bracket in the left front corner of the case. The bracket is installed by pushing it forward and down. *Gently* push forward on the bracket and pull up. This should free it from the logic board, and pushing on the interrupt and reset buttons should push the switch out.

The logic board can be removed by sliding it toward the front of the case and lifting it out. Note the location of the button over the power switch in the right rear corner of the case and make sure it is reinstalled the same way.

Installation of three-slot Mac components is just the reverse of the above.

PDS Macs

PDS Macs, the new modular Macs that use a PDS slot for expansion, include the LC, LC II, and the IIsi. Like all other modular Macs, the LC, LC II, and IIsi can be opened by simply removing a Phillips-head screw just below the back of the case lid and lifting up on two tabs.

To start disassembling the Mac LC, first remove the plastic fan/speaker assembly. This is in the center of the case and can be released by gently pulling back on a locking tab at the front of the assembly. The LCII fan and speaker are each held down by plastic locking tabs and can be released separately (Figure 3.28).

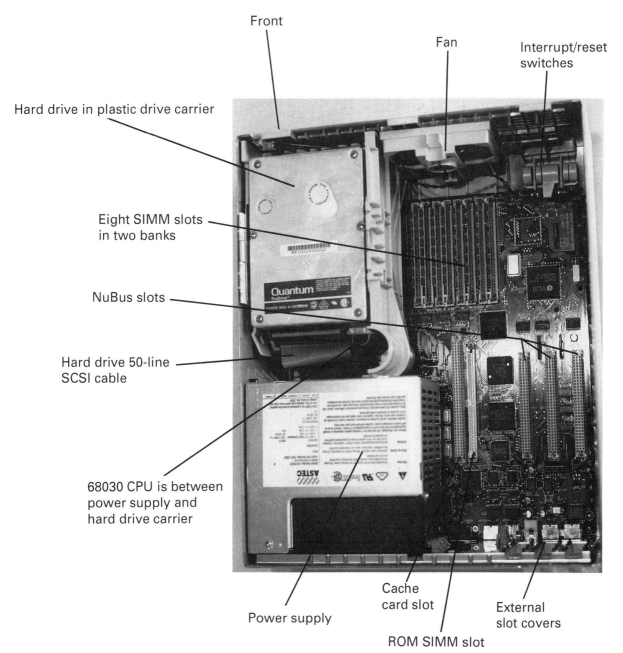

Front

Fan

Interrupt/reset switches

Hard drive in plastic drive carrier

Eight SIMM slots in two banks

NuBus slots

Hard drive 50-line SCSI cable

68030 CPU is between power supply and hard drive carrier

Power supply

Cache card slot

ROM SIMM slot

External slot covers

FIGURE 3.24:   Internal arrangement of the three-slot Macs

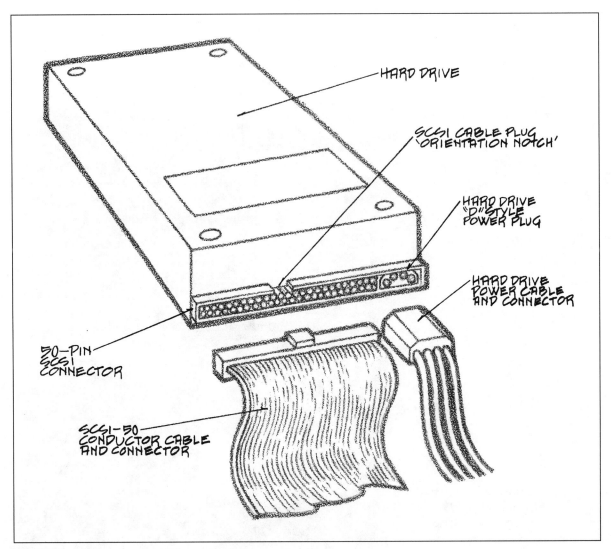

FIGURE 3.25:   The hard drive SCSI and power cables

In the LC and LCII, the hard and floppy drives are also held down by plastic locking tabs. Disconnect the floppy and hard drive cables, unlock the plastic tabs, and lift the drives out (Figure 3.29). The hard drive and floppy drive are in their own metal brackets and can be removed by taking out the mounting screws. If you decide to replace the hard drive in the LC, make sure that the replacement is a low-power version designed for the machine.

Squeeze the locking latches and
lift the drive bracket out

Locking latches

Front

FIGURE 3.26:   Lifting out the hard drive carrier

The LC power supply is held down by two locking tabs on either side. With these unfastened, the power supply can be unplugged and removed (Figure 3.30). It's probably easier to remove the power supply before inserting or removing SIMMs. There's only one SIMM bank with two slots. Looking from the front, it's on the right side of the logic board next to the power supply.

A long, 68-pin slot for video expansion memory (VRAM) is right next to the SIMM bank (Figure 3.31). The 96-pin PDS expansion slot(or "LC Slot") where you can add internal modems, FPUs, video cards, and the Apple II emulator board, is on the far left (once again, looking from the front) side of the logic board (Figure 3.32). The LC case has a plastic cover on the back plane behind the slot to accommodate any plugs associated with add-in boards.

Like the LC, the Mac IIsi's hard and floppy drives are held in place by plastic locking tabs. But unlike the LC these tabs are quite wide. To remove a IIsi hard or floppy drive, just unlock the tabs, disconnect the cables, and pull the drive out. The IIsi's SIMMs and PDS slot are behind the hard drive, in the left rear corner of the case. Numerous suppliers make adapters for the IIsi slot to add NuBus and multiple-slot capability, as well as cache cards and FPUs. The IIsi case back has a long horizontal cutout, behind the PDS slot, that can be removed to allow plugs from slot adapters to pass through.

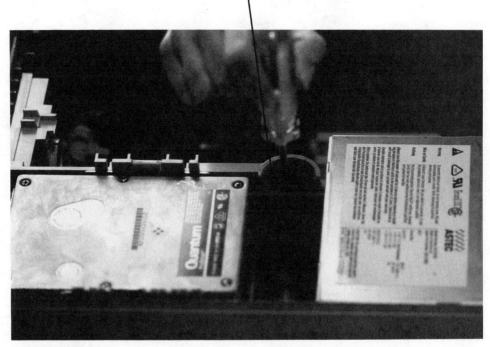

The hold-down screw for the IIci plastic drive carrier is at the base of this support

FIGURE 3.27:   Removing the hold-down screw for the drive holder

The Quadra 900 and 950

The Quadra 900 or 950 tower case is easily accessible by removing the side access door, using the two unlatching buttons at the back of the case. The Quadra SIMMs are near the front of the case, just below the power supply. The NuBus slots are totally unobstructed and designed to accommodate large cards that require high power.

Getting to the Quadra's VRAM SIMMs is a little harder, requiring the removal of the power supply.

The Quadra drive bay, right on top of the 300-watt power supply, can accommodate up to two removable media drives at the front of the bay and two half-height, nonremovable devices at the back. You can remove the hard and floppy drives easily by removing the cable connections and the mounting screws on the drive mounting plate, which is at the top of the power supply. Then just lift the drives out.

The floppy drive 20-pin connector is below the power supply and beside the SIMM banks. The two SCSI connectors are in the middle of the logic board just below the power supply, and just beside the external SCSI connector, between the power supply and the case backplane. The drive power cables are just

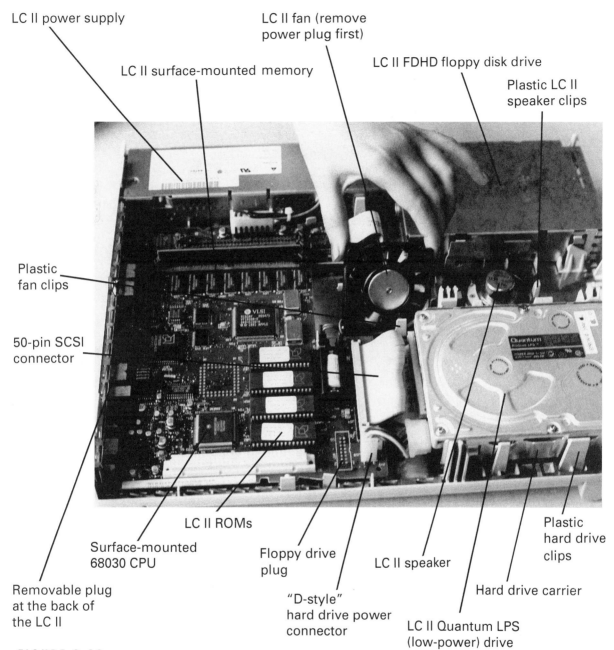

LC II power supply

LC II fan (remove power plug first)

LC II surface-mounted memory

LC II FDHD floppy disk drive

Plastic LC II speaker clips

Plastic fan clips

50-pin SCSI connector

LC II ROMs

Surface-mounted 68030 CPU

Floppy drive plug

LC II speaker

Plastic hard drive clips

Removable plug at the back of the LC II

"D-style" hard drive power connector

LC II Quantum LPS (low-power) drive

Hard drive carrier

FIGURE 3.28:   Removing the fan/speaker assembly

underneath the power supply. These cables have to be quite long, so you may have some "cable threading" to do when you add and remove drives in the Quadra.

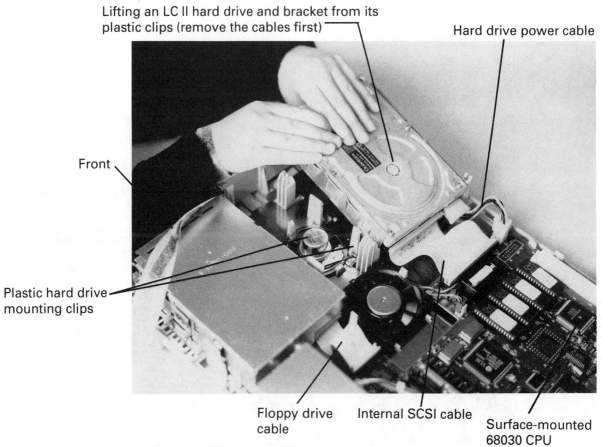

Lifting an LC II hard drive and bracket from its plastic clips (remove the cables first)

Hard drive power cable

Front

Plastic hard drive mounting clips

Floppy drive cable

Internal SCSI cable

Surface-mounted 68030 CPU

FIGURE 3.29: Removing the drives

Opening a Mac Portable

The original Mac portable was designed to be upgraded and is easy to open. The PowerBooks, unfortunately, are another matter. Both, however are eminently do-able, and I will describe how here.

The Original Portable

Opening Apple's original Portable is quite straightforward. Set your portable down, in the closed and locked position, so that it's facing you. Reach around both sides and place your fingers on two square tabs on either corner of the case back. These are the lid latches. Press them in and lift the cover up about 45° and off. You'll see a hard drive on the right and a battery cover on the left (Figure 3.33).

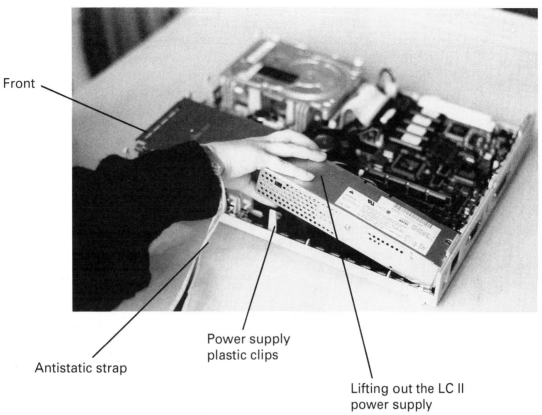

Front

Antistatic strap

Power supply
plastic clips

Lifting out the LC II
power supply

FIGURE 3.30:   Removing the power supply

 Remove the battery cover and take the battery out, then REPLACE THE BATTERY COVER. With the battery cover off, reserve power is supplied to the machine and inserting or removing expansion boards could damage the machine. Before proceeding, replace the cover!

You have the alternative of removing the 9-volt backup battery, at the rear of the case behind the main battery. This is basically a transistor radio battery, and removing it will also remove your parameter RAM settings—for instance, things like time, date, and cache memory size.

The Portable has four expansion slots between the hard drive and the battery. Viewed from the back of the Portable these are, from left to right, the PDS slot, the RAM expansion slot, the ROM slot, and the modem slot.

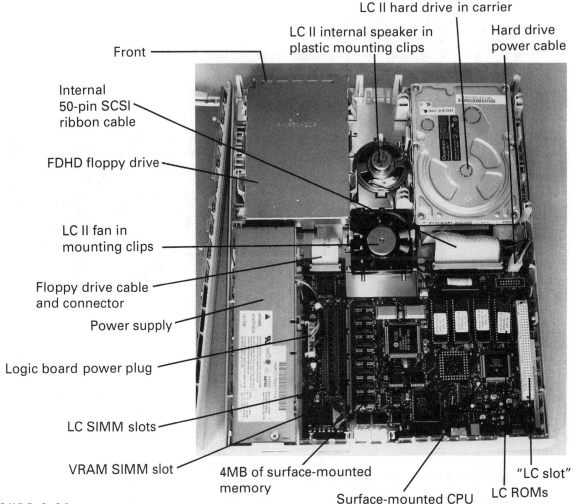

Front

LC II internal speaker in plastic mounting clips

LC II hard drive in carrier

Hard drive power cable

Internal 50-pin SCSI ribbon cable

FDHD floppy drive

LC II fan in mounting clips

Floppy drive cable and connector

Power supply

Logic board power plug

LC SIMM slots

VRAM SIMM slot

4MB of surface-mounted memory

Surface-mounted CPU

"LC slot"

LC ROMs

FIGURE 3.31:   Location of the LC SIMMs and VRAM

The PowerBooks

Opening a PowerBook case is a bit of an adventure, but then, so is opening the case on a compact Mac. The PowerBooks are certainly no harder.

To open a PowerBook 100, begin by turning the computer off and closing the screen. Remove the PowerBook 100 battery from the right front corner of the computer. Then remove the backup battery from the right rear corner, pulling it out gently. Remove the rubber feet from the bottom of the PowerBook and take the three Phillips screws out of the case bottom. *Hold the PowerBook together* and gently turn it over so the screen latch is toward you. Release the latch and *carefully* swing the screen open, until it lies flat on the table. Grasp the rear edge of the keyboard, lift slightly, and pull about ¼" toward the rear of the computer. Grasp the side of the keyboard and flip it over on top of the

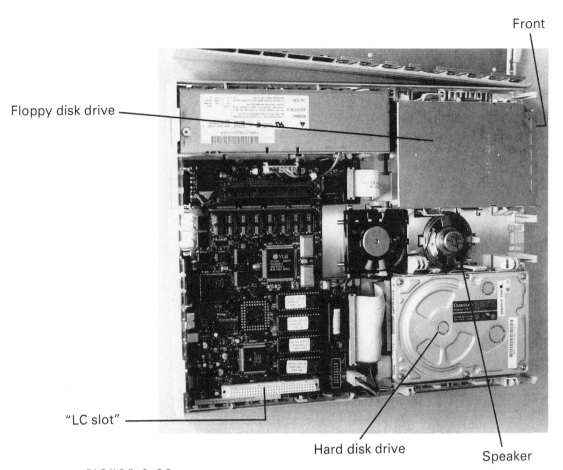

Front

Floppy disk drive

"LC slot"

Hard disk drive

Speaker

FIGURE 3.32: Location of the 96-pin LC PDS slot

screen (Figure 3.34). You can now get at the memory expansion connector, which is by the right front corner of the case.

To restore the PowerBook 100 to its original state, replace the keyboard, hooking its front edge under the trackball deck. *Carefully* swing the screen closed, lining up the rear edges of the case halves first. Replace the three screws and rubber feet.

To open a PowerBook 140 or 170, you'll need #8 and #10 Torx screwdrivers (try an auto parts store). Start by turning the portable off, and closing and latching the screen. Remove the battery, from the left front corner of the machine. Turn the computer over and remove four #10 Torx screws from the bottom of the case, two below the hinges, one by the serial number plate, and one at the front edge of the case.

Carefully turn the computer right side up with the back toward you and open the rear door. Remove the single #8 Torx screw. Gently lift the top of the computer from the rear until you can get at the keyboard ribbon cable. Gently

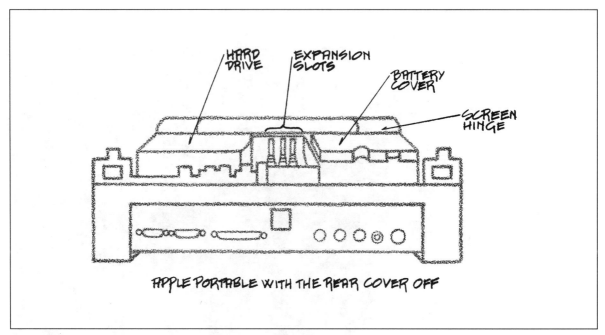

HARD DRIVE

EXPANSION SLOTS

BATTERY COVER

SCREEN HINGE

APPLE PORTABLE WITH THE REAR COVER OFF

FIGURE 3.33:   Expanding Apple's original Portable Mac

pull up on the ribbon cable to disconnect it from the base of the case and lift the top of the computer away from the bottom. You can now get at the internal memory expansion and modem connectors (Figure 3.35).

To close a PowerBook 140/170 case, set the top of the computer in place, lining up the front edges of the case. Lift the rear of the case up slightly, reconnect the keyboard ribbon cable and push down gently. Close and line up the case halves. Carefully turn the case over and replace the four #10 Torx screws in the bottom, and the #8 Torx screw in the back, of the PowerBook. Replace the battery.

Some Thoughts about Slots

With the variety of Macs that have been produced, there's been a profusion of expansion slots as well. Fortunately, some slot types, if not standards, have appeared often enough to merit discussion. Apple appears to be making an effort to maintain the NuBus slot standard on its high-end modular Macs. This makes it easier for users to continue with their existing NuBus hardware, and for developers to produce new hardware without having to continually reinvent product interfaces for new slot types.

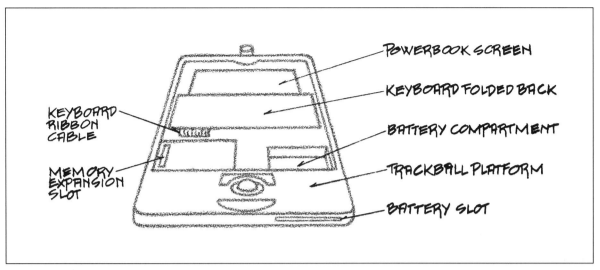

FIGURE 3.34: Inside the PowerBook 100

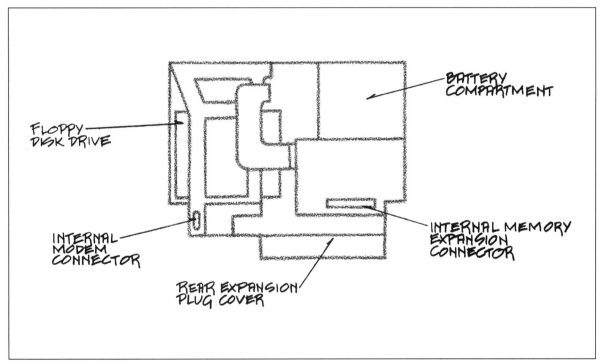

FIGURE 3.35: The PowerBook 140/170 memory and modem connectors

NuBus Slots

With the Mac II, Apple adopted the NuBus standard (which was developed by Texas Instruments). NuBus boards do not require extensive setup and are self-configuring. In effect, any board can go in any available slot. This is a boon to anyone who has fiddled with expansion card software and hardware setup problems on other machines.

The speed restrictions imposed on earlier NuBus slots by clocking them to the 16MHz Mac I/O (input/output) bus have been removed in the Quadra— Quadra slots now run at the 25MHz system speed. The Quadra's NuBus slots utilize some developing NuBus90 standard features, including a burst mode that allows for almost 80MB/sec data transfer between boards. NuBus boards that are set up as bus masters (that is, capable of taking control of the expansion bus) can transfer data to system memory at up to 9MB/sec.

Cache Slot

The Macintosh IIci is the first and only modular Mac (so far) with a dedicated cache slot. Adding a cache memory board to the slot can boost a IIci to the equivalent of IIfx performance. The cache slot, like PDS slots, operates at 25MHz system bus speed. Other machines, like the SE/30 and IIsi can add a cache through expansion boards.

PDS Slot

Modular Mac PDS slots became common with the Mac LC and are a feature of all later machines. The LC II, which adds a 68030 processor but retains LC architecture, will retain the PDS slot, now called the "LC slot." Apparently, the plan is to maintain compatibility with LC PDS boards. But complete compatibility is the exception rather than the rule, so check LC boards for compatibility before using them in an LC II.

Because PDS slots are hooked into the CPU bus, each type of slot is normally slightly different, to take advantage of different processors. For instance, the Mac SE PDS slot, or "SE Slot," has 96 pins while the SE/30 PDS slot has 120 pins. This reflects the increased complexity of the 68030 (versus the 68000) processor.

THE JOY OF MAC CRACKING

Now that you've seen how to open various models of Macs, I hope you realize that there is little difficulty in opening a Macintosh case for a hardware upgrade, even if it belongs to a compact Mac or a PowerBook. The keys lie in careful preparation and step-by-step assembly or disassembly, keeping in mind the cautions necessary for each model. If you take precautions (such as an antistatic strap) and take your time, you should be able to work around any difficulties.

If you *do* run into trouble, then backtrack and check all your work, including connections and SIMM seats. If, after trying everything, you still can't get an upgrade to work remember that it is possible to get defective upgrade parts. Try sending them back for replacement or refund. To provide some help with troubleshooting problems I've included a list of Macintosh error codes in Appendix B.

TROUBLESHOOTING

Problem	Cause	Solution
Cables can't be removed	Probably just a snug fit	Wiggle *gently* and work until connector comes free
Parts do not fit easily	Wrong reassembly	Check fit of parts
Bent pins	Forced chip insertion	Straighten carefully!
Video problems after board removal	Power/video connector not inserted properly	Open the Mac, remove the power/video connector, and reinsert
Floppies don't insert correctly	Drive misaligned	Reopen Mac and realign
Drives don't spin up	Loose power connector	Reopen Mac and reinsert.

CHAPTER FOUR

Memory Upgrades

You're doing fine with 1MB? I envy you! It's possible to get by on 1MB these days, but it isn't easy. Shoehorning a complete operating system plus some basic applications into a meg takes a lot of planning and patience. Most programs, including the Macintosh operating system, require a substantial amount of memory to run properly. This is not the only reason to expand your Mac's memory, however.

WHY ADD MEMORY TO YOUR MAC?

A lot of enhancements that require expanded memory can markedly increase your system's performance.

So What's a SIMM?

SIMMs were first introduced as expansion memory for the Macintosh Plus. They have since become the standard for Macintosh memory expansion. *SIMM* stands for *single inline memory module*—an appropriate name, since Macintosh SIMMs consist of memory chips (usually eight) soldered to a small printed circuit board.

A SIMM is installed in a special, often angled, SIMM slot (see Figure 4.1.) It's inserted into the slot and tilted back toward a set of "fingers" (retainers) that holds it in place. Another set of supports behind the SIMM supports and secures it.

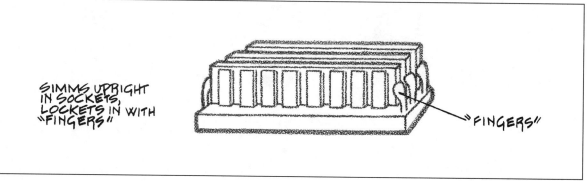

FIGURE 4.1: Installed SIMMs

Current standard SIMMs come in 256K, 1MB, 4MB, and 16MB sizes. Other sizes may work with your machine, but it's wise to check this first.

SIMMs come as DIP and SOJ versions. *DIP*, or dual inline package, SIMM chips are soldered in through holes in the SIMM board. The SIMM is larger as a result and will not fit in a Plus or SE. *SOJ SIMMs* use surface-mounted chips and are more expensive than DIP models. However SOJ SIMMs will fit any Mac SIMM socket and are the more common memory upgrades available today.

SIMMs come in different speeds. The SIMM speeds indicate how quickly the SIMM can be read or written to. Faster Mac CPUs require faster SIMMs. You can use fast SIMMs with a slow CPU, but you won't see any performance advantage in paying the higher price. However, if faster SIMMs are not overly expensive, you can buy them with an eye to transferring memory to a faster machine later. The suffix numbers on SIMM chips indicate their speed: –15 is 150 nanoseconds, –12 is 120 nanoseconds, –10 is a 100 nanosecond SIMM, –80 is an 80 nanosecond SIMM, and –70 is 70 nanosecond chip. In this case less is better—lower numbers refer to faster chips.

Not All Macs Use SIMMs

Not all memory for Macintosh computers comes on SIMMS. A number of manufacturers produce a 3MB memory card for the Mac Classic that has all of the memory chips surface-mounted to the card and is a good price deal. Apple's own card uses SIMMS for the last two megabytes of memory expansion. Some third-party memory cards won't give you the option of recycling SIMMs in a new machine, a possible disadvantage. Recycling is only an option, though, if your SIMMs are fast enough to be used in faster Macs.

The original Portable uses a special expansion card with static RAM. The backlit version of the Portable uses a card with pseudo-static RAM. The PowerBooks use special expansion cards with *pseudo-static thin small outline packages* (TSOPs).

Virtual Memory, 32-bit and 24-bit Addressing

Virtual memory is disk space used by your Macintosh as system memory. Blocks of memory, or pages, are swapped out of memory and on to disk, and vice versa, as required. This system was first used by Unix to extend system memory.

The Macintosh requires a paged memory management unit (PMMU) to handle virtual memory under A/UX, System 7, or System 6 with Virtual (a virtual memory management application by Connectix). The PMMU is built into Motorola's 68030 CPU and is available separately as the 68851 PMMU for the 68020 CPU. A PMMU is available from Connectix for the Mac II, and from Novy/Systech for the LC (which runs virtual memory with Connectix's Virtual).

A Macintosh 68000 CPU cannot run virtual memory unless upgraded with a 68030 accelerator board and Compact Virtual 3.0. Compact Virtual lets a "non-68030" compact Mac access up to 16MB of memory on the accelerator board and up to 4MB of system memory as a RAM disk. See Figure 4.2, a Mac Classic running Compact Virtual. A "native" 68030 Macintosh can use System 7's virtual memory feature.

Program and file sizes on a system with hard disk virtual memory are limited only by available disk space. Virtual memory is slower than RAM memory because it depends on hard disk, and not RAM, speed.

Note... A large amount of virtual memory file access will result in constant disk access, and may cause undue wear and tear on your hard disk drive.

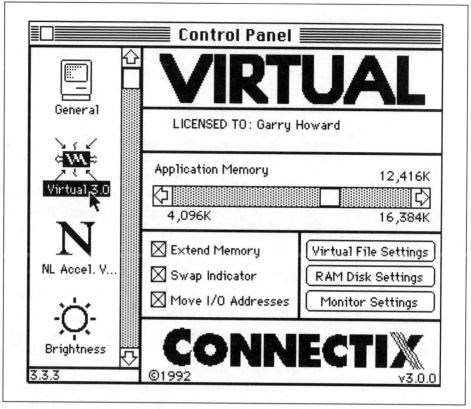

FIGURE 4.2:   Compact Virtual running on a Classic with a NewLife Accelerator! board.

The 68000 CPU uses 24-bit addressing and has an upper memory limit of 16MB. Only 4MB of the 68000 address space are available to compact Macs.

System 6 supported only 24-bit addressing and the resulting 16MB address space. Older modular Macs, such as the Mac II, use the upper 8MB of this for system purposes, leaving 8MB of RAM available under System 6 for machines that can use it.

The Apple IIci and newer 68030 Macintoshes support 32-bit addressing. This addressing mode allows Macs to access up to 4 gigabytes (10^9 bytes). "32-bit clean" applications can be relocated anywhere in the available 32-bit address space.

Unfortunately, applications that are *not* 32-bit clean can crash spectacularly when run in 32-bit mode.

Connectix's Maxima provides up to 14MB of free memory, plus a RAM disk, to a modular system using 24-bit mode. It does this by extending the Mac's address space to include unused system memory. Each NuBus card you add uses one additional megabyte of system memory, which reduces the amount available for virtual memory. Older programs are written for compatibility with 24-bit addressing and will run in this space with no problems. Owners of older 68030 Macs without 32-bit clean ROMs can run in 32-bit mode by using Connectix's Mode32, now available free of charge through an arrangement with Apple. Mode32 is a "ROM patch" similar to those installed in each new version of the Macintosh operating system. Machines that require Mode32 to use 32-bit addressing include the Mac SE/30, Mac II, IIx, and IIcx.

The Costs and Benefits of Upgrading Mac Memory

Memory upgrades are usually the cheapest, easiest, and most effective (in $/MB) upgrade for your Mac. See Figure 4.3—the declining cost of Macintosh memory—for a graphic demonstration of the price breaks that Mac users are getting on SIMM memory. SIMM prices have decreased by an average of 40%

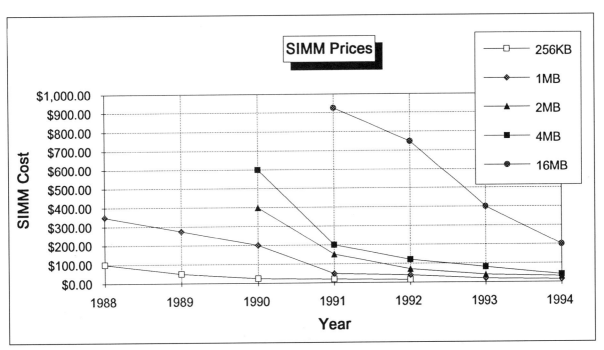

FIGURE 4.3: The declining cost of Macintosh memory (1993 and 1994 figures are projections at press time)

per year, and the price of a memory upgrade typically makes up 5% or less of total Macintosh system cost. You can be sure that memory costs will continue to decline and that the availability of large SIMMs will continue to rise. (By large SIMMs, I'm referring to the 4MB and 16MB SIMMs typically used in memory-intensive operations such as mathematical and engineering modeling and rendering in 24-bit color.) If you go shopping for a good deal on memory, you'll probably find one. However, it's a good idea to know what you're looking for before you go searching for those deals.

SOME ADVANTAGES OF EXPANDED MAC MEMORY

There are a lot of good reasons to expand the memory on your Macintosh, and they're not all spelled "System 7." Memory is the workhorse of your Mac and can be used for a variety of functions—RAM disks, RAM caches, spoolers, and other goodies. Of course, there's still the old-fashioned reason—program space.

A Little More Program "Elbow Room," Please!

System 6 will run with 1MB of memory and run reasonably well with 2MB. System 7 will run in 2MB, but will run well and *multitask* (that is, execute more than one program "simultaneously") with 4MB of memory or better. The more large applications you run, the more system memory you need.

It's not unusual for modern applications to demand 1MB of memory to run and 1.5MB to run well. Using System 6.08 and allowing some working space for things like fonts and inits, 2.5MB will be required. If you add one or two programs running under MultiFinder, you approach 4MB of memory very quickly. With a fully enhanced System 7 and one program in memory, the 4MB "wall" is in sight. Multitasking a number of large programs under System 7 will require 6MB and more.

An 8½ × 11" 8-bit color document occupies 8MB; the 24-bit version occupies 23MB. Figure 4.4 shows the size of an 8½ × 11" black-and-white graphic scanned at 300, 400, and 1200 *DPI* (*dots per inch*, a measure of printer or scanner resolution). As you can see, the 300-dpi scan takes about 1MB of memory. Even black-and-white graphics are memory hogs.

Avoiding Memory Fragmentation

Under low memory conditions, a Mac has only a few, relatively small, contiguous blocks of memory. As the Mac's memory manager struggles to fit available programs into this small amount of memory, increasing numbers of memory blocks too small to use for programs or data are created.

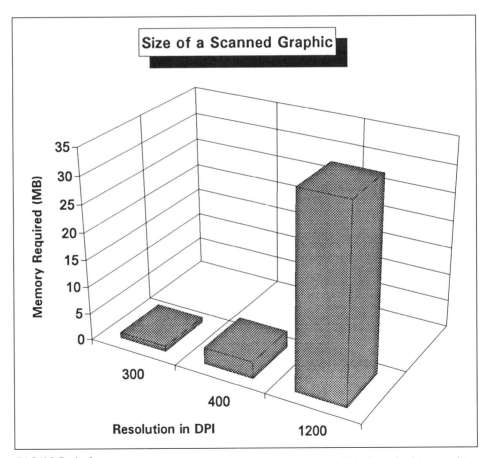

FIGURE 4.4:   Estimated memory requirement of a scanned black-and-white graphic at different resolutions

Eventually this *fragmentation* starts to take up significant amounts of system memory. Under low memory conditions, these small blocks cannot be recovered. Applications may refuse to load in available memory, or may unexpectedly quit due to insufficient memory.

Many programs respond to low memory conditions by loading only the program modules that are immediately required. This means that as each new module is required, it is loaded and existing modules removed, using an "overlay" method. This results in repeated disk access, slowing program execution. If enough RAM is available, most applications will load into memory to increase execution speed.

A Larger System Heap

The system heap contains system code, fonts, DAs, inits, device management data, and a variety of other system data. Each application also has its own heap space.

If your Mac, running under System 6, is short on memory, the system heap may run out of space, resulting in a variety of errors and bombs. You can allow your system heap more space by allocating more memory for the system, or by running a utility like HeapFixer, which allocates extra heap space on bootup.

System 7 shouldn't have system heap problems, since it dynamically allocates heap space based on available RAM.

Using Extra RAM as a RAM Disk

Extra RAM in a Macintosh can be used as a RAM disk. A RAM disk is an area of memory that can be used like a disk drive. In other words, executable programs or data can be copied into the RAM disk and accessed at RAM speeds, considerably faster than ordinary disk drive speeds. RamDisk+ is a utility that allows the System file to be copied into RAM, speeding program execution. Most compact Mac accelerator boards include a copy of Compact Virtual, which will allocate up to 4MB of system (nonaccelerator board) memory as a RAM disk and automatically load the Mac operating system into it.

A Larger RAM Cache

A RAM cache is built into the Macintosh operating system. Cache memory stores the last information used by the system, resulting in quick data access and eliminating some hard or floppy disk input and output. This speeds up system operation considerably.

The more memory allocated to the cache, the more speed improvement you'll see from your system—up to a point. With a very large RAM cache, your system can spend more time searching the cache than retrieving disk data.

A Faster Font Cache

Adobe Type Manager uses a font cache to speed access to outline fonts being used by your system. In a Macintosh system with a large number of fonts (not an unusual situation), you can experience significant slowdowns as ATM pulls font outlines from your hard disk drive. Allocating memory to ATM's font cache should result in a significant speed improvement when many fonts are being used.

Space for a Print Spooler

Macintosh memory can be used as a *print spooler*. When files are printed on a system with a spooler, the print files are sent to a "spool file" in memory, freeing up an application for immediate use, instead of freezing it until a print job is completed. As the Mac's CPU becomes available, it ships out portions of the spool file to the printer. This is called *background printing*. If a printer is unavailable, many spoolers will save a print file to disk. Printing is resumed when the printer becomes available.

A number of spooler software packages are available for the Mac, among them SuperLaserSpool (SLS) from Fifth Generation Systems. SLS can be used as a spooler for a variety of Mac printers, not just lasers. System 7 users printing to an Apple Laser have a built-in spooler and background printing available to them as part of the system.

THE MECHANICS OF MEMORY UPGRADES: TUNE-UP, ANYONE?

If you've decided that you need more memory (on your Mac, that is) your best approach is usually to add SIMMs. Fortunately, adding SIMMs is easy. Figures 4.5 and 4.6 show just how easy. The SIMM is inserted in a SIMM slot, generally at a 45° angle, depending on the Mac model, with the chips facing up, toward the SIMM retainers. The SIMM is then leaned toward the metal or plastic retainers on either side of the slot, and *gently* pushed until the retainers snap into place and the chip seats in the slot. Rock the SIMMs back and forth *slightly*, and gently lean them back to make sure they're seated properly.

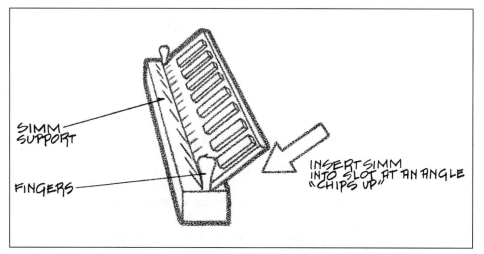

FIGURE 4.5:   Inserting a SIMM

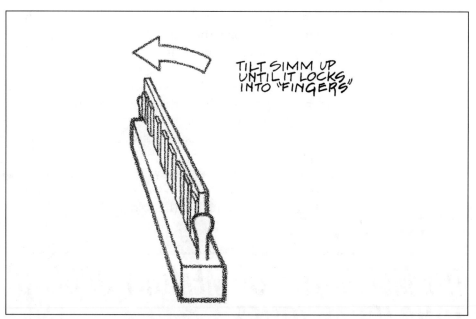

FIGURE 4.6:   Snapping it into place

Removing SIMMs is just as easy, but requires a little more care, especially if the SIMM slot uses plastic retainers. Using a small, nonmagnetized screwdriver, *carefully* move one retainer away from the SIMM and lean the SIMM slightly forward until the retainer is held back by the edge of the SIMM. Figure 4.7 illustrates this. Now move the other retainer away from the opposite edge of the SIMM and lean the SIMM forward. It should tilt forward at a 45° angle and come out of its slot easily. Be very careful with plastic retainers, as they can break if forced. SIMMs should come out of their sockets with no problems once the retainers are moved out of the way, so if you can't remove the SIMMs, *don't* force them. Look for the problem before trying again!

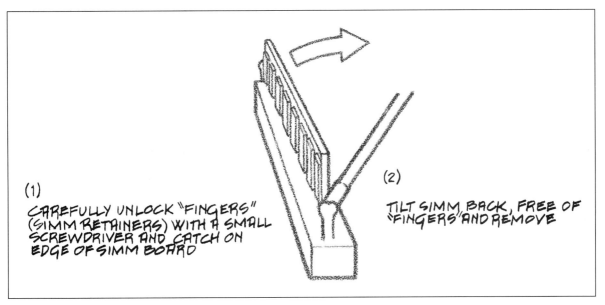

FIGURE 4.7:   Removing a SIMM

The Five Commandments of SIMM Installation

There are five basic commandments to engrave on your brain when installing SIMMs. These are:

Commandment #1:   Each of your SIMM banks must be completely full or completely empty.

Commandment #2:   Use the correct SIMM speed and size.

- The Mac Plus requires 150ns (*nanosecond*) or faster SIMMs. It can't use 4MB or larger SIMMs.

- The Mac SE to Mac IIcx, the Mac LC and the Classic II all require 120ns or faster SIMMs. The SE and Classic can't use 4MB or larger SIMMs. The LC can use 2MB SIMMs, and the Classic II cannot use SIMM sizes smaller than 1MB.

- The Mac IIci, IIsi, IIfx, and the Quadras require 80ns or faster SIMMs. The IIci and IIsi can use 512K SIMMs and the IIsi can use 2MB SIMMs. The IIfx and the Quadras require 1MB or larger SIMMs and the IIfx requires 64-pin SIMMs (whew!).

Commandment #3:   Fill each SIMM bank with SIMMs of the same size.

Commandment #4:   If you fill only one SIMM bank, make it Bank A. (Excepting only later jumper versions of the SE, where you should use Bank B.)

Commandment #5:   Usually put the largest SIMMs in Bank A. This rule no longer holds completely for SIMMs over 1MB in size.

A FEW COMMENTS ABOUT MEMORY EXPANSION

Before you purchase SIMMs or a memory expansion board for your computer or printer, be sure of what you need. Take note of how much memory you already have and how it's installed. Make sure that the memory configuration you plan to add is compatible with what's already in the machine. If you're completely replacing memory or adding completely new expansion memory, once again make sure that your proposed memory configuration is compatible with the machine you're using.

Be sure that the SIMMs you use are the correct speed and type. Sixty-four-pin, 80ns or faster for the IIfx, no DIP SIMMs on the SE or Plus—these and other considerations are important. Select a good, reliable vendor for your SIMMs and tell him what machine they are for.

Try to buy from vendors who supply good quality SIMMs. Technology Works produces quality Mac memory expansion products.

Take your time installing SIMMs and make sure they are seated properly. Make sure you follow the rules for SIMM configuration on your particular Macintosh. If these two items are done correctly, you're less likely to have to reopen your Mac to check the SIMMs later.

Always remember to wear an antistatic wrist strap *whenever* you work inside your computer and printer. This is not only fashionable attire for every good hacker, but will prevent the ever-present danger of frying chips on your logic or expansion board with a jolt of static electricity.

If you handle memory expansion with care and follow the "rules" you should have no problems. When you're done, go to the Apple menu on the finder, select About the Finder… and enjoy the sight of all that memory!

Installing Memory on Compact Macs

The first step is to crack your Mac. This is covered in Chapter 3. Once your compact Mac is open to the world, you can don your antistatic wrist strap, pick up your small, flat-bladed screwdriver, and go for it!

Early Macs—the 128, 512, and 512KE

The early Macs had no built-in memory expansion capability, but they can be expanded with the addition of an accelerator/expansion board. These boards are available from many manufacturers. SIMMs should be purchased for a board according to the manufacturer's recommendations. If the installation manual does not provide details on the preferred SIMMs to use, call the board's manufacturer. This is a whole lot easier and cheaper than buying the wrong SIMMs.

SIMMs are installed on an accelerator board according to the instructions given above. Installation of SIMMs takes place *before* the expansion board is installed.

The Mac Plus

The Plus has four SIMM slots in two banks of two. It needs 150ns or faster SIMMS, in 256K or 1MB sizes. Maximum memory expansion is 4×1MB SIMMs for 4MB. Other configurations are 4×256K SIMMs for 1MB, 2×1MB SIMMs for 2MB, and 2×1MB plus 2×256K SIMMs for 2.5MB. Figure 4.8 gives some further details. The Plus can gain up to 16MB of memory expansion with a 4MB RAM disk if a 68030 accelerator board with Compact Virtual is installed.

Remove the Mac Plus logic board according to the directions in Chapter 3. The Plus uses resistors to define the amount of memory installed. Figure 4.8 shows the location of these resistors, R8 and R9, and their installation for different memory configurations. In the standard 1MB Plus configuration, a 150-ohm resistor is installed at R8. Bank A, slots 1 and 2 and bank B, slots 3 and 4, all contain 256K SIMMs. For a 2MB Plus, the 150-ohm resistor at R8 is cut at one end and bent up to break contact with the logic board. Enough wire "pigtail" should be left so that the resistor can be soldered back in if necessary. A 150-ohm resistor is installed at R9. Two 1MB SIMMs are installed in Bank A, Slots 1 and 2. Bank B is empty.

For more than 2MB of system memory, both R8 and R9 are removed. A 2.5MB Plus has two 1MB SIMMs in bank A, slots 1 and 2, and two 256K SIMMs in bank B, slots 3 and 4. A fully configured 4MB Plus has 1MB SIMMs in all 4 slots, banks A and B.

Early (Pre-Jumper) Mac SEs

Remove the SE logic board as instructed in Chapter 3. Figure 4.9 shows the location of the SIMM banks and memory configuration resistors on an early SE. The slot setup and SIMM banks are changed from the configuration in the Plus. The four SIMM slots on the SE are located across the front of the logic board. Bank A, slots 1 and 2, are the two rear SIMM slots on the left and right sides of the board, respectively. Bank B, slots 3 and 4, are the two slots, left and right, at the front of the logic board.

The memory configuration resistors are located directly behind slot 1 on the left front side of the logic board. They are numbered R35 and R36. For a 1MB SE, a 150-ohm resistor is installed at R35 and all SIMM slots are filled with 256K SIMMs. In a 2MB SE, R35 is cut or removed and a 150-ohm resistor is installed at R36. Two 1MB SIMMs are installed in bank A, slots 1 and 2—the two rear SIMM slots. Like the Plus, SEs with over 2MB have both resistor R35 and R36 removed.

A 2.5MB machine has 1MB SIMMs in bank A, slots 1 and 2—the two rear SIMM slots, and 2×256K SIMMs in bank B, slots 1 and 2—the two front SIMM slots. A "fully populated" SE with 4MB of RAM has 1MB SIMMs in all slots in both banks. Like a Plus, an SE can access over 4MB only with a 68030 accelerator board and Compact Virtual installed.

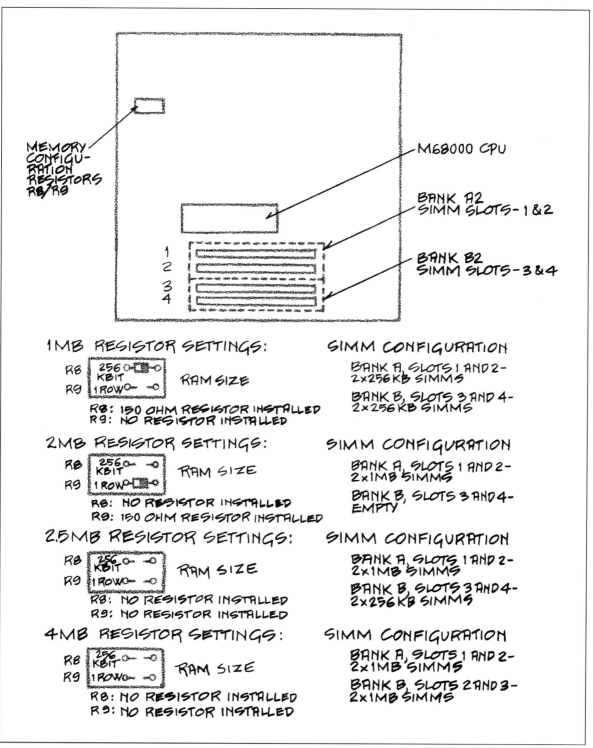

FIGURE 4.8:   Mac Plus memory configurations and resistor settings

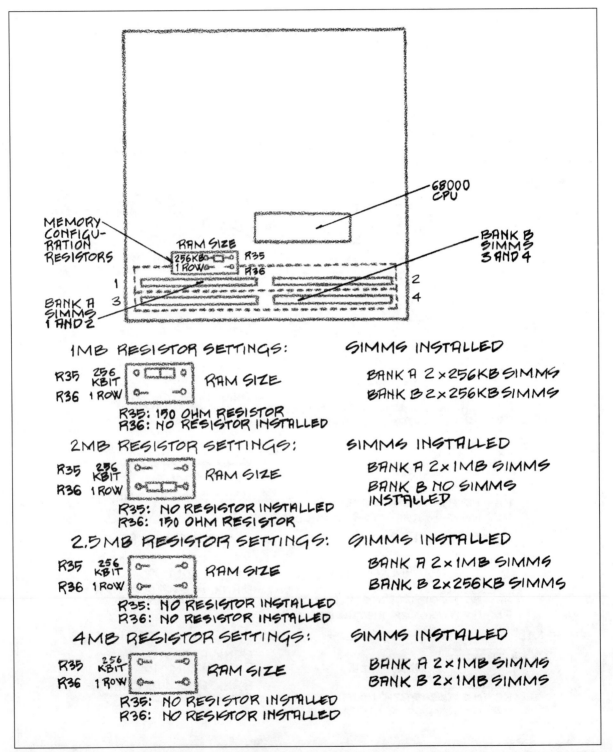

Later (Jumper Model) SE

Later models of the Mac SE use memory-select jumpers instead of soldered-on resistors. This makes adding memory much easier, as it eliminates cutting and soldering resistors on the logic board. The SIMM banks and memory-select jumpers on later SEs are shown as Figure 4.10. The jumpers are a three-pin "block" located in the same position as early SE memory-select resistors. A jumper fits over two of the three pins, "shorting them out" and selecting the SE's memory configuration.

A 1MB jumper model SE has a jumper on the right two pins of the block (looking toward the rear of the logic board) and 4×256K SIMMs installed, filling all available slots. A 2MB SE has a jumper over the left two pins of the jumper block and 2×1MB SIMMs installed in *bank B, slots 3 and 4* (just to keep you guessing). For memory greater than 2MB, there are no jumpers on the configuration pins, or you can leave the jumper on *only* the farthest right pin, to keep it available. A 2.5MB jumper SE has 2×1MB SIMMs in bank B, slots 3 and 4 (at the front of the logic board), and 2×256K SIMMs in bank A, slots 1 and 2. A fully configured 4MB jumper SE has 4×1MB SIMMs in the slots.

The Mac Classic

Although memory expansion for Classics requires cracking the case, it doesn't require removal of the logic board. That's because the Classic's special 22-pin memory expansion slot is located on the right rear corner of the logic board (see Figure 4.11). A nonexpanded Classic has 1MB of memory chips surface-mounted to the logic board. Adding an Apple memory expansion card increases the total memory to 2MB. Adding a memory expansion card with 3MB of *surface-mounted* expansion memory increases system memory to 4MB (as discussed in Chapter 1, surface-mounted memory expansion puts all the chips on one card instead of a number of SIMM boards). Adding two 256K SIMMs to the SIMM slots on the Apple Classic memory expansion board brings the system memory up to 2.5MB. Replacing the 256K with 2×1MB SIMMs brings the Classic's memory up to 4MB.

Before you reinstall a Classic memory expansion card with SIMMs mounted, look for a jumper marked "SIMMs installed—SIMMs not installed" and move it to the "SIMMs installed" position. Surface-mounted Classic memory is 150ns, but add-on memory must be 120ns or better. As with the Plus and SE, virtual memory is not available on a nonaccelerated Classic. The Classics can't handle 32-bit addressing.

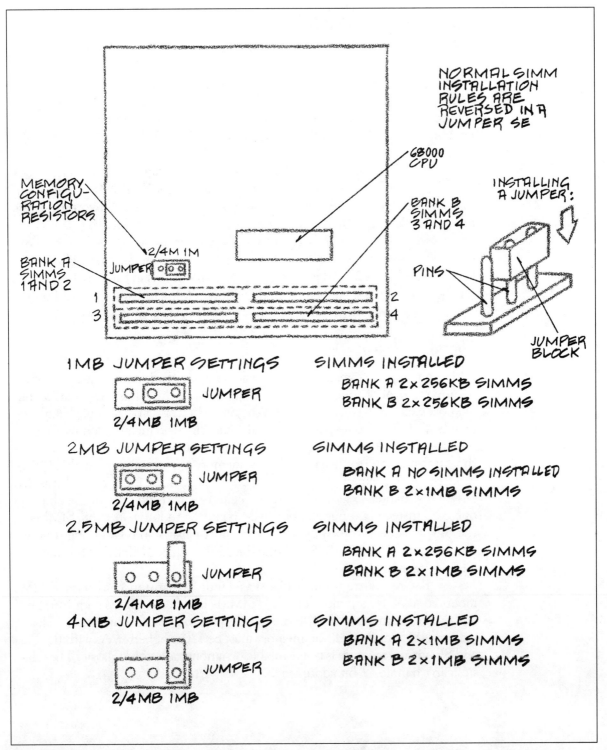

FIGURE 4.10:   Mac SE memory configurations and jumper settings

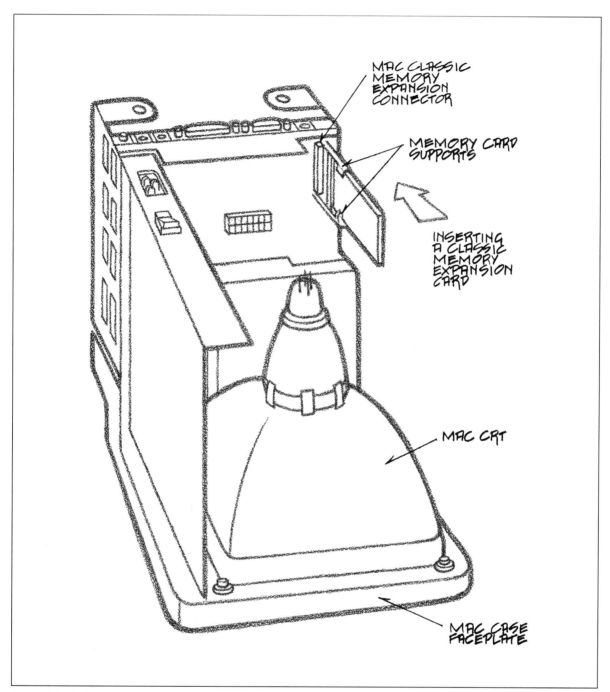

MAC CLASSIC
MEMORY
EXPANSION
CONNECTOR

MEMORY CARD
SUPPORTS

INSERTING
A CLASSIC
MEMORY
EXPANSION
CARD

MAC CRT

MAC CASE
FACEPLATE

FIGURE 4.11:   The Macintosh Classic memory board

The Mac SE/30

The SE/30 has two SIMM banks with four SIMM slots in each. The machine requires a minimum of 120ns SIMMS and can use virtual memory. 32-bit addressing requires installation of the Mode32 ROM patch. SE/30 memory expansion requires removing the logic board.

Figure 4.12 shows the memory configuration for a number of eight-SIMM slot Macs, including the SE/30. Bank A, slots 1– 4, are the SIMM slots closest to the left front corner of the SE/30 logic board. Bank B, slots 5–8, are just behind them. The SE/30 can use 256K and 1MB SIMMs in the standard configuration for modular Macs. In other words, either bank A or B must be *completely* filled with the same size SIMMs. The standard SE/30 configuration is 1MB, with bank A filled with 256K SIMMs. Filling both banks gives you 2MB. Filling bank A with 1MB SIMMs gives you 4MB. Filling both banks gives you 8MB. This is the limit of normal memory on the SE/30. Filling all SIMM slots with 16MB SIMMs, the SE/30 can have up to 128 MB of RAM installed. To use this much RAM, Mode32 and System 7 must be added to allow 32-bit addressing. Normal cautions apply here—programs that are not 32-bit "clean" can cause a lot of problems in such a system.

As mentioned, Virtual's Maxima will allow up to 16MB, 4×4MB SIMMs installed in bank A, to be used under ordinary 24-bit addressing. Older programs will use this program space without difficulty.

The Classic II

The Classic II, with its 68030 processor, has the same potential for memory expansion as the SE/30. Because the Classic II's ROMs are 32-bit clean, the machine is potentially capable of using 32-bit addresses without further software. The machine can also use virtual memory directly under System 7.

The Classic II has 2MB of memory on the logic board and *one* bank of two-SIMM slots. Because the Classic II uses SIMMs, the logic board has to be removed to add memory. The machine requires 120ns or faster SIMMs. 4MB SIMMs are the maximum size recognized by the machine, which gives a maximum memory of 10MB under System 7 with 32-bit addressing. Larger configurations are not possible. As the minimum SIMM size used by the Classic II is 1MB, minimum memory with both SIMM slots full is 4MB.

The Classic II can access up to 1 gigabyte of virtual memory under System 7.

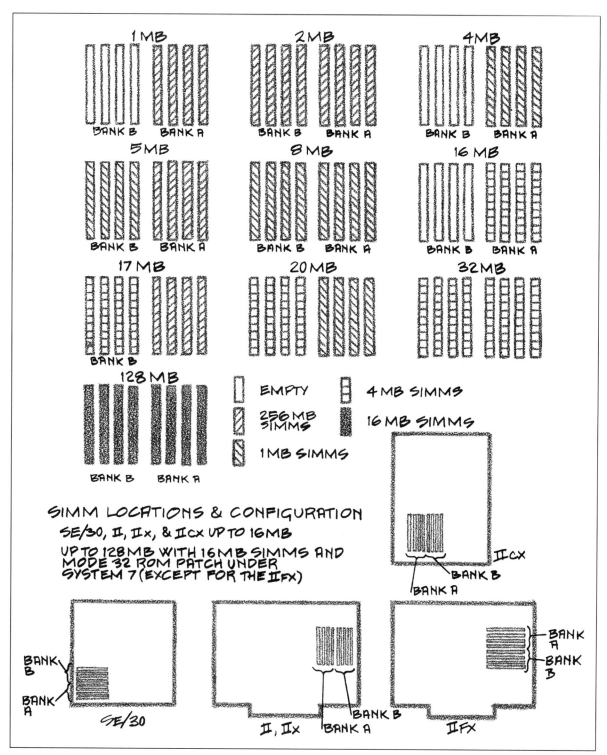

FIGURE 4.12:   Mac II and SE/30 memory configurations

Modular Macintosh Memory (Say That 100 Times Fast, Please)

Memory expansion for modular Macs is much easier than for compact Macs. And you can add much more memory to modulars than to compacts (with the exception of the compact SE/30). To give an idea of how much, the Mac II through the IIfx have two banks of four SIMMs. The Quadra 700 has 4MB of memory on the logic board and four SIMM slots. The 900 also has 4MB on the logic board and *twelve* SIMM slots.

Before venturing into the world of modular Mac memory expansion, *make sure* you have that antistatic wrist strap on. Once again, a small flat-bladed screwdriver can be useful when removing SIMMs.

The Macintosh II

All members of the Macintosh II series have two banks of four SIMMS. To get at the SIMM banks in the Mac II, you'll have to remove the drive platform. As described in Chapter 3, the drives don't have to be removed from the platform. Just unplug the drive cables as described, undo the screws in the corners of the platform, and lift it out. Viewed from the front of the Mac II case, the SIMM slots are located by the right wall of the case just behind the mid line of the logic board. The slots are oriented "front/rear." SIMM slots 1 to 4 on the right are in bank A and 5 to 8 on the left are in bank B.

Figure 4.12 shows Mac II and SE/30 memory configurations. The Mac II requires 120ns or faster SIMMs. As mentioned, under normal 24-bit addressing, the Mac II can use 8MB of memory. Maxima from Connectix allows the use of some of the remaining 8MB system memory; how much depends on the number of NuBus cards installed. A Mac II with Mode32 and System 7 can address up to 68MB (4×16MB and 4×1MB SIMMs) with the original ROMs installed. With a high density floppy drive (FDHD) upgrade, the Mac II can address up to 128MB of expansion memory using 16MB SIMMs.

To use virtual memory under System 7 or System 6 with connectix's program Virtual, the Mac II requires a paged memory management unit (PMMU).

The Macintosh IIx

The Macintosh IIx is the 16MHz 68030 upgrade to the Macintosh II. The IIx has the FDHD ROM upgrade and so is capable of addressing up to 128MB with all eight SIMM slots fitted, System 7 running, and Mode32 installed. Mode32 is required because, once again, the IIx doesn't have 32-bit clean ROMs.

Upgrading Mac IIx memory requires the removal of the drive platform. SIMM location is the same as in the II, namely on the right side of the case, just behind the center point of the logic board. Bank A SIMM slots are the four on the right, bank B slots are the four on the left.

The IIx with System 6 and Connectix's Virtual, or running System 7, can use up to 1 gigabyte of virtual memory.

The Mac IIfx

The IIfx has a 40MHz 68030 CPU and requires special 64-pin SIMMs that support rapid 64-bit equivalent data transfer. Unfortunately, with the introduction of the Quadras, it appears that the IIfx's days are numbered.

If the fx fades away, you can expect those rare, expensive, 64-pin SIMMs to get scarce as well. This is something for prospective IIfx owners to consider.

The IIfx is fully 32-bit clean and requires 80ns memory. The fx can address up to 128MB under System 7. The machine has the standard Mac II configuration of two banks of four SIMMs. Filling SIMM slots is the same as for other Macs, except that it requires 64-pin, 80ns SIMMs, and that the slots are oriented "right/left" instead of "front/rear" like those on the II and the IIx.

Virtual memory is available to the fx under System 6 with Virtual and under System 7.

The Mac IIcx

The Mac IIcx was the first of the compact (what the "c" stands for), three-slot, modular Macs. The IIcx uses the standard eight-SIMM-slot Macintosh II configuration, but the location of the SIMM slots is now the left front side of the case. All SIMM slots are easily accessible—nothing needs to be moved or removed. The SIMMs have "front-rear" orientation and bank A, slots 1–4, is on the right side, bank B on the left. Figure 4.12 once again shows the standard Mac II SIMM fill patterns. Because the Mac IIcx has a 68030 CPU but not 32-bit clean ROMs, the Mode32 software ROM patch is required in order to address more than 16MB of memory. Like the other Mac IIs, the IIcx can access up to 128MB with 16MB SIMMs and 32-bit addressing.

Virtual memory is available to the IIcx under System 6 with Virtual or under System 7.

The Mac IIci

The Mac IIci was the first compact 68030 Mac with 32-bit clean ROMs. Figure 4.13 shows the Macintosh IIci SIMM fill pattern.

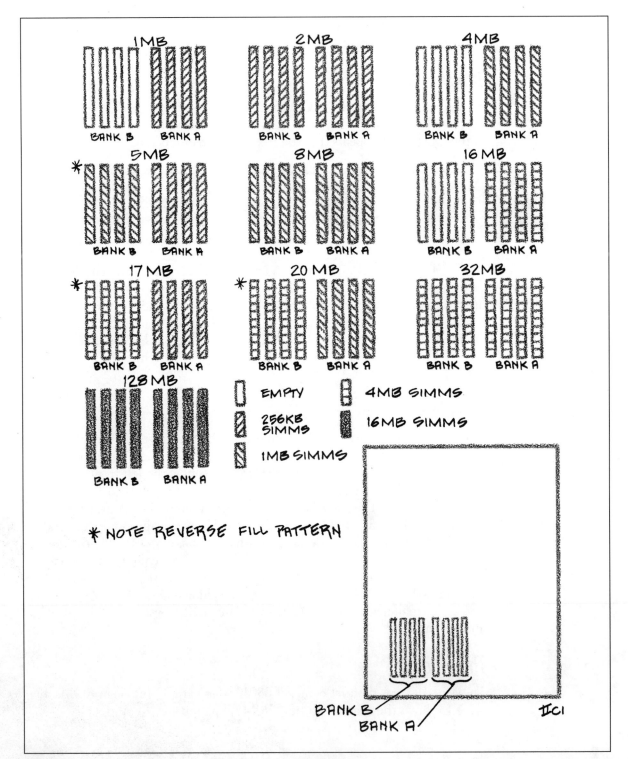

FIGURE 4.13: Macintosh IIci SIMM memory configuration

The ci can use SIMMs ranging from 256K to 16MB. As usual, each bank must be completely filled with a specific SIMM size. SIMM slots are once again oriented front to back at the left front corner of the IIci case (see Figure 4.14). As with the IIcx, the SIMMs are completely accessible. Bank A, slots 1–4, is on the right side and always filled first. Bank B, slots 5–8, is on the left. IIci memory chips must be 80ns or faster. If completely filled with 16MB SIMMs, the IIci SIMM slots contain 128MB. The ci's 68030 CPU and 32-bit clean ROMs allow the machine to address its maximum 128MB under System 7 with no additional hardware or software. Virtual memory to 1GB is available under System 6 with Virtual or System 7.

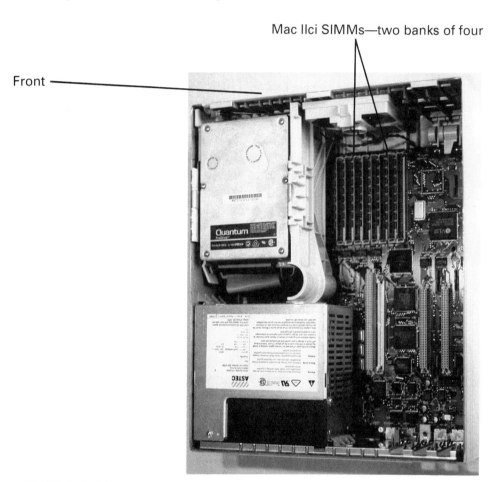

Mac IIci SIMMs—two banks of four

Front

FIGURE 4.14:   SIMMs installed in the Mac IIci

Some IIci machines designed for government applications have an optional parity-checking chip installed (parity checking insures RAM accuracy). The IIci requires special 9-chip parity SIMMs.

The Quadra 700

The Quadra 700, one of the 68040 modular Mac screamers, is compact enough to fit the same case as the Mac IIci. Unfortunately, in the Quadra 700 the SIMMs are covered by the floppy and hard drive carrier, which must be removed to gain access to them. Four megabytes of memory are surface-mounted on the logic board and four SIMM slots in one bank are available for memory expansion. Using 16MB SIMMs, maximum 32-bit memory expansion is 68MB, including logic board memory. The 700, not surprisingly, accepts a minimum of 1MB, 80ns SIMMs.

The Quadra 700 also has six VRAM, or video RAM, slots. These can be equipped with up to 2MB of RAM for 24-bit color at 832×624 pixels on 16" third-party RGB monitors or 8-bit color at 1152×870 pixels on the Macintosh 21" Color Display. The 700 has 512K of VRAM soldered in (a 13" monitor at 8-bit color). The VRAM SIMMs are the same 256K (only), 68-pin VideoSIMMs that the LC uses.

The Quadra 900 and 950

The Quadra 900 has no soldered-on motherboard memory, but comes with 4×1MB SIMMs in the first bank. The 900 and 950 have four banks of SIMMs, sixteen slots, for a total of 256MB when fully filled with 80ns or faster 16MB SIMMs. The SIMMs are fully accessible when the Quadra access door is opened.

Bank A SIMMs on the Quadra are the left two slots of the upper row of eight and the left two slots of the lower row of eight. Banks B,C, and D are the same.

The Quadra 900 and 950 have 1MB of VRAM soldered in and four slots in two banks of two. Once again, the VRAM required is LC-style 68-pin 256K VideoSIMMs. Note that the Quadras take *LC Style*, not LC, VRAM SIMMs.

The PDS-Slot Modular Macs

Modular Macs with single processor direct slots include the LC, LC II, and IIsi.

The LC has a 68020 CPU with (normally) no PMMU expansion capability, although Novy/Systech offers a PDS-slot PMMU with Virtual from Connectix to add virtual memory.

The Mac LC II and IIsi both have a 68030 processor, so they can use virtual memory with System 6 and Virtual, or System 7. All three machines have 32-bit clean ROMs, so they can use 32-bit addressing. However all three machines are somewhat limited in the maximum memory that they can address.

The LC has 2MB on the motherboard, a single bank of two RAM SIMM slots, and a single 68-pin 256K VRAM slot. The LC can address up to 4MB of 24-bit memory and 10MB of 32-bit memory with System 7.

The LC II has the same SIMM setup as the LC, but comes with 4MB on the logic board. Because the LC ROMs were not completely upgraded in the LC II, 2 × 4MB SIMMs in the RAM SIMM slots will only give you 10MB of 32-bit memory. Even if you insert 8MB of SIMMs for a total of 12MB of system memory, the LC II recognizes only 10MB.

The Mac IIsi has 1MB of memory soldered to the system board and one bank with four SIMM sockets, requiring 80ns SIMMs. With 16MB SIMMs, maximum system memory is 65MB under System 7 32-bit addressing.

Adding Memory to Macintosh Portables

All of Apple's portables are designed for up to 8MB of memory expansion. This is significantly easier to add to the original Portable.

The Original Macintosh Portable

The original Mac Portable, for all the bad press about its weight, is a beautifully engineered machine and is easily upgraded. As noted in Chapter 3, getting at the memory expansion slot is a matter of opening the rear case lid. Fold the screen down, "hug the Mac," press the release latches at the left and right rear corners, and pop the rear lid up. Lift the lid off, then turn the machine around so that you're facing the back of the case. Then remove the plastic battery cover on the right side. Remove the battery, replace the battery cover, and place your RAM card in the second slot from the right. That's it—easy, no?

The Mac Portable has 1MB of memory on the logic board and a special slot for RAM expansion. The Portable uses a special card for memory expansion which can hold 1, 2, 3, or 4MB of memory. Although the machine is technically capable of addressing up to 8MB, no large RAM card was ever produced for it. The original Portables use *static* RAM. Static RAM chips do not have to be continually refreshed like dynamic RAM, the chips used in most computers, so they take a lot less power. Static RAM is also much faster. Unfortunately, it's also much more expensive. Later backlit Portables use pseudo-static RAM. The two types of memory boards are *not* interchangable and they cannot be used on any other Macs.

Because the original portable uses a Motorola 68000 CPU, it has no PMMU, and no virtual memory capability. The original Portable cannot use 32-bit addressing.

The PowerBooks

The Macintosh PowerBooks set new standards for compact size, light weight, and power in a Mac portable. But like the original Portable, the PowerBooks are too small to use SIMMs for memory expansion, and instead use a special RAM card.

The PowerBook 100 has a 68000 CPU, so it doesn't use 32-bit addressing or have the capability for virtual memory. The machine has 2MB soldered to the logic board, and up to 8MB can be added with a memory expansion card. As mentioned earlier, PowerBook RAM is of a special variety called TSOPs, pseudo-static thin small outline packages.

The PowerBook 140 uses a 68030 CPU, and thus has 32-bit addressing and virtual memory capability. But 32-bit addressing is of no use because of limited PowerBook memory, and virtual memory use would quickly drain the batteries on the machine. The PowerBook 140 memory card, like the Power-Book 100, uses TSOPS in 2, 4, 6, and 8MB configurations.

Like the PowerBook 140, the 170 has a 68030 CPU, 32-bit addressing, and virtual memory capability. Again, the use of 32-bit addressing is unneces-sary and the use of virtual memory can shorten battery life. The 170 uses the same memory expansion cards as the 100 and 140, and thus has up to 8MB of expansion memory available. The machine has 2MB installed and 2MB on the expansion card in its standard configuration.

The PowerBook TSOP expansion cards are interchangeable among all three machines, but not usable by other machines.

As detailed in Chapter 3, cracking the PowerBooks is fairly easy. Open-ing the machines involves removing the battery or batteries, the case screws (which in the 100 are under the rubber feet), and the keyboard. In the 100, this just involves carefully opening the screen and folding the keyboard back, and with the 140/170, it involves unplugging the keyboard and lifting the top of the case off. The memory expansion connector for the 100 is along the left edge of the case, just above the trackball platform. The connector for a 140/170 is parallel to the back of the case and just forward of the rear plugs. The memory expansion card just has to be plugged in and the case closed, as described in Chapter 3. Some enhancement boards for the PowerBooks have a "pass-through" port. In other words, you first plug in the enhancement board, then the PowerBook memory card.

Adding Memory to Laser Printers

The larger and more complex a document, whether it's a PostScript file or not, the more memory your laser printer will need to compile and print it. Printers use memory to store fonts and images or to act as a buffer. Most lasers use SIMMs to add this expansion memory, and Apple LaserWriters are no exception. Third-party laser printers have their own memory expansion schemes and you should consult your manual, and contact the manufacturer if necessary, to get the details on SIMM requirements and installation.

Need I say it—use your antistatic wrist strap when playing with printer internals! Static is bad news for printer electronics. Once again, a small, flat-bladed screwdriver is useful for installing SIMMs.

Apple's Personal LaserWriter LS has 512K of memory and the Laser-Writer IINT has 2MB. Neither printer has memory expansion capability.

The LaserWriter IINTX has three RAM expansion banks with four sockets each (see Figure 4.15) and comes with 8×256K SIMMs installed in banks A and B, for a total of 2MB. The IINTX uses 64-pin SIMMs like the IIfx, but only requires SIMM speeds of 100ns, instead of the IIfx's 80.

To install SIMMs on a LaserWriter IINTX, you'll have to remove the printer logic board. As discussed in Chapter 3, turn off the printer and remove any cables. Go to the printer connector panel (where the printer cable connector plugs are located) and remove the two screws on either side. Slide the printer logic board out. SIMM banks A, B, and C should be on the right hand side of the board from top to bottom, respectively. Look at Figure 4.15 for the available IINTX memory configurations. As you can see, the IINTX has a maximum expansion capability of 12MB.

Apple's LaserWriter IIf and IIg both have two banks of four SIMM slots and use standard SIMMs, 100ns or faster. The standard IIf has 2MB — 8 × 256K SIMMs—installed. The IIg has 5MB in a 4×1MB and 4×256K SIMM configuration. Both machines will use up to 32MB of memory—8×4MB in standard SIMMs.

Apple's Personal LaserWriter NTR, introduced at the same time as the Mac LC II, has 3MB installed and 1MB of expansion capability.

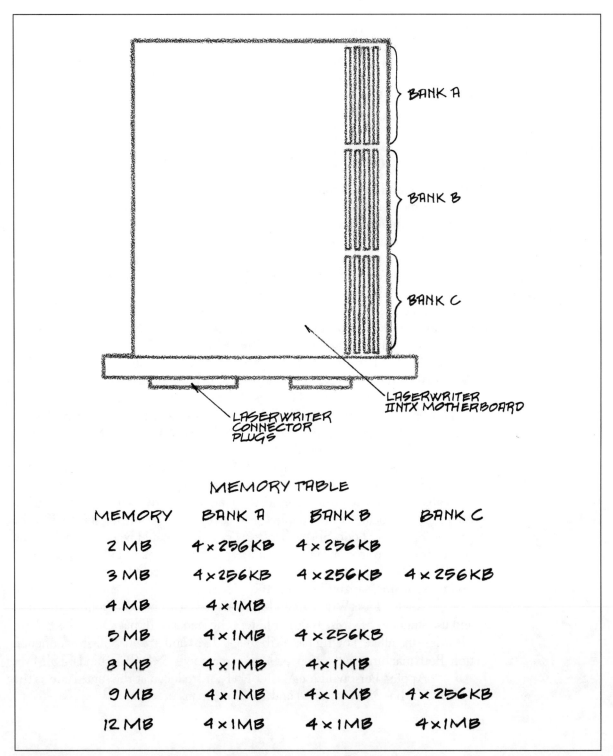

MEMORY TABLE

MEMORY	BANK A	BANK B	BANK C
2 MB	4 × 256KB	4 × 256KB	
3 MB	4 × 256KB	4 × 256KB	4 × 256KB
4 MB	4 × 1MB		
5 MB	4 × 1MB	4 × 256KB	
8 MB	4 × 1MB	4 × 1MB	
9 MB	4 × 1MB	4 × 1MB	4 × 256KB
12 MB	4 × 1MB	4 × 1MB	4 × 1MB

FIGURE 4.15: Apple LaserWriter IINTX memory configuration

TROUBLESHOOTING

Problem	Cause	Solution
After installing memory, you see a "sad Mac" error in the middle of your computer screen	You have done something wrong in your memory configuration scheme or in seating the SIMMs	See Appendix B for a list of the "sad Mac" error codes to help you diagnose the problem
After checking the SIMM configuration and reseating the boards, the problem is not rectified	You may have a bad SIMM (or SIMMs)	Return it (or them)
Memory errors occur	SIMMs are loose or have been inserted in the wrong slots	Reinsert SIMMs carefully—they are fragile and breaking them requires replacing a SIMM slot
A SIMM connector has a poor connection	You handled the SIMM with your fingers, and oil got on the SIMM	Never handle the SIMM connectors with your fingers. If the connectors get smudged, carefully clean them with a *clean* eraser tip or a small amount of 99% isopropyl alcohol (be careful what you get this stuff on, as it may damage some materials)

CHAPTER FIVE

Accelerators...

In this chapter I'll be concentrating on hardware accelerators. These products are designed to speed up your Mac by adding a faster CPU or system clock, along with some combination of RAM memory, cache memory, SCSI acceleration, an FPU, and a fast graphics adapter.

A Mac is a balanced system. The speed of the CPU, ROM, RAM, and ports all influence overall speed. Just adding a faster CPU will not guarantee a big boost in the performance of your system. In fact, if a Mac accelerator does not take a balanced approach to improving system speed, it can actually cause incompatibility problems with memory, system ROMs, video, or other areas. Because of this, accelerator packages should use compatible onboard components, designed to replace or work well with your Mac's systems.

512K Macs and the Mac Plus have slow processors, slow RAM, slow screen redraws, and a slow SCSI port. Accelerators generally enhance some or all of these features to achieve high performance. Companies that build accelerators for these early systems often include an additional power supply and cooling fan to improve reliability.

More recent enclosed systems don't need SCSI acceleration or an add-on cooling fan, but accelerators often add a fast processor, fast RAM, an FPU, an additional power supply, and a large-screen graphics adapter.

Modular Macs, with the exception of the compact LC, LCII, and IIsi, shouldn't have power or cooling problems. That lets accelerator board developers concentrate on accelerating the CPU and FPU, and forget about bringing the rest of the system up to snuff. Accelerators for these systems often combine slot expansion, cache memory, and an FPU/accelerator. The SCSI ports for these machines are quite fast, but SCSI accelerators and fast RAM disk boards can improve data access dramatically, even on the high-performance modular machines.

ACCELERATING A MAC

To understand how an accelerator board works, you should understand the function of each of the components. The first and most important accelerator component, as I've discussed, is the CPU. Second only to the CPU is accelerator RAM or cache memory. Additional enhancements can include an FPU, a graphics adapter, and a fast SCSI port. Let's look at each one individually.

ADDING A FASTER AND MORE ADVANCED CPU

The most obvious hardware accelerator enhancement is a faster and/or more advanced CPU. This can range from a 68000 to a 68040 chip at speeds from 16 to 40MHz.

You may recall from my previous discussion of CPUs that clock speed is a measure of how fast a system operates. The clock controls how many instructions a CPU executes in a second. More advanced processors, such as the 68040, have complex instructions taking five cycles or more. However, one of these complex instructions can take the place of a number of instructions executed by simpler processors. This means that clock speed is not the only consideration in evaluating accelerator speed.

More advanced chips use full 32-bit addressing and more and larger on-board caches. These advanced processors can be used in accelerator boards with 32-bit buses and high-speed memory for maximum acceleration effect.

Some accelerators achieve their effect by replacing the system clock with a faster chip. This is a dangerous practice for CPUs that aren't designed to operate at a high clock speed.

ADDING MORE RAM

The effects of adding more RAM to your Macintosh system were discussed in the previous chapter. Basically, the advantages of additional RAM include adding more swap memory for programs running under System 6, more multitasking memory for programs running under System 7, more System cache or font cache memory, and more memory for RAM disks and print spoolers.

Adding an accelerator's high-speed CPU, especially to early Macs, often necessitates adding high-speed memory (80-100ns) to the accelerator board to eliminate the speed bottleneck of slow system memory. Once programs and data are in accelerator memory, the system has to access the slower system bus only to transfer data to and from disk (and the system video display if fast video is not available). It can do everything else at accelerator speed.

Accelerator boards for compact Macs add RAM in two ways. One approach uses a relatively small cache of extremely fast (up to 20ns) static RAM, (SRAM), on the accelerator board. Data and instructions are loaded into the fast RAM cache and the accelerator CPU goes to the cache first. If the instructions that the CPU requires are found in the cache (a "cache hit"), then the accelerator can continue to process the instructions at a high speed. If the processor has to go to slow system memory, probably clocked at 150 to 120ns, the system slows down. The more functions that can be executed at accelerated speed, the closer your system will come to the speed of the accelerator CPU. Harris Labs' Performer, a low-priced 16MHz 68000 accelerator that uses an onboard cache, helps accomplish this.

Another approach to adding RAM to the accelerator board is to place a large amount of fast accelerator RAM directly on the board. If the accelerator has a 68030 processor and an onboard 32-bit bus, accelerator RAM can transfer data at full CPU speed. Some accelerators copy the contents of the Mac ROMs into fast memory so that the accelerator doesn't even have to go to the system to access the Mac's toolbox.

Putting fast RAM on the accelerator board is a common practice for high-performance systems. Extremely fast accelerators (i.e., with 33MHz 68030 processors) may require scarce, very fast RAM (i.e., 50ns or faster). In this case the manufacturer uses what are called *wait states*, which slow the processor down for data transfers and allow the use of slower RAM memory.

Unfortunately, adding wait states to an extremely fast CPU degrades the performance of the system somewhat.

ADDING AN FPU

An FPU, or floating point unit (also called a numeric coprocessor, to further confuse the issue), provides a substantial speed boost to applications using transcendental functions. Transcendental functions include logs, natural logs, and trigonometric functions. FPUs can provide a speed boost not just to complex engineering programs and spreadsheets, but to your graphics and CAD applications as well.

ADDING A FAST GRAPHICS ADAPTER

A large-screen monitor is a popular enhancement for compact Mac owners, especially those who do a lot of desktop publishing. But if you add a graphics adapter to your compact Mac without acceleration, the graphics performance of a standard machine with a large monitor will be poor. For that reason, accelerator board-graphics adapter combinations are quite popular. (If this adapter runs off a 32-bit data bus, it will benefit from the same performance enhancement as accelerator RAM and an FPU.)

Buying an accelerator board with a graphics adapter also eliminates the possibility that a graphics upgrade will be incompatible with an existing accelerator board (this isn't unusual). Timing conflicts between accelerator board and graphics adapters from different manufacturers can produce some interesting glitches.

ADDING A FAST SCSI PORT

Accelerators for early Macs, as mentioned, attempt to add a fast SCSI port for 512KE machines or replace a slow SCSI port on the Mac Plus with a faster one. Generally, accelerated SCSI options are not needed or provided by accelerator cards for modular machines. The most common location for an expansion SCSI connector in an early compact Mac is in the battery compartment door.

HOW ACCELERATORS ARE INSTALLED

Accelerators for the Mac are mounted in a variety of ways. Those for compact machines without a PDS slot mount on the CPU with a Killy clip (see Figure 5.1). A Killy clip is a plastic device with spring-loaded metal clips that fasten tightly over a DIP or surface-mounted 68000 CPU, while making secure contact with all of the CPU pins. After an accelerator "daughter board" is clipped onto the Mac CPU, it is secured with nylon or plastic "standoffs." The Mac Classic II does not have a PDS slot and the pins on the surface-mounted CPU are too close together to allow mounting of a Killy clip.

The Mac SE and SE/30, with a PDS slot, will accept a "plug-in" accelerator board, which must frequently be "tied down" with standoffs like the clip-on variety.

Modular Mac accelerators are far easier to install, unless they require removal of the original CPU and installation of a daughterboard in the socket (as in the Mac II). Installing an accelerator in a NuBus, PDS, or Cache Card slot is a piece of cake.

Whether your Mac is compact or modular, and has a PDS slot or not, installation of an accelerator usually involves the installation of software "patches," drivers, or cdevs (Control Panel devices). This software can control

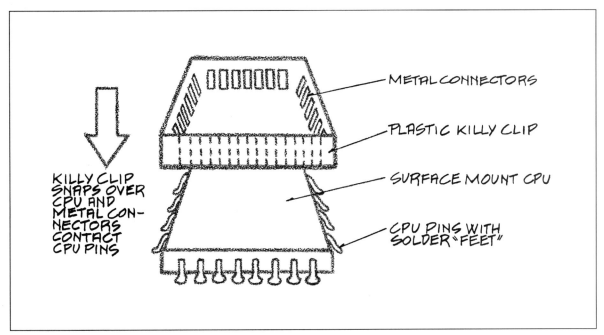

FIGURE 5.1:   A Killy clip for mounting devices in compact Macs

the speed and enable or disable the accelerator, make a 68882 FPU recognizable to applications that use a numeric coprocessor, or partition memory between system memory and a RAM disk.

Thinking about an Accelerator Upgrade

Before jumping with both feet into an accelerator upgrade, you should look at its cost and economics, as I indicated in Chapter 2. This is especially important for upgrades to the Mac Plus or earlier, where substantial improvements may be required. If the cost, performance, compatibility, and features of the upgrade don't match those of your other options, then reconsider. But for many older systems, an accelerator is a reasonable, economic solution to a performance problem.

YOUR MODULAR MAC ACCELERATOR ALTERNATIVES

Table 5.1 lists a variety of compact Mac accelerators with features and relative speeds (the Classic = 1). Accelerators based on the 68030 processor have largely replaced earlier models, based on fast 68000 and 68020 processors.

Novy Systems/Systech has an accelerator solution for owners of the Mac 128, 512, or 512KE. Of these, the Mac 512KE is the most logical and economical choice for an upgrade, as it doesn't require a disk drive and ROM upgrade as well. The Quick30 accelerator board comes with or without an FPU in speeds of 16 to 33MHz. A fan and power supply, SCSI port, and video board adapter are available. The board can mount up to 16MB of SIMM memory. The Quick30 is also available for the Plus and SE. Figure 5.2 is the Quick30 Plus.

The NewLife 25 and 33c accelerators, for the Mac 128 through SE, include a high-speed CPU and FPU with an optional video upgrade. The versions for early Macs include a fan with the installation kit. A high-speed SCSI port is available with a battery-door mounting kit.

Total Systems produces the 16MHz 68030 Mercury and the high-performance 25 and 33MHz Gemini accelerator boards. When purchased for a 128 to 512KE Mac, the installation kit includes a fan and power supply. A high-speed SCSI port is available for both boards.

FIGURE 5.2: The Novy Quick30Plus Accelerator(photo courtesy of Novy Systems/Systems Technology)

The Final Decision

Installing an accelerator board is quite similar for all of the clip-on Macs, which include the Mac 128 to 512KE, the Plus and the Classic.

As I've mentioned before, the Mac 128 and 512 have to be upgraded to make them usable with an accelerator. This upgrade involves replacing the 64K ROMs with newer 128K ROMs and replacing the single-sided 400K drives with 800K drives. I'll be discussing this upgrade in Chapter 7. If you decide to upgrade your early Mac to a high-performance machine, make sure that the cost is worth it. The software compatibility of the accelerator should be a key issue in your purchase decision. I cannot suggest strongly enough that if you decide to upgrade an early Mac, or even a Plus, you should also purchase a power supply and fan upgrade. The power supply in these machines was never meant to handle the draw of a high-performance accelerator. Overheating, already a problem in early Macs, will be a bigger problem with a lot of extra electronics "in the box."

ACCELERATOR	SPEED(MHz)	MACINTOSH	MAXIMUM MEMORY	VIRTUAL MEMORY	FPU	AUXILARY POWER SUPPLY	ON–BOARD VIDEO	RELATIVE SPEED (CLASSIC=1)
Applied Eng. Transwarp LC	25–40MHz	LC	System Memory	None	Included	None	None	11× (40MHz)
Applied Eng. Transwarp 040	25MHz	II, IIx, IIcx, IIfx, IIci	128MB	None	Included	None	None	14×
DayStar PowerCache	33–50MHz	SE/30, LC, II, IIx	System Memory	Apple's	Option	None	None	10× (50MHz)
Dove MaraThon Racer 030 II	32MHz	Mac II	System Memory	Apple's	Option	None	Option	6-×
Dove MaraThon Racer 030 Classic	16MHz	Classic	System Memory	Compact Virtual 3.0	Option	None	Option	3×
Dove MaraThon Racer 030 SE	16MHz	SE	System Memory	Compact Virtual 3.0	Option	None	Option	3×
Fusion TokaMac CI/LC/SX 25	25MHz	IIci, LC, SE/30, IIsi	System Memory	None	Included	None	None	9–12×
Harris Labs Classic Performer	16MHz 68000	Classic	System Memory	None	Option	None	None	2×
Mobius One Page 030 Display	25MHz	SE, Classic	System Memory	Compact Virtual 3.0	Option	None	One Page Mono	5×
NewLife 25	25MHz	128, 512, Plus, SE	16MB	Compact Virtual 3.0	Option	Optional	Optional	3–4×

TABLE 5.1: Macintosh Accelerators

ACCELERATOR	SPEED(MHz)	MACINTOSH	MAXIMUM MEMORY	VIRTUAL MEMORY	FPU	AUXILARY POWER SUPPLY	ON-BOARD VIDEO	RELATIVE SPEED (CLASSIC=1)
NewLife 33 SE	33MHz	SE	4MB	Compact Virtual 3.0	Included	None	Optional	4–5×
NewLife Accelerator! Classic	16MHz	Classic	16MB	Compact Virtual 3.0	Included	Included	Optional	3–4×
NewLife Accelerator! SE	16MHz	SE	16MB	Compact Virtual 3.0	Included	None	Optional	3–4×
Novy/Systech Quick30	16–33MHz	128, 512, Plus, SE, Classic	16MB	Compact Virtual 3.0	Included	Optional	Optional	3(16MHz)– 7(33MHz)×
Novy/Systech ImagePro	16–33MHz	512, Plus, SE, Classic	16MB	Compact Virtual 3.0	None	Optional	Optional	3–7×
Radius Rocket	25MHz 68040	II, IIx, IIcx, IIci	128MB	None	Included	None	None	7–10×
Total Gemini Classic	20–50MHz	Classic	16MB	Compact Virtual 3.0	Optional	Included	Optional	3–8(50MHz)×
Total Gemini Ultra	20–50MHz	512, Plus, SE	16MB	Compact Virtual 3.0	Optional	Optional	Optional	3–8(50MHz)×
Total Mercury 030/SE	16MHz	128, 512, Plus, SE	4MB	Compact Virtual 3.0	Optional	Optional	Optional	2–3×
Total Mercury Classic	16MHz	Classic	16MB	Compact Virtual 3.0	Optional	Included	Optional	2–3×
Total Voyager 030	33–50MHz	II, IIx	System Memory	None	Included	None	None	4–7×
Total Magellan 040 CI/LC/SI	25MHz	IIci, LC, SE/30, IIsi	System Memory	None	Optional	None	None	7–10×

TABLE 5.1: Macintosh Accelerators (continued)

To illustrate the installation of a typical clip-on Mac accelerator board, I've chosen the NewLife Accelerator! Classic. This is a well-engineered accelerator "daughterboard" for the Macintosh Classic. Because of the Classic's low-cost, no-frills construction, it is very similar to earlier clip-on Macs, with the exception of internal hard drive mounting capability and the memory expansion slot. Therefore, you should be able to use the installation directions that follow no matter which clip-on Mac you own.

The NewLife Accelerator! Classic includes a 16MHz 68030 processor, an optional FPU, and up to 16MB of fast 80ns memory on a 32-bit bus. A video connector for Apple monochrome, EGA, VGA, or MDA monitor interface boards (the Classic versions of NewLife's video boards should be available by the time this book is released) can be added. Figure 5.3 shows all of the NewLife Classic mounting components. The accelerator board is in the upper left corner of the picture. If you look carefully, squinting slightly, you'll notice four SIMM boards in the lower right corner of the board. These are 4MB SIMMs for a total of 16MB on the accelerator (you may recall that an unenhanced Classic only recognizes 4MB of memory).

The (socketed) 68882 FPU is just opposite the left corner of the lower SIMM bank. The accelerator 16MHz CPU is just above and to the left of the upper SIMM bank. Like the Classic 68000 processor, the accelerator 68030 is surface-mount device (as discussed in Chapter 1). You'll notice the accelerator ROM in the form of a large, square, ASIC (application specific integrated circuit—can I sling the slang, or what?), just above the middle of the SIMM banks.

Just to the right of this is the cutout for the Classic logic board power plug. The white plug on the right side of the cutout is the accelerator's own power plug. Right of the accelerator power plug, on the edge of the board is the Accelerator!'s graphics adaptor plug. You can see the solder pads for the board's Killy clip, which is used to mount an accelerator or other "daughterboard" over the CPU of a clip-on Mac, just above and to the left of the Classic power plug cutout. The Killy clip, obviously, is on the underside of the board.

On the upper left edge of the board is the cutout that fits over the Classic's battery. Clockwise from the accelerator board are the two software installation disks that contain the NewLife init/cdev (board initialization and Control Panel software), Bootman (a utility to adjust system heap size under System 6), Speedometer 3.06 (a nifty little utility that will tell you just how fast your accelerated system *is*), and NewLife's FPU SANE patch (SANE, Apple's Standard Apple Numeric Environment, is the Mac's built-in calculator. The patch allows software to use the built-in FPU and run SANE a lot faster).

In the lower right corner of the photo you can see a copy of Connectix's Compact Virtual. Virtual lets you use your Classic's system memory as a RAM disk that will autoload the Mac system or a selected program at bootup. Virtual also lets you allocate accelerator memory between system memory and the RAM disk. In the lower left of the picture is the auxiliary power supply for the board and just right of it, the plastic Killy clip installation tool and standoffs.

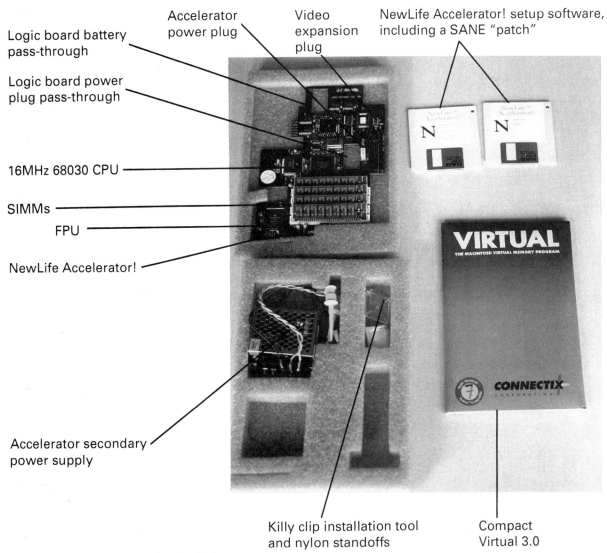

Logic board battery pass-through

Logic board power plug pass-through

Accelerator power plug

Video expansion plug

NewLife Accelerator! setup software, including a SANE "patch"

16MHz 68030 CPU

SIMMs

FPU

NewLife Accelerator!

Accelerator secondary power supply

Killy clip installation tool and nylon standoffs

Compact Virtual 3.0

FIGURE 5.3: The NewLife Accelerator! Classic system components (photo courtesy of Newlife Computer Corporation)

Down to the Nitty Gritty

To begin an accelerator installation, gather up your Mac cracking tools, adding a Phillips screwdriver and a small adjustable wrench or set of nut drivers to your basic toolkit. Place the Mac on a clean, soft pad, undo the screws, and crack the case. Drain the CRT anode. Remove the main power, drive power, and drive controller cables from the Mac's logic board and remove the logic board from the case.

Place the logic board on a smooth, firm surface, such as a neoprene mouse pad, or, if possible, an antistatic bag. Place the accelerator board Killy clip over the Mac CPU (orient and line it up carefully!) and press down until the clip is sitting snugly on the Mac's logic board. With any system that comes with a Killy clip installation tool, (like the NewLife Accelerator!), you can use the tool to make sure the clip is seated properly.

If you're installing an accelerator in a compact Mac with a PDS slot, you'll plug the accelerator board into the PDS socket. Some accelerators use different adapters for each machine. In that case, plug your accelerator into the PDS adapter, then plug the whole thing into the PDS slot. In a Mac SE, the board will install horizontally and will probably have nylon standoffs to stabilize it. In an SE/30 the accelerator board will mount vertically.

Standoffs

With the accelerator firmly attached to the Mac logic board, it's time for you to add standoffs. Many accelerator "daughterboards" use these small nylon bolts and screws to maintain the distance between an accelerator board and a Mac's main logic board as well as to keep the accelerator board securely fastened down. (See Figure 5.4.)

Installing a Power Supply (Och, Captain, She Can't Take Much Morra This!)

If your compact Mac accelerator board has an auxiliary power supply (and pre/SE Macs should), you should mount it to the compact Mac frame and attach it to the Mac power supply board (using the manufacturer's instructions) now. Figure 5.5 demonstrates how to hook up the auxiliary power supply for the New-Life Accelerator! board to a compact Mac power supply.

Getting the Motherboard (Logic Board) Back In

Getting a compact Mac logic board back into the machine with an accelerator daughterboard installed is an interesting operation, to say the least. To reinstall the logic board with the NewLife Accelerator!, my Mac Classic's internal frame had to be gently spread, and the logic board fitted in so that the bottom end of the daughterboard could slide under the Mac drive platform and into the case. Figure 5.6 illustrates this operation.

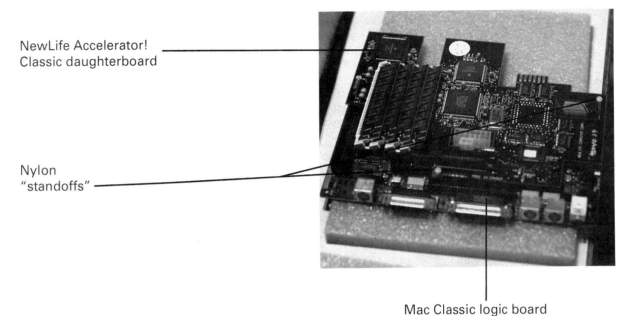

NewLife Accelerator!
Classic daughterboard

Nylon
"standoffs"

Mac Classic logic board

FIGURE 5.4:   Installing the NewLife daughterboard and standoffs

Reinstalling the Cables

With the logic board back in, the drive and main power cables should be reconnected and the accelerator board power cable plugged in. Figure 5.7 shows the accelerator installed and all power cables connected.

Installing Control Software

With your accelerator board installed, you can "close the hood" on your compact Mac and install the accelerator memory management software—usually Compact Virtual (Figure 5.8).

As you can see, Compact Virtual allows your machine to use any or all of the onboard accelerator memory as system memory, and slower Mac main memory as a RAM disk. Virtual lets you include part of the onboard accelerator memory in the RAM disk if you wish. Apparently, the latest version of Compact Virtual also supports the use of your hard drive as virtual memory.

You'll also need to install SANE patches if you have an FPU. Since most compact Macs don't support an FPU, if you install one with your accelerator, you'll have to find a way to tell your Mac and SANE that it is

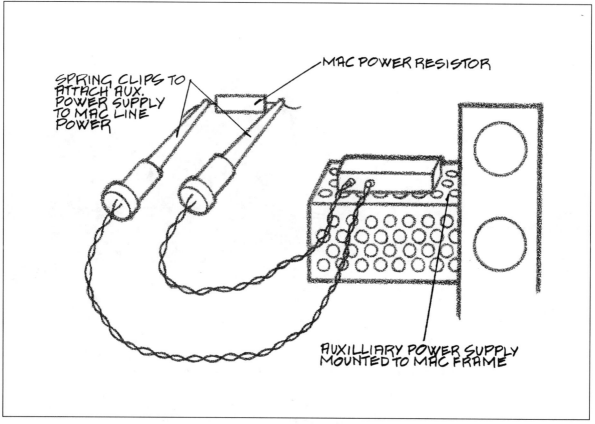

FIGURE 5.5: Hooking up the NewLife Accelerator! auxiliary power supply

installed. This is done with a software patch, usually a small assembly language program that redirects your Mac to the FPU when it uses certain SANE functions. A Mac with an FPU can execute complex SANE operations much more quickly than a standard machine.

Speed Traps

Speedometer 3.06, a $30 shareware Mac CPU evaluation program (see Figure 5.9), will evaluate your accelerator-equipped machine as compared to standard high-end Macs.

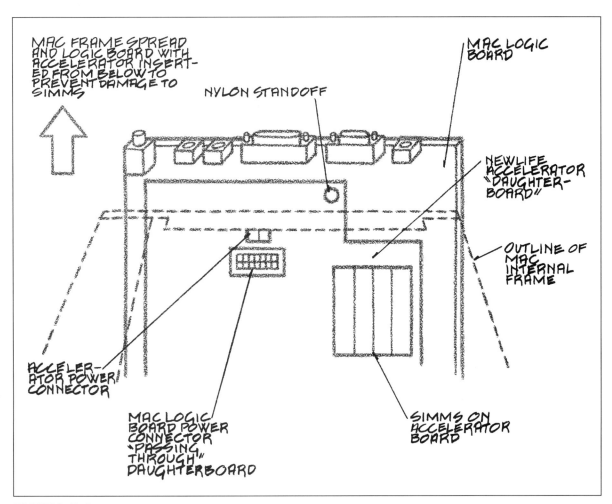

FIGURE 5.6:   Reinstalling the Mac logic board and accelerator

With the accelerator board installed, you may want to test your machine's speed. You can get a good idea at this point if all the claims the accelerator manufacturer made for his product are true.

You may want to try reformatting your hard drive and change its interleave to match its performance to your new, fast machine. Be sure you have the correct formatting software—see Chapter 7.

ACCELERATING YOUR MODULAR MAC

As with a lot of other upgrades, adding an accelerator to your modular Mac is a breeze—that is, of course, unless your accelerator is one of the models that

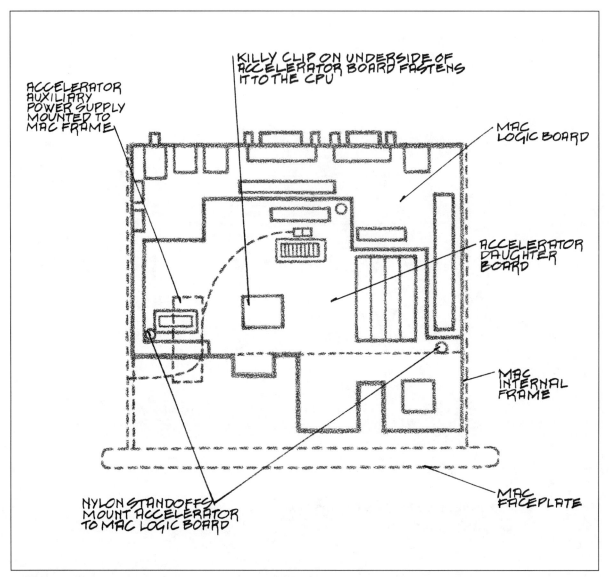

ACCELERATOR
AUXILIARY
POWER SUPPLY
MOUNTED TO
MAC FRAME

KILLY CLIP ON UNDERSIDE OF
ACCELERATOR BOARD FASTENS
IT TO THE CPU

MAC
LOGIC BOARD

ACCELERATOR
DAUGHTER
BOARD

MAC
INTERNAL
FRAME

NYLON STANDOFFS
MOUNT ACCELERATOR
TO MAC LOGIC BOARD

MAC
FACEPLATE

FIGURE 5.7:   A NewLife Accelerator! and power cables installed

plugs in to a Mac II CPU socket. (DayStar uses this approach with the Mac II version of its PowerCache accelerator boards (see Figure 5.10).)

You may have to plug your accelerator board into an adaptor before installing it, as some manufacturers use one accelerator and a number of different adapters.

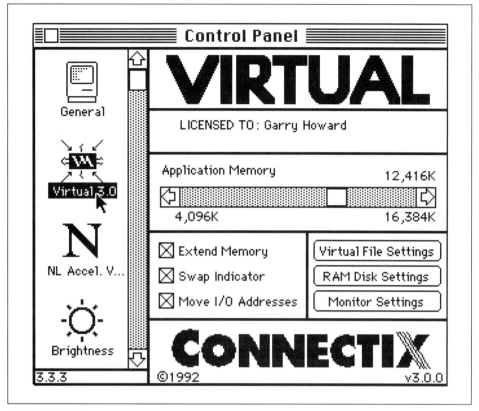

FIGURE 5.8:   Compact Virtual memory allocation screen.

Most 68030 accelerators used in modular Macs plug into the PDS slot. Because this gives the accelerator direct access to the Mac's system bus, performance is greatly enhanced. Many Mac accelerators add a variety of options such as extra cache memory and additional PDS slots. Be careful, however, because some of these slots are a proprietary design of the manufacturer.

Some boards, like the Radius Rocket 25i, plug into a modular Mac's NuBus slots. Installation is easy, but speed enhancement for some NuBus boards may not be as great as PDS accelerators, because they have bus speed, other devices on the NuBus, and system bus access to contend with.

Once you've installed an accelerator in your modular machine, you'll need to install control software to turn the accelerator on and off as well as a control for an FPU patch if you added the chip. These controls are usually in the form of a cdev or possibly an init.

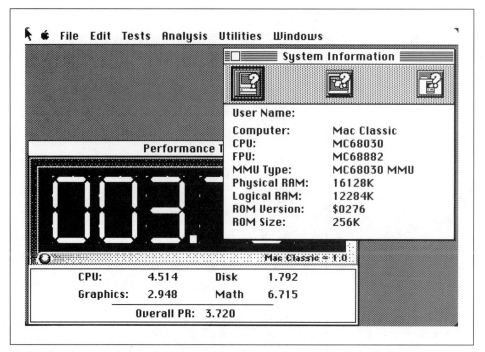

FIGURE 5.9:   Speedometer 3.06, a Mac hardware evaluation utility

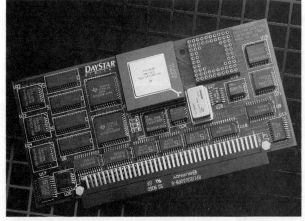

FIGURE 5.10:   DayStar's Universal PowerCache Card (photo courtesy of Daystar Digital, Inc.)

ACCELERATOR INSTALLATION PROBLEMS, SOLUTIONS, AND TIPS

The main problem with installing an accelerator in a compact Mac is opening the case. Having done this, the rest of the installation is pretty straightforward if you follow the manufacturer's instructions. *Make sure* you use a wrist strap to avoid killing your fancy new accelerator board with a shot of static.

And—another thing I've mentioned before that bears repeating—if you install an accelerator in a Mac Plus or earlier, get a fan and power supply upgrade.

Check hardware reviews or your local user's group for news about potential software conflicts with your accelerator. If there are conflicts, ask the board manufacturer if new control software, upgrades, or patches are available to eliminate them.

Make sure that your preferred accelerator can be easily turned off in case some unresolved software conflicts exist. If you're installing a Killy-clip accelerator, make sure that the clip is on snugly and that standoffs are properly attached. This should (God willing!) keep your accelerator board from loosening up and sending your Mac to an untimely end. In single-slot PDS Macs choose your accelerator carefully. If the accelerator or an adaptor board offers an additional (Apple-compatible) PDS slot, you won't be locked in to just one board in your single slot. However, the power budget for single-PDS-slot Macs is pretty tight, so make sure that your machine can handle the accelerator and any subsequent cards you may want to add.

CONSIDERING YOUR ALTERNATIVES

As I've suggested previously, though accelerators are frequently a good option, you should determine if they are a good option for *you*. Are the economics of buying a fully loaded accelerator better than purchasing a new machine? If they are—great! If not, better think some more.

Don't ignore the potential of used equipment. Older high-end machines will often outperform accelerated equipment and are a better deal if the price is right. Don't get me wrong—now that Apple has committed to releasing new hardware every year, adding an accelerator may be the SANE (sorry) way to stay current.

Advantages of an Accelerator Upgrade

So, in summary, what are the advantages of adding an accelerator to your older Mac?

The obvious first answer is faster program execution. If you've used PageMaker on a Classic, you know where I'm coming from. Some programs, as a matter of fact most programs these days, are a whole lot more reasonable to use when they're run at a higher speed.

The second advantage is one I've referred to before—a new large-screen monitor. With all that additional monitor real estate, you wouldn't expect scrolling and screen updates to be as fast. And they aren't. An accelerator makes a large-screen monitor on *any* Mac a whole lot more usable. Many accelerators include a large-screen monitor adapter or a plug for one. If the monitor is running on a 32-bit accelerator bus, performance will be *much* better.

The third reason to use an accelerator? It'll speed up your hard disk. With a fast processor, read-write operations can take place much more quickly. As a matter of fact, as I've mentioned, you may want to reformat your hard drive to take advantage of the faster processor.

And reason number four to add an accelerator—a "bundled" FPU. The FPU, especially running at accelerator speed, can cut the time it takes to do complex calculations.

Disadvantages of an Accelerator Upgrade

Now, the disadvantages of adding an accelerator.

The first and most obvious disadvantage of an accelerator is the bane of a hardware designer's existence—software incompatibility. As long as programmers insist on bypassing the Mac's ROM "toolbox" for a gain in performance, they risk causing problems with hardware and other software. They're also forced into a string of "maintenance upgrades." Sound familiar?

The second disadvantage of an accelerator is the cost/benefit situation that I mentioned. The upgrade has to make economic sense.

A third, and potentially very serious, disadvantage of an accelerator is getting "left behind" by Apple's hardware and software evolution. If you have a good, reliable hardware manufacturer behind your accelerator this may not be as big a problem as it appears.

Finally, when accelerators are used with video upgrades from other manufacturers, there is always the possibility of hardware incompatibility between the video adaptor and the accelerator. Sometimes this is due to timing conflicts. This is why I recommend, at least for compact Macs, that you go for an "all-inclusive" upgrade if you're planning on adding better quality video.

TROUBLESHOOTING

Problem	Cause	Solution
Intermittent problems or "flaky" behavior	Possible accelerator/System init, cdev conflict	Selectively remove or deactivate
No power and computer plugged in	If accelerator has separate power supply, check	Otherwise check logic board power
Strange video, i.e., checkerboard or vertical lines, on boot	Possible bent pins, poor video connection	Check and correct
Wavering vertical lines after power-up	If board has auxiliary power supply, not properly connected	Otherwise check main board supply
Sad Mac on power-up	Incorrect or incorrectly installed memory	Incorrect logic board memory
Intermittent sad Mac or system bombs	Software conflicts, poor connection with Killy clip, or intermittent power	Check

CHAPTER SIX

Coprocessors and Cache Cards

Cache memory has become a popular method of increasing the performance of computer hardware and software at a relatively low cost. In its most basic form, a *cache* is an area of computer memory used to store the data last accessed. As mentioned in Chapter 4, when the computer needs data, it goes to the cache first instead of to slower memory or a disk drive. If the computer finds the data it needs in the cache (a cache hit), it can process faster. Overall, the improvement due to a cache is somewhere between cache speed and slower system or disk speed.

DID YOU BRING THE CACHE?

Mac caches can be implemented in a variety of ways, using both hardware and software. The Mac system uses a built-in adjustable software cache to improve performance. If you have Adobe Type Manager, you've seen Adobe's font cache, which is used to improve the speed of font scaling.

A variety of hard drives now have onboard data caches to improve performance. Accelerator boards like Harris Labs' Performer use a hardware cache to achieve a speed increase. This type of cache memory is provided by cache cards for 68030 and 68040 processors. This cache, when installed on the fast PDS bus, stores processor instructions in fast memory and improves processor instruction access and system performance.

TYPES OF CACHES

There are a number of commonly used caching systems. A *write-through cache* writes updates to main memory as well as to cache memory. This ensures data integrity as no cached data will be overwritten.

A *copyback cache* is not updated with a write to main memory until necessary. Cache snooping monitors the contents of a copyback cache and updates main memory if the contents are changed. A copyback cache can also be updated on command.

Processor Internal Caches

Motorola 68030 and 68040 processors have built-in instruction and data caches to increase chip performance. The '030 caches are 256 bytes in size, and the '040 caches are 4K in size. If either CPU contains necessary information in its cache memory, program execution will be much faster. Unfortunately the 68000 processor in older Macs has no internal caches, so that adding a fast external cache board would have no appreciable affect on performance. The only caches associated with these CPUs may be on an accelerator board. The 68020 processor in the Mac II and the Mac LC has only an instruction cache; an external cache would probably have limited value. There hasn't been a stampede to produce an LC or Mac II cache board, in any case.

Cache Boards and PDS Slots

Many of Apple's 68030 and '040-based machines have a PDS slot, allowing an external board to access the CPU instruction and data buses directly. This gives PDS boards a substantial speed and performance advantage over, for example, NuBus boards.

Cache cards for '030 Macs achieve a large speed boost with maximum compatibility by just extending the 68030's cache memory with fast cache memory installed on the PDS bus. Any program that accesses the 68030 caches can get more than the 256 standard bytes from cache memory. The cache thus doesn't achieve a speed increase by accelerating the standard Mac '030 processor, but by allowing the CPU to operate at maximum speed without the bottleneck of slowing down to read from, or write to, slow system memory. The speed improvement can be as much as 35%. Wait states are the main problem for Macs with CPUs running faster than 16MHz. Cache memory can result in the virtual elimination of these wait states.

Most cache cards use static RAM instead of the dynamic RAM used by main memory. Compared to a dynamic RAM speed of 80ns, static RAM can operate as quickly as 25ns, allowing the 68030 to transfer information to and from the cache at system bus speed.

'040 Cache Boards and Compatibility

The caches on the Quadra's 68040 processor cause compatibility problems with many current software programs that aren't designed to work with them. A number of software utilities designed to turn off the 68040's internal caches have sprung up recently. Turning off the '040 caches slows the Quadra down considerably.

Cache boards for the 68040 processor may suffer from the same sort of compatibility problems. This would substantially reduce the value of an '040 cache board with most software.

MACINTOSH CACHE BOARDS

Cache boards were first produced for the Macintosh IIci, but various manufacturers now produce them for most 68030-equipped Macs and some 68040 Macs. Some manufacturers produce one cache board and a variety of adapters for different machines. Caches are available in combination with FPUs, extra PDS expansion slots, and accelerated '030 and '040 chips. The boards plug into the PDS slot on an '030 or '040 machine and give the CPU access to fast 25ns cache memory, eliminating or reducing processor wait states.

Cache card memory sizes of 64 to 128K seem to be optimal. Smaller sizes don't produce the maximum performance boost while larger sizes waste processor time searching the cache contents.

I've mentioned possible problems with 68040 cache cards, but 68030 cards experience very few problems. As a matter of fact, these cards are the cheapest and most compatible speed improvement you can install on your Mac.

Cache Card Compatibility (CCCurumba)

You'll remember that I talked about compatibility problems with accelerator boards. Well, you won't find them with cache cards, at least not to the same extent. Accelerators have to play some major tricks with the Mac system to add a faster processor, FPU, fast memory, and graphics expansion. Some of these tricks include using system *interrupts*, a process with major potential for problems if not done properly. But because cache cards are just an extension of the 68030 instruction and data caches, the potential for problems is considerably reduced.

If, on the other hand, you *do* have some compatibility problems, most cards have a utility to allow you to shut the cache down. If you have an FPU on your cache card, the software patches that came with it may be the source of compatibility problems and can usually be shut off if necessary.

Types of Macintosh Cache Cards

As I've mentioned, a variety of single purpose and multifunction cache boards are available from Mac hardware developers.

First, there are the "ordinary" cache cards with only fast cache memory installed. Figure 6.1 shows DayStar's FastCache '040, FastCache 64K, and Fast-Cache 32K cards. The original FastCache, for the IIci, was released with the IIci in September 1989. The latest of these cache boards, the FastCache '040, was the first cache board released for the Quadra. Many of DayStar's cache boards use a slot adapter to mount one type of board in a variety of different machines.

FIGURE 6.1:   Clockwise, DayStar's FastCache '040, FastCache 64K, and FastCache 32K (photo courtesy of Daystar Digital, Incorporated)

Other cache cards include Applied Engineering's Cache-in IIci and QuickSilver IIsi-SE/30 cache cards, the UR Micro MacCache LP32 for the IIci, Total Systems QuickCache IIci, Micron Xceed IIci, and the ATTO cache IIci.

Cache-Accelerator Combos

A number of manufacturers build fast static RAM and an accelerated CPU into one cache board. The fast cache memory on the board is more likely to be used as a cache for the accelerated CPU than the main system CPU. DayStar's PowerCache series is a good example. I consider these products to be accelerator boards and have mentioned them in Chapter 5.

Cache-Slot-FPU Combos

Another very popular combination for a cache board is the addition of an FPU and slot expansion. For single-slot PDS machines such as the LC, LC II, and IIsi, this combination offers you more speed, a math coprocessor, and often, an additional PDS slot. Good examples are DayStar's DualPort IIsi and Combo-Cache IIsi boards. (See Figure 6.2, the ComboCache IIsi board.) Check carefully, though—some of these boards use special-purpose, proprietary slots. Also, as I mentioned, a built-in FPU and its associated patches may be a source of incompatibility for these boards. Another thing to consider when adding a multislot adapter is the power budget for your Mac. The IIsi's power supply runs pretty tight, so you're going to have to be careful of the power requirement for any expansion boards you add to an adapter.

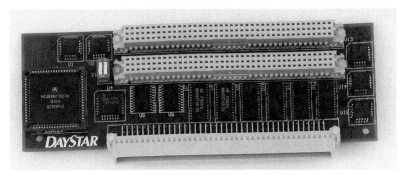

FIGURE 6.2: DayStar ComboCache IIsi, with 32K RAM Cache, 2-'030 PDS slots, and a 20MHz FPU (photo courtesy of Daystar Digital, Incorporated)

Installation Details

With the exception of the Mac SE/30, installation of cache boards is a breeze. (And once the case is cracked, an SE/30's PDS slot makes the addition of a cache board almost as straightforward as for a modular machine.) Regardless of the Mac you're upgrading, *make sure* you're well grounded with an antistatic strap. Take your time and work the board in slowly and carefully, rocking it *gently* (front to back, not side to side) if necessary. Like any other expansion board, do not attempt to force an installation. This can bend pins and bend or break connections or expansion plugs.

An SE/30 Installation

To install an SE/30 cache board, crack the case as shown in Chapter 3. Remove the RFI shield from the base of the SE/30 case, replacing it before you "button up." If your cache board uses an adapter, the board is plugged into the adapter and then slid in between the PDS slot brackets and plugged into the PDS slot. Otherwise, the cache board is plugged in directly. Make sure the board is installed snugly and securely, but don't get over-enthusiastic. Once the cache board is installed you will have to install the control software, which may be a cdev and/or an init. Don't forget that you can shut the board or an FPU off if things start to get strange.

A Modular Mac Installation

Installing a cache board in a modular Mac just requires you to pop the lid and plug the board, or adapter and board, into the modular Mac's PDS or cache slot. You then install the controller and SANE patch software (for the FPU) if required. The cache board is ready to go! Easy, wasn't it? (By the way—you did wear that anti-static wrist strap, didn't you?)

THE ECONOMICS OF CACHE UPGRADES

Cache boards are a relatively cheap, easy, and effective speed upgrade for a Mac. As I've mentioned, there are not a lot of hardware "tricks" or "work-arounds" involved in accelerating a Mac with a cache card. The straightforward hardware also keeps cache card prices low. When combined with FPUs, slots, and even accelerators, a cache can provide an "all-in-one" upgrade and make effective use of an available PDS slot. Of course, combining a cache with an accelerator raises the possibility of hardware and software conflicts again.

The cache card is probably the most economical and effective upgrade for an '030 or later model Mac with a PDS slot.

MACS AND COPROCESSORS

A coprocessor is a device that "takes the load" from the Mac CPU. It performs a specific operation and lets the CPU get on with other things. Some coprocessors built into the Mac include the SCSI controller and the serial communications chip (SCC), which controls the serial ports.

FPUs

Add-on coprocessors are available to perform a variety of functions for your Mac. The most common Mac coprocessor upgrade is the numeric coprocessor or floating point unit (FPU) discussed in Chapter 5.

 The FPU is designed to speed the execution of transcendental math functions such as logs, trigonometric functions, powers, and roots, not to mention floating point math (hence the "FPU"). Thus, ordinary arithmetic will not see any benefit from the chip. Complex calculations will *definitely* benefit.

FPUs improve the performance of a variety of applications. However, only software written to take advantage of the FPU will see any significant benefit. Spreadsheets with complex (for instance, engineering) calculations will see large performance benefits from an FPU.

Pure mathematical modeling software such as Mathematica, Maple, and other programs make heavy use of an FPU, as do lab, modeling, and mapping packages.

Interestingly, complex draw and CAD packages use advanced mathematical functions, so that an FPU can speed these packages up substantially.

Software PostScript emulators do a lot of calculations to create and scale fonts and graphics. Many of these packages will receive a speed boost from an FPU.

Mapping and *GIS* (Geographical Information System) programs on the Mac do millions of calculations for every operation. Once again, an FPU is a necessary addition if you're going to be using these programs.

High-Performance Floating Point Accelerators

Spectral Innovations produces two floating point accelerator cards for the Mac. These are the MacDSP AP1M for the Mac SE/30 or IIfx and the MacDSP APN for the Mac II family. The cards can accelerate a system up to 50 times and are used for signal, image, and graphics processing, as well as general floating point acceleration.

PMMUs

For a Mac II to use virtual memory, you must replace its memory management chip with a PMMU. The PMMU allows a 68020 CPU to treat drive space like memory, transferring memory a "page" at a time to and from disk.

A Mac LC can use virtual memory with Novy/Systech's MMU board. The Novy board also has an FPU option.

Video and Graphics Coprocessors

A number of video boards come equipped with dedicated graphics coprocessors or RISC chips to handle the heavy load of high-resolution, large-screen color. I'll be talking about a number of these in Chapter 8. There are other video coprocessor boards available. The RasterOps ProColor 32 is a high-powered NuBus coprocessor board designed specifically for color desktop publishing, or color prepress. The board has separate banks of VRAM (video RAM) chips for CMYK (cyan-magenta-yellow and black) color separation and a custom chip to convert from CYMK to *RGB* (red-green-blue) and do color calibration. The board also has space for up to 8MB of RAM for image handling, hardware zoom and pan, and a plug for a RISC accelerator.

Hardware Compression and Decompression

Another common Mac coprocessor card is a hardware compression/decompression card. Very large Mac graphics and sound files are becoming common; hardware compression and decompression dramatically improve their file storage.

Sigma Designs produces the NuBus Double Up hardware compressor/decompressor. The NeoTech Image Compressor board from Advent Computer Products, Inc. does fast *JPEG* (Joint Photographic Experts Group) hardware image compression at ratios up to 100:1, with average compression ratios of 10:1 to 25:1.

The Picture Press Accelerator from Storm Technology is a NuBus image compressor card that lets users open compressed files at the same rate as uncompressed files. Storm claims compression ratios of up to 1:100 for 24-bit graphics files.

Signal Processor Boards

Signal processors are devices that quickly enter, digitize, analyze, and manipulate an input signal. They can be used for signal processing, image and graphics processing, spectral analysis and process control. Spectral Innovations Inc. markets the MacDSP64KC for the Mac II or better. The board is based on AT&Ts DSP32C digital signal processor, has two 16MBit/sec serial ports and 4MB of *zero-wait state* static RAM.

Spectral Innovations also markets a higher performance signal processor called the MacDSPII, with two AT&T DSP32C signal processors, 1MB of SRAM per processor, 2MB of shared DRAM, and 8K of dual-port SRAM.

Macs with and without Coprocessors

A number of newer Macs include built-in coprocessors. The IIci has a built-in 68882 FPU. The IIfx has an advanced SCSI controller and enhanced serial port controllers. The fx's DMA and coprocessor chips, supposedly optimized for Apple/Unix (A/UX), never quite worked properly. The Quadras have SCSI controller chips that provide true direct memory access (the chip accesses Mac memory directly, without the intervention of the CPU).

INSTALLING A COPROCESSOR

Once again, compact Macs are much more interesting (so to speak) to upgrade than modular Macs. Most of the interest involves opening the case. Of course, modular Macs are still the class of the field for upgrades. Just plug in the coprocessor board and go.

FPU Boards

Many compact Mac accelerators have an FPU option. You can purchase the coprocessor with the board or install it later if the FPU is socketed. (Installing an accelerator board was covered in the previous chapter.) The Mac Classic II has a dedicated ROM/FPU slot and a number of manufacturers build plug-in FPU boards for the slot. ATEC builds the FPU Classic for the Classic II, and Quantum Leap Systems markets the Classic II C2FP fast floating point board. Newer Technology and MacTel Technology market the FPU-882 and Index Gold Mathmate, respectively. Addition of an FPU to the Classic II expansion slot, once the case has been opened, is easy.

Modular Macs are easy to open and modular Mac PDS FPU cards are simple to install. In a Mac LC or IIsi, all you have to do is plug in the FPU adapter and install control software. FPU boards for the LC include FastMath LC from Applied Engineering, the FPU LC V2.0 from ATEC, the Index Gold Mathmate LC from MacTel Technology, and the LCFP board from Quantum Leap Systems. Figure 6.3 is a Novy/Systech QuickMath LC and Figure 6.4 shows DayStar's PowerMath and Equalizer LC cards. The PowerMath card is a 16MHz 68882 FPU for the LC and LC II and the Equalizer is a 68030 and 68882 upgrade for the LC. DayStar provides an FPU upgrade for the ComboCache IIsi and DualPort IIsi cache/slot upgrades. Quantum Leap builds the SIFP FPU card for the IIsi.

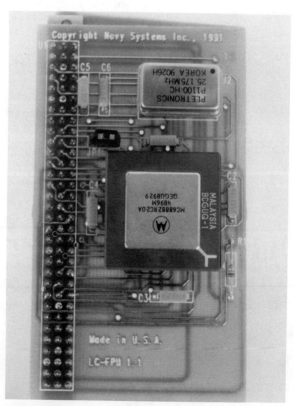

FIGURE 6.3: The Novy/Systech QuickMath LC (photo courtesy of Novy Systems/Systems Technology)

FIGURE 6.4:   Left, DayStar's PowerMath LC and Right, the Equalizer LC (photo courtesy of Daystar Digital, Incorporated)

The 68020 Chip and the PMMU

In order to use a Mac II, which has a 68020 CPU, with virtual memory, you'll have to remove the Mac II's built-in chip and install a PMMU. Open the case and remove the drive platform. Locate the HMMU using the Mac II schematic, Figure 3.19. The chip is between the Mac II SIMMs and the 68020 CPU. *Gently* pull the HMMU with a chip puller or small flat-bladed screwdriver. Install the PMMU with the line on its surface pointing to the Mac speaker.

You can install the PMMU option for the Mac LC using Novy/Systech's MMU board. Pop the lid and carefully insert the board into the LC PDS slot. You may have to add an init or cdev.

A PMMU, once installed, gives the Mac LC the same ability to use virtual memory that 68030 Macs have. This means that you can use your hard drive as an extension of system memory. This is great for very large files, if somewhat slow. However, be aware that a number of applications do not support virtual memory.

NuBus Coprocessor Boards

Video coprocessors, hardware compression boards, and other NuBus cards are simple to install in Macs with NuBus slots. Depending on the board, you may have to remove the NuBus back panel slot cover before inserting it. Finally, some initialization and control software may have to be installed.

TROUBLESHOOTING

Problem	Cause	Solution
Mac will not boot, or locks up	Cache or FPU card software conflicts with System extensions and cdevs	Selectively remove or disable
Still having problems after above	Possible corrupted System file	Repair or replace
Don't get a normal start sound, or get a different sound	Possible defective or damaged board	Return

CHAPTER SEVEN

Storage Options: Hard Drives and Such...

If you're looking for program and data storage for your Mac, you're faced with a bewildering range of options. You can choose from third-party high-density floppy drives, hard drives, cartridge drives, tape drives, optical drives, floptical drives, CD-ROMs, and RAM drives. This chapter will help you select the storage devices that meet your needs, taking into account price, speed, capacity, and other variables. It will also give you some suggestions for preventing problems, such as SCSI bus conflicts, and present some ideas for troubleshooting.

The right storage device can give programs a performance boost, give you the program and archive "elbow room" you need, and even add extra RAM if you're using a Mac that's capable of running System 7 virtual memory.

A MAC DISK PRIMER

Why explain disk formats and the structure of the Mac operating system in a hardware upgrade book? I can think of a number of reasons. If you understand formats and the Mac operating system, you'll have a better idea of how storage devices work, why some are faster than others, and why your current system may have trouble with some older programs and data disks. You'll also have a better understanding of what your operating system is and how to keep it healthy, not to mention how to restore or repair it when something goes wonky. Your upgraded hardware is only as good, fast, and reliable as the operating system setup that runs it.

Disk Structure and the Low-Level Format

There are two disk preparation processes, or formats, that are applied to Macintosh hard and floppy disks. The first is the hard, physical, or *low-level format*. This process writes physical tracks and sectors to your drive. The second is the *logical format*. In this process, the Mac's catalog and disk organization information are written to a hard or floppy disk.

Tracks, Sectors, and Cylinders

I mentioned that a low-level format writes *tracks* and *sectors* to a Macintosh disk. So what the devil are tracks and sectors? Tracks are like concentric circles on the surface of a Macintosh disk. When the disk *read-write heads* travel across the surface of a disk, they can stop on one of these concentric circles to read or write data. Macintosh hard or floppy drives write data to tracks with magnetic pulses.

While it is possible to read from and write data to an entire track, the variable size and number of programs, drivers, and files on a Macintosh disk make this impractical. It's not likely, for instance, that you'd want to use an entire track for a file that might only take up one-tenth of the track space. For this and other reasons, the tracks on Mac disks are divided into sectors. Basically, a sector is just a small portion of a track. The common sector size for Mac devices is 512 bytes. A program can be efficiently divided into sectors, and the partially filled final sector wastes very little disk space.

With old Macintosh 400K floppy disk drives, tracks and sectors are all you have to worry about. However, when double-sided floppy and hard disk drives are considered, you need to know about cylinders as well (see Figure 7.1).

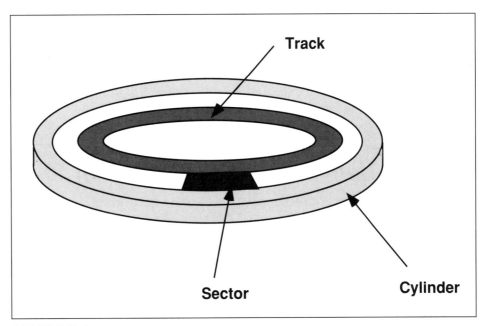

FIGURE 7.1:   Tracks, sectors, and cylinders

Tracks are numbered from the outer edge of a disk starting with track 0. On a double-sided disk, track 0 is written on the top *and* the bottom of the disk. The top track is called track 0, side 0, and the bottom track is track 0, side 1. Mac 800K disks have 80 tracks, numbered 0 to 79 (from the edge of the disk to the spindle). Each pair of top and bottom tracks is called a cylinder.

Mac 400 and 800K floppies have eight sectors on inside tracks and twelve on outside tracks. Because the number of sectors changes, the drive has to alter speed to read or record the floppy. You'll notice this as a change in the pitch of the sound that the drive makes when reading or writing data.

Hard drives store data on solid metal platters and drive space is increased by adding more platters to the central spindle. For a two-platter hard drive, the numbering scheme for platter one is track 0, sides 0 and 1, while for platter two, it's track 0, sides 2 and 3. All four tracks numbered 0 are one cylinder. Multiple platter hard drives are just an extension of this numbering scheme. Hard drives can have over 600 tracks per inch.

Recording a Sector

Macintosh disk sectors have to be labeled in some fashion when they're recorded to allow the disk drive to find them on the disk. This labeling is called *soft sectoring*. The address of each sector is written into the sector during formatting. The sector address is part of a sector "header" that also includes synchronization (sync) bytes, which occur before each sector to let the drive controller know that a sector address is coming. *Gap bytes* are written between sectors to allow enough time for the drive to read each sector. When a sector is written to, a sum of bytes in the sector, or *checksum*, is written to a location following the sector data. When the drive reads the sector, it does its own checksum and compares it to the sector checksum. This is called a CRC, or cyclical redundancy check. If the CRC comparison fails, you'll get a report of a disk read failure.

Interleaving for Fun and Profit

If you've been around Macintosh hard drives for a while, you've probably heard of something called *interleave*—some folks call it "skew." Interleave is the adjustment of a hard drive's recording pattern to match the speed of the Macintosh that's using it.

A fast computer can read consecutive disk sectors as fast as they come, in the sequence 1-2-3-4-5-6-7.... This is known as a 1:1 (one-to-one) interleave. A slower machine needs more time to "digest" and transmit data, and might use a 2:1 interleave. The sector sequence in a 2:1 interleave might be something like 1-10-2-11-3-12-4. A very slow machine uses a 3:1 or higher interleave. A 3:1 interleave might be something like 1-7-13-2-8-14-3. You'll get a better idea of how this works from Figure 7.2.

The Logical Format

As I've mentioned, the logical format is the "map" that your Mac system uses to find its way around a disk. A logical format divides a Mac disk into six areas: the boot blocks, the volume information blocks, the catalog tree, the extents

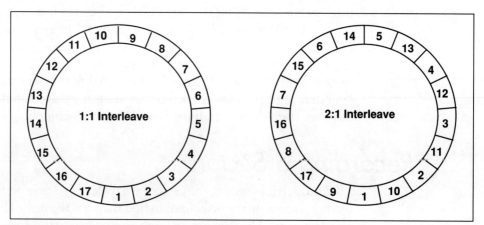

FIGURE 7.2: Mac disk interleave

tree, the partitioning information (if used), and the data area. Logical format-ting divides a device into blocks, consisting of one or more sectors. Because the Mac operating system sees storage space in terms of blocks, and not tracks and sectors, it is device-independent. A device controller looks after actual track-sector addresses, while the Mac operating system only worries about blocks. Dif-ferent devices have different block sizes. For instance:

20MB or less	512-byte block, one sector
20–60MB	1024-byte block, two sectors
60–100MB and greater	1536-byte block, three sectors

Larger block sizes provide better disk performance. A Mac can write a lot more contiguous data without having to locate the next sector(s) when the blocks are large.

The performance benefit of large block sizes is not without a penalty. This penalty is called slack space. When a file is written, available blocks are filled until the end of a file is reached. The remaining bytes of the file are writ-ten to the last block, with some block space left over—the slack space.

With larger block sizes, the same file will have more slack space. This is why files seem to shrink when you move them from a large hard drive to a smaller drive or floppy. Larger amounts of slack space are the price you pay for the increased performance of large hard drives.

The Mac logical format organizes blocks in terms of volumes, which are "logical devices" (as opposed to physical devices like hard drives). Volumes can consist of separate drives, individual drive partitions, or an area of RAM desig-nated as a RAM drive. The Mac operating system treats each volume as a separate disk.

The Boot Blocks

The first two sectors of a Mac volume contain the *boot blocks*. These start the Mac boot process by reading the Mac system file in use, the names and location of critical system files, and other information. Boot blocks contain a code that starts the booting process, then loads the rest of the boot code from the Mac ROMs. If a Mac's boot blocks are damaged, or *corrupted*, your drive will *hang*, refusing to load data.

The Volume Bitmap

The volume bitmap is exactly what it says—a series of bits whose pattern of 0s and 1s correspond to empty and full blocks, respectively, on a Mac device. The first-to-last bits in the bitmap are equivalent to the corresponding blocks in a Mac device. This is the way a Macintosh keeps track of which device blocks are occupied and unoccupied.

The Extents Tree

While the volume bit map keeps track of occupied blocks, the extents tree keeps track of which file pieces (*extents*) are in the occupied blocks. The extents tree has *b-tree*, or binary tree, structure. The b-tree stores the location of extents information in *index nodes* and the information itself in *leaf nodes*. This structure gives the Macintosh the ability to index very large devices and keep track of scattered file pieces throughout a device. When too many files get split into too many small pieces, you've got a *fragmentation* problem. Figure 7.3 illustrates fragmentation.

The Catalog Tree

The MFS (Macintosh File System), which was used by pre-Plus Macs, could handle only 128 files and had trouble with large storage devices. Folders were a convenient illusion in this system.

With the Plus, Apple introduced HFS, the Hierarchical File System. In HFS, folders are a real part of the file structure, like Unix or MS-DOS subdirectories without the pain. Together with the introduction of the SCSI port in the Plus, HFS allowed the Mac to, theoretically, keep track of an unlimited number of files.

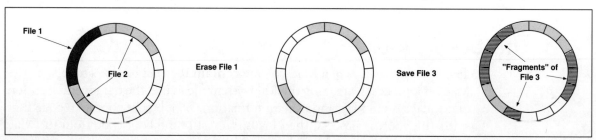

FIGURE 7.3:   Fragmentation and the single disk

The Mac catalog tree stores a variety of information about files on a device. Each file has a single entry, including the file name, what folder(s) it is located in, position on the desktop, and the location and size of the file data and resource forks. The catalog tree, like the extents tree, has a b-tree structure. Figure 7.4 is a schematic diagram of the Mac's file blocks.

The Partition Map

When a Macintosh device is "partitioned," it's divided into a number of logical devices, or volumes, with separate boot blocks and volume information blocks for each. Partitioning creates a partition map on a series of blocks, beginning with block 1. Each partition has an entry in the partition map containing the name of the partition, processor type, partition type, status, size, and other details. Every block on the disk, including free space, belongs to a partition. A Mac disk driver has its own partition. The operating system on the boot partition will recognize its own and other partitions as separate devices.

Why partition a device? If one partition's directory structure becomes corrupted, programs and data on your remaining partitions will be safe. Want to install separate operating systems on different partitions? No problem! For instance, you might want to install System 7 on one partition and 6.07 on another. To boot a different system, just change the boot device in the Control Panel. Using different partitions can provide some protection against a virus infection, and can allow you to organize your work by partition or use a partition for archives. Partitioning also controls disk fragmentation, because the majority of copying, moving, and deleting files can be restricted to one partition.

How the System Works and What to Do When It Doesn't

When you save a file, the Mac file manager receives the file name, the directory ID of the file folder, the size, and other information. The file manager checks the volume bitmap to find out where disk free space is, marks it as reserved, and writes the file to the free space. The file manager then checks the catalog b-tree

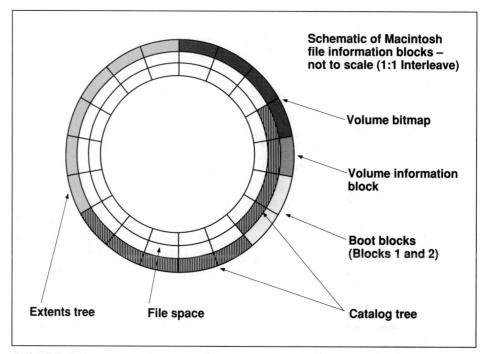

Schematic of Macintosh file information blocks – not to scale (1:1 Interleave)

Volume bitmap

Volume information block

Boot blocks (Blocks 1 and 2)

Catalog tree

Extents tree

File space

FIGURE 7.4: The circular file

with the folder ID to find the next-to-last level for leaf nodes, where information is stored. When the correct leaf node is found, information is stored if the file name is not already taken. The information stored includes the location of the file's data and resource forks.

Opening a file sends the file manager back to the catalog b-tree with the file's directory ID to find the correct leaf node and the filename to find the file "leaf" record. When the file is located, the file manager creates an area in RAM called the file control block (FCB), which holds the file location and other information. The number of open files is determined by a number in the volume information block that indicates how many FCBs your setup can support. The file manager flags the current file as "in use" and your application has the use of the file until you're finished with it.

If you add to a file, the file manager locates additional free space and writes the information in the catalog tree. If the file contains more than six fragments, the location of the pieces is noted in the extents tree.

Deleting a file removes the file's bit entry in the volume bit map and erases the file's catalog "leaf" entry.

If you do not do any file operations after deleting a file, the odds of recovering it with an "undelete" utility are good. Programs like Norton Utilities and MacTools Deluxe use special files that preserve your Mac's file records and do "delete tracking" of files. This means that the catalog entry of deleted files is saved in a special data file so that the deleted files can be restored.

Corruption of the file blocks can cause a lot of nasty problems when you try to use your Mac. If the boot blocks are even slightly corrupted, your Mac will refuse to boot. A corrupted volume bitmap can result in two files claiming the same block, called "cross-linked files." Your Mac won't recognize a disk with a corrupted catalog tree, and the machine will try to initialize it.

 A normal quit and shutdown from your Mac applications will prevent a lot of problems. Quitting or rebooting without closing files properly, unless you have no choice, is the road to trouble. If you have no choice, rebuild the desktop upon rebooting by holding down the ⌘ and Option keys before the desktop comes up on the screen. A Norton utility called Disk Doctor can check for and repair any desktop problems.

If you do run into problems with your Mac's filing system, a good recovery utility can give you a chance of backing out with your dignity (and your files) intact. Microcom Disk and File Utilities, Fifth Generation Systems Public Utilities, Norton Utilities for Macintosh, and MacTools V.2.0 all have good disk and file recovery utilities, although I'm partial to Norton. If all else fails, you can still restore the last version of your file from a backup (you do make backups, don't you?).

SCSI—WHAT IS IT AND HOW DOES IT WORK?

SCSI (or "scuzzy") stands for *small computer system interface* and is one of the standards that Apple has adopted for hooking internal and peripheral devices to your Macintosh.

Some SCSI History

The SCSI specification was developed as a nonproprietary standard for small computer input/output bus hookups. Apple adopted it with the release of the Mac Plus in 1986. The trouble with the SCSI-1 standard, as it is known, is that it is *not* standard. Not all of the specifications are used by all devices, resulting in some interesting hookup problems. SCSI-2 has just been released, and an early implementation is used in the Quadras. The SCSI-2 specs promise much faster data transfer and greater compatibility between SCSI devices. SCSI-3 is in the works.

SCSI is a parallel bus interface with 50 lines—9 data lines, 9 control lines, 31 ground lines, and an unused line, number 25. The Mac, to save space, has a 25-pin (DB-25) SCSI connector. A number of the SCSI ground lines are connected to the same pins at the "Mac end" of a SCSI cable. A standard SCSI connector has 50 pins on an "edge card," "centronics," or "parallel-style" connector. Figure 7.5 shows a Mac-to-50-pin SCSI, or Mac system cable, and a 50-to-50 pin peripheral interface or 50-50 cable.

The 50-50 cable is used to interconnect the 50-pin SCSI ports of devices in a SCSI chain. A third type of SCSI cable, not shown, is the SCSI cable extender, used for just that purpose. Your Mac SCSI cables should be high quality, preferably from the same manufacturer, and use double-shielded, twisted-pair, 28 AWG wire. A good conservative length for a SCSI bus is 3 meters (roughly 10 feet) or less.

The SCSI bus can handle up to eight devices, one of which is the computer. The nine data lines in the SCSI bus are reserved for these devices plus one parity line. SCSI devices are identified by an ID number from 0 to 7, which is set by a switch or switches on the device case, or "jumpers" on the device itself. The computer always has device ID 7, an internal hard drive generally has ID 0, and an external boot drive generally has SCSI ID set to 6.

On bootup, your Mac checks the internal floppy drive first. If there is no bootable disk there, the machine goes down the SCSI chain starting from the highest number. If it doesn't find a bootable device before it counts down to zero, your Mac will boot from the internal hard drive. This is the main reason for setting your internal hard drive ID to zero. Setting the internal drive ID to six guarantees that you can boot from a floppy or the internal hard drive, but no external device. Not a good plan!

The Mac SCSI bus must also be *terminated* on both ends, and devices on the ends of the bus must provide terminator power. A terminator is a set of resistors designed to damp out signals traveling in either direction on the SCSI bus, preventing "echos" and noise. Improperly terminated devices will not work. This includes "over-termination." Adding external termination to a device that already has internal terminators can make its behavior extremely flaky. The Mac IIfx comes with a special terminator which *must* be used with any external devices. Using any other terminator can result in damage to the fx. Figure 7.6 shows two external terminator blocks.

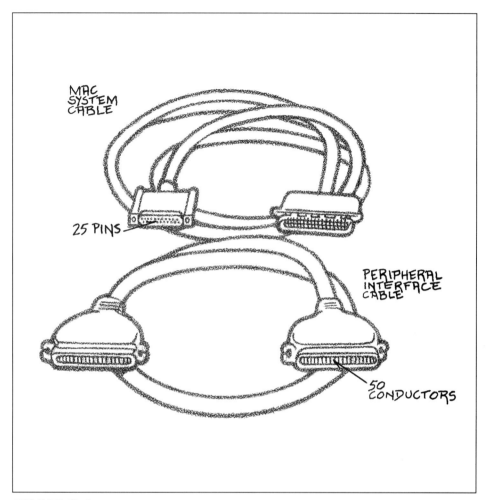

FIGURE 7.5: Mac system cable (top) and peripheral interface cable (bottom)

SCSI devices are "smart." The device controller electronics are on the device, and the computer only needs a "host adaptor" to communicate with SCSI device controllers. This "smart" capability was supposed to make SCSI devices independent. However, differences between manufacturers ensure that each device still requires separate driver software.

Most Macs use NCR 5380 and 53C80 SCSI device controller chips. The Mac communicates with these chips in two ways: Normal Mode and Pseudo-DMA. In Normal Mode, the Mac CPU constantly monitors input and output on the SCSI bus. In Pseudo-DMA, the Mac CPU checks in once, and then leaves I/O to the SCSI controller chip. DMA refers to direct memory access, in which a SCSI controller has direct access to Mac memory for reads and writes, without involving the CPU. The Mac IIfx was an ill-fated attempt at implementing true DMA on a Mac using a 53C80 and a DMA controller on a custom

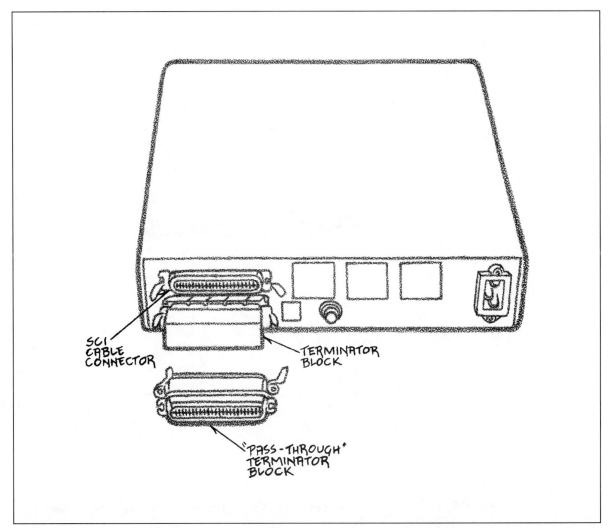

FIGURE 7.6:   External terminators. The "pass-through" terminator block is not attached.

chip. Mac Quadras finally support true DMA, using the NCR 53C96 controller, and can transfer data at up to 8MB/sec.

Hooking Up Your SCSI Bus

Adding new SCSI devices to your Mac shouldn't be a problem. But it often is. There are a number of things you should keep in mind when adding devices to your SCSI bus. The first thing is SCSI termination. As I've said, the *first* and *last* device on a SCSI bus must be terminated. Make sure that terminating devices can supply terminator power. Your Mac SCSI internal port or internal hard drive should have terminator resistors installed. *Any* other device terminators should be removed. This may mean opening up your SCSI device to remove terminator resistors (a good reason to make sure you buy a device with an external terminator block). The IIfx requires the special terminator block provided to avoid damage to the machine.

The second most important thing to be sure of on a SCSI bus is device ID. As I've mentioned, the Mac internal hard drive generally has ID 0, to allow an external device to boot the machine, if desired. The Mac is 7, which leaves ID numbers 1 to 6.

Many Mac devices come with their ID numbers pre-set. If the device has an external ID switch or switches, check to make sure that there are no device ID number conflicts.

Note that having two devices with the same ID on a SCSI bus can damage both devices.

If your Mac will not recognize and mount the device on the desktop, even after properly terminating the bus, you may want to try changing the device's SCSI ID.

The third thing that can affect SCSI devices is the quality of cables and the length of the bus. As I've mentioned previously, try to use high-quality, well shielded cables and keep the length of the bus to 3 meters (10 feet) or less.

Make sure that you have the correct drivers for your SCSI device. If you consider buying a SCSI device from a "non-Mac" hardware discounter, be sure that you can obtain the correct drivers from another source.

Don't try to use more than one removable media device on a SCSI bus. This includes cartridge hard drives, tape drives, optical drives, and others. The SCSI bus only has one "backup channel" and sees these drives as archival devices.

If you absolutely can't get your SCSI device to mount, try installing the SCSI Probe freeware cdev from Robert Polic (see Figure 7.7). If your device is identified on the SCSI Probe list but won't mount, check the SCSI bus for correct termination, try a different cable, and/or change the device ID.

SCSI Storage Choices

As I've mentioned, you have a large selection of storage devices available for your Mac. Most of these are SCSI drives, but some of them plug into your Mac's floppy drive port or a NuBus slot. Apple and a number of third-party hardware developers produce 800K and 1.44MB Mac external floppy drives. Hard drives are getting cheaper almost daily, and a great variety of internal and external hard drives is available for the Mac. Modern drives are fast, reliable, small, and not too power-hungry.

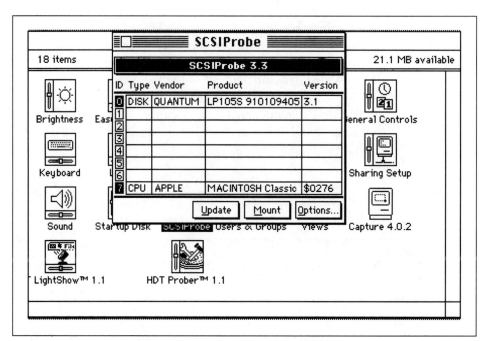

FIGURE 7.7:   SCSI Probe

The biggest trend in storage is rugged, small "transportable" hard drives and removable hard drives. SyQuest and Bernoulli disk cartridges are the most popular removable drives. Tape drives are most valuable as backup devices for large hard drives or hard disk arrays. Older DC2000 and DC6000 mechanisms are available at reasonable prices, and newer DAT drives are fast and reliable, with high capacity.

CD-ROMs (compact disk-read only memory) are a hot item for Macs these days. Their large capacity (600MB+) and stability make them good storage media. However, they don't have the data access speed of hard drives and cannot be written to.

Optical drives, also called magneto-optical (MO) drives, have the large capacity of CD-ROM drives, coupled with read *and* write capability. With the advent of newer and faster 3½" MO drives, optical drive speed is moving toward the mainstream. Optical drives still have two major problems, though. One is cost, the other standards. Regarding the latter, MO drives built to ISO (International Standards Organization) standards are finally being released. Exchanging data with cartridges built for these devices is still somewhat "hit and miss," however.

Floptical drives are kind of interesting. They can write to 20MB floptical cartridges, 1.44MB floppies, and 800K floppies. They are about the price of a removable hard drive, but are significantly slower. There are no formatting standards for floptical media so cartridges cannot be exchanged.

WORM (write-once read-many) drives are expensive, high-capacity, stable archiving devices best used where a lot of data has to be stored safely.

Last, but not least are volatile NuBus RAM drives used to speed up program and data access for CAD, 3-D rendering, and multimedia projects.

Evaluating SCSI Storage Devices

If you're going to evaluate Mac storage devices, you should understand how such devices are rated, and how to cut through the jargon to do a meaningful evaluation. First, let's consider some of the common terms used when describing SCSI devices.

Access Time

This is one of the most misunderstood evaluation criteria for Macintosh storage devices, but it does have its uses. *Access time* is the average time required for the read-write heads on a device to move from some arbitrary location to the point on the disk you want to read. It averages out to the time required to seek across one-third of the tracks on a disk. Fast hard drives have access times as low as 9ms (milliseconds or one-thousandth of a second). Moderately fast hard drives average about 24ms, and slow ones average 40ms or more. Cartridge drives have access times in the vicinity of 19ms, while CD-ROMs average about 300ms (one of the reasons they're not great as regular storage devices). Floppy drives, the snails of the bunch, come in at 800 to 1200ms.

Track-to-Track Seek Time

This is the length of time required to move from one track to the adjacent one. The values for hard drive track-to-track *seek time* are typically in the range of 8–40ms. Floppy disk drives have considerably slower track-to-track seek times.

Average Latency

Latency is the time a device's read-write head spends idle on the desired track until the desired sector comes around. *Average latency* for hard drives stays around 8ms and doesn't change appreciably from drive to drive. Thus, it's not much good for hard drive comparisons. Latency may have some value for "inter-device" comparisons.

Data Transfer Rate

This is the number of bits per second that a device can transfer to and from your Mac. Fast, optimized SCSI drives for the Quadra are capable of transfer rates of 5MB/sec or more.

MTBF

This is *mean time between failures*, and is a statistical measure of your SCSI device's life span. Because MTBF is a statistical measurement, there's no guarantee that your hard drive will last this length of time. A MTBF value of 50,000 hours is adequate, 100,000 hours is very good.

Cost, and Cost per Megabyte

Cost is the ultimate deciding factor for Mac owners trying to evaluate storage devices. If you can't afford it, it doesn't matter what it can do. While many manufacturers and magazines will sell you the old $/MB story, a *great* many things should influence your storage decision. If, however, you're trying to decide between two hard drives, cost per megabyte can be a big help in your decision. See Figure 7.8 for a graph comparing Mac peripherals.

Formatted vs. Unformatted Capacity

What's the reason for the reduction in a device's capacity when it's formatted, compared to when it's unformatted? Is this some kind of scam by manufacturers or does it have some significance? You can relax—drive manufacturers aren't

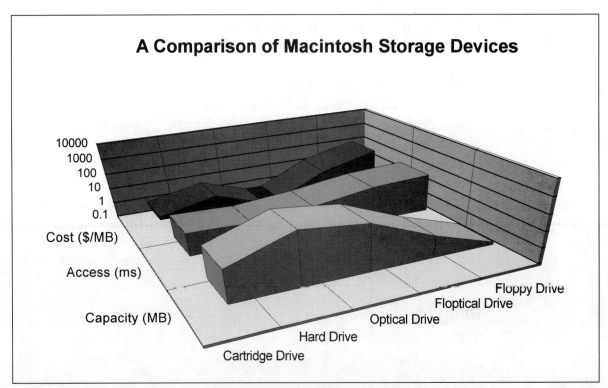

FIGURE 7.8:   A comparison of Macintosh storage devices

engaged in any heinous plots. You'll remember from the Mac "disk primer" section that formatting a device adds things such as a driver partition and a partition table. These take up drive storage space and are the reason that your available data space doesn't match your device's total capacity.

Quality

When buying internal devices, go for established, reliable components and buy from a reputable dealer, so that a defective drive can be returned. If you're buying from a "non-Mac" dealer, know what you're looking for, what components you're going to need, where to get mounting hardware, and what mounting hardware to get. You'll need utility software that can load the drivers and mount your device (make it visible to the operating system). A Mac reseller will ship you the correct drive, formatting software, mounting hardware, and cables for your Mac if you give him the details.

If you're buying an external Mac device, look for a sturdy steel case, two 50-pin SCSI connectors, an external SCSI ID switch, and an external terminator resistor pack. Most devices will need a cooling fan and should have a shielded switching power supply (the power supply may be hard to check).

Storage Methods

The Mac's SCSI bus gives you considerable flexibility when choosing storage devices. You can go for speed, storage capacity, stability, or some combination of the three.

You can also choose between internal and external devices. External devices are easy to install—just plug them in—and they let you avoid cracking the case. And if you decide to trade up to a newer Mac, you can still keep your old external drive.

You can't do that with an internal drive. And internal devices can sometimes cause overheating. Internal devices have only one advantage: they take up less desk space.

Mac Floppy and Hard Drives

The original Mac's 400K, 3½", single-sided floppy marked a revolution in disk storage, followed rapidly by a double-sided 800K drive in the Mac 512KE, Plus, SE, and Mac II. Next came the 1.44MB floppy drive. Macs may have a 2.88MB floppy or floptical drive in the near future.

In floppy drives, the recording heads contact the disk surface. The resulting friction severely limits the drive's top speed.

Hard drives float the read-write heads on a cushion of air just above the disk. This give hard drives substantially faster data access times, but makes them much more sensitive to shock.

MAC 400 AND 800K FLOPPY DRIVES

All single- and double-sided low-density Mac floppy drives use an encoding method known as GCR, or group code recording. This system records from 12 sectors in track 1 (at the edge) to 8 sectors in track 79 (by the hub). Gap bytes (the bytes between sectors) are constant throughout the disk. Sector size stays fairly constant from the edge of the disk to the center. The drive varies its speed when recording sectors from the edge to the center.

400K drives can read, write, and format only single-sided 400K floppies. 800K drives can read, write, and format 800K and 400K floppies.

400K floppy drives were great in their time but make great door stops these days. If you have an older Mac with one of these and want to upgrade, you're going to have to upgrade the ROMs first. 800K drives are still common enough that most software is distributed on double-sided, double-density disks. However, if you want to use double-sided, high-density (1.44MB or HD) disks or read MS-DOS disks with your older Mac SE or II, you're back into ROM/drive upgrade country. For a Plus, a number of third-party SCSI drives provide high-density capability.

MAC 1.44MB OR FDHD DRIVES (SUPER DRIVES)

Starting with later models of the Mac SE and 68030 Mac IIs, Macs came with 1.44MB drives. These drives use modified frequency modulation (MFM) encoding—discussed in the next section—and have 18 sectors on the edge *and* at the center of the disk. Edge track 1 has more gap bytes than center track 79. Sector size gets smaller from the edge to the center of the disk. MFM-capable drives run at a constant speed unless recording 800 or 400K disks. Figure 7.9 shows the difference between 400 and 800K GCR and 1.44MB MFM disks.

HARD DRIVES

Pre-Mac Plus machines used slow hard drives that plugged into the floppy disk drive controller port. With the introduction of the SCSI port on the Plus, Macs entered the wonderful world of fast, high-capacity hard drives.

In order to get more information on a hard drive, the controller packs in more tracks per inch (*TPI*) than on a floppy. This requires a *much* more precise disk controller. As mentioned above, in order to access their densely encoded information quickly, hard disk read-write heads "float" on a cushion of air just above the disk surface, which rotates at speeds of 3600 RPM or higher. Hard disk platters are solid to prevent vibration and contact with the read-write heads. Like other double-sided devices, hard drives have a read-write head above *and* below the disk surface. Adding capacity to hard drives involves adding additional platters and read-write heads.

To write data to disk, Macintosh SCSI drives use one of two methods (encoding schemes). The more popular method is called modified frequency modulation (MFM); the other is called run length limited (RLL). SCSI drive specs usually list the method used. Let me tell you more about how they work.

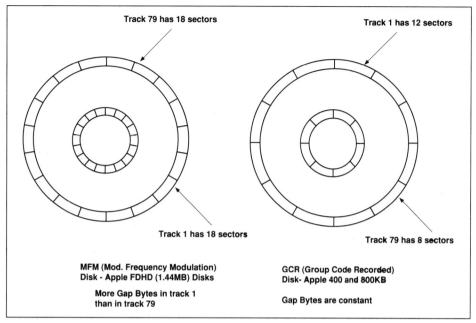

FIGURE 7.9:   Mac GCR and MFM disks

Frequency modulation is how hard drives stay in sync with the drive controller. Frequency modulation involves "clock pulses," or regular magnetic timing pulses, which provide the background upon which "data pulses" record the data. The MFM scheme codes more data into fewer bits, using 8-bit data pulse patterns. The RLL scheme uses 16-bit data pulse patterns—squeezing up to 100% more data onto a drive than MFM. But there's a downside to RLL, which is why it's less popular—it's been less reliable then MFM. The RLL approach risks loss of sync, and thus data problems, if the drive controller loses track of the read-write head's position (though RLL reliability does seem to be improving).

To control the read-write heads, older hard drives used *stepper band* and *rack and pinion* drive mechanisms. Stepper band drives use a stepper motor with detentes that convert rotary motion to linear movement by coiling and uncoiling the stepper band, shifting drive heads back and forth with a characteristic "squeek-thunk." Stepper band drives are easily affected by thermal or mechanical shifts, losing previously created tracks. Drives with access times greater than 40ms are probably stepper band drives. Rack and pinion drives use a gear system and are more accurate and reliable than stepper band drives. They can have access times of 28-42ms and make a whirr-thunk sound as they work.

Good quality modern drives control the read-write heads with a *voice coil mechanism*. This mechanism uses a magnetic coil to move the read-write heads over the drive. Voice coil drives are fast, quiet, stable, and reliable. Figure 7.10 is a schematic drawing of a voice coil drive.

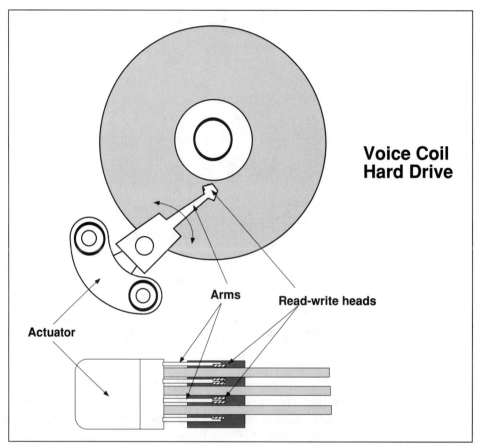

FIGURE 7.10:   A voice coil hard drive

Another feature of a good quality modern drive is *autopark* capability. When a drive loses power, the read-write heads drop to the disk surface. If this happens quickly and at the wrong time, it can cause a head crash, in which the read-write heads hit the hard drive platters and may actually gouge them. Autoparking places a hard drive's read-write heads in a safe place to settle when a drive is powered down. This protects your disk, your data, and your read-write heads. Older hard drives required you to manually park the heads before powering down.

Modern drives have caching capability and can read a track at a time into a track buffer. A drive with caching capability and a track buffer can run at a 1:1 interleave even on a relatively slow Mac.

Even with the large number of companies providing external drives for the Macintosh, certain names are fairly frequently associated with high-quality cases, mechanisms, and software. These include APS, TMS Peripherals, Micronet, FWB, and LaCie.

DISK DUPLEXING, MIRRORING, AND RAID   Three approaches use an "array" of multiple hard drives to increase system speed and/or data security. In *disk duplexing*, one drive exactly duplicates the read-write actions of the other. In *disk mirroring*, two drives are connected to one controller. The controller reads from one drive but writes to both. If one drive goes down, the other one takes over and the user is notified of the failure.

RAID (redundant arrays of inexpensive drives) is a disk mirroring scheme taken to a larger extent. The drives in a RAID are synchronized so that all the drives spin in unison. There are a number of levels of RAID, characterized by greater complexity, higher speed, and better data security. The cost of this type of system ensures that it will be used only for large, complex networks which require high data security.

Golden Triangle's hardware and software versions of DiskTwin implement disk twinning on a small scale. PLI's QuickSCSI implements disk twinning for up to seven drives.

Removable and Transportable Hard Drives

Transportable hard drives are small, light, sturdy hard drives that can be easily carried and mounted on your computer. These drives have autopark and shock resistant mountings to withstand the bumps they're likely to undergo. Transportable drives must also have a low power requirement. LaCie's Pocket-Drive is a $2\frac{1}{2}$" "palm-size" transportable.

Transportables are a good choice to add hard drive storage to a Mac PowerBook, but you're going to need a special PowerBook SCSI cable. You can make a standard $3\frac{1}{2}$" hard drive into a transportable with the use of a plug-in hard drive bracket, the WX2877 from Wetex International Corp. This device will fit in a $5\frac{1}{4}$" drive enclosure in an external case, and has a key lock.

With one modified case at home and one at work, you have a standard hard drive "to go." This may be an option if you work with large amounts of data and require a convenient way to transport large-capacity hard drives. Keep in mind, however, that most standard hard drives are not designed to be regularly moved around.

The most popular removable hard drives today use the SyQuest, Ricoh, or Bernoulli hard drive mechanisms. The SyQuest mechanism is a $5\frac{1}{4}$" aluminum hard disk with magnetic alloy coating in a plastic case. When the SyQuest cartridge is inserted, the metal hub is "grabbed" by a magnetized drive spindle and sets of voice-coil-powered read-write heads swing into place. The SyQuest mechanism has a 32K cache to speed data access and transfer by the mechanism. The SyQuest cartridge has an arrow indicating the correct direction of insertion.

This insertion arrow is important because it's possible to insert the cartridge incorrectly, causing damage to the mechanism.

The SyQuest mechanism had some early reliability problems not shared by the Ricoh mechanism, but the manufacturer now claims a mean time between failures of 60,000 hours (quite respectable).

Iomega is the manufacturer of the Bernoulli cartridge mechanism and distributes it as a drive known as the Bernoulli Box.

Unlike SyQuest, which distributes its mechanism to third parties, Iomega retains the Bernoulli technology patent. Bernoulli drives are more expensive, but very reliable and immune to dust and head crashes. In a Bernoulli mechanism, a flexible disk is spun at 2368 RPM, raising it up close to the read-write heads. This is accomplished by the Bernoulli Effect, the same process that lets airplanes fly. If power is shut off suddenly, the disk falls down and away from the heads, preventing a crash. The cartridge is spring-loaded and seals up when it's removed from the drive mechanism, reducing problems with dust and grit. The flexing of the Bernoulli disk will eventually cause failure, so Bernoulli formatting software keeps track of media wear and indicates when a cartridge needs replacing. Iomega builds a 32K cache into its cartridge drives. Bernoulli cartridges have an effective access time of 19ms, and a MTBF of 60,000 hours.

Cartridge hard drives work fine as Mac boot devices. If you insert a new cartridge after the Mac has booted up, you'll need a mounting utility in your system to show it on the desktop.

The Quadra 900 and 950 are the only Macs with enough space and a removable blank face plate to allow removable drives to be mounted internally.

Fast SCSI Adapter Cards

If you have a Mac with NuBus slots, you can replace the standard hard drive adapter with a fast SCSI adapter board. The most recent generation of these boards supports the SCSI-2 standard. A SCSI adapter that supports "bus mastering" can take control of the relatively slow standard NuBus and initiate extremely fast data transfers.

Fast SCSI adapters achieve their speedup in a variety of ways. Many use the latest version of the NCR 53C90 SCSI-2 controller chip. Some have an onboard coprocessor to offload SCSI control from the CPU and many have fast onboard RAM. Unlike the relatively slow Mac SCSI port, these boards can fully utilize the data transfer speed of fast, modern SCSI-2 compatible drives.

DayStar produces the SCSI PowerCard with up to 16MB of onboard memory, a 5MB/sec dedicated 68000 controller, and a DMA controller.

Fast SCSI-2 boards include PLI's QuickSCSI, Storage Dimensions Data's Cannon PDS/FX, MicroNet's NuPORT-II, and ATTO's SiliconExpress II.

CD-ROMs

CD-ROMs use the same type of disks used by audio CD players—metallized disks with digital data recorded as laser-cut "pits." The metal disk is covered with a plastic coating for protection. The disks are read by reflecting a laser beam off the pits. The most common CD-ROM recording standard is called the "High Sierra" standard.

CD-ROMs are quite slow because the mass of their optical heads is much larger than hard disk read-write heads. This makes it difficult to move the head and change directions quickly.

The "read-only" nature of these disks is because of the destruction of the substrate involved in creating them. This makes recording and erasure of data by this method pretty much impossible.

CD-ROMs have become very popular in the Mac and PC worlds because of their large data capacity—600MB or greater—stability, and reliability. 'ROMs are generally used where large volumes of data must be exchanged. Common uses are online encyclopedias, atlases, collections of programmer's tools, sound, graphics, and outline fonts. One unique use is games with "photo-realistic" graphics and digital sound. Apple now distributes the QuickTime starter kit on CD.

Apple, Toshiba, NEC, and Chinon CD-ROMs are quite popular and reasonably priced. NEC bundles their drives with an extensive collection of software. Before the Quadras, Mac owners didn't have the option of internal installation of CD-ROMs, but the Quadra makes this feasible. Generally speaking, installation of an external 'ROM just involves adding it to your SCSI bus, setting the ID number and termination if necessary, loading the drivers and mounting it on your desktop.

Optical, or Magneto-Optical, Drives

The idea of an optical drive with 600MB capacity that can be written to was a beautiful dream—until Steve Jobs included one as the primary storage device for the NeXT computer. Unfortunately, like many optical drives, this Canon magneto-optical device was too slow for routine use and has been replaced by more conventional devices.

Since that time, however, there has been a proliferation of Mac magneto-optical drives (many folks just call them optical, but this can be confusing). The most common magneto-optical drive mechanisms are built by Sony, Ricoh, Teac, MOST, and IBM and now come in both 3½" and 5¼" sizes. I've mentioned that magneto-optical media now meet ISO standards, which should make cartridge data exchange easier. However, don't expect guaranteed compatibility with your friend's M-O drive, unless it's built by the same manufacturer. Hopefully, the popularity of these devices will lead to better standards.

Optical drives are not susceptible to head crashes because the drive head is roughly 1000 times farther from the disk surface than a hard drive read-write head. The optical disk case is made of polycarbonate and the disk itself is covered with plastic. Since an optical drive's laser reads the layer below the plastic coating, the disk is not easily affected by scratches and smudges. Optical drives have a recording density of about 15,000 tracks per inch (TPI), ten times the density of a hard drive.

There are actually three types of rewritable media optical disks: dye-polymer, phase change, and, of course, magneto-optical. Dye polymer disks use a heat-sensitive dye to record laser pulses. This technology is somewhat expensive because it uses two lasers and the media only handles 1000 to 10,000 write cycles. Phase change optical disks use lasers to heat a special metal layer embedded in a plastic disk. The heat of a drive's laser changes the metal of the disk from an amorphous state to crystalline. The read head detects differences in brightness as data. This type of optical drive is expensive and the disk medium is short-lived.

This leaves magneto-optical recording, the common method used by read-write optical disks. Magneto-optical drives erase and write data to a disk by heating the disk media to a temperature of about 150° Celcius, called the Curie Point, with a laser beam and applying a magnetic field. This changes the magnetic polarity of the disk at a point. The disk is then read with a laser (at lower power) using a property called the Kerr Effect, where plane polarized light is rotated when reflected off of a magnetized surface. Because magnetic polarity is set while heating the disk surface, magneto-optical storage is extremely stable and a safe way to archive data. The only potential problem is mechanical damage to the cartridge. Figure 7.11 shows the M-O recording process and a schematic of a $3^1/_2$" mechanism.

Historically M-O drives have been very slow, because, like CD-ROMs, the entire mechanism has been built into the read-write heads. The mass of the heads made the process of moving them slow. $3^1/_2$" M-O drives and newer $5^1/_4$" drives, such as the Pinnacle PMO-650, use the split optical system, shown in the Figure 7.11 schematic. This makes these devices significantly faster, by removing the mass of some optics from the read-write heads. PLI assigns their PMO-650 drive a 19ms effective access time.

$5^1/_4$" cartridges hold 650MB of data, 325MB/side, and have to be flipped to read or record both sides. $3^1/_2$" cartridges, the size of a Mac floppy, but about $1/_2$" thick, hold 120MB of data when formatted.

M-O drives are expensive, but the price is coming down rapidly. If you need very large storage capacity, these devices may be the only way to go.

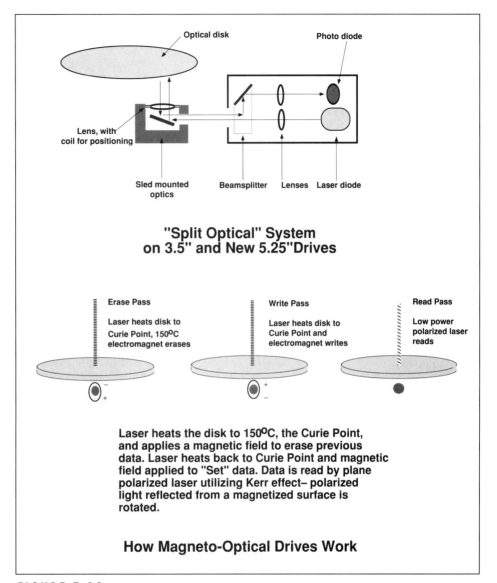

Optical disk

Photo diode

Lens, with
coil for positioning

Sled mounted
optics

Beamsplitter   Lenses   Laser diode

**"Split Optical" System
on 3.5" and New 5.25"Drives**

Erase Pass

Laser heats disk to
Curie Point, 150°C
electromagnet erases

Write Pass

Laser heats disk to
Curie Point and
electromagnet writes

Read Pass

Low power
polarized laser
reads

**Laser heats the disk to 150°C, the Curie Point,
and applies a magnetic field to erase previous
data. Laser heats back to Curie Point and magnetic
field applied to "Set" data. Data is read by plane
polarized laser utilizing Kerr effect– polarized
light reflected from a magnetized surface is
rotated.**

How Magneto-Optical Drives Work

FIGURE 7.11:   Magneto-optical recording and a 3½" drive schematic

When choosing an external M-O drive, use the standard checklist for
SCSI device cases, pick a fast, reliable mechanism, and make sure the case has
a good fan and is well ventilated. Because of the laser, M-O drives run *hot*.
Hookup and installation are the same as for other SCSI devices—you'll need
driver software and a terminator if the M-O drive is at the end of the SCSI bus,
and you should use care when setting the SCSI ID to eliminate conflicts with
existing devices.

Note that because of the length of time that M-O drives take to spin-up, they can't be used for primary storage devices. Your system won't boot from one. Manufacturers are working on this problem and we may see a solution soon.

Floptical Drives

These drives use mechanisms developed by Brier and Insite. The Insite floptical can format special media up to 21MB, and can read and write to standard Mac 800K and HD floppies. The Brier mechanism formats cartridges up to 100MB, but will not handle floppies.

Floptical disks are exactly the same size as regular Mac floppies, but include special optical servo tracks that allow the drive to increase track density from 135 TPI to over 1000 TPI. Dual-use floptical drives have heads with two different gaps, narrow for high-density floptical media and wide for regular floppies. The drive senses which type of media has been inserted and uses the appropriate head. Seek time for these drives is approximately 135ms and they spin at 600 RPM. The media is magnetic and susceptible to erasure. Flopticals are fast floppy drives but very slow hard drives and are about the same price as removable hard drives. PLI and Procom use the Insite floptical mechanism and the Quadram FLEXtra drive uses the Brier mechanism.

WORM Drives

WORM drives have 600–800MB data capacities. WORM drive lasers cut pits in an optical disk, making a permanent record. These drives are ideal for long-term, stable archives.

Tape Drives

Tape drives are of no use for primary storage or boot devices. They are archiving devices only. If you have a lot of large hard drive storage to back up, whether on a network or your own machine, these devices are the way to go. Older technology fixed-head DC2000 and DC6000 tape drives with high density tape can back up as many as 525MB. Helical scan drives, such as 4 mm Digital Audio Tape (DAT), use rotating read-write heads at an angle to the tape path to record high data densities. DAT cassettes can hold up to 2GB or 5GB (gigabytes, or millions of K) with compression. APS, FWB, MicroNet, PLI, and others produce Mac DAT tape drives. DAT drives use mechanisms from Archive, Hewlett-Packard/Sony, WangDAT, and WangTek. Tape drives will not mount on the Mac desktop, but they are often bundled with backup software such as Dantz's Retrospect. This can be mounted and used to control the tape drives.

Large RAM Drives

RAM drives are faster than any hard drive, but are volatile and of small size. Any application that continually reads or writes a lot of large files can benefit from the speed improvement of a RAM drive. Applications that fall into this category include CAD, rendering, multimedia, and 24-bit graphics. A RAM drive is a good location for files that will be dynamically compressed and decompressed, avoiding disk "lag." DayStar's RAM Powercard is a RAM card that allows the creation of RAM drives up to 48MB in size. Installation of a RAM drive is as simple as installing the NuBus card and driver software.

FLOPPY UPGRADES

If you have an older Mac and want to upgrade it, the floppy drive is often the best place to start. Since floppy upgrades involve a ROM upgrade, you're also bringing your machine further up to date.

400 to 800K

To upgrade a Mac 512 to 512KE, you'll need to replace the 64K ROMs with 128K ROMs, and the 400K floppy drive with an 800K drive. Crack the Mac, pull the logic board, and remove the 400K drive, as described in Chapter 3. Locate the ROMs on the logic board (marked ROM Hi and ROM Lo—see Figure 3.15) and pull them with a chip puller or, *carefully*, with a small screwdriver. Reinsert the 128K ROMs, numbered (Hi ROM) 342-0341-x and (Lo ROM) 342-0342-x. Unplug the floppy drive cable, remove the screws on the underside of the drive mounting platform, and remove the 400K floppy. Mount the 800K floppy, reinsert the logic board, and install the cables. You're done! If you have a 128K Mac that you're planning to upgrade with an accelerator board, you can update the ROMs and drive without going through a Mac 512 upgrade, or so I'm told.

800K to 1.44MB (FDHD)

Older Mac SE and II computers require a ROM upgrade to use the Apple FDHD (floppy drive high density), or 1.44MB, drive. To upgrade an older SE, crack your Mac as instructed in Chapter 3. Unplug the cables and remove the logic board. Unplug the hard drive power plug, then remove the floppy drive mounting screws, *while holding the floppy and hard drive housings*. This ensures that the drives will not fall into the Mac CRT. Lift the drives out. Remove the hard drive bracket from the top of the floppy drive housing (assuming that a hard drive is present), and install the hard drive on top of the new FDHD drive housing. Then reinstall the hard and floppy drives by screwing them into the SE's drive mounting plate. Remove the old SE ROMs from the logic board (see Figure 3.16 for the location of the SE ROMs) and replace with the upgraded ROMs. Apple's upgrade package is part number M6052/B and costs $450. Reinstall the logic board and close the case.

To upgrade the Mac II ROMs, pop the case top, unplug the drive cables, and add a new 1.44MB FDHD drive. Unscrew and lift out the drive platform as shown in Chapter 3. Remove and replace the following ROMs, whose location is shown on Figure 3.19, U6-High ROM 342-0639, U5-Med High ROM 342-0640, U4-Med Low ROM 342-641, U3-Low ROM 342-642. You will also have to replace the IWM (Integrated Wozniak Machine) drive controller chip, just behind the front drive platform support post, with a SWIM chip. SWIM stands for Super Wozniak Integrated Machine (just in case you didn't guess). Replace the drive platform, plug in the drive cables, and you're ready to go! Installing the ROM upgrade in the Mac II gives you one additional benefit—32-bit address capability, up to 128MB.

External Floppy Drive Upgrades

If you want to attach a high-density 1.44MB drive to a Mac like the Plus that doesn't have the high-density SWIM chip installed, consider the Drive 2.4 and controller kit from Kennect. This is just one more upgrade option, but one whose economics you'll have to consider carefully. It might make more sense to invest in a more advanced Mac.

The Future

What is Apple's next floppy storage option going to be? Will the choice be the new 2.88MB drive, to keep data exchange compatibility with 2.88MB PC drives, or will Apple go to floptical drives with up to 20MB capacity? Apple apparently has plans to include built-in CD-ROM drives in some of their upcoming machines. The one thing you can look forward to is larger, faster storage devices and hopefully a continuation of Apple's upgrade policies.

CHOOSING A HARD DRIVE

If you're considering a hard drive upgrade, you have some thinking to do. Modern hard drives come in three "form factors"—$2\frac{1}{2}$", $3\frac{1}{2}$", and $5\frac{1}{4}$". *Form factor* is a fancy-Dan way of referring to the drive's platter diameter. The actual drive housing is much larger than the platter diameter. The other measurement you'll need to know is what drive height your Mac will accommodate. New hi-tech drives need fewer platters to accommodate greater amounts of data and thus do not have to be as high. Most Macs require half or third-height devices. A *half-height* 5¼" drive is 1.625" tall, and *third-height* 2.5" and 3½" drives are 1" tall.

The compact Macs, Mac IIcx, and Mac IIci use 3½" half-height drives. The Mac IIsi and LC use 3½" third-height drives. The Mac II, IIx, and IIfx can use 5¼" half- and full-height drives and the Quadra 900 and 950 can handle full-height 5¼" drives (with capacities up to 1.6GB). The PowerBooks use 2½" third-height drives.

When choosing a drive for your Mac, physical size is not the only consideration. The compact Macs, the LC, LC II, IIsi, and the PowerBooks require low-power-requirement drives such as the Quantum LPS series.

Now that you know what type and size of hard drive you're going to need you should consider things like capacity and speed. The physical size requirement will affect the maximum storage capacity of the drive you choose. Generally a good rule of thumb (mine) is to select a drive size 40% larger than your first estimate. To evaluate drive performance, you can use a program such as SCSI Evaluator by William A. Long. This shareware utility ($20 fee) can be used to evaluate any Mac SCSI hard drive. Another good hard drive evaluation utility is Benchtest, part of FWB's Hard Disk Toolkit. Your only problem then is to find an individual or hardware retailer who'll let you test the drive you're interested in.

When you're considering hard drive speed, average access time is only useful for comparisons between drives. But access time will put you in the performance ballpark. A drive with a 20ms or lower access time is a fast drive, 20-28ms is intermediate, 28-40ms is slow, and greater than 40ms is very slow. However, the actual speed of a drive attached to your machine depends on your machine's SCSI transfer speed and the interleave and block size you chose when you formatted the hard drive. The fastest hard drive in the world on a slow machine with the wrong formatting is slooooowwwwwwww.

Manufacturer

You'll also want to choose your drive manufacturer carefully. Quantum, Micropolis, Core, CDC, and Hewlett-Packard all have reputations for quality.

Mechanism

Your hard drive should have a voice coil mechanism, autoparking capability, and, if possible, a track buffer and data cache. If you have something in mind and are looking for specs, try contacting the manufacturer or an authorized reseller.

MTBF Rating

Mean time between failure ratings will give you some idea of the potential reliability of your drive. These numbers are only statistical estimates, but may help you select a drive with better longevity. As I've mentioned, an MTBF rating of less than 50,000 is mediocre, 50–80,000 is average to good, and 100,000 is excellent.

Price/MB

The $/MB rating can be very helpful in deciding which hard drive to buy. Smaller external hard drives, in the 40-50MB range, run approximately $5.50/MB. Intermediate external hard drives, in the 80-120MB ballpark, will run you about $4.25/MB. Very large external hard drives, 400MB and better, can run $2.50/MB and lower. As you can see, there are some considerable economies of scale at work here. It pays to buy the largest hard drive that you can afford. Applying the $/MB rating to drives available by mail order or from local sources will give you a good test of the deal you're getting on a hard drive.

INSTALLING A HARD DRIVE

Installing a hard drive on a Macintosh is not a difficult chore. External hard drives are a snap, and internal drives a little more challenging, especially on a compact Mac. I don't want to trivialize the chore of doing an installation on a compact machine, but once you've got the machine open, the actual hard drive installation is quite simple.

External Hard Drives

First let's look at the installation of an external hard drive. You'll need a Mac DB-25 (25-pin connector) to 50-pin SCSI cable if your external device is the first on your SCSI bus. If this is the case, you'll also need a terminator resistor pack or terminator block. The terminator resistor pack plugs in to the free 50-pin SCSI connector on the back of your drive. If your external hard drive, as purchased, didn't have an external terminator, make sure that the drive is not internally terminated by asking your hardware supplier before adding external termination. If the drive is already terminated and it is your only device, you can probably leave it as is for now.

If you're adding a hard drive to a SCSI bus that has other devices, things get a little more interesting. Instead of a Mac 25-to-50 pin system cable, you'll need a 50-to-50-pin peripheral interface cable. The device already on your SCSI bus should already be terminated, so you don't have to worry about that.

However, if your hard drive is externally or internally terminated, you have two options. You can remove the terminator from the device currently at the end of your SCSI bus, reinstall it on your new drive, and make your new drive the last device on the bus. Or you can remove the hard drive terminator, plug your current device into the hard drive's spare SCSI plug, and use the system cable to plug your hard drive into the Mac. Removing an external terminator is as easy as unplugging the resistor pack from the free SCSI port on the back of your hard drive.

Removing an internal terminator takes a little more work. If your drive has an access window on the bottom, you may be able to open it and carefully remove the terminator with a small screwdriver. If not, you're going to have to open the hard drive case and remove the drive to get at the terminator. The main way to identify a terminator is that it's socketed (the chip is meant to be removable, and so is placed in a socket). I'm hoping here that your drive's controller board doesn't have anything interesting like socketed ROMs. The terminator may be a "pencil-yellow" color or a black, linear, multipin chip. In any case, carefully pry the resistor out of its socket and put the drive and case back together. If you don't have an external SCSI ID switch or an easy way of getting at the SCSI device select pins, you might as well set the drive ID before reinstalling the drive and closing the case.

Setting a SCSI hard drive's device ID is the other very important procedure to do before finishing your drive installation. If your hard drive has an external switch or switches, you can set the drive ID with them (follow the case manufacturer's instructions). However, if your drive case has a window allowing you access to the hard drive, you may have to set the SCSI ID using the drive's *device select pins*. If there is no other easy way to do it, you'll have to remove the hard drive from the case, which is about where I left you when I discussed how to remove hard drive terminators. Figure 7.12 is a picture of a Quantum LP105S drive showing the terminator resistors and the drive select pins.

Figure 7.13 is a schematic diagram of how to set SCSI drive ID using the drive select pins. Note that different SCSI drives have their select pins in different locations.

Many Seagate drives have the pins beside the SCSI connector. In this case the low pin is right next to the SCSI connector. Hopefully your drive manufacturer will number the select pins. As you can see from the diagram, leaving all pins clear gives the drive an ID of 0. All other IDs are set by putting "jumpers" over the drive select pins. Jumpers are small metal connectors, enclosed in plastic, that create settings on circuit boards by "shorting out" sets of select pins. If there are no jumpers already installed on your drive controller board, any good electronics store can sell you some. Drive select pin sets have values, low pins to high, of 1, 2, and 4. Setting a drive ID of 1 requires a jumper on the first pin set. An ID of 3 requires jumpers on the first two pin sets. An ID of 6 requires jumpers on the second and third pin sets, since 2 + 4 = 6. You use the same principle of addition to get 5 or 7.

When I mentioned SCSI ID previously, I introduced you to some of the conventions of SCSI ID numbering. The Mac is *always* ID=7. Your internal drive is usually 0. You may remember that this is so you can boot from an external SCSI device if desired. An external boot drive usually is given an ID of 6. This is so that the Mac will boot immediately after checking the floppy drive(s), without working its way down the SCSI bus first. *Do not* give two devices on a SCSI bus the same ID. There is real potential for damage here!

Drive select pins

SCSI terminator resistors

FIGURE 7.12:   A Quantum LP105S with terminator resistors and drive select pins shown

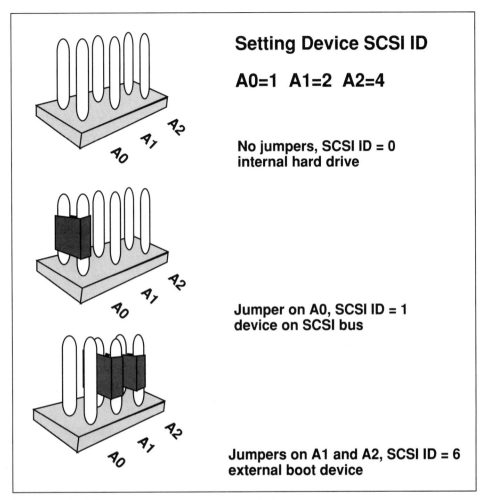

FIGURE 7.13:   Setting SCSI drive ID with drive select pins

Once you've terminated your hard drive, set the ID, and plugged it into another device or the Mac, you should be ready to go. A word of caution here. It is good practice to use the best SCSI cables you can get and to buy both system and peripheral interface cables from the same source. I *strongly* advise against buying hard drives that use 25-pin instead of standard 50-pin SCSI connectors, and I highly recommend that you buy a case with two 50-pin connectors on the back for "daisy-chaining" your drive to other SCSI devices.

In any case, your drive should now be ready for formatting and partitioning, so you can move on to that section.

Installing Internal
Hard Drives in Compact Macs

As I mentioned, the hardest part about installing an internal drive on a compact Mac is cracking the case. When you have your compact Mac open, remove the logic board, as I described in Chapter 3, unplug the floppy and hard drive cables, remove the screws holding the floppy and existing hard drive (if one is installed) to the drive platform, *while holding the drives*, and lift the assembly out. The hard drive and mounting bracket screw into the floppy drive housing. Remove the hard drive and bracket and then remove the hard drive from its bracket.

If you are installing a hard drive in a compact Mac for the first time, be sure to get 50-pin SCSI and power cables, as well as the correct bracket for the drive. Your new drive should have a terminator resistor installed—if it does not you will have to get a terminator and install it.

I recommend that you set your drive ID to zero. To do this, remove all jumpers, or leave each jumper on only one of a pair of drive select pins. Mount your new hard drive in its bracket (see Figure 7.14; do not overtighten—you can torque and damage the hard drive) and attach the bracket to the floppy drive housing with the mounting screws provided.

Drive mounting bracket   Hard drive (controller board shown)   Mounting screws

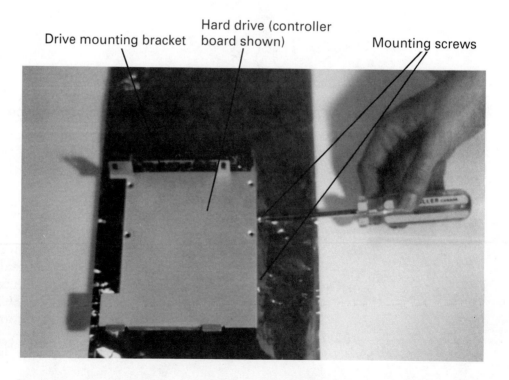

FIGURE 7.14:   Installing a hard drive in its mounting bracket

Install the SCSI ribbon cable in the drive plug (see Figure 7.15) and the hard drive power cable on the compact Mac power supply board (see Figure 7.16).

Carefully reinstall the hard and floppy drives and screw them into the drive mounting plate. If your Mac did not have an internal hard drive, there will be a SCSI resistor terminator pack plugged into the internal SCSI connector. You'll find this on the logic board right behind the external SCSI plug. Remove the terminator pack and re-install the logic board, connecting the main power, 50-pin SCSI, and floppy drive controller cables. Plug the hard drive power cable into the drive. Check to be sure that all cables are snug and "button up" the case.

Installing Internal Hard Drives in Modular Macs

Installing a hard drive in a modular Mac is considerably easier than a compact Mac installation because, obviously, the modular Mac case is meant to be opened. Release the cover latches, and lift the top—observing due caution with machines like the Mac II to avoid breaking the cover hinges. The hard drive will be easily accessible.

In six-slot Macs like the II, IIx, and IIfx, just unplug the hard drive SCSI ribbon and power cables, unscrew the drive bracket, and lift the old hard drive out. In three-slot Macs like the IIcx and IIci, and in the Quadra 700, the hard drive is held in place by tabs on the drive bracket. Unplug the SCSI and power

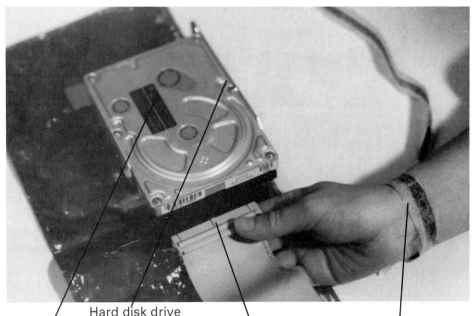

Hard drive   Hard disk drive mounting bracket   50-conductor SCSI cable   Antistatic strap

FIGURE 7.15:   A 50-conductor SCSI cable on a Mac hard drive

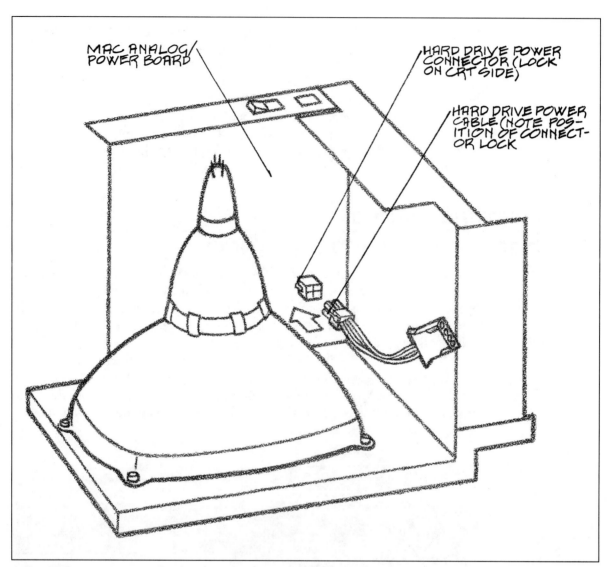

FIGURE 7.16:   Location of a compact Mac hard drive power connector

cables, squeeze the tabs to release the drive, and lift it out. The Mac LC, LCII, and IIsi all have plastic tabs locking the hard drive bracket into place. Disconnect SCSI and power cables, free the plastic locking tabs, and lift the drive out. (Assembly and disassembly of these machines is really a dream.) Be careful with the hard drive locking tabs—break these and you're toast.

Replacing the drives on these modular machines is just like removing them—a piece of cake. Just reverse the procedure. One exception is replacing an older Mac II 5¼" hard drive with a 3½". This is not a serious problem, but you will need the correct mounting bracket.

Internal drives added to modular Macs should be terminated and have a SCSI ID of 0. Remember that some of these machines have specific drive requirements. The LC, LCII, and IIsi all take one-third-height, low-power-requirement hard drives. If you're going to buy from a non-Mac supplier, *know the drive* you need.

The Quadra 900 and 950, like other modular machines, are no problem for hard drive installation. Hard drives mount on the mounting plate above the power supply. Unlike other modular Macs, the 900 and 950 have provision for a cartridge device, with mounting room and a removable bezel right below the floppy drive. The Quadra 900 and 950 have room for four half-height devices, two front, two rear—one of the front drive bays is used for the FDHD floppy. These Quadras can mount 3½" and 5¼" drives, and can use a variety of configurations and form factors. Because these two machines have two SCSI buses, termination and numbering of drives should be done with care.

Building Your Own External Drive

At one time, the cost of Mac external hard drives made a "do-it-yourself" approach very appealing. You could save a considerable amount of money by building your own external drive. But these days the price advantage is not all that great. Still, some good reasons remain for building your own external drive. Some of these are:

■   You can be sure of top-quality components.

■   You can still save a lot of money on a large hard drive project.

■   You can customize the external case any way you like.

■   You can salvage an old, "dead" hard drive.

Figure 7.17 shows sketches of three "homebrew" hard drives. One is a Seagate ST296N in an old Ehman drive case, another is the same mechanism in a double drive case, and the third is a Quantum in a new case with front-mounted power controls. These three drives illustrate some of the points I was making above.

A case for a homebrew drive should meet a number of criteria. The case should have a switching power supply that provides at least 30 watts/drive. For drives over 150MB, you may want to double this—check the drive power

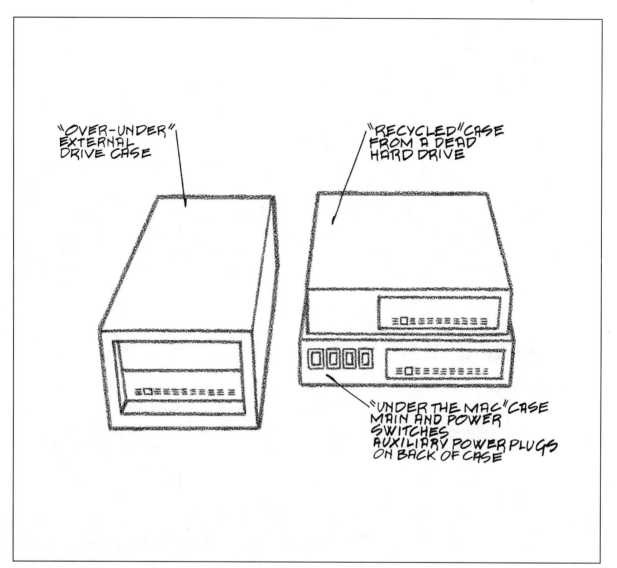

FIGURE 7.17: Three different "homebrew" hard drives

requirement and remember that startup will draw more than the average power requirement. There should be a fan—today's hard drives run cooler, but they still generate a fair bit of heat. The power supply should be shielded to prevent interference with the drive data cable. The case should have room on the back for two 50-pin SCSI connectors. Preferably, the case should have an easily accessible power switch, a "power-on" light, and, if the drive will be enclosed, a disk access LED.

Your project case should match the form factor and height of the drive you'll be using, and you should make sure that you'll receive all necessary mounting hardware to do a proper job. A great variety of external drive cases are available—try checking Computer Shopper for some sources. I've had some good luck with Wetex International—the double-drive case in Figure 7.18 is a Wetex WX2866 case.

It has most of the features I've been talking about except, unfortunately, a shielded power supply. The case does, however, come with a 60-watt switching power supply, *three* internal hard drive power plugs, and other goodies. Some cases, such as those sold by Tulin Corp., come with SCSI and power cables. With other cases, you may have to provide your own SCSI cables. Both Tulin

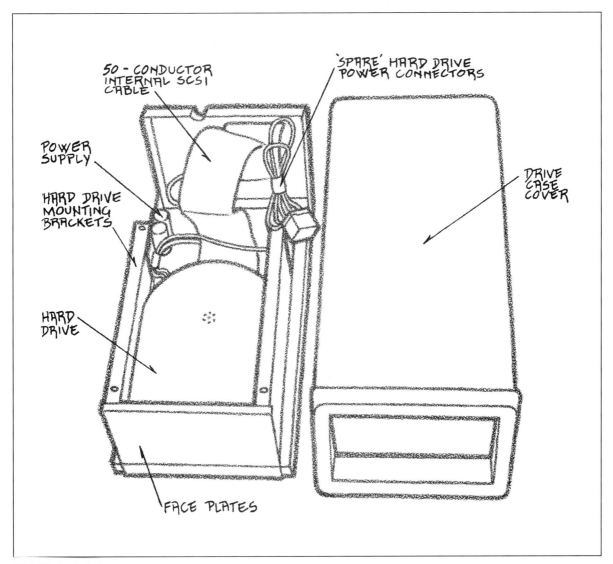

FIGURE 7.18:   Wetex WX2866 external SCSI device case

and Wetex can supply 50-pin internal to 50-pin external SCSI connectors for your project case. If you're not planning on buying the SCSI drive for your project from a Mac dealer, *make sure* that you have a source of formatting software for the drive. FWB's Hard Disk Toolkit, LaCie's Silverlining, and Tulin's Formatter all work with a variety of drives—just make sure one of them works with yours!

Low- and High-Level Formatting, Mounting, and Partitioning

A new Macintosh hard drive has to be formatted. Because SCSI hard drives from different manufacturers are different, their formatting specs are different and many are shipped with specific formatting software, some of it pretty primitive. Formatters from FWB and LaCie, Hard Disk Toolkit and Silverlining respectively, let you optimize a variety of hard drive parameters, including block size and interleave. They also install high-speed SCSI drivers. Either package may be a better bet than the rudimentary software supplied with your drive. If you plan to use the virtual memory feature of System 7, make sure that your formatting software supports it.

Good formatting software should allow you to set hard drive interleave as well as block size. The Mac Plus uses a 3:1 interleave, the SE and Classic 2:1, and faster machines 1:1. While most formatting software should automatically adjust the interleave for the machine that a drive is running on, adding an accelerator board could change the preferred setting. A utility, such as FWB's Hard Disk Toolkit, that allows you to manually set drive interleave will enable you to optimize a hard drive for the speed of an accelerator. Choosing the wrong interleave for a hard drive can kill performance. A slow machine reading a 1:1 hard drive will miss sectors (that's called "blowing a rev"), and will have to wait for one complete rotation of the hard drive before reading the next sector. Using too high an interleave on a fast machine will leave the machine waiting for the next sector to show up.

After formatting at a specific interleave, your formatter should ask you if you want to partition the hard drive. This is generally a good idea, especially with large drives, for reasons I've already discussed. You will be able to customize partition sizes to your own preferred settings. A word of advice don't make your boot partition too small. Adding fonts, DAs, cdevs and the like can swell your system file quickly and your boot partition will run out of room.

Once your drive is up and running, you'll want a good backup package to protect your programs and data. A large variety of packages are available to Mac owners, including Dantz's Retrospect, 5th Generation's FastBack II, and MicroSeed's Redux.

I've mentioned the effects of drive fragmentation on performance. A variety of drive optimizers, or "defragmentation utilities," are available for the Mac. These include the hard drive optimizers in Norton Utilities for the Macintosh and MacTools deluxe. Both of these products are also good choices for data security and recovery software—something I heartily recommend to hard disk drive owners.

Drive Organization

Finally, a word about hard drive organization. When you're faced with the terrific amount of (relatively) low-cost space on a modern hard drive, its easy to dive right in and not worry about organization. This is a *big* mistake, and something that will cost you later. The larger the hard drive, the easier it is to "misplace" programs and files and the more useful a file-finding utility becomes. Basically, there are three ways to organize a hard drive—by application, by type of application, or by project. Organizing by application puts a bunch of program files, Word 4.0 for example, on your desktop with subfiles containing data inside. Organizing by type of application creates a master folder, such as Communications, with subfolders containing your communications programs such as ZTerm and related files inside. Organizing by project creates specific project files and puts specific applications inside. All of these methods have merit, but you may want some sort of hybrid, like leaving your applications in folders and creating project files in their own separate folders. Clicking on the file will launch the appropriate application anyway. System 7 aliases make this type of organization even easier.

Whatever organization you adopt, I highly recommend that you keep your organization fairly flat—no more than three folders deep if possible. This will make it a lot easier to stay organized and keep you away from having to use File Finder.

TROUBLESHOOTING

Problem	Cause	Solution
Happy Mac appears, then a floppy and question mark	Corrupted boot blocks, System file, or disk logical structure	Use disk recovery program, reinstall system and driver
Flashing Happy Mac, drive does not boot	Corrupted boot blocks or System files	Use disk recovery or reinstall System

Problem	Cause	Solution
Happy Mac, drive seeks constantly before boot	Hard reset without proper exit, Mac reverifying data structures	No current problem; rebuild desktop and run a disk repair utility to be safe
Sad Mac	OF or OOOF software; otherwise, hardware	Check for source of hardware or software problems
No drive activity	Blown fuse or power supply problem	Open the Mac and check for a blown fuse. If not blown, check if drive power connectors are connected
Partial drive mount followed by crash	Virus, corrupted System, not enough 6.0x heap space, multiple System files, corrupted logical structure	Virus checker, disk repair utility, heap expander, remove one system file, or restore from backup
Device does not mount	Potential connection, media, SCSI, or other problems	Try each of the above
"Do you want to initialize?" message	Corrupted logical structures	Run recovery program
Drive mounts but cannot be used for startup	Bad boot blocks or hardware problem	Check startup Control Panel, hardware connections, system software

CHAPTER EIGHT

Monitors

When Henry Ford released the Model T, he gave buyers a choice of any color as long as it was black. When the Mac was released, you had a choice of any monitor as long as it was monochrome.

The situation has changed almost as radically with Mac monitors as it has with Fords. You can now choose from a wide selection of monitor sizes and types—from 9" monochrome to 21" 24-bit color. This chapter surveys the territory and gives advice on choosing and installing an upgraded monitor.

HISTORY

The original Mac monitor, still used by compact Macs, is a 9" blue-white monochrome screen with a resolution of 512 × 342 pixels. This screen is sharp, easily read, and has a density of 72 dots per inch. These Macs have true WYSIWYG, or what you see is what you get, when printed on an ImageWriter. This is by design and it helped make Macs so intuitive.

Unfortunately, the small compact Mac screen begins to seem cramped and hard to use rather quickly. Third-party hardware suppliers started providing large-screen monitors and adapters for compact Macs as a way to improve the situation. With the introduction of modular Macs, Apple started producing its own monitors. Table 8.1 is the current "state of the Union" for Apple monitors and display cards.

HOW THEY WORK

Monitors and display adapters both have important roles to play in the final appearance of your display. If a monitor has a sharp picture and very high resolution, but your video card won't drive it at maximum resolution, you're wasting money on the monitor. If a monitor is cheap and has a resolution "ceiling" lower than a high-performance video card will support, you won't get much benefit from the card. Keep these relations in mind when you're looking for a Mac monitor.

The Video Card

Matching the speed and performance of the controller to the type of monitor you want will prevent a lot of frustration. The closer the synchronization of the board's electronics with the monitor, the better quality the image. With a compact Mac, you have to do the best you can from the available graphics (and accelerator/graphics combination) boards. This, of course, doesn't apply as firmly to the SE/30.

When adding a large-screen monitor to a compact Mac, you should seriously consider a video upgrade on an accelerator board. The standard 8MHz compact Mac CPU just doesn't have the poop to drive a large-screen monitor. If you are considering one of the external large-screen monitor upgrades that plug into a compact Mac's SCSI port, you're once again limited to the monitors supported by the manufacturer you choose, and don't have the option to swap devices and monitors to find the best combination. The good side to this is that, depending on your choice of upgrade, you often receive a graphics driver/ accelerator/monitor combination that's optimized to work together well. The SCSI port option is a good choice for original Mac Portable and PowerBook owners as well.

If you didn't have to open the case to get at the expansion slot, you'd probably say that the Mac SE/30 has more in common with PDS-slot modular Macs than with compact Macs. The SE/30 has a good selection of color and monochrome video expansion boards. If you choose a hi-res monitor for the SE/30, you may want to consider a card with a video coprocessor or an accelerator. The SE/30 is fast enough, but pretty poky by today's graphics standards.

DISPLAYS/ CARDS	MAC 12" MONO	MAC 12" RGB	APPLECOLOR HR RGB 13"	MAC 16" COLOR	MAC 21" COLOR	APPLE 2 PAGE 21"MAC PORTRAIT MONO	MAC PORTRAIT
LC Onboard Video	16 grays	256 colors	16 colors	N/A	N/A	N/A	N/A
LC with 512K VRAM	256 grays	32,768 colors	256 colors	N/A	N/A	N/A	N/A
IIsi Onboard Video	256 grays	256 colors	256 colors	N/A	N/A	N/A	16 grays
IIsi with 8.24 Card	256 grays	16.7 million colors	16.7 million colors	256 colors	256 colors	256 grays	256 grays
IIsi with 8.24GC Card	256 grays	16.7 million colors	16.7 million colors	32,768 colors	256 colors	256 grays	256 grays
IIci Onboard Video	256 grays	256 colors	256 colors	N/A	N/A	N/A	16 grays
IIci with 8.24 Card	256 grays	16.7 million colors	16.7 million colors	256 colors	256 colors	256 grays	256 grays
IIci with 8.24GC Card	256 grays	16.7 million colors	16.7 million colors	32,768 colors	256 colors	256 grays	256 grays
IIcx,II,IIx,IIfx 4.8 Card	256 grays	256 colors	256 colors	N/A	16 colors	16 grays	16 grays

TABLE 8.1: Apple Monitors and Display Cards (from Apple's "Macintosh Compatibility Chart")

DISPLAYS/CARDS	MAC 12" MONO	MAC 12" RGB	APPLECOLOR HR RGB 13"	MAC 16" COLOR	MAC 21" COLOR	APPLE 2 PAGE 21"/MAC PORTRAIT MONO	MAC PORTRAIT
IIcx,II,IIx,IIfx 8.24 Card	256 grays	16.7 million colors	16.7 million colors	256 colors	256 colors	256 grays	256 grays
IIcx,II,IIx,IIfx 8.24GC Card	256 grays	16.7 million colors	16.7 million colors	32,768 colors	256 colors	256 grays	256 grays
Quadra 700 Onboard Video	256 grays	256 colors	256 colors	256 colors	16 colors	16 grays	16 grays
Quadra 700 512 VRAM	256 grays	16.7 million colors	256 colors	256 colors	256 colors	256 grays	256 grays
Quadra 700 1.5MB VRAM	256 grays	16.7 million colors	16.7 million colors	16.7 million colors	256 colors	256 grays	256 grays
Quadra 900 Onboard Video	256 grays	16.7 million colors	256 colors	256 colors	256 colors	256 grays	256 grays
Quadra 900 512K VRAM	256 grays	16.7 million colors	16.7 million colors	16.7 million colors	256 colors	256 grays	256 grays
Quadra 950 2MB VRAM	256 grays	16.7 million colors	16.7 million colors	16.7 million colors	16.7 million colors	256 grays	256 grays

TABLE 8.1: Apple Monitors and Display Cards (from Apple's "Macintosh Compatibility Chart") (continued)

Onboard video for most compact Mac accelerator boards is monochrome and often an afterthought. Exceptions are the Mobius and Lapis video boards, which seem to have excellent output.

External video expansion adapters often come as SCSI peripherals with video circuitry and a graphics accelerator built in. Unfortunately, this also raises the price of the upgrade unit. Aura Systems' ScuzzyGraph is an external video expansion box that supports a fairly wide selection of monitors. In this case you're not limited to the manufacturer's choice of video board and monitor. This can be a blessing or a curse depending on how careful you are with your choice of monitor for the ScuzzyGraph.

Video cards for modular Macs are easy to install and give you a lot of selection. The only thing that limits your choice of video cards is PDS slot compatibility. NuBus video adapters, of course, can be used with any NuBus-equipped modular Mac. The problem with NuBus is that for compatibility you sacrifice the speed of the Mac system bus available with PDS slots.

Mac video cards have several common components. ROM for the card's operation is found in a video general logic unit (GLU). Many cards have fixed and/or expandable banks of VRAM, or fast video memory that stores image and color/grayscale data. The VRAM is commonly *dual-ported*, which means that it can be read and written to at the same time, increasing video performance. A frame-buffer controller chip controls receipt of image data and the writing of data to VRAM, and also generates the *sync timing*. Sync timing is done in conjunction with an oscillator crystal and controls the rate at which video data is sent to the monitor. A custom ASIC (application specific integrated circuit, an acronym you may recall me mentioning before) reads image data and sends it to a RAMDAC (random access memory digital to analog converter—ooooh, alphabet soup!) at rates determined by the frame buffer controller. The RAMDAC converts digital image data into an analog signal to drive your monitor. High-performance video controllers often include faster timing oscillators along with components designed to work with them, more VRAM, and high-speed RISC controllers and/or specialized graphic coprocessor chips. These become necessary when working with 24-bit color on large, high-resolution monitors.

Monitors

Mac black-and-white monitors fall into two classes—monochrome and grayscale. Monochrome monitors produce grays by a process called dithering, simulating grays with a pattern of black and white dots. Grayscale monitors receive gray-level signals from their controller boards and can vary the brightness of individual monitor pixels.

Separate controller boards generally improve video performance by 50% or more over built-in Mac circuitry because of their VRAM and optimization. In the Quadras, this improvement is not as great because these machines already sport high-speed, high-performance video.

Apple and other high-performance color monitors are *analog*. Old *digital* RGB monitors carried image data to the monitor on three separate digital data lines, but this severely limited maximum resolution and color capability. Modern monitors can send and receive much more complex data by encoding it as analog signals, hence the RAMDAC that I talked about earlier. When a Mac monitor receives an analog signal it is decoded into red, green, and blue signals that drive the respective electron guns in your monitor. The intensity of each of the red, green, and blue signals will determine the color you see on your monitor. The larger the range of signal intensity your controller card and monitor will support, the more RGB combinations, and hence more colors, that are available to you. The increasing amount of image data handled by 4-, 8-, 16-, and 24-bit graphics controllers provide ever-increasing numbers of RGB combinations.

Of course, the single electron gun in a grayscale monitor limits the amount of gray levels that are available at common controller card resolutions. (You've only got one beam instead of some combination of three.)

The incoming monitor signal also includes a sync signal that controls the creation of a *raster*, or scanning pattern, on the Mac monitor screen. The *vertical-scan rate* is how many times per second a raster is completed. In Mac monitors, this is 60–75 times per second. A higher scanning rate increases your viewing pleasure, as I will explain later. *Horizontal-scan rate* is the number of times per second that the electron beams sweep each line on the raster.

In order to produce sharp, clear pictures, monitors use something called a *mask*. This helps to align and sharpen the monitor's electron beams. Older monitors used a *shadow mask*, or a perforated sheet of metal. This had a number of undesirable effects. The shadow mask reduced the intensity of signal reaching the monitor screen, resulting in a somewhat "washed out" picture. When a monitor got hot, the shadow mask had a tendency to warp, creating focusing and alignment problems. Most modern manufacturers use Trinitron technology, pioneered by Sony. The Trinitron screen uses a mask made of vertical wires, resulting in a brighter, sharper picture and no warping problems. Newer shadow-mask tubes, using an alloy called Invar, are much more resistant to warping.

MONITOR SIZE, RESOLUTION, AND COLOR CAPABILITY

Monitor size is measured diagonally, like your TV. A 12", 14", or 21" monitor is 12, 14, or 21 inches diagonally. Computer resolution is measured in pixels, or "picture elements." The Mac's graphic control hardware forms text and pictures by patterns of pixels. On a monochrome screen, these pixels are only "on" or "off," white or black. This is called a "bit depth" of one. Macintosh color monitors use red-green-blue to form all colors. RGB monitors have three electron guns that activate red, green, and blue phosphors on a monitor screen, producing colors. The most basic Macintosh color controllers use four bits to describe mixtures of red, green, and blue that make up the colors on the screen. This is called a bit depth of 4, and the number of colors available with this type of controller are 2^4 or 16. 8-bit controllers can generate 2^8, or 256, colors. 16-bit controllers, such as those used by the Mac LC and appropriate monitors, can display 32,768 colors. The latest Apple computers and 24-bit color adapters can display up to 16.7 million colors for almost photographic quality. Grayscale monitors display shades of gray instead of colors. Good grayscale monitors are sharp, clear, and generally display up to 256 shades of gray. They are not just glorified monochrome monitors!

A medium-resolution Mac monitor can display 640×480 pixels, a high-resolution monitor 1024×808 pixels, and a very high-resolution monitor 1600×1200 pixels. This translates into 307,200, 827,392, and 1,920,000 pixels respectively. Now you know why compact Mac large-screen monitors come with an accelerator, and why large-screen 24-bit NuBus boards often use a RISC graphics accelerator.

Before you install 24-bit display adapters in a Mac, it must have 32-bit QuickDraw in ROM, or Apple's 32-bit graphic system extensions installed. The IIci and later modular Macs, as well as the Classic II and the PowerBook 140 and 170 have 32-bit color capability. Pre-IIci modular Macs and the SE/30 need the 32-bit QuickDraw extensions. Why 32-bit QuickDraw and 24-bit display adapters? The remaining 8 bits are for something called the alpha channel, used by some programs for special functions.

MORE ABOUT MONITORS

Some monochrome display cards for compact Macs let you use low-priced PC TTL, or transistor-transistor-logic, monitors. Higher quality blue-white monochrome monitors for the Mac come in full-page (portrait) and two-page (landscape) display sizes. The Radius Pivot one-page display even rotates between one-page vertical and horizontal orientation. Graphics adapter cards for the Apple original Portable and the PowerBook 100 can use a variety of monochrome monitors and VGA grayscale monitors. Grayscale monitors such as the NEC GS2A can be used with the Mac SE/30 and a display adapter, and with the modular Macs. A variety of RGB monitors are available for the SE/30 and modular Macs in sizes from 12 to 21 inches.

EVALUATING MONITORS

When you're trying to decide on a monitor upgrade, you'll have to determine what types of monitor your Mac can drive. Your choice will also be limited by what kind of monitors your graphics adapter upgrade will support—check your manual or call the hardware manufacturer. Compact Macs, excluding the SE/30 and Classic II, have no built-in color or grayscale capability and even with an upgrade will require a monochrome monitor. The SE/30 and modular Macs support up to 24-bit graphics with the appropriate upgrade. A number of manufacturers are producing color videoSIMM upgrades for the Classic II.

Once you've decided on a video board for your Mac and determined what monitors it will support, you can start looking for the right monitor. If you're looking toward a future system upgrade you may want to buy a monitor and adapter combination that is a little more than you need at the moment. This will let you keep your equipment a little longer and may save you some money in the long run.

In your search for the right monitor, there are a few things you should consider. Go for the best screen resolution, in horizontal and vertical pixels, that you can afford. Generally, a Mac's pixel density should approximate 72 dots per inch for a WYSIWYG display. Multiresolution Mac monitors are also available. Sigma Designs Multiview offers resolutions varying from 36–120 dots per inch (dpi). Unfortunately, on a Mac monitor, increased resolution does not translate into a sharper picture, but tends to crowd pixels together, actually making your display harder to read. Lower resolution than 72 dpi makes for a coarse, easier-to-read, but visually unappealing picture.

In addition to high resolution, your monitor should have a sharp, bright, high-contrast picture. The monitor scan rate should be higher than 65Hz to eliminate flicker. Slow, cheap, monitors try to eliminate flicker with monitor interlacing (double-scanning a screen image), and slow or long-persistence phosphors. You can tell if your monitor uses long-persistence phosphors by whether a moving object on screen leaves a "tail." Also, a high-quality monitor should have sharp *convergence*, the distance between the red, green, and blue electron beams in an RGB monitor. Many monitors have adjustable convergence.

Monitor advertisements often give dot pitch values. This is the distance in millimeters between the phosphor dots on a monitor screen—the lower the better. Less than .31 is good. You shouldn't see any "blooming," the deterioration of a monitor image at high picture intensities. Another important thing to notice is any monitor variance like jitter, swim, or drift. These look just like they sound.

Some of the highest quality monitors for Macs are "multiscanning" monitors. These automatically synchronize their scan rate to a wide variety of graphics adapters rather than being fixed to specific frequencies. This means that if you buy a multiscanning monitor, you buy an insurance policy against future changes in graphics standards.

Be sure to get the right cable for your monitor. Mac-specific cables use three pins, called *sense pins*, to tell the Mac the size, type, and resolution of monitor that's connected. An incorrect cable won't do that, and it won't drive your monitor at maximum resolution.

MONITOR UPGRADES

Large-screen monitors are among the most common compact Mac upgrades. But because the larger number of pixels in these monitors requires a lot of work from compact Macs with a 68000 CPU, these upgrades often include an accelerator. Accelerator packages often include a monochrome graphics adapter plug. Buying an accelerator with a graphics adapter eliminates the possibility of incompatibility between a large-screen monitor adapter and a Mac accelerator.

Modular Macs that require higher resolution graphics and a large-screen monitor can be upgraded using a PDS or NuBus graphics slot upgrade. Using a 21" monitor with 24-bit graphics will require an adapter card with a fast graphics coprocessor.

Compact Mac Monitor Upgrades

While stand-alone graphics adapters are available for compact Macs, adapters are usually offered as part of an accelerator board, because of the load that a large monitor places on a compact Mac 68000 CPU. One adapter, the Galileo stand-alone video board from Total Systems, drives a large variety of monitors including Apple, Radius, and multiscan VGA, and has an accelerator option. I strongly suggest that you do *not* install an unaccelerated video upgrade in a compact Mac.

Compact Mac Video Upgrades and Accelerator Boards

Some video boards are built to work with an accelerator board. You just plug them into the board, then install the board in a compact Mac. You can mount a video board's monitor plug in the battery door of an early compact Mac, in the expansion port of an SE or SE/30, or the video control access door on the Mac Classic.

I've mentioned video options available for accelerator boards. NewLife, Novy/Systech, Total Systems, and others all provide them for their accelerator boards. Mobius produces accelerated video boards as a matter of course. SIMM-based video expansion called, surprisingly, videoSIMMs is available from Envisio for the Classic and Classic II, giving an outlet for the Classic II's LC-compatible video capability. Numerous monochrome, color, and grayscale controllers are available for the Mac SE/30. These just plug into the SE/30's PDS slot and mount a connector in the machine's expansion "window."

Color on a Compact Mac

There are a number of external large-screen monochrome and color upgrades available for compact Macs.

For the Classic, earlier SCSI-equipped Macs, and the Mac portables, external monochrome and color monitor adapters can be plugged into the SCSI port. These devices contain accelerated 68000 graphics processors. Some of the most popular external video adapters for the 68000 compact Macs are made by Aura Systems Incorporated. This is the ScuzzyGraph series of monochrome and color display adapters. The ScuzzyGraph adapter provides eight colors on black-and-white Macs and 256 colors on color-capable Macs. The device accelerates graphics about four times and allows you to use a variety of monochrome, grayscale, and color monitors. It supports Apple, VGA, and MultiSync graphics standards. Installation consists of setting the SCSI ID, terminating the device if necessary, and installing control software.

Plug-in Monochrome Monitor Upgrades

Aura Systems ScuzzyGraph adapter will drive a monochrome monitor, but a number of manufacturers are making monochrome monitors with built-in graphics accelerators that mount on the SCSI bus of any Mac. These are particularly useful for compact and portable Macintosh monitor upgrades. Outbound produces the Outrigger full-page monitor with a 20MHz 68000 graphics accelerator and a SCSI daisy-chain port. The adapter is compatible with compact Macs and portables. Lapis markets the Displayserver SCSI, compatible with the Classic II and the PowerBooks. The Displayserver has a 16MHz 68000 video controller. Installing these devices is as simple as setting the SCSI ID and adding termination if necessary, then installing any control software.

Classic II and SE/30 Video Options

The Mac Classic II is somewhat limited in the expansion department, but a number of vendors, including Envisio, are producing videoSIMMs for it. These fit in the SIMM slots and act as a graphics adapter without destroying the slots' memory expansion capability. The Classic II has Mac LC color-capable ROMs.

The Mac SE/30 is fully color-capable, and a variety of video adapter cards have been built for its PDS slot. Video adapters plug into the SE/30 PDS slot and the video plug mounts in the SE/30's expansion port. A number of manufacturers offer '030 slot color graphics boards, including Lapis and RasterOps.

Monitor Options for Modular Macs

Modular Macs, with their easy access and slots, are good choices for video upgrades. In addition, newer Macs like the LC, LC II, and Quadras are designed to run popular VGA monitors right out of the box with the correct cable.

If you own a modular Mac, your machine's graphics potential is limited only by the size of your pocketbook. A large monochrome monitor may be adequate for a network server or some limited desktop publishing applications, but for modular Macs, you should probably consider at least a grayscale monitor. 8- or 16-bit color-capable monitors and upgrade boards are good choices for most common applications, but for high-end publishing, color prepress, and graphics jobs, a 24-bit color capable system will probably be necessary.

To upgrade a Mac LC or LC II to 16-bit color, just pop the case and add video RAM SIMMs. The same applies when upgrading a Quadra 700, 900, or 950 to 24-bit graphics. An LC or LC II can use certain VGA monitors with the appropriate video cable, as mentioned. Table 8.2 lists the pinouts, if you'd like to try building one.

A number of manufacturers make LC-slot video expansion boards, including Lapis, RasterOps, and Sigma Designs. The IIsi can use a variety of NuBus and '030 PDS slot boards, but has very tight power requirements. Check before you buy!

SIGNAL	LC PINS	VGA MONITOR PINS
Red Ground	1	6
Red Signal	2	1
Green Signal	5	2
Green Ground	6	7
Wired together on LC Side	7 and 10	-
Blue Signal	9	3
Composite/Vert. Sync Ground	11	4
Vertical Sync	12	14
Blue Ground	13	8
Horiz. Sync Ground	14	10
Horiz. Sync	15	13
Not Connected	3, 4, 8	5, 9, 11, 12, 15

VGA monitor side uses "mini" 15-pin connector, Apple side uses Apple 15-pin connector. Works with *selected* VGA monitors.

TABLE 8.2:   Mac LC Video Cable Pinouts

Both the LC and IIsi accept a PDS slot adapter with monitor connectors installed in the machines "knock-out" expansion plugs. Installing video boards in a PDS slot involves a certain amount of care. When you're feeding in the monitor cable and plugging it into the PDS board, *be careful* not to torque the board. IIsi boards are quite easy to torque because of the adapter required. Choose and mount your adapter carefully.

Macs with NuBus slots have a variety of video upgrade options, including Apple's 4•8, 8•24, and 8•24GC graphics cards and high-end options like SuperMac's Thunder24 24-bit graphics card (see Figure 8.1). Adding a NuBus video card is straightforward. Pop the top, remove the rear slot cover, and insert the board.

Apple's PowerBooks and original Portable have a number of large-screen monitor options, among which are Envisio's PowerBook 100 large-screen expansion board, pictured in Figure 8.2. These boards install in the PowerBook memory expansion connector and the expansion slot in Apple's original Portable (the slot closest to the hard drive). The video cable is threaded out through the case.

FIGURE 8.1:   SuperMac Thunder24 24-bit graphics card (photo courtesy of SuperMac Technology)

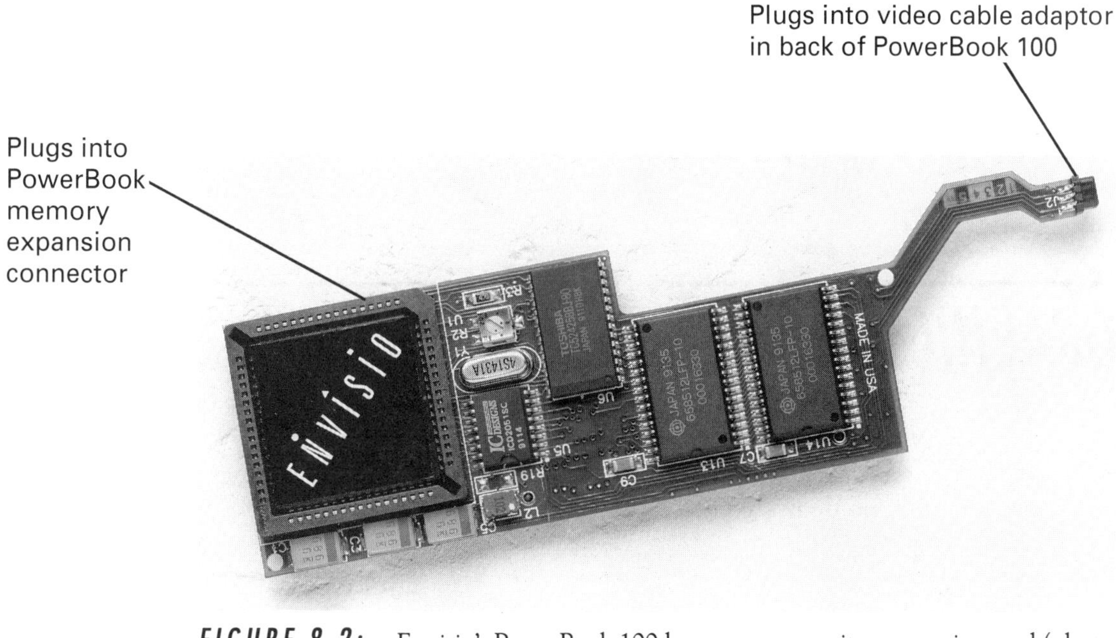

Plugs into video cable adaptor in back of PowerBook 100

Plugs into PowerBook memory expansion connector

FIGURE 8.2:   Envisio's PowerBook 100 large-screen monitor expansion card (photo courtesy of Envisio Inc.)

All of the upgrades described may include a software installation as well, possibly a Control Panel cdev and/or an init. If you have more than one monitor connected to a modular Mac, you'll need to install the startup monitor Control Panel (Figure 8.3).

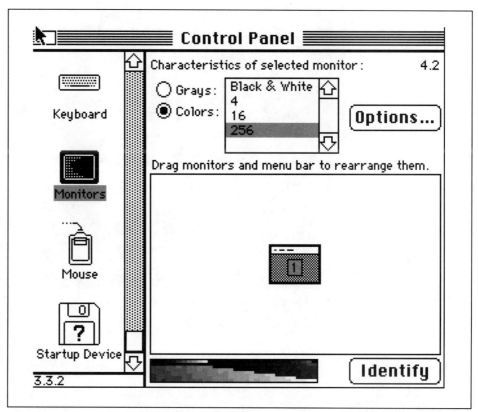

FIGURE 8.3: Apple's startup monitor Control Panel for modular Macs

GRAPHICS ACCELERATORS

A number of Mac video expansion boards provide plugs for add-on graphics accelerators to improve performance. This feature allows you to add a speed boost to your video card when you can afford it. These graphics accelerators are based on dedicated graphics processors or RISC chips.

LCD SCREENS

If you do a lot of presentations, you may want to look at the Mac LCD screens built for use with overhead projectors. These devices provide a ready way to do a presentation for a large group economically. The screens are not cheap, and many tend to be somewhat slow. However, they can be packed and carried easily and adapters are not overly difficult to install—although some adapters may require some modification of a compact Mac's power/video cables.

PROJECTION TV

Under normal conditions, Macs are not equipped with circuitry to synchronize their output to television scanning frequencies. However, adapters are available to allow a Mac to drive a TV monitor. When hooked to a projection TV, this makes a good presentation device.

MONITOR RADIATION

Lately, the exposure of workers at CRTs to extra low frequency (ELF) and very low frequency (VLF) electromagnetic radiation has become a concern.

A number of standards have arisen to govern the amount of low frequency electromagnetic radiation a monitor can emit. Some of the more popular and stringent regulations were developed by the Swedish National Board of Measurement and Testing and are called the MPR II standard. If your monitor meets these, you can be sure that any emissions are pretty low. A variety of products claim to provide protection from low frequency electromagnetic radiation produced by older monitors. These include screens that fit in front of the monitor and gizmos that sit over the monitor housing. Measurements done on these devices have almost never found a reasonable reduction in ELF and VLF. Your best bet, if you're concerned about this, is to purchase a monitor that follows the MPR II standards. Recommended distances to minimize ELF exposure are about 30 inches ("arms length") from the front of the monitor and 45 inches from the rear. You may want to maintain 45" "intermonitor" distances in an office to minimize exposure.

FINALLY, DOES IT FIT?

Before you take that final big step and upgrade your Mac's monitor, consider a few more details. Will the monitor fit your desk space or will you need to make changes? Can you sit it on a desk or on your Mac? Keep in mind that very large monitors can literally crush a Mac.

Your eyes should be level with the top of the monitor and light should hit it at no less than 50° degrees from the horizontal, to prevent glare. Failing this, try a monitor screen cover. Consider a tilt and swivel stand to allow you to adjust the monitor to the perfect angle for you. A lot of mysterious neck and eye strain is prevented by proper monitor placement.

QUICKDRAW AND THE FUTURE OF MAC GRAPHICS

Apple has admitted that the Mac's graphic toolbox, called QuickDraw, is getting a little long in the tooth and that its slow performance is hindering Mac graphics capability. In an attempt to provide some third-party solutions, Apple has licensed portions of the QuickDraw code to Macintosh graphics hardware developers.

Apple has also announced plans to upgrade QuickDraw to an object-based system with more speed and power, as well as possible compatibility with Display PostScript. It's high time that Apple improved Mac graphics performance, so we can only hope that these upgrades happen quickly.

TROUBLESHOOTING

Problem	Cause	Solution
Display on compact Mac is dark or shows a checkerboard	CRT video card or power-video cable may be loose	Open machine and re-seat cable connectors

Problem	Cause	Solution
A thin horizontal line about 2¼" from the bottom of AppleColor Hi-Resolution RGB Monitor	No problem, it's a standard part of the CRT	Nothing to do
Colored blotches on the display	Possibly a magnetized CRT	Manually degauss the monitor if able to
Black screen with power on	Brightness and contrast likely turned down	Turn up brightness, adjust contrast
Two CRTs on a Mac, a rippling line through one	RFI interference from one monitor is causing the line	Move one monitor
Cable supplied with monitor does not mate with Mac plug	Wrong cable for your Mac	Talk to a Mac hardware supplier, local custom cable dealer, Apple dealer, or build your own

CHAPTER NINE

Of Mice and Keyboards (and Trackballs, and...)

When the Macintosh was young, the only input devices you had to think about were the keyboard and the mouse. Now that the Mac has matured, you have an amazing variety of devices to choose from. What you choose and how you decide will depend on which Mac you've got, what type of input you have, what kind of device you're comfortable with, and what you can afford.

THE APPLE DESKTOP BUS

Before we get into the decision process, let's discuss the Apple Desktop Bus (ADB). The ADB serves the same function as the Mac's SCSI bus. Both offer you the option of "daisy-chaining" a number of devices to your Mac (daisy-chaining means connecting a number of devices with cables; the end of the chain is plugged into the computer). The ADB bus, like the SCSI bus, allows input to and output from your Mac. The ADB bus, however, is somewhat specialized and most often used to connect Mac input devices.

The ADB port was introduced with the Mac SE and replaced the mouse connector and *RJ-11* (modular telephone jack) keyboard connector on earlier Macs. As a standard, the ADB lets Mac hardware manufacturers produce a variety of input devices without worrying about differing hardware standards for different devices and Macintosh models. That's one reason why Mac ADB devices have proliferated.

The ADB is a slow-speed serial bus, as compared to the high-speed SCSI parallel bus. But while the ADB is a *serial* interface, devices on its bus are interconnected in *parallel* fashion (confusing, no?). The ADB provides "intelligent" support for a Mac ADB keyboard and mouse, and allows you to connect a variety of additional input devices. It has its own microcontroller or coprocessor (which I mentioned in Chapter 6). Devices on the ADB are interconnected with inexpensive four-conductor cable and four-pin mini-DIN connectors. The ADB supplies +5 volt power at 500 milliamps to devices. Up to 15 devices can (theoretically) be connected on the ADB, with device cables not to exceed five meters (16⅔′) in length. It's probably a good idea to keep your ADB chain to about three devices and the total length to something less than eight meters (26⅔′).

The ADB gives you a great deal of versatility and peripheral expandability, but you should consider your options with some care. While plugging devices into the ADB frees up your other ports, remember that ADB devices are proprietary and work only on Apple products. They cannot be used with PCs like a serial modem can. This limits resale of these devices to owners of Apple equipment with ADB capability. In a number of cases, for instance when purchasing a modem, you may want to stay with a more generic non-ADB product that will have a wider resale market. This isn't an option with a variety of Mac input devices like keyboards and mice, so for these devices you should choose carefully for comfort and convenience and then for resale value. A good-quality product will serve you well now and sell easily later.

ADB Quirks and Quarks

If you will be plugging and unplugging Apple ADB devices frequently, watch them carefully. Apple's keyboard and CPU ADB connectors are secured only at the base and after repeated fastening and removal of connectors they can work loose. This will result in your keyboard or mouse "going dead" and it will require replacement of the ADB connector(s). Apparently, this can happen after as few as 500 connect-disconnect cycles. Try to avoid as much of this repeated stress on the connectors as possible. Third-party products should not (hopefully) have this problem. You'll be able to tell if you're in potential failure territory if your ADB plug can be wiggled after connection. I don't recommend, however, that you continually jerk the plugs around to check for impending doom.

Another helpful hint for ADB users applies to most computer peripherals. Don't plug in or unplug devices on the ADB bus with your Mac turned on! The ADB connectors can flex, shorting the power pin to the ground pin. This will blow some ADB fuses and may fry the ADB controller.

NON-ADB DEVICES

Before the ADB, there was anarchy. Well, not quite, but there were few standards for Macintosh devices. Older Macs, meaning the Plus and earlier models, required a mouse compatible with the Macintosh DB-9 mouse connector and a keyboard designed to use the built-in RJ-11 connector. Additional input devices could use the SCSI port and/or the Mac serial ports. There are, all the same, plenty of expansion products that can be used with these Macs. The Key-Tronic MacPro Plus keyboard, for instance, provides both ADB and RJ-11 keyboard connectors. A number of third-party hardware developers build mice that can use the older Mac mouse connector. A number of hand scanners and other devices plug into the Mac's SCSI port and have a "pass-through" SCSI connector to attach other devices to.

REASONS FOR UPGRADING

Why upgrade your Mac input devices? In the case of keyboards, you may not like the feel, the key arrangement, the size, or the features of standard Apple keyboards. Third-party keyboards are a way to solve most or all of these problems, not to mention the ADB connector wear problem that I mentioned above.

Apple's mechanical mouse is not the be-all and end-all. It frequently has a tendency to jerk and move inaccurately, especially if it's not cleaned regularly. Some third-party mice may fit your hand better and be more accurate and less prone to wear than Apple's standard model.

Touchpads are a relatively new solution to the pointing device problem. These devices literally put cursor control "at your fingertips," allowing you to move the cursor by touching a pad with your finger. They may solve both the desk space and the pointing accuracy problem for Mac users.

Trackballs, or "upside-down mice" are a solution for Mac users with limited desk space, or for folks who want a little more control over the cursor. I'm not a big fan of these devices, but maybe I haven't met the trackball of my dreams yet.

Graphics tablets allow you to move the cursor and enter data using a pen and pad device. These products give artists more control over Mac paint and draw programs than a mouse does (doing art with a mouse is sometimes described as "drawing with a bar of soap"). Engineers, who call these devices *digitizer pads*, use them with CAD or Geographical Information System (GIS) programs. They're useful for detailed drafting and for calculating the areas and volumes of irregular shapes and solids.

The *touch screen* is a specialized Mac input device that fits over your monitor screen and allows you to control the Mac cursor by touching the screen and moving your finger. The main use of this device, at least to my limited imagination, is running an interactive demo or virtual control panel.

John Sculley tells us that the Mac is strictly a business machine, but for us closet game players, help is finally at hand in the form of the *mouse stick*. This is a joystick that plugs into your Mac's available ADB port, controlling game play. For a lot of games this is a welcome alternative to the Macintosh mouse.

A new development for the Mac is the *voice-controlled interface*. This device uses voice commands to execute a number of operations usually controlled with a keyboard or mouse. The voice interface is useful for hands-free operation or for individuals who don't have the use of their hands.

Individuals with special needs have felt somewhat left out by the Macintosh's graphical user interface (GUI). The dependence of the Mac's interface on a mouse made it difficult to use for individuals who cannot use a conventional pointing device. This is changing, however, through the efforts of Apple and third-party hardware vendors.

As you can see, there are almost as many reasons for upgrading your Mac input device as there are Mac peripherals. Upgrading these devices is not a trivial or spur-of-the-moment decision. The wrong decision can get you a peripheral that is irritating to use at best and a disaster at worst. Take your time, select your device carefully, and make sure it fits the way you work. If you do that, you're much more likely to find an input device that meets your needs.

MAC INPUT OPTIONS

For the rest of this chapter, I'll give you some details on the wide variety of devices available to the Mac user. My examples represent the most common input options and are not exhaustive (I want to get this done before I hit 90). But they'll probably help you find a device that solves your most difficult problem.

To make your choice, think about what you want to do on your Mac and what irritates you about your current setup. Could your input devices be more accurate, operate faster, have more options? If your upgrade will be expensive, does it have resale value and upgrade potential? Most importantly, does your upgrade device fit how you work? Does it feel comfortable when you use it? What's the quality of the device? Don't forget that input devices see a lot of mileage. Those with shoddy workmanship won't last long.

Keyboards

Despite all the innovations in Mac input devices, the device of necessity for most Mac owners is still the keyboard. Because of the importance of the Mac keyboard, you should have a number of features in mind when you go shopping for a new or used one.

First, size. How big are your hands and how long is your reach? Will you be happy with a big, roomy, extended keyboard, or would you prefer one of the more compact regular boards?

Second, "feel." Many keyboard manufacturers give their boards gradually greater resistance until a "trigger point" is reached and the key goes down. The key will then come up immediately, pressed against your finger. This is called "tactile feedback." It helps you feel whether your keypresses have been recorded, something that's very important to touch typists. Another feature, key clicks, can be thought of as "sonic feedback" for typists. How much tactile feedback and key click is ideal? It's a subjective matter. Some keyboards, notably the MacPro Plus from Keytronic, let you customize the keyboard for a feel you're comfortable with.

Third, keyboard arrangement. The standard Mac keyboard, for use with the SE, SE/30, and other early ADB Macs, is a jewel. It has perfect keyboard feel, large "bar" shift keys and a large "L-shaped" return key. On the left side, the Escape key is in the top left corner, on the row with the number keys, with large Tab and Control keys below. The Caps Lock key is in the lower left corner, easy to find.

The keyboard for Mac Classic, Classic II, LC, and LC II, has been inexplicably changed—not for the better (see Figure 9.1). The Return key is a small bar instead of an L-shaped pad. The Escape key is, are you ready, on the right side of the space bar at the bottom of the keyboard. Huh? The Tab, Caps Lock, and Control keys on the left side of the keyboard are all rearranged. With the release of the "Classic" keyboard, Apple has given a great example of how a poor keyboard arrangement can mess up your work habits. After a long history of good keyboards, it's amazing that Apple could come up with something like this.

Fourth, extra keys and function keys. The appeal of extended keyboards is that they add those nifty function keys for things like Undo, Cut, Copy, and Paste, as well as a number of user-definable functions if a keyboard macro package is used. Another nicety of extended keyboards is the area between the main keyboard and numeric keypad. It's used for an intuitive T-shaped cursor key

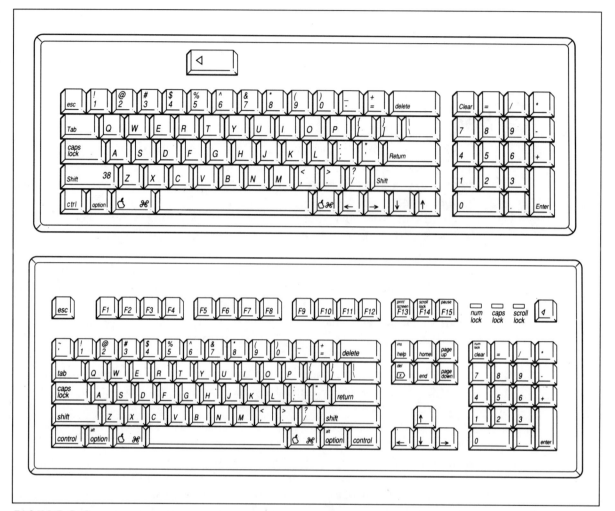

FIGURE 9.1: The Apple Extended and Apple Classic keyboards.

layout and neat keys like Page Up, Page Down, Home, End, Ins/Help, and Delete. The extra document movement keys are handy to quickly navigate documents in applications that support them, like Microsoft products and Lotus 1-2-3 for the Mac.

Fifth, dual-connector capability. The KeyTronic MacPro Plus keyboard (Figure 9.2), for instance, supports both the RJ-11 connectors on older Macs like the Plus and the newer ADB connectors. This means that you can buy the keyboard for your Mac Plus and use it with another Mac if you decide to upgrade later.

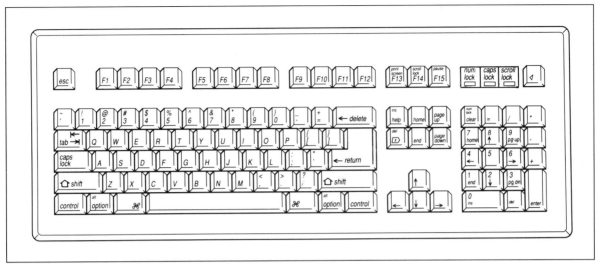

FIGURE 9.2: The KeyTronic MacPro Plus keyboard.

Sixth, angle adjustment. To keep things easier on your hands, arms, and wrists, a keyboard should ideally have a keyboard angle adjustment. Many do, including Apple's latest extended keyboard.

Non-ADB Keyboards

The original Mac keyboard, used with the Mac Plus and earlier, is basically a typewriter keyboard with no function keys. (The Plus was the first to add a numeric keypad.) The keyboard has the same crisp action as newer keyboards, with more key travel. KeyTronic's MacPro Plus, with its RJ-11 connectors, is a good replacement keyboard for a Mac Plus or earlier model.

Regular Keyboards

Apple builds two "small" keyboards, without a special cursor keypad, document "movement" keys, function keys, or status lights. The size of these keyboards is an advantage for those who prefer a more compact layout and are short on desktop space. The keyboard feel is comfortable, as with most Apple keyboards, and the keyboard angle is fixed or two-position adjustable (legs up and down) as in the Apple standard keyboard.

I've already vented my spleen on the problems I have with the Apple Classic keyboard (above, Figure 9.1) and I won't bore you with them again. If you use the Classic keyboard and love it, bully for you. If you don't like the Classic keyboard, consider an older standard keyboard (or an Apple IIgs keyboard) or buy a third-party enhanced keyboard.

Extended Keyboards

So why an extended keyboard? Well, for starters, the third-party keyboards for the Mac are extended, so you have a lot more choice than Apple, Apple, or Apple. Apple and most third-party extended keyboards have the layout I mentioned above: intelligent key location, large Return key, function and movement keys, and status lights. I recommend that you choose between keyboards until you find the one that has just the feel you're looking for.

If you find the right deal at the right time, you might even get a keyboard macro package like QuicKeys bundled with your keyboard. A keyboard macro package will allow you to automatically execute a sequence of keypresses by hitting one function key on an extended keyboard. For instance, you might program F12 to save, and then quit, each currently running program and shut the Mac down. The uses are limited only by available keyboard equivalents and your imagination. Frontier, the new scripting language for the Mac, suggests even more interesting possibilities for function key equivalents.

The first four function keys on a Mac extended keyboard, F1–F4, are usually assigned to Undo, Cut, Copy, and Paste— the four most commonly used commands. This setup is more convenient than the usual command-letter combinations.

I prefer large L-shaped Return keys because they're easy to hit and reduce the chances of making errors with this important key. Unfortunately, while third-party extended keyboards add this enhancement, Apple's extended keyboards, including the newest ADB Extended Keyboard II, do not.

As for page-movement and cursor keys, the T-shaped arrow layout allows you to navigate with one hand on the cursor pad. The middle finger selects the up or down arrow and the second and fourth fingers select the left and right arrows. This is neat and intuitive, and makes it hard to get lost.

Many extended keyboards provide the option of customizing your keyboard with a switch and/or keycaps. Some, like the KeyTronic keyboard, allow you to set key sensitivity with a special kit.

All extended keyboards have three status lights in the upper right corner—Num Lock, Caps Lock, and Scroll Lock. All Mac programs support Caps Lock status, but only specific programs (often by Microsoft) support Num Lock and Scroll Lock.

Apple's extended keyboard has terrific feel, a decent layout—except for the Return key—and an angle adjustable between 4° and 16°.

I've mentioned KeyTronic's MacPro Plus (Figure 9.2) keyboard frequently because I use it and I like it. The keyboard has two adjustments, up and down, a sane keyboard layout, and 15 function keys. The keyboard also has customizable key layout, ADB connectors located on the back of the keyboard instead of the sides, RJ-11 connectors for the Plus and older Macs, and a keyboard adjustment kit that allows you to set key "feel." Most reviewers rave about the feel of the keyboard. I find it kind of mushy when compared to Apple keyboards, but I haven't made any attempts at customization.

KeyTronic also makes the TrackPro keyboard, with a built-in trackball. There have been some quality control problems with the trackball, but these may be resolved by the time this book goes to press.

Prometheus Products' Mac-101E extended keyboard can be used on all Macs. The 101E has switchable control and caps-lock keycaps. The keyboard has a plastic cover and a function key template. It gives a clear "click" when you press its keys—the "audio feedback" that I mentioned. Prometheus, in conjunction with CE Software, offers a discount on the QuicKeys keyboard macro package.

The Switchboard is a neat product from Prometheus that allows you to "build your own keyboard" from custom modules, including a trackball. The Switchboard works with Macs and PCs, giving it definite resale value.

Most of you have probably heard the story of the evolution of the conventional (QWERTY) keyboard layout, derived from the typewriter. Supposedly, the first typewriters were so slow that the keyboard was designed to keep fast typists from outrunning them. Whether this is true or not, keyboards haven't changed substantially since the introduction of the typewriter. Different layouts (like the ergonomically sound Dvorak) have been tried, but none has caught on so far.

Still, some imaginative alternatives to the standard keyboard are appearing. One of these is the Bat, from InfoGrip. Keyboard input on the Bat is by way of "chording," or pressing several keys at once. The design of the device apparently also reduces strain on the wrists of a typist.

It will be interesting to see if any of the new alternative keyboards stakes a claim on the Mac market. You may find that one of these devices is just what you've been looking for. With these and all keyboards, I recommend that you try before you buy, if possible.

Mice

Every Mac user would probably agree that the mouse is one of the best and most user-friendly input devices ever invented. (It was invented, by the way, as part of the Xerox Star system that eventually became the Apple Lisa and finally the Macintosh.)

The mouse is a relative positioning device. In other words, its absolute location doesn't matter—only the distance that it travels between two points. That's why you can pick your mouse up and move it back when you run out of space.

There are three main types of mice: mechanical, opto-mechanical, and optical. Mechanical mice use two rollers at right angles that are moved by the mouse ball and transmit their rotations as changes in cursor X and Y coordinates. Opto-mechanical mice use a combination of rollers and optical detectors to count X and Y "ticks." Optical mice have no roller ball but use an LED and a photo-detector in the mouse in combination with a special mousepad. The mousepad has an x-y grid over a mirrored surface, encased in transparent plastic. Optical mice are accurate, reliable, and, because they have no moving parts, long-lived. Older Apple mice were opto-mechanical, newer mice are mechanical.

One recent development that frees up your mouse, eliminating the long cord that can often get in the way, is the infrared mouse. Infrared mice use an infrared light source in the mouse and a detector that you plug in to your Mac. A great use for these mice is when the mouse and Mac have to be a fair distance apart, such as in presentations.

You may hear references to the "resolution" of pointing devices, including mice. Resolution is a measure of how many points or pixels can be detected for each inch of mouse movement. Most Mac pointing devices provide resolutions of 75 to 150 counts per inch. If your device of choice claims higher resolution, make sure that this resolution translates into better control. Devices with higher resolution should have smoother, finer movements and more precise control. The Apple mouse, for instance, is adequate, but can create cursor movements that are somewhat jerky.

Another aspect of some Mac input devices, including mice, is "dynamic resolution" or "ballistic tracking" (see Figure 9.3). This refers to the relation of device resolution to speed. A fast movement of the device translates into a larger cursor move across the screen, a slow movement results in a smaller cursor move. This is especially valuable on a large-screen Mac where there's a lot of space to cover with device movements.

Your Choices

Mouse Systems is the main supplier of optical mice. These include the A3 mouse and LittleMouse ADB. The small size of the LittleMouse may be perfect for smaller hands. The A3 mouse is a two-button model.

Logitech's Mouseman is an accurate, smooth, reliable, two-button mouse that has a slope to fit the contours of a right-hander's grip. Unfortunately, a left-hand model isn't available for the Mac. Left-handers, here's an opportunity to write some letters!

Advanced Gravis provides the contoured, two-button SuperMouse. SoftCode Canada makes the SICOs Fancy Mouse, a low-profile, "designer" mouse. And AirMouse and Z-Nix make cordless infrared mice, the AirMouse Remote Control and the Z-Nix Super Cordless mouse. The Z-Nix device works from a distance of up to 6' and has rechargeable batteries, one in the mouse and one in the holder-receiver. The mouse has a resolution of 400 dpi.

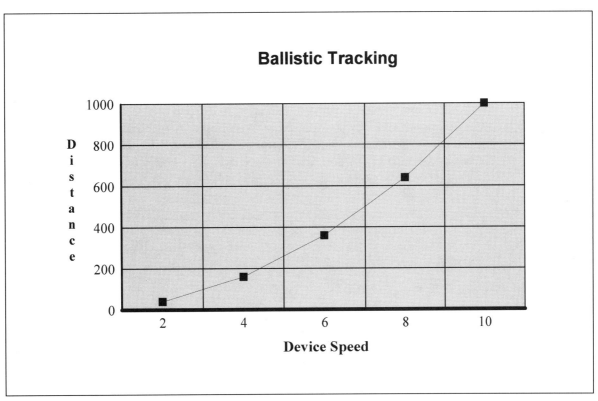

FIGURE 9.3:   Ballistic tracking

Try 'em Before You Buy 'em

Mice, like keyboards, all have a distinctive "feel" and performance. They may look great in the ads, but feel terrible in your hand. Your best bet is to try before you buy. But, you say, my dealer doesn't have most of these goodies. This is my chance to get in a plug for your local Mac user group. These are made up of enthusiasts and, if the group is a fair size, the odds are good that one of them may have the device you're looking for. He or she may even let you try it if you promise to wipe the fingerprints off afterwards.

The most important accessory for a mouse user is a good mouse pad. Unless you've got an optical mouse, the best pads are neoprene-backed with a rough or slightly tufted cloth cover. They may not be pretty, but they work like a darn. Take my word, you don't want to try to roll a mouse around on a smooth surface unless you like jerky movement and poor accuracy.

Touchpads

Touchpads are a new and exciting entry in the world of Macintosh pointing devices (see Figure 9.4). The UnMouse from Microtouch is a 3½" × 4" 1000 × 1000 point touchpad. The device uses the same principle as touchpads for kitchen appliances. Putting your finger on the pad changes the capacitance, or the amount of electricity stored, at that point. A movement of your finger is translated into a cursor movement onscreen. The UnMouse button is mounted at the left side of the pad nearest the cable. These devices have a lot of potential, especially for small desktops and graphics applications.

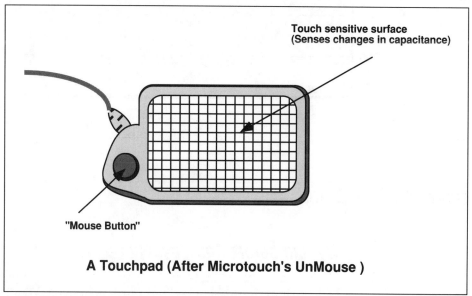

Touch sensitive surface
(Senses changes in capacitance)

"Mouse Button"

A Touchpad (After Microtouch's UnMouse)

FIGURE 9.4:   A touchpad

Trackballs

Ah… trackballs. The "upside-down mice" of the Mac world, they use the same sensing mechanisms as mice. Some people *love* trackballs. I'm not one of them. However, you may find that a trackball is your ideal input device, especially for applications that need more control or less desk space than a mouse.

A trackball will keep your wrist above the desk surface at an angle that may be uncomfortable, so a lower profile one may be more acceptable. Trackballs have different masses, and you may want to try them for comfort. A high-mass trackball will be smooth, but could be hard to move rapidly.

A trackball should have a "drag" button for drag-and-drop actions. How these buttons are placed is critical for comfort.

Many trackballs include control software to customize their operation, including ballistics.

Kensington produces the TurboMouse ADB (Figure 9.5), with a large, responsive trackball and easy-to-use buttons. The TurboMouse also comes with special customization software.

CoStar Corporation's Stingray is a low-profile trackball with large buttons. The MVP Mouse, from Curtis Engineering, has a sloping contoured case with a wrist rest and an optional floor foot switch. Kraft Systems' Trackball ADB is also available with a foot switch.

The Silhouette Trackball, from EMac, has a "side-mounted" colored trackball. You can choose from four different trackball weights.

Thumbelina, from Appoint, is a neat little hand-held trackball designed to be operated with a thumb. Logitech's Trackman for the Macintosh is a thumb-operated trackball designed for right-handed users. What is this with Logitech and lefties, anyway?

FIGURE 9.5: The Kensington TurboMouse ADB (photo courtesy of Kensington Microware Limited)

Graphics Tablets

Artists call them graphics tablets, engineers call them digitizer pads, but both groups find them indispensible. A graphics tablet, unlike a mouse, is an absolute pointing device. This means that an X-Y location on a graphics tablet corresponds to an exact X-Y location on your computer screen. (Software is available for some graphics tablets to make them perform like a mouse if required.) The electromagnetic sensing grid in a graphics tablet can sense the radio signals of an attached pen or puck to within one ten-thousandth of an inch. Mac graphics tablets have available resolutions of 200–1000 points per inch.

A graphics tablet puck has a window with cross-hairs and may have a numeric keypad to enter values at a point. The puck normally has a data-entry button. A graphics tablet pen, or stylus, normally enters data by clicking on a switch in the point. A number of pads, including the Wacom products, have a pressure-sensitive point and with appropriate software can behave like a paintbrush tip.

Graphics tablets can connect to your Mac through a serial port or the ADB. If your tablet is an ADB device, make sure it has a pass-through or *daisy-chain* port, unless you have an ADB port to spare.

Kurta Corporation makes the IS/ADB Mac graphics tablet, Summagraphics Corporation produces the Summasketch II ADB, and Calcomp produces the DrawingBoard II. The DrawingBoard II tablet is available with a pressure-sensitive stylus and in a cordless version. Wacom Technology Corporation's SD-421E and SD-510C each have a pressure-sensitive stylus. The 510C has a smaller 6" × 9" pad.

Touch Screens

Touch screens have never taken off as Mac input devices, but they have their moments. Specific uses include educational programs and "self-guiding" automated displays. Edmark Corporation's Macintosh TouchWindow is the primary touch-sensitive screen cover for the Mac.

MouseSticks

Up to now, ignoring Mac games hasn't been that hard, because playing games with a mouse is, well, kinda dull. But now my prayers for a joystick have been answered with the ADB MouseStick, from Advanced Gravis. Fire up the Lear, honey, and let's try out Flight Simulator.

Voice-Activated Devices

Ever since you saw Scotty talk to the computer on the Enterprise, you knew it was possible. Up till now, though, using voice recognition control software with a Mac has been somewhat hit or miss. But Articulate Systems has made voice control of a Mac feasible with its Voice Navigator SW, for Macs with built-in microphones, and Voice Navigator II for machines without microphones. Voice Navigator has to be *trained*, but apparently works acceptably. This software has real potential for Mac users who require "hands-off" operation, especially special-needs users without the use of their hands.

Special-Needs Devices

Special-needs users have typically had more options available with PCs or Apple IIs than with Macs. But Mac special-needs devices are coming. The Foundation for Technology Access, originally created with the aid of Apple Computer, can help special-needs individuals find the products that best suit their needs. The number of the Foundation is (800)992-8111 or (510)528-0747.

Don Johnson Developmental Equipment makes Ke:nx, a hardware and software interface that attaches a variety of alternative input devices to a Mac. Unicorn Engineering manufactures the Smart Keyboard. The keyboard comes with seven overlays with large keys. It works with standard software programs. Tele-Sensory makes a braille translator and printer for visually impaired Mac users. Apple's CloseView software magnifier control panel for visually impaired users makes standard programs accessible with little PCs effort. The Easy Access control panel gives users access to key combinations without having to hold down two keys at once.

Other Input Devices

Finally, there are the oddballs—the variety of Mac input devices that don't fall into any easy category. Some, like the Mac itself, may just define their own "insanely great" category.

Among these are Kensington's new NoteBook KeyPad (Figure 9.6) for the PowerBooks. The KeyPad isn't wild or wacky. In fact, it's better described as the right product at the right time. The KeyPad adds a full numeric keypad and 15 function keys to a PowerBook or any other ADB Mac.

The MousePenPro Mac, from Appoint, certainly falls into a category of its own. The MousePen can be used on most surfaces and provides a natural, useful input device with special application to graphics.

Felix, from Altra, is a 6" square box with a small plastic handle topped with a button—sort of a short joystick. This is an interesting idea, anyway.

FIGURE 9.6:   Kensington's NoteBook KeyPad
(photo courtesy of Kensington Microware Limited)

CAN YOU CHOOSE, OR ARE YOU CONFUSED?

You've seen that there really is a profusion of input devices for your Mac. You probably also realize that picking the right input device or devices is going to take a little work. I *highly* recommend that you try before you buy if at all possible. Otherwise, you could get stuck with an expensive lemon that drives you crazy. My opinions may not coincide with yours, so don't take my word; but, if a device sounds good, take it out for a spin.

TROUBLESHOOTING

Problem	Cause	Solution
The device is plugged in, but doesn't work	No other problems apparent	Check ADB connections, control software, settings
The device is connected, but doesn't work	ADB connector wiggles	You may have a bad ADB connector
Again, the device is connected, but doesn't work	You plugged it in to the ADB with power on	You may have blown an ADB fuse or cooked the controller
Your mouse doesn't track well and the pointer moves erratically	The mouse ball may be dirty	Remove ball, wash it with warm, soapy water, dry with a lint-free cloth, replace
Your optical mouse doesn't work	The mouse got zapped with static electricity	Unplug and replug. Hopefully, this will do the trick
You spilled soda pop in your keyboard and it sticks	The soda pop is sticking keys and may corrode contacts	CAREFULLY pry up keys and clean keyboard with isopropyl alcohol (watch for reactions!)

CHAPTER TEN

"Software Upgrades"

Software upgrades—in a book about Macintosh hardware? An explanation is in order. Like the gasoline in your car, software makes your Mac's "wheels go round," and good software is the high octane that makes the wheels go faster.

Utilities, applications, and system software can help your Mac run faster and avoid crashes. They can give you more system memory and disk space, keep your system healthy, and let you do more than one thing at once—something you've probably wanted to do for years. Heard enough? Then let's discuss some of these high octane hardware improvers.

A TUNE-UP WITH SYSTEM 7

System 7 is a Mac idea whose time has come (Figure 10.1). It's the Ferrari of operating systems, which once more puts the Mac ahead of competitors in the MS-DOS world. System 7 solved a number of Mac performance, organization, and enhancement problems previously handled by a mitt-full of software add-ons. The most spectacular of the enhancements are cooperative multitasking, the ability to run multiple programs at the same time, and virtual memory, the ability to use disk space as system memory.

Should You Consider the System 7 Upgrade?

Should you upgrade to System 7, or are all the horror stories about "out of memory" errors and unending application upgrades true?

If you have a Mac with 2MB of memory or less, System 7 is not for you—at least at the moment. I know that Apple ads say you can run System 7 with 2MB. They're right—you can run System 7, but *nothing else* (of any size, at least). To actually use System 7, you'll need 4MB. System 6.07 and 6.08 can live reasonably happily with 2MB and let you have more than one (reasonably sized) program in memory.

If you have lots of memory, and a load of older software that System 7's compatibility checker (Figure 10.2) doesn't like, you can still run System 7 as well as System 6 with the use of a software utility like System Switcher or Blesser (see Figure 10.3). These utilities let you have more than one System file on your boot volume (normally a major no-no) and easily switch Systems. You can keep your older programs and use System 7 too. Nirvana, right? Well, almost, except for the duplication of DAs and fonts in the system folders. Even this can be "worked around" by using Suitcase or MasterJuggler, which let you keep fonts, DAs, and sounds outside of the system folder.

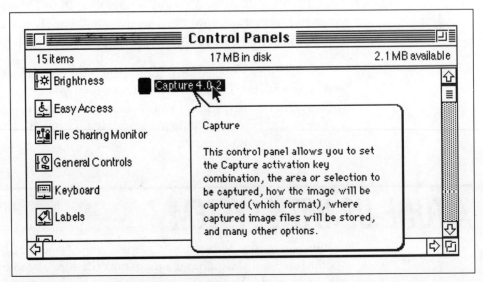

FIGURE 10.1:   The System 7.0 Desktop

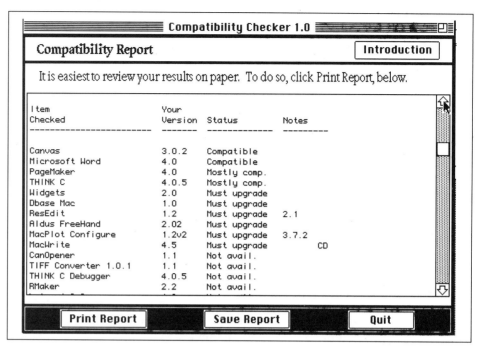

FIGURE 10.2:   The Compatibility Checker

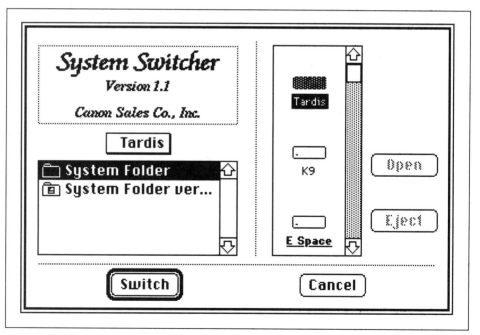

FIGURE 10.3:   System Switcher

If you've just bought a Mac Classic II, you'd better get some memory too, because the Classic II has to use System 7.

How Does System 7 Improve Your Mac's Hardware?

System 7 is an example of how software can provide some very real improvements to your Mac hardware. It gives you crash protection in the form of heap space, more speed when launching programs, print spooling, more memory with 32-bit addressing and virtual memory, and outstanding print quality on a non-PostScript printer. System 7 also provides better network access, file sharing, and access to a central database, as well as 32-bit graphics and QuickTime multimedia compatability for appropriate Macs.

My comment above concerning "appropriate Macs" is very important. System 7.0 will run on every Mac from a Plus to a Quadra 950, but it will run better on a fast Mac with lots of memory. QuickTime runs under System 7, but requires a minimum of an SE/30. In any case, here are some details about System 7's "hardware" upgrades.

More Heap Space

You may recall my discussion of the Mac system heap in Chapter 3. The system heap contains a variety of system data. Each application also has its own heap space. A Mac that is short of memory, and running System 6 or lower, may run out of system heap space, resulting in a variety of errors and bombs. System 7 prevents this problem. It has something called *dynamic heap allocation*, which automatically allocates any necessary heap space to the system from available memory. This results in faster, more reliable Mac operation because a multitude of heap-related problems are made obsolete.

Multitasking and System Speed

How can a larger, more complex program *improve* system speed? System 7's *multitasking* capability lets your Mac execute multiple programs at the same time and quickly switch between them. This is much faster than loading and running individual programs, and the background execution of a multitasking program can let you get a task done while you execute another one in the foreground.

The concept of multitasking implies that your Mac is executing more than one program simultaneously. In fact, that's not quite what happens. The CPU in your Mac just switches between different programs so quickly that it appears to be executing them simultaneously. Programs running "in the background" on your Mac have a lower priority than the program you're currently working with and receive less attention—that is, fewer clock cycles—from the

CPU. This ensures that the program you're working on will receive the most attention from the CPU and run faster.

Slower Macs, like the Classic, don't have enough speed and power to multitask quickly or handle a large number of programs at once. However, just by bringing multitasking to Macs from the Plus to the Quadra 950, System 7 is a giant technical step forward.

System 7 mediates between multitasking programs. These programs have to be "well-behaved"—they need to access the Mac operating system in consistent and well-defined ways. If one program goes down, it can pull the whole system with it (this is called *cooperative multitasking*). Still, because most Mac programs are designed according to well-defined guidelines, system crashes are not all that common. Incompatibility with multitasking is one reason that programs have to be upgraded for System 7.

By the way, Windows, OS/2, and Unix use a system called *pre-emptive multitasking*. Pre-emptive multitasking allows the multitasking operating system to isolate crashed programs while continuing to run others. Sounds great, doesn't it? It is when it works. Generally speaking, System 7's cooperative system works well because of Mac program compatibility.

Faster Program Launching and System Speed

System 7's aliases let you access a single program in different folders, on different devices (including floppies), and even on different Macs. This eliminates a lot of folder shuffling and device access, speeding up your jobs. This may not improve absolute system speed but it sure improves system efficiency. But like the hard drive folder organization I described in Chapter 7, aliases will only help organize you if you organize *them*.

Creating an alias under System 7 is as easy as picking the program that you want to create an alias for and selecting Make Alias from the System File menu. The alias is created in the same file as your program. You can move the alias anywhere and it will remain linked to the original program. The Alias is a tiny file with the same name as the program it accesses, and can be treated just like any other file. Clicking on the alias launches the program it's linked to.

You can create your own custom program launcher by putting your aliases in the System 7 Apple menu Items folder. They will then appear under the Apple menu. By the way, placing a bullet (Option-8) in front of your aliases will put them at the bottom of the Apple menu, where they're easy to find (Figure 10.4).

Print Spooling and System Speed

When printing to an Apple LaserWriter, System 7 activates a built-in print spooler. The spooler sends data to a file on disk and then feeds it to the printer a piece at a time. This frees your Mac and you to do other things. While this doesn't increase speed, it does increase efficiency. System 7's print spooler *does* use disk space, memory, and CPU time, so print spooling is not without a price.

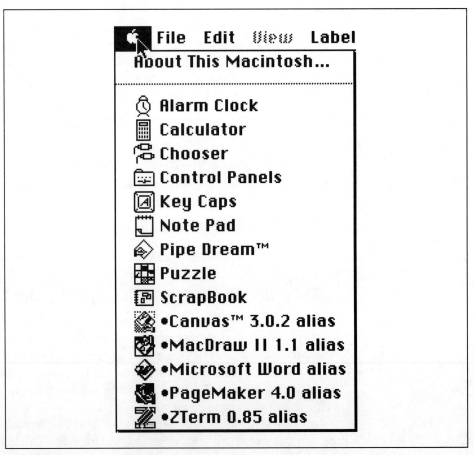

FIGURE 10.4:   Aliases in the Apple menu

Working in the Background

System 7's multitasking capability will let you execute a number of common utility functions in the background. Copying, duplicating files or folders, emptying the Trash, or using System 7's Find command can all be done this way.

The program you want to use must be open before you start your background process.

When you're executing a background process, you'll notice a speed penalty in the program running in the foreground.

Running utilities in the background, like a number of other System 7 processes I've mentioned, won't accelerate your Mac. However, using this capability will free up your time and speed up the completion of your jobs.

32-Bit Addressing and Mac Memory

If your Mac has a 68030 processor, it is capable of using 32-bit addressing with System 7. Theoretically, 32-bit addressing will soon allow a Mac to address up to 4 gigabytes of memory. Current Macs with sufficient SIMM space and 16MB SIMMs can access from 64–256MB with 32-bit addressing under System 7. You turn 32-bit addressing on and off from the memory control panel.

The Mac SE/30, II, IIx, and IIcx all have older ROMs and can't use System 7's 32-bit addressing without a software utility called Mode32. This is a commercial product produced by Connectix that "patches" a Mac's ROMs with the 32-bit address code. Mode32 has been purchased by Apple and, by agreement with Connectix, released to public domain. It is available to owners of older Macs from user groups and on Mac bulletin boards.

Virtual Memory and System 7

Virtual memory is disk space that the Mac treats as system memory. Virtual memory is only available on Macs with a 68030 processor or a 68020 processor upgraded with a PMMU (paged memory management unit—see Chapter 6). Until recently, only operating systems like Unix have given their users access to virtual memory. Now, with the right hardware, you can have it too.

Virtual memory is not the ultimate answer to a memory shortage. Hard drives and other storage devices don't approach the speed of RAM memory, so virtual memory is *slow*.

Continual virtual memory disk access will shorten the life of your hard drive or other storage device.

You should allow yourself enough disk space for the largest application and file you'll be running with virtual memory. With System 7 multitasking and virtual memory active, your disk space should be used only for file swap space. This means that you'll only be using slow virtual memory when it's necessary.

Before you can use virtual memory with your Mac hard drive, you'll have to format the drive with a System 7-compatible low-level formatter. You don't need a specially formatted drive to use System 7 by itself, however. Table 10.1 lists a variety of System 7-compatible low-level formatters. Don't worry if your formatter is not on the list. Just check with your supplier to find out if it's compatible with System 7.

System 7.0-compatible hard drive formatters		
VENDOR	**FORMATTING SOFTWARE**	**VERSION COMPATIBLE WITH VIRTUAL MEMORY**
Alliance Peripheral Systems	Alliance Power Tools	2.0
CMS Enhancements	CMS SCSI Utilities	6.1
FWB Incorporated	FWB Hard Disk Toolkit	1.1
GCC Technologies	Drive Manager	7.0
LaCie	Silverlining	5.3
SuperMac	Manager	4.2
Third Wave	Disk Manager Mac	2.24

TABLE 10.1: Some System 7.0-Compatible Low-Level Formatters

Should You Upgrade?

Well, now you've seen how System 7 can upgrade your Mac and you have an idea of what it requires. To use System 7 effectively, you should have at least 4MB of memory. To use 32-bit addressing, you'll need a 68030 processor. For virtual memory, you'll need a 68030 or a 68020 processor with a PMMU. As I've mentioned, System 7 is not for everybody. It is, however, the wave of the future. You'll just have to determine if it's in your future.

A "SOFT DISK"—RAMDISK+

RAMDisk+ is a *great* shareware init, by Roger D. Bates, that lets you set aside a portion of your system memory as a file storage device up to 32MB in size.

You may remember some comments about RAM disks. They are fast, convenient, and, unfortunately, *volatile*. This means that when your Mac goes off, your files are gone. If you've got enough memory, a RAM disk will let you access files like large 24-bit graphics at RAM speeds which are much quicker than even the fastest hard drive.

RAMDisk+ has some nice features. It's compatible with System 7 and earlier operating systems, will optionally switch control to the RAM disk, ejecting a startup floppy, and will activate a *crash saver* function to allow a graceful exit from a system bomb.

A SANE CALCULATOR

OmegaSANE is a freeware patch init for FPU and non-FPU Macs. This patch is in its early development stages, but apparently provides *substantial* speed improvement for calculations using the Standard Apple Numeric Environment (SANE). OmegaSANE enhances SANE in a number of ways. These include a faster non-FPU divide algorithm, a faster non-FPU square-root algorithm, correctly rounded binary-to-decimal conversions, faster executions of transcendental functions, and improvements in SANE "trapping" speed (the speed with which SANE detects and executes functions). Table 10.2 is from the OmegaSANE documentation and details SANE speedup for the utility on FPU and non-FPU Macs.

OPERATIONS	NON-FPU SPEEDUP	FPU SPEEDUP
Add/Subtract	2.39×	3.15×
Multiply	1.55×	2.95×
Divide	2.37×	2.99×
Square Root(Exact)	3.08×	3.55×
Square Root(Inexact)	1.75×	3.22×
Cosine	2.33×	7.82×
Sine	2.4×	6.29×
Tangent	2.37×	8.70×
Logarithm	2.53×	9.32×
Exponential	2.61×	10.12×
Compound	2.53×	8.05×
Annuity	2.67×	8.91×

TABLE 10.2: SANE Speedup with OmegaSANE

CRASH PROTECTION

Crash Barrier from Casady and Greene, Inc. is a commercial utility that, like RAMDisk+, gives you a graceful exit from system bombs. Crash Barrier claims to provide:

- Error prevention by system memory protection, reducing crashes.
- Error recovery, as I mentioned above, with a dialog offering you a variety of options.
- Auto-save, with application and desk accessory automatic saving ability.

I don't know how you feel, but when I'm installing and using new hardware and software, especially in a low-memory situation, this kind of utility looks pretty good to me.

A HEALTHY SYSTEM

After a hardware upgrade, you may be concerned about possible problems that could occur from incorrect installation or component failures. Two utilities, Snooper from Maxa, and MacEKG from Micromat, provide a set of diagnostic tests to evaluate the condition of your Mac. Even when things are running well, a good diagnostic package can be useful—you've heard of preventative medicine, I presume?

Snooper is a software utility and optional plug-in board that does a complete hardware check on your Mac, including benchmarks, audio and video tests, RAM and SCSI tests, I/O and System tests, and serial port *loopback tests*. A loopback test sends signals back and forth between two Mac serial ports connected with a serial loopback cable. Snooper also produces an error log if requested.

MacEKG performs 35 benchmark tests in logic, SCSI, and QuickDraw categories. MacEKG also produces a test log, accessible through a cdev. The test log is used to monitor system performance history and warn of potential failure.

These utilities also have potential as evaluation tools for expensive new and used hardware. If there are any problems with the equipment you're buying, you have a decent chance of locating them with Snooper or MacEKG.

SYSTEM 6 — A HEAP OF TROUBLE?

I mentioned earlier that System 7 prevents problems with the system heap, the area of memory that stores a variety of critical system parameters. In pre-7 operating systems, system heap size is normally fixed, so the possibility of a "collision" between the heap and application memory in a loaded Mac system is great. This results in bombs and a variety of system errors.

Mac developers jumped on this deficiency with HeapFixer, from CE Software, Bootman (Figure 10.5), a freeware utility from Bill Steinberg, and other applications.

Bootman allows you to edit three values which are normally not available to you, on your startup disk's boot blocks. These are the system heap size, the maximum number of open files, and the maximum number of operating system events. When you boot from a disk set with Bootman, the parameters you updated are passed to the system for you. I suggest you proceed with care and read the documentation for these programs before using them. If you get over-enthusiastic when resetting heap size, you could cause more problems than you're trying to solve.

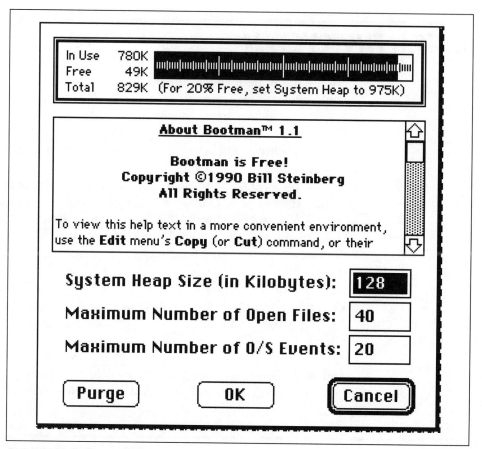

FIGURE 10.5: Bootman

FRAGMENTATION—PUTTING THE PIECES BACK TOGETHER

I mentioned disk fragmentation and optimizers in Chapter 7. To bring you back up to speed, fragmentation is the splitting up of file "pieces" that occurs with continual copying and erasing of files on a hard drive or other storage device. Optimizers are utilities that take the separate file fragments on your hard drive and put them back together in contiguous chunks. This can take some time on a machine with low memory and a large, loaded, badly fragmented hard drive. That's because optimizers load file chunks into memory for speed and have to continually swap them to and from the fragmented storage device. If your Mac device has a lot of small chunks, not much device storage space to write them to, and not much memory to read them to, you can see that optimizing could take some time.

OPTIMIZING YOUR FILE SIZE

A lot of good disk optimizers are available for the Mac. Norton Speed Disk (Figure 10.6) is part of Norton Utilities for the Macintosh. Alsoft's Disk Express is now part of the Alsoft Power Utilities package. Fifth Generation Systems produces the Public Utilities package, including a disk optimizer. Last, but certainly not least, is the MacTools V.2 disk optimizer from Central Point Software.

A disk optimizer won't make a slow hard drive into a fast one, but it will make your badly fragmented drive *seem* like the newest, fastest model—at least until you fragment it again.

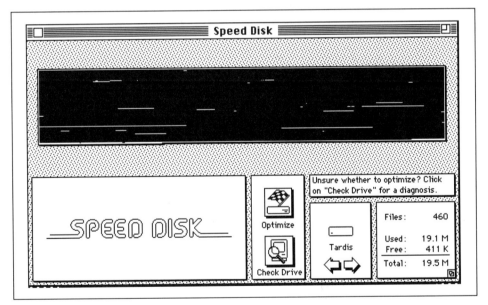

FIGURE 10.6:   Norton Speed Disk

LAUNCHING YOUR PROJECTS

I mentioned System 7's program launching capabilities. Well, even with this built-in launcher, software developers are producing a variety of program launching utilities for System 7, and in some cases, earlier operating systems.

One of the neat new ideas used by some program launchers is the concept of program and data "groups"—program and data files grouped together by project. Program launchers dealing with data groups allow you to open all necessary files at once and arrange them on your desktop any way you desire.

Kiwi Power Windows

Kiwi Power Windows (KPW), from Kiwi Software is a system extension (init) that puts a new menu in the Finder menu bar. The menu lists all open windows and applications and allows you to move rapidly to any of them. The utility also lets you customize window displays. Finally, an aspect of KPW that especially appeals to me lets you create worksets of specific applications and documents. These can be opened from an alias in the Apple menu, from the KPW menu, or by double-clicking on a workset file.

HAM

HAM, from Microseeds Publishing, adds hierarchical menus to your Apple menu. With the launching capabilities of System 7, the Apple menu can become pretty crowded. HAM gives you a simple way to organize and display the Apple menu, with folders popping out as submenus. The possibilities are endless. You could wind up with twenty layers of hierarchical menus—yikes! Still HAM is a good, simple idea.

MEMORY AND DISK SPACE

Two useful memory and space-saving utilities are Suitcase from Fifth Generation Systems and MasterJuggler from Alsoft. These products are system extensions, or inits, that allow you to compress and place fonts, sounds, DAs, and FKeys in folders *outside* of the system file. This was a very useful feature in System 6 and remains so even in System 7. In the section on System 7, I discussed the use of these products when you put Systems 6 and 7 on the same startup disk. These utilities have other space- and time-saving benefits that you may want to explore.

FILE COMPRESSION UTILITIES

Get 30-50% more disk space without buying a new hard disk? Halayleewyuh, aaaave beyun sayuved! File compression utilities are a hot software product for Macs. They've been released by a number of manufacturers, including Alysis, with More Disk Space, Aladdin Systems with SpaceSaver, and Salient Software with Disk Doubler and Auto Doubler.

DiskDoubler may be the best of these utilities (Figure 10.7). A system extension that adds an expansion/compression menu and automatic compression and decompression to files, DD runs acceptably even on a Mac Classic. The program has multiple data checking systems to maintain compressed file integrity. Salient even provides file recovery utilities, in case disaster strikes. The program is completely System 7-compatible, does batch compression and decompression, automatically decompresses and launches the associated application for an opened file, works in the background under System 7, and makes self-extracting archives if desired.

AutoDoubler automatically compresses and decompresses files that you designate. AutoDoubler also includes a manual decompression utility, keeps a user-specified amount of disk space free, automatically compresses specified network volumes, is safe if interrupted by a power outage, and is capable of running in the background under System 7.

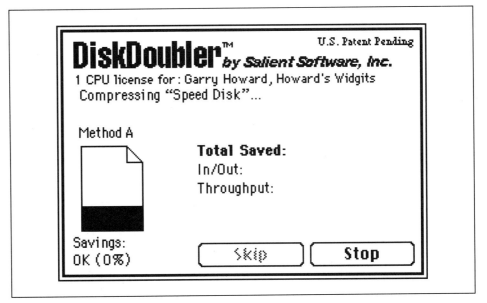

FIGURE 10.7: DiskDoubler

When I say that file compression/decompression utilities are "quick" on a Classic, this doesn't mean that you should keep all of your applications in compressed form. Life is just too short. However, if you keep large, less frequently used data files compressed, you'll save a lot of disk space, and decompression times shouldn't be too onerous. I used to think that file compression utilities on low-end machines were just too slow, but I've been won over. They are considerably faster than I anticipated, and the sight of all that extra disk space is hard to resist.

PASS THE SCRIPT

A software upgrade long overdue for Macs is a scripting language. This is available in a primitive form to MS-DOS users as batch files. Batch files allow DOS users to automate, customize, and improve on a lot of basic functions. Now scripting comes to the Mac, in Userland's Frontier Mac Scripting software. The possibilities are endless, extending a good bit past automating backups and creating extended keyboard functions.

HOW TO BUILD A GREAT PROGRAM

Last but definitely not least on my list of upgrades are small, fast, optimized Mac programs I've come to know and love. They're usually written in assembly language, which is why they're so compact and blazingly fast. These programs are a great "upgrade" for low-powered Macs like the Plus, Classic, or PowerBook 100. And, on a Fast Mac, the performance and small size of these products will seem like a dream.

Programs falling into this category are PublishIt Easy, the "low end" desktop-publishing, word-processing database program from TimeWorks; WriteNow, the fast, efficient, word processor from T/Maker; the Light version of Nisus, the powerful full-featured word processor from Nisus Software; and the super-integrated programs BeagleWorks, ClarisWorks, and GreatWorks. These three give a lot of basic word processor, database, and spreadsheet "bang for the buck" and are a good choice for Mac portables. BeagleWorks actually implements a very efficient version of publish-and-subscribe under System 6. All three products have draw and/or paint modules as well and import a variety of files from numerous programs including AppleWorks, making them a good choice for Apple II owners deciding to move to a Mac. ClarisWorks, like all

Claris products, supports XTEND file translators. These software utilities can be easily added to Claris programs, giving them the ability to translate to and from a variety of file formats from other computer systems.

SUMMING UP

I hope you see how Mac software can actually upgrade your hardware. Take the time to decide where your system performance is lacking and have a look at the software option first. Maybe a software upgrade is all you need right now. And if you do get a hardware update, good software may be just the high-octane fuel your sporty new system needs.

TROUBLESHOOTING

Problem	Cause	Solution
Unexpected application bombs	Not enough memory	Close some applications. Eventually add memory
Frequent "Out of Memory" errors with lots of system memory	Not enough application memory	Select application and choose "Get Info" from File menu. If application memory too small, increase
Frequent bombs and unexplained quits on a loaded System 6	Running out of system heap memory	Use HeapFixer or BootMan to increase heap size
Strange behavior of an application under System 7	Program may not be System 7-compatible	Check and upgrade if possible
Application bombs under 32-bit addressing	Program may not be "32-bit clean"	Check and upgrade if possible

CHAPTER ELEVEN

Repacking Your Mac

Ever feel the need for "speed"? Want a bigger screen? Is your power supply anemic? You might consider repacking your Mac.

WHAT DO I MEAN BY "REPACKING"?

By "repacking" I mean upgrading a Mac by swapping the logic board, or placing a board in a new case and then "tweeking" it. This is also called cloning the Mac.

A number of third-party hardware manufacturers have gotten around the problems of copying Apple's proprietary ROMs by repackaging genuine ROMs or entire logic boards, often by agreement with Apple. As we've seen from the number of lawsuits over the "look and feel" of the Macintosh system, Apple guards the contents of the Mac ROMs jealously. Many a clone builder has met an ugly fate at the hands of Apple's legal department. A company called

NuTek, in an interesting turn of logic, has tried to clone the Mac ROMs using entirely original code. This is similar to the process Phoenix went through when they cloned the PC's ROM BIOS (Basic Input-Output System, in case you're interested). NuTek has even declined to use Apple's operating system with their clone, choosing instead to go with Motif, a windowing system often used by Unix systems. NuTek's progress is worth watching, as it may have an impact on the entire Mac market.

A variety of manufacturers produce cases that accept a Mac system board, enhancing it with more power, better cooling, a faster, more advanced CPU, more enhancement potential, and so forth. Some of these companies will do the repackaging for you. You send them the Mac, they return an upgraded screamer. You may be nervous about parting with your machine in this fashion, however, and I don't blame you.

If you don't want to part with your machine, or you don't like any of the available kits, you may want to try building your own Mac. This has its own set of advantages and disadvantages, and represents a heck of a lot more work than building an external device. To do it, you try to pick up high-performance components cheaply, a piece at a time, as they become available.

Finally, you may want to consider an authentic Apple upgrade. This too has its own set of advantages and disadvantages.

THIRD-PARTY REPACKS

I mentioned that a number of companies circumvented problems with Apple by buying or obtaining genuine Apple ROMs or logic boards and repackaging them in a new case with a number of hardware upgrades. Outbound uses this system for their Macintosh portables. Until the Macintosh PowerBooks were released, these third-party portables represented the only true portable alternative for Macintosh users. They still have a number of advantages over PowerBooks.

MicroMac and Aztech Micro Solutions have nifty repackaging kits for Macintosh logic boards. Perspect and Sixty Eight Thousand offer repackaging solutions for high-end modular Mac boards.

Outbound Systems

Outbound has the most intelligent arrangement of the Mac clone makers. They have licensed Mac ROMs, by agreement with Apple's legal department, and use them with a board of Outbound's own design (Figure 11.1). A neat arrangement, and on the whole, it works well. Unfortunately, some software incompatibilities have been reported with the systems.

FIGURE 11.1:   The Outbound Notebook computer (photo courtesy of Outbound Systems, Inc.)

Outbound Notebook computers all come standard with a SuperDrive-compatible 3½" 1.44MB floppy drive that reads Mac or MS-DOS disks, a ten-inch diagonal 640×480 pixel LCD screen with fluorescent backlighting, and a full-size standard Apple-style keyboard. Outbound portables also have a neat pointing device called a *trackbar*, a bar at the front of the Outbound keyboard that rotates and slides from side to side to move the cursor. The portables come with a SCSI port, two serial/AppleTalk ports, an ADB port, and an audio port. The systems run for up to three hours on a camcorder battery, and have an AC recharger for the battery.

Outbound's CPUs range from the 68000 to the 68030. A system's hard drives and memory can easily be removed and upgraded via doors at the side and back of the unit.

The Outbound System 2000 weighs 6¼ pounds and uses a 20MHz 68000 CPU, upgradable to a 68030 with or without a PMMU (the Outbound 2030). It has 68882 FPU and a "solid-state disk" using standard 80ns SIMMs. The portable feeds power to the SIMMs to preserve the contents of the RAM disk. It also has a low-power "sleep" mode.

The Outbound System 2030 uses a 20MHz 68EC030 (non-PMMU) processor running at five times the speed of a Mac Classic and gives the option of adding a 68881 FPU.

The Outbound 2030E uses a 25MHz 68030 and optional 68882 FPU. The model 2030S has a 33MHz 68030 and an optional 68882 FPU. It can run virtual memory, although, as I've mentioned, this is not a good idea when using a portable's battery power.

Outbound makes a variety of peripherals for their notebooks including software that allows the portables to act as a SCSI drive for another Mac. Obviously Apple was impressed with this feature, because they included it in ROM with the PowerBook 100.

Outbound Notebooks versus PowerBooks

Outbound supported the Macintosh notebook market before Apple decided that there *was* a notebook market, but now that Outbound has Apple as a direct competitor, what will happen to the market for their portables?

Your decision regarding Outbound vs. Apple will have to be based on a number of factors. These should include software compatibility, expandability, price, speed, and "ergonomics" (things like the quality of keyboards and comfort factor of the track*bar* vs. the track*ball*). Like all purchase or upgrade decisions, the best choice here is the one that does what you want and does it as economically as possible.

Aztech Micro Solutions

Aztech Micro manufactures the Merida Upgrade Kit, a "repacking" solution for Mac 512ke, SE, or Classic computers. The upgrade consists of a new enclosure with a "universal" power supply, fan, speaker, cables and brackets as well as an accelerator, video board, and a full or dual-page display. The Merida upgrade sans monitor is about the price of a Mac Classic. The Merida case itself, for do-it- yourself upgrades, is less than half of the price of a Classic. On the whole, it's not a bad deal.

You can do the Merida SE upgrade yourself or send the board in to Aztech for installation. Aztech will solder the upgrade directly to a 512ke or Plus logic board, eliminating the loosening that can occur with a Killy clip upgrade. Other options that Aztech supports include shipping your entire 512ke/Plus/SE to them for the upgrade, exchanging your system for an upgrade, or trading in your Plus logic board for an SE board when buying the upgrade.

The SE upgrade uses the SE PDS slot, making it easy to do yourself. The Merida upgrade supplies a "pass-through slot" for an additional SE upgrade board installation.

The Merida B&W upgrade kit offers the following:

- Plastic enclosure with cables, brackets, fan, and speaker.

- 65-watt "universal" power supply.

- 25 or 33MHz 68030 processor.

- 68882 FPU.

- Option to upgrade Plus to SE logic board.

- 4, 8, or 16MB RAM upgrade with Connectix's Virtual.

- Choice of do-it-yourself or factory-installed upgrade.

- Full- or dual-page Panasonic, Sony, NEC, and Triam monitors supported.

- Color/grayscale upgrade with the Merida Color kit.

- Support for most third-party displays.

Aztech provides a color, speed, and virtual memory upgrade using a Mac LC system board core. The basic color system less monitor is roughly half of the price of a Mac LC. The Aztech Merida Color Upgrade consists of:

- A plastic enclosure, half as large as the standard Merida enclosure.

- A 65-watt "universal" power supply.

- A modified LC logic board upgrade/swap with Plus or SE board.

- 33, 40, and 50MHz accelerator options.

- 4MB of RAM.

- Supports 1.44MB FDHD drive.

- 33MHz+ upgrade includes support for 8-bit two-page color or gray-scale monitors.

- Internal 3$\frac{1}{2}$" bay for standard or removable devices.

- Internal 3$\frac{1}{2}$" bay for nonremovable devices.

- Full-page, dual-page, or large-screen color displays supported.

The Aztech color systems, like their monochrome cousins, can also be purchased as stand-alone units for significantly less than Apple systems with similar performance.

Aztech provides another neat product that solves some of the problems common to Mac LC and IIsi system units as well as Mac SE/30 upgrades. They call this the Galexa Upgrade. The Galexa LC/IIsi Upgrade includes:

- A taller enclosure top for additional expansion cards.

- An internal 5¼" hard drive bay for fixed or removable drives.

- An internal 3½" hard drive bay for fixed, removable, or optical drives.

- 65-watt "universal" power supply upgrade (3 times the 20-watt standard supply).

- Dual-slot adapter for the LC or IIsi '030 PDS slot.

- Optional accelerator or video board upgrade.

Mac SE/30 upgrades can be difficult because of the case height required to accommodate expansion cards. The Galexa SE/30 Upgrade solves this and some other problems. The upgrade includes:

- A taller Merida-style enclosure designed to accommodate additional expansion cards.

- One 3½" internal hard drive bay for nonremovable or removable hard drives.

- One 3½" internal nonremovable drive bay.

- A 65-watt "universal" power supply upgrade.

- A dual-slot adapter that supports most SE/30 PDS cards.

Aztech's basic Galexa upgrades are about one-third the price of the Apple units they're designed to upgrade.

I can't personally vouch for Aztech's system units as I haven't used one for an upgrade, but I am impressed with their "repacking" ideas.

Common problems with "in the case" Mac upgrades include a weak power supply, no fan, limited room for electronics and hard/floppy drive expansion, and limited memory expansion capability. Aztech has addressed and solved all of these problems. The LC/IIsi expansion solves the small case and anemic power supply problem. All in all, good ideas, but ideas whose economics you're going to have to evaluate for yourself.

MicroMac Technology

MicroMac Technology provides another repackaging system for Mac Plus, SE, and SE/30 logic boards.

The MicroMac Plus has a $12\frac{1}{2}$" × $12\frac{1}{2}$" × $2\frac{1}{2}$" low-profile modular case, worldwide power supply with fan, a full- or half-page video card with system battery and SE expansion slot, all cables, including an internal SCSI cable, and an optional full-page monitor.

MicroMac indicates that only the Mac Plus logic board and 800K drive are required. Apparently, there are no modifications to be done and the upgrade takes less than an hour (but I'd take this with a grain of salt if I were you).

The MicroMac SE and SE/30 upgrade system puts SE and SE/30 logic boards in a slimline case with monochrome and VGA video capability. It leaves the SE or SE/30 board free for more upgrades (however, an SE/30 upgrade board in a small case will need an adapter of some sort to allow expansion cards to lie flat).

The Plus upgrade system costs about as much as a basic Mac Classic. The SE-SE/30 upgrade system varies from this price level to about twice the price of a Classic.

Perspect

Perspect Systems offers the Perspect Nexus fx upgrade. This is a prime example of a "factory-installed" system upgrade for a Mac IIfx. You send Perspect your IIfx and they send you back a powerhouse. Perspect's upgrade speeds up the fx system clock, an occasionally chancy proposition. The upgrade is a CPU socket card with extra cache memory and a faster clock with a speed of 55MHz. The card is built by a company called Tech Noir (hmmm… "Black Tech"). The upgrade includes heat sinks to avoid CPU damage and is permanent—that is, it can't be removed easily. The IIfx upgrade has a one-year guarantee.

Sixty Eight Thousand

Sixty Eight Thousand Inc. should be located in Texas because they do things in a BIG way. In the Sixty Eight Thousand dash 30fx, they repack a Mac IIfx board in a tower case. Like the Perspect upgrade, this one is done entirely as a "factory job." You send Sixty Eight Thousand your IIfx and wait for the result. However, as I mentioned before, this kind of thing makes me a tad nervous.

The 30fx upgrade includes a 2′ locking tower case with a 250-watt power supply and two fans, a 50MHz accelerator, 8MB of 70ns RAM, a fast SCSI-2 card, and a number of device storage bays.

REPACKING YOUR OWN—BUILDING A PROJECT MAC

If none of the third-party options for a Mac repackaging job rings your chimes, you can build your own. You have a lot of choices to make when you go this route, but you have a lot of options, too.

The Case

Most Mac repackaging jobs use a PC case. The reason for this is that there are literally thousands of different models to choose from in all sizes and shapes, and their power supply and mounting equipment is fairly standard.

When you're choosing a project case, look for one that fits the Mac logic board you're upgrading. Mac 512ke, Plus, and SE boards will fit nicely in a low-profile PC case, but the SE/30, which mounts expansion cards vertically, will need the "head room" of a wide PC mini-tower case. You will need to modify the back end of the case for your Mac logic board expansion plugs, so you should pick a case that won't require you to cut some heavy-gauge steel to do this.

If you decide to modify a PC case for a modular Mac logic board, you'll have to be sure you have enough room for the board. You'll also have to plan on some major modifications to allow NuBus boards to mount properly in the PC case. A PC tower case is probably a good choice for modular Mac repacks. After a case is modified, you may want to design an RFI shield for the back of the case out of aluminum or thin sheet steel to prevent interference from the computer's electronics.

A standard PC 150- to 200-watt switching power supply should be more than adequate for a compact Mac repack, but a 200- to 250-watt supply is advisable for modular logic boards.

Your PC case should have a fairly large drive-mounting area and mounting brackets, at least two power connectors (for hard drives), a good cooling fan, and some plastic or nylon "standoffs" to use when mounting your Mac logic board (make sure the standoffs are the right size). You should make a template or at least have a complete set of measurements of your logic board when selecting a case. A template is advisable eventually, because you'll have to mark the PC case to drill and mount the standoffs. With the standoffs installed, the Mac logic board can be mounted in the case.

Power to the Logic Board

The logic board power cable for a Mac is not compatible with the power connectors (or connector) on a PC power supply, so some modifications will be required. These entail cutting the Mac logic board power cable and creating one cable end that can be plugged into the PC power supply plug. To build a connector that you can plug into a PC power supply, you'll need a couple of 6-pin polarized, locking header connectors to attach your Mac power connector to the PC. See Figure 11.2 for the details of wiring a Plus and SE-SE/30 power cable. Table 11.1 provides some modular Mac power cable pinouts. I can't help but consider the Mac LC a prime candidate for a repack. Apparently Aztech agrees with me—see the description of the color Merida upgrade, above. You'll need LC power cable pinouts for this, however.

Once your power cable has been built, you have the hardest part done: power to your Mac logic board.

Hard and Floppy Drives

The FDHD drive has taken over, and MS-DOS connectivity is a necessity in today's world. Having said that, I highly recommend that you mount a high-density *Mac* (the PC drives won't work) floppy drive in your project case. You can probably use a standard PC floppy bracket to mount the high-density 3½" drive in your case. You may have to modify a PC 3½" drive faceplate, or create your own from finished soft metal or plastic. Don't forget to create a hole for a drive ejection pin on the right side of the floppy slot.

Mounting a SCSI hard drive in a PC case is a simple matter of providing the appropriate bracket and face plate, which any knowledgeable PC vendor should be able to help you with, and plugging the drive into the PC power supply's standard four-pin "D" power connector.

Because both the floppy and hard drives will need long cables to reach the Mac logic board, you should choose Mac II or Quadra kits for the floppy signal and power cable and the hard drive 50-pin SCSI cable.

Video Connection Options

Mac logic boards with a PDS slot or on-board video can easily be upgraded for a large-screen external monitor with a video card, accelerator/video card, or compatible monitor cable. Older Macs or those without slots can generally be upgraded with a clip-on (Killy clip) package, often with an accelerator. This is another place that a Mac LC logic board could shine. Its onboard video is compatible with a number of low-priced VGA monitors.

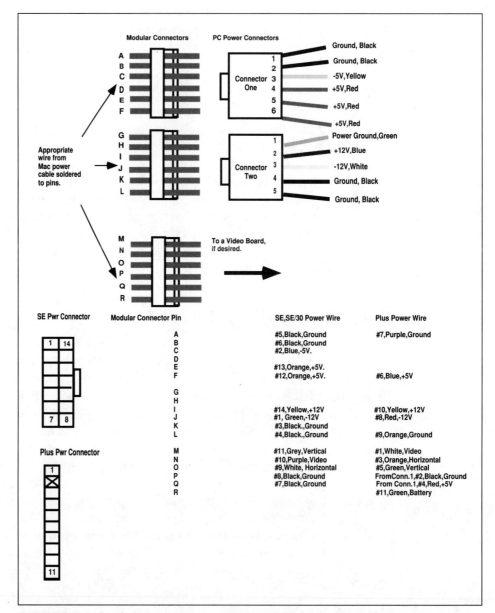

FIGURE 11.2: Compact Mac-to-PC power cable hookups

SIX SLOT (II, IIX, IIFX)	PIN NUMBER	THREE SLOT (IICX, IICI)	PIN NUMBER
+12V	1	+12V	1
+5V	2	+5V	2
+5V	3	+5V	3
+5V	4	+5V	4
+5V	5	Ground	5
+5V	6	Ground	6
Ground	7	Ground	7
Ground	8	−5V	8
Ground	9	−12V	9
Ground	10	/PFW	10
Ground	11		
Ground	12		
Unused	13		
−12V	14		
/PFW	15		

TABLE 11.1:   Modular Mac Power Cable Pinouts

Bob Brant, in his book *Build Your Own Macintosh and Save a Bundle* (Windorest Books, 1991), gives instructions for a nifty compact Mac video upgrade using the power/video cable's video signal and a PowerR connector. If you'd like to go this route, I recommend Bob's book.

Selecting Project Mac Peripherals

To complete your project Mac, you'll need to decide on some peripherals. Your video adapter may decide part of this for you. You can use this book to help you decide on the rest of the peripherals, however.

THE PROS AND CONS OF "DOING IT YOURSELF"

A project Mac allows you to build a lot of power into a custom Macintosh at a relatively low cost. However, with Apple dropping prices on state-of-the-art equipment daily, and used Mac equipment at reasonable prices becoming more common, the project Mac has lost the economic advantage it once had.

So what are the advantages of a project Mac? Well, once the hard parts—the power cable, floppy drive faceplate, and accelerator/video installation—are finished, the rest of the project essentially uses off-the-shelf components. A lot of these are PC components—very easy to find, cheap to purchase, and easy to sell. The project machine has lots of drive expansion, a strong steel case, and will support a variety of monitors. In addition, *all kinds* of power (it's going to be hard to strain the power supply *at all* with Mac components) will run cool because of its high-capacity fan.

The downside of a project Mac? Well, it's one of a kind, nonstandard, can't be used in any Apple upgrade, will be hard to resell—at least in one piece—and will require specialized repair work. You can send most project Mac components out for repair work and drop them back in, so that last concern is not a serious one. However, the resale argument is legit. Be prepared to resell your project as components.

BUILDING A MAC FROM COMPONENTS

Yet another way to get a high-powered Mac on the cheap is to build it from genuine off-the-shelf Apple components. Why do it this way? Won't it cost about twice as much?

Not necessarily. If you keep an eye out for sales of local enthusiasts' equipment or price deals in Mac magazines, you can gradually build up the parts you need to construct a Mac at a bargain price.

You may want to check local users groups, newspapers, bargain tabloids, and resellers such as Pre-Owned Electronics, Shreve Systems, and Maya Electronics for spare parts.

What to Look For

A modular Mac is the best choice for this kind of bargain-basement assembly project, and the Mac II series is the best of this bunch. Keep an eye out for Mac

II cases and II and IIx logic boards. Look for deals on old FDHD drives and old NuBus 8-bit video cards and compatible monitors.

 Make sure you have all the mounting hardware you'll need before beginning a bargain-basement Mac assembly project. Don't try to force-fit or jury-rig anything. The parts are available for a proper assembly. Get the right ones! Don't force any screws or connectors—make sure you have the right ones and put them in carefully.

Should You Do It?

Like all of the upgrades I've described so far, building a Mac from parts has to fit your economics. If you're not getting some high-quality hardware for much less than you'd pay for new or good used equipment, then maybe you should consider buying instead of building.

APPLE UPGRADES

If you don't want to build or buy a third-party upgrade, you might want to consider one of Apple's official "board swaps." Table 11.2 is taken from Apple's January 1992 "Macintosh Compatibility Chart" and will give you an idea of which official Apple upgrades are still being supported and what their official part numbers are.

Pre-Mac Plus to Plus

Apple no longer supports the upgrade from older Macs to the Mac Plus, but it is still possible to do by purchasing a Mac Plus case back and logic board from a Mac parts distributor such as Pre-Owned Electronics. You may also want to upgrade your power supply and add a fan. These upgrades are available from many accelerator board manufacturers such as Novy/Systech. You have to ask yourself if this is really worthwhile. If you want a bargain-basement machine and can get all the components *really* cheap, it may be.

Classic to Classic II

The Classic upgrade is relatively cheap and gets you up to 10MB of SIMM expansion, a 16MHz 68030 CPU, a ROM/FPU slot, sound input capability, and

MACINTOSH MODEL	LOGIC BOARD UPGRADE	PART NUMBER
Mac Classic	Mac Classic II logic board upgrade	M1545LL/A
Macintosh SE	Macintosh SE/30 logic board upgrade	M1102LL/A
Macintosh IIcx	Macintosh IIci logic board upgrade	M5816LL/A
Macintosh IIcx	Macintosh Quadra 700 logic board upgrade	M5950LL/A
Macintosh IIci	Macintosh Quadra 700 logic board upgrade	M5950LL/A
Macintosh II	Macintosh IIfx logic board upgrade	M0375LL/A
Macintosh IIx	Macintosh IIfx logic board upgrade	M0375LL/A

TABLE 11.2:   Apple logic board upgrades (from Apple's Macintosh Compatibility Chart)

potentially color/grayscale video. Should you do it? If you don't have a lot of money and want a low-cost upgrade, maybe. However, the Classic II is a dead-end machine. Its 16/32-bit bus and 16MHz processor are not very fast, memory expansion is limited, and it has no PDS slot to give you future upgrade potential. The pins on the surface-mounted 68030 chip are too close together to allow a Killy-clip upgrade. If you're still interested, the upgrade is Apple part number M1545LL/A.

SE to SE/30

The Mac SE to SE/30 upgrade is still the best deal going. For a Mac SE and some cash, you get a 16MHz 68030 CPU and a 16MHz 68882 FPU on a 32-bit bus, with eight SIMM slots, stereo and color capability, two ADB ports, and the heavy-duty power supply and fan that came with your SE. Apple's part number for this upgrade is M1102LL/A.

Mac II, IIx to IIfx

Upgrading a six-slot Mac II or IIx to a IIfx is probably not a bad deal, but it is still expensive. The IIfx is fast, but uses a poor implementation of DMA SCSI and is susceptible to damage if a special terminator is not used. The specialized SIMMs for the IIfx may become scarce in the near future. I guess if you have older Mac IIs, this is the only upgrade game in town, but you may want to look at purchasing a newer Mac instead. The II and IIx upgrades to IIfx are Apple part number M0375LL/A.

Mac IIcx, IIci to Quadra 700

The IIci is a nice, fast machine and easily upgraded, so I hate to recommend a board swap. However, the Quadra 700 is a screamer, so upgrading a IIci to a Quadra starts to look kind of attractive. The cost of the upgrade should be your main determining factor.

If you have a IIcx, the Quadra 700 upgrade is *very* attractive. It allows you to leapfrog the IIci upgrade and go straight to a state-of-the-art machine. The upgrade number is M5950LL/A.

Quadra 900 to 950

The Quadra 950 is an exciting, fast machine on the cutting edge of Mac hardware development. However, the upgrade costs for 900 owners are high for the advantage gained, at least at this point. I would recommend that Quadra 900 owners give this one a pass.

BRING ON THE CLONES

Because of the way Apple jealously guards the proprietary Macintosh design and firmware, clone makers have not had much success in the Mac market to date. Companies like Outbound, who have made deals with Apple, are exceptions.

NuTek and Mac ROMs

As I mentioned at the beginning of this chapter, a new and exciting player on the scene is NuTek, a company trying to produce a true clone of the Mac ROMs using entirely nonproprietary code and running the Motif windowing system. NuTek has had limited success running common Mac programs. But it's planning to produce a cheap, "low-end" 68030 clone for Mac beginners. If the NuTek ROMs, like the Phoenix BIOS on the PC, can successfully clone the Mac operating system, it could give the entire Mac market a boost. Since Apple is gradually moving into higher end, RISC-based systems, they may be inclined to let this happen.

If You Want to Take
a RISC, We'll Need a Quorum

A company called Quorum is now developing a Mac software emulator for RISC workstations. Given the power of RISC machines and the decline in workstation prices, this emulator may be the source of new Mac "clones."

IS THERE A REPACK IN YOUR FUTURE?

Repacking your Mac is an exciting, engrossing way to upgrade. If you've got the stomach for it, repacking will let you keep up with, and even leap ahead of, the leading edge of current Macintosh computing technology. If you're a computer hobbyist, repacking a Mac is *fun* and lets you get into the guts of the machine.

TROUBLESHOOTING

Problem	Cause	Solution
You get only a checkerboard, lines, or garbage on the video screen	Your video card or cable is loose	Tighten up the card or cables
Your drives won't power up	You may have bad connections or power supply	Check connections and the power supply
You've got a Sad Mac error after adding memory	You've installed the wrong memory, done it in the wrong order, or the SIMMs are loose	Check SIMMs and reinstall
"Flaky" behavior of some software	May be accelerator or control software incompatibility	Turn off accelerator or FPU patch, if installed

CHAPTER TWELVE

Printers and Plotters

The Mac and the ImageWriter I (a moderately fast 9-pin printer) were designed for compatibility from day one. Compact Macs have square pixels and 72 dpi (dot per inch) resolution, just like the ImageWriter I. When a Mac screen image is printed on an ImageWriter I, everything you see on the screen will appear the same way on the printed page—the first example of WYSIWYG (what you see is what you get). That helped make Macs easy to use, and also helped make them popular. Early users found that they could sit down, do a job, print it out, and get what they expected. No muss, no fuss, no setup strings, no weirdness, garbage, or half-printed pages. The ImageWriter II maintained WYSIWYG on the Mac and added higher speed, bidirectional printing, downloadable fonts, an enhancement slot for things like printer buffer memory, and color capability.

APPLE PRINTER HISTORY

The ImageWriters were and are good printers, but the printer that really made the Mac was the LaserWriter (see Figure 12.1). The laser's quality and speed were amazing. Taking advantage of them, Aldus PageMaker created a niche for the Mac and LaserWriter in corporate America. That niche was desktop publishing. It took some work from Aldus to convince Apple that the niche existed, but when Mac desktop publishing systems started selling like hotcakes, Apple got the idea.

Now the Mac is accepted not just as a desktop publishing platform, but as a CAD, graphics, and mapping workstation as well. With this popularity has come a host of printers and plotters for all manner of black-and-white and color Mac applications.

Early Macs used only *bitmapped fonts*, descriptions of type faces composed of dots. To get good printed results at a specific type size, you had to have that size in your Mac System folder. If you didn't have the type size you needed, the Mac would build it for you, resulting in an ugly, blocky typeface. QuickDraw printers, or printers controlled directly by the Mac, printed letter-quality documents only when the fonts used by Mac documents matched the printer's internal fonts. A typeface built by the Mac and sent to the printer would result in the same ugly output that the Mac produced on screen. It was a good idea to have the same fonts in your system folder as on your printer. Then, if your screen image was ugly, you knew what to expect from the printer.

A number of companies produced *page-description languages*, that defined type and graphics on a printed page by *primitives*—simple graphical

FIGURE 12.1:   A Mac IIci and Personal LaserWriter (photo courtesy of Apple Computer)

items like circles and lines. Adobe was one of these companies and its language, PostScript, was adopted by Apple for its laser printers. PostScript has now become the de facto standard page description language in the Apple world and is very strong in the PC world as well.

Using a PostScript laser printer with built-in fonts, you can build a page on your Mac using screen versions of the LaserWriter fonts present in your printer. No matter how ugly some of the odd font sizes might appear on screen, PostScript scales them to look sharp at any point size.

The next step was to produce printers with expansion memory and the ability to accept *downloadable fonts*. Downloadable fonts use graphic primitives to create font *outlines* (that's why they're also called *outline fonts*), which are downloaded to the printer. A Mac user with LaserWriter screen fonts and downloadable fonts can create a page using the screen fonts, and the Mac automatically downloads the equivalent outline fonts to the laser. Another alternative is to download fonts directly to laser memory before printing, using a utility. With downloadable fonts, Mac users were no longer saddled with only the PostScript fonts built into their laser printer.

Enter Adobe yet again with Adobe Type Manager (ATM). ATM, using PostScript technology, resizes fonts on the screen and sends these fonts to a printer, either QuickDraw or PostScript. Because ATM fonts are outline fonts, they look great on screen at any point size and just as great when they're printed. With ATM, WYSIWYG is back for Macs. ATM is especially useful for QuickDraw, or non-PostScript, printers, where it produces *great* type at a reasonable cost.

But we're not through yet. Apple, to compete with Adobe, added its own font technology, which comes standard with System 7. This is, of course, TrueType. TrueType outline fonts look just fine at any point size, on-screen or printed. TrueType gives Mac users a free or cheap upgrade to outline fonts without getting ATM. This is especially nice for new Mac users with Quick-Draw printers. However, TrueType fonts have displayed some incompatibilities with PostScript printers, TrueType is slower on both PostScript and QuickDraw printers, and ATM fonts are sharper at small sizes. Because of this, there's not much incentive for existing ATM users to make a change.

Moreover, Apple has decided to do an about-face by allowing Mac users to get a low-cost upgrade to ATM. Apparently, the next Mac operating system upgrade will incorporate ATM. What will happen to TrueType? It appears that it won't be developed further, but who knows?

In yet another creative installment of the Macintosh printing saga, Apple released the StyleWriter inkjet printer, which was meant to compete with Hewlett-Packard's DeskWriter. Then came the LaserWriter IIf and IIg with PostScript Level 2 and Apple's PhotoGrade image-enhancement technology, and the "moderately priced" LaserWriter NTR, with an ultra-fast RISC graphics processor.

You can reasonably expect that there will be newer and faster printers in Apple's future, probably incorporating newer, faster versions of PostScript and image-enhancement technologies. High-resolution printing for the Mac will continue to get cheaper, and Apple may release a new Mac graphics system based on Display PostScript, with QuickDraw compatibility.

A FONT PRIMER

Understanding printing and printers requires an understanding of fonts. A font is a design for a specific character set. Its size is measured in points, which equal 1/72 of an inch. Its spacing can be measured by *pitch* or the number of characters per inch.

In a *monospaced* font, all the characters are a single width. Examples are Monaco and Courier. A *proportional* font varies character width depending on the character. To see the difference, fully justify a paragraph of text in a proportional font and print it. Then change the font to Monaco or Courier and print it again. You see a bad case of "gaposis" in the latter, right? If you see this effect with your printer when you were expecting to see nice proportional text, you can bet that your printer substituted a monospaced font for what you had on screen—an example of *font substitution*. (Monospaced fonts, by the way, are useful for tables.)

I mentioned bit-mapped fonts above. For each font point size, bit-mapped font files have individual characters defined by specific bit patterns. If these are scaled up or down by the Mac, bit patterns are just doubled or halved. As mentioned earlier, this results in a very ugly screen font.

Outline fonts consist of a screen font and an outline file. The outline file is a PostScript description of the font's character shapes. When ATM is used, it needs the screen font and the outline file to build screen bitmaps of any size.

WHY ALL THE FOLDEROL ABOUT FONTS?

Why did I spend all this time on fonts when this chapter is about printers? Because the kind of printer you're using will influence what sort of font software you'll need in order to get the best printed output.

If you have only bitmapped fonts on your system, you'll get good-quality document output on QuickDraw printers by using the bitmapped font sizes available in the system folder. If you have a PostScript printer, you'll get best results by building documents with fonts that are available on the printer.

If you want the best screen and print output available, you should use scalable fonts. For users of System 6.07 or later, Apple's TrueType fonts are available via the TrueType upgrade kit. The kit contains a TrueType fonts and software disk and a TrueType printing tools disk. An init called TrueType is installed in the system folder and the TrueType fonts Helvetica, Times, Courier, and Symbol are installed using an updated version of Font/DA Mover. The printing tools disk includes updated drivers for the ImageWriter, StyleWriter, and LaserWriter. The TrueType upgrade kit is available from bulletin boards and Apple user groups.

Your other option is to obtain System 7 and get TrueType fonts as part of your new system installation. System 7 is available from user groups, or you can purchase Apple's upgrade package and get manuals and some toll-free phone support. TrueType will give you excellent screen and print output for your QuickDraw printer, but some problems have been reported in using it with PostScript printers.

Another scalable font option for Mac users—probably a better one, since Apple seems to be switching to it—is the original Adobe Type Manager package. ATM works fine with both System 6 and System 7, on both Quick-Draw and PostScript printers, with no hitches. Note the ATM package offered by Apple and Adobe for the cost of mailing. You can contact Adobe at 1-800-833-6687 to check on the status of the upgrade or obtain further information. ATM requires system 6.02 or later. On System 6, you have to install Adobe's icon, the ATM 68000 or 68020/68030 driver init, outline font files, and bit-mapped font files. You can install Adobe's screen fonts (the bitmapped font files) with Font/DA Mover, or just use the Font Porter utility included and drag the screen font suitcases into the system file. With System 7, you don't need Font Porter, but just drag the Bitmapped Font folder to the System file.

I highly recommend outline font packages for Mac users. They give you the WYSIWYG output that your machine is famous for on virtually any printer. The only drawback is memory. These packages need enough memory to build outline fonts and for font caching (at least in ATM). If you're running System 6 or 7 with multiple inits and programs in memory, you may need as much as 4MB to use ATM comfortably.

TYPES OF PRINTERS

Several types of printers are commonly used with Macs. These include 9- and 24-pin, or LQ, dot-matrix printers, inkjet printers, PostScript and QuickDraw laser printers, and specialized thermal printers. Let's look at each type in more detail.

Dot-Matrix Printers

The dot-matrix printhead is a vertical row (matrix) of steel pins that are "shot" at a ribbon and page by small electromagnetic coils (Figure 12.2). 9-pin dot-matrix printers use a small, inexpensive printhead with, obviously, 9 pins. These printers have relatively low-quality output, but are fast, tough, and can print multipart forms or invoices as well as continuous tractor-feed sheets and single sheets with a cut-sheet feeder.

Now that price wars have made inkjet printers affordable, there's not much point to buying a dot-matrix except for printing multipart forms or for data-logging on tractor-feed paper.

The ImageWriter II is a relatively fast, relatively good 9-pin printer, but it's costly. With appropriate printer drivers, you can choose from a list of much cheaper PC printers that includes, literally, thousands of candidates. If you go the PC printer route, you'll probably want a printer that is Epson FX and/or MX compatible. You should look for printers with a paper path that's as straight and simple as possible. This will reduce the potential for paper jams. Printer tractor feeds should be adjustable for wide or odd-shaped sheets, and should feed easily and repeatedly without jamming. You should look for a bottom-feed or rear-feed tractor. You will want a printer with a simple, front-mounted control panel and

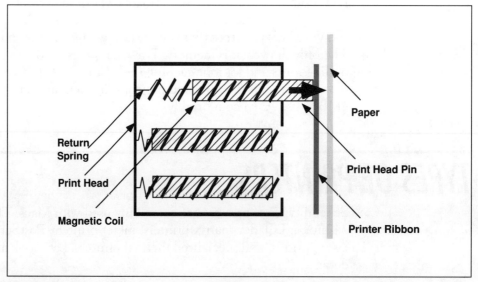

FIGURE 12.2: How a dot-matrix printer works

front-mounted DIP switches for setting preferences. In addition to driver software, you'll need a third-party serial-to-parallel port cable. These are sold by Orange Micro (the Grappler series) and GDT Toolworks with their PowerPrint package (Figure 12.3). Some dot-matrix printers have a serial port, and you may be able to connect to them with a Mac Plus-to-ImageWriter I cable.

PC 9-pin printers from Citizen, Epson, CItoh, or Panasonic are all good choices. A better choice might be one of the Mac-compatible ImageWriter substitutes: the Olympia NP60APL or Seikosha SP2000.

LQ (letter quality) dot-matrix printers have resolutions of 360 × 360 dots per inch, more than the Apple LaserWriter. These printers are ideal where

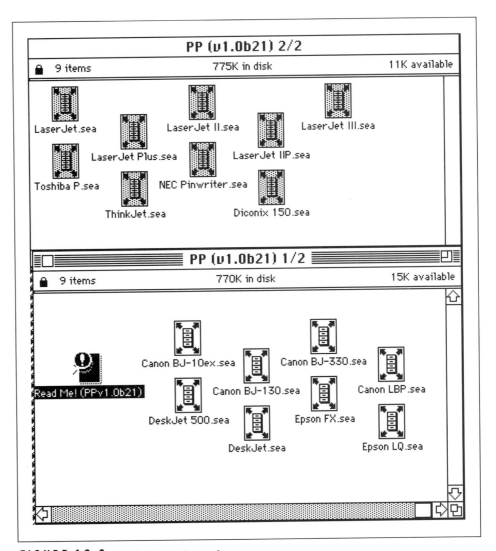

FIGURE 12.3:   The PowerPrint drivers

letter quality is required for forms or mass mailings. Epson LQ emulation should be available for whatever printer you select. Try Epson, NEC, or Citizen for good-quality LQ printers.

Apple builds no 24-pin or LQ printers. The ill-fated ImageWriter LQ was discontinued some time ago and I don't recommend it as a used-equipment purchase.

When looking at LQ printers, use the same evaluation process as for 9-pin printers. Good paper-feed mechanisms and the paper path are crucial for efficient and trouble-free operation.

Dot-matrix printer speeds are measured in characters per second. Slow printers operate at speeds less than 40 cps, intermediate printers at 40–110 cps, and fast ones at speeds greater than 110 cps.

Both 9-pin and 24-pin LQ printers are prone to printhead problems, so treat the printhead with care. Clean it as necessary according to the manufacturer's instructions. Lubricate the printer only as indicated by the manufacturer. If your printer seems to need lubrication other than what you can give it, take it into the shop for service. Keep your printer ribbons in good shape, and don't re-ink them too many times. Also, use a good-quality ink. A damaged or gummed-up printhead will cost a lot more than you save from re-inking. Clean the printer to keep it free of paper dust, which can get into the mechanism and cause problems.

Installing a dot-matrix printer on your Mac can be as simple or as complicated as you want to make it. Before you choose a dot-matrix printer, be sure you can get Mac printer drivers that will give you all of the printer's special features. This includes things like page control, high-quality printing, and color. You'll need a compatible cable. To get the best speed and compatibility with most PC-compatible dot-matrix printers, you'll need a Mac serial-to-parallel cable. If your printer accepts a serial cable, you may be able to connect it to your Mac with a Mac Plus-to-ImageWriter I serial cable. This has a mini-DIN 8 connector at one end and a standard DB-25 RS-232C connector at the other. Orange Micro's Grappler serial/parallel cable and driver package and GDT SoftWorks' PowerPrint drivers and ParaLink cable will work well with most Epson-compatible 9- and 24-pin printers.

The ImageWriter II uses a LocalTalk cable, like Apple LaserWriters, with a mini-DIN 8 connector at each end. All that's necessary for this setup is a copy of Apple's drivers, provided with every copy of System software they sell. If you want to get better ImageWriter control and faster printing, try GDT Softworks' BetterWriters package.

If you want the best print quality with your dot-matrix print jobs, I highly recommend that you install TrueType, System 7, or Adobe Type Manager.

Inkjet Printers—Cheap Lasers?

Inkjet printers offer laser-quality printing at dot-matrix prices. Color inkjets are a high-quality option for color printing that's significantly cheaper than most high-resolution color printers.

Inkjet cartridges come as an ink bladder and printhead in one unit. The printhead has a number of nozzles with built-in heating units that, when activated, vaporize some printer ink, creating a bubble of ink which sprays onto the paper. Color inkjets have cartridges with red, green, and blue ink reservoirs. The knock against color inkjets is that the blacks produced by a combination of the three colors lean toward brown and are a little "muddy." However, if you use a black-ink cartridge, the blacks look great—and you can switch cartridges on a single document, using the black cartridge for black type and the color cartridge for color sections.

Inkjets, like dot-matrix printers, are QuickDraw devices. This means that they receive all of their printing instructions from the Macintosh CPU and its built-in QuickDraw graphics "toolkit."

Most Mac inkjet drivers, like lasers, compile a print job a page at a time before sending it to the printer. Therefore, laser and inkjet print speeds are both measured in pages per minute. Most lasers produce 4–8 pages per minute, whereas inkjets print about 1–2 pages per minute. Converting pages per minute to characters per second for an average page can be done with the formula

$$\text{ppm} \times 2000 \text{ char. per page}/60 \text{ sec. per min.} = \text{cps}$$

For an inkjet speed of 1 ppm this translates to 33 cps and for 2 ppm, 66 cps. Inkjets in character mode, using built-in fonts, are *considerably* faster than this. GDT's drivers, and some public domain utility programs, allow you to use HP DeskJets in character mode. If you create a document with proportional fonts and then print it out with a DeskJet's monospaced fonts, however, you'll see the same sort of "gaposis" I described previously.

The Apple StyleWriter prints with a resolution of 360×360 dots per inch, roughly one and a half times greater than HP DeskWriter/DeskJet resolution of 300 dpi. Don't be too impressed, though—your eye probably won't be able to tell the difference. And print times are correspondingly greater.

Unlike lasers, which use electrostatic charge to glue "ink" to a page and a fuser to fasten it, inkjet print tends to "spread" slightly as the ink soaks into paper fibers. This degrades inkjet print quality slightly. High-quality hard-surfaced paper reduces this effect to a minimum, and special clay-coated paper prevents it entirely, resulting in laser-quality print from an inkjet printer. Much has been made of the degradation in print quality that results from inkjet print spreading, but for normal work with reasonable quality paper, you'll need a magnifying glass to see any print degradation.

The other knock against inkjets is the price of the ink cartridges, a legitimate concern. Inkjet cartridge cost per ream (500 sheets) of paper is roughly $22.10 versus 50–88 cents for dot-matrix printer ribbon. Refill kits for HP DeskWriters/DeskJets and Apple's StyleWriter are now available for $9.50 each (see Figure 12.4). Using these will cut inkjet ink costs per ream of paper approximately in half. This is roughly the cost of laser-printed sheets. Inkjet printers, like lasers, are single-sheet devices and cannot use tractor-feed paper. Unlike dot-matrix printers, inkjets do not exert any pressure on a printed page and so cannot print multipart forms.

The most common inkjets used with Macs are built by Hewlett-Packard and Apple. HP printers include the DeskWriter and DeskJet, which have the same print engine but slightly different controller electronics. The Apple Style-Writer uses a Canon BubbleJet print engine. Hewlett-Packard also produces the 180-dpi PaintWriter and PaintWriter XL, as well as the newer 300-dpi Desk-Writer/DeskJet C color printers. Sharp produces the JX-730 color inkjet printer and Tektronix builds the ColorQuick inkjet.

Generally, HP printers with the "Writer" suffix are Mac-specific and "Jets" are PC printers. The DeskJets (Figure 12.5) were once cheaper than DeskWriters, even including the cost of purchasing driver software and a cable, but price wars have pushed the DeskWriter cost so far down that it's now a better deal. It costs the same as a DeskJet, but you don't have to spend an extra $100 on conversion software and hardware. The DeskJet still enjoys a resale advantage because it includes serial and parallel ports, making it PC compatible.

FIGURE 12.4:   HP DeskWriter/DeskJet cartridge and refill kit

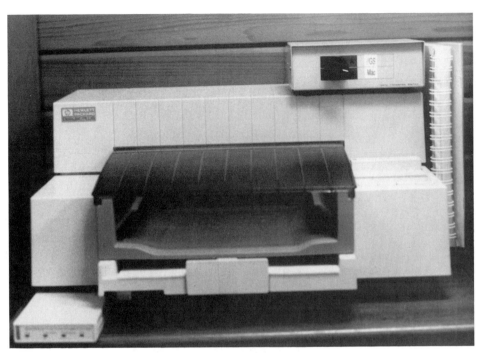

FIGURE 12.5: An HP DeskJet Plus with a serial switchbox

Installing Mac-specific inkjets is a breeze. They already come with cables, drivers, and often font packages. The StyleWriter and DeskWriter can both use Apple LocalTalk cables. You'll hear about how slow the StyleWriter is with Apple's drivers, and it's true. However, you can speed up the printer with GDT Softworks' BetterWriters package.

Your Mac can use HP DeskJet and Canon BubbleJet inkjet printers if you install cable and driver packages from GDT Softworks, Orange Micro, or Insight Development Corp.

Like dot-matrix printers, inkjets benefit from scalable font packages. With their 300-dpi resolution and scalable fonts, inkjets are great high-quality print packages.

Lasers

Laser printers are some of the highest-quality Macintosh print devices, outside of computer Linotronic imagesetters. Laser printers use *xerographic* technology, as in the photocopier. In a laser printer, an image is "written" with a laser (surprise!), liquid crystal shutter (LCS), or light-emitting diode light source to a light-sensitive, negatively charged drum. The light source creates areas of positive charge where it hits. The drum rolls through a reservoir of negatively charged toner, picking up the "picture" on the drum. Laser copier paper is drawn into the printer under a *corona wire*, which gives the paper a positive charge. The positive charge transfers toner from the drum to the paper. The laser paper then passes between heated rollers, fusing the toner onto the page.

A laser consists of a controller board and a print engine. The most commonly used and reliable print engines are the Canon SX and LBP-SX units, with an estimated life of 300,000 pages. Most major laser manufacturers, including Apple, use the Canon engine.

Because laser printers compile and print one page at a time, they are true "page printers." Whether a page is nearly blank or completely filled with a graphic, the printer still has to compile the entire page before it is printed. This is why laser printer speeds are measured in pages per minute, or ppm. Lasers with the original Canon engine print at 4 ppm. Current "average" lasers print at a true speed of 6 ppm, though they are rated at 8 ppm. High-speed, high-output lasers with RISC processors can print at rates of up to 18 (text) ppm.

Using the equation I gave in the inkjet section above, laser ppm speeds translate to cps as follows:

PPM	CPS
4	134
8	267
10	334
18	600

The fastest print speeds don't apply at higher print resolutions. Lasers printing at 600 and 1000 dpi have considerably more information to deal with than at standard 300-dpi resolution. High print resolutions have almost photographic quality. That's why, combined with PostScript, high-resolution lasers are good choices for print shops. Like high-resolution monitor cards, hi-res lasers have to move and process an incredible amount of information. Because of this, most modern hi-res lasers use blazingly fast RISC processors.

A number of laser manufacturers, including Apple, have introduced laser-enhancement technologies. These improve on standard laser printing technology by making documents seem much sharper than their rated resolution. Apple's version, called *PhotoGrade*, was introduced with the LaserWriter IIf and IIg. PhotoGrade uses modulated laser pulses to change the size of the dots that make up a laser-printed graphic. This is similar to a technique called *halftoning*, used when printing graphics in magazines and newspapers, to simulate grayscales. Apple also provides a technology called *FinePrint* with the IIf and IIg that smooths the jagged edges of printouts. Hewlett-Packard uses a similar technique, called Resolution Enhancement Technology (RET), on its newest printers.

Mac lasers come in two forms—QuickDraw and PostScript. QuickDraw printers, as I mentioned, rely on your Macintosh to compile a page and send it to the printer. QuickDraw lasers have the same engines as PostScript lasers in most cases, but they are slowed down by your Mac's compilation time. Faster Macs will produce faster print jobs with these printers. QuickDraw lasers are generally *significantly* cheaper than PostScript lasers because they don't include Adobe's PostScript licensing fee and the cost of PostScript page compilation hardware. Low-priced QuickDraw lasers are produced by GCC, Okidata, and Hewlett-Packard. GCC provides its own drivers with the PLP II and PLP IIS, which can be upgraded to PostScript. HP, and Okidata in HP emulation, can be used with cables and driver packages from GDT SoftWorks, Orange Micro, and Insight Development (MacPrint 1.3).

In attempts to make QuickDraw lasers simulate PostScript, several companies offer generic PostScript emulator packages. Some examples are CAI's Freedom of Press and Freedom of Press Light, QMS UltraScript and UltraScript Plus, and TeleTypesetting's T-Script. Keep in mind that these are slow, even on a fast machine, though their speed may be improved by adding an FPU to your Mac. Also remember that because these packages are emulators, they typically don't work as well as true PostScript printers. Graphics professionals probably shouldn't mess with them.

Figure 12.6 shows Apple's older LaserWriters, Personal LaserWriter LS, Personal LaserWriter NT, LaserWriter II NT, and LaserWriter II NTX. The LaserWriter II NT and II NTX, which used a 68020 print engine, have now been superseded by Apple's latest IIf, IIg, and NTR lasers. The LS and NT have been retained. The LS, Apple's lowest priced laser, is a QuickDraw model. The LS uses a Canon LX engine at 300 dpi and includes TrueType. The printer is (supposedly) compatible with ATM, uses page-compression technology, and connects to the Mac via a SCSI interface.

The LaserWriter NT is a PostScript printer with a 12MHz 68000 processor and 2MB onboard, expandable to 8MB. It uses a 4 ppm Canon engine. The IIf and IIg use PostScript 2 and PhotoGrade image enhancement technology. The LaserWriter NTR, released with the Mac LC II, has a 16MHz AMD Graphics RISC chip, PostScript Level 2, up to 4MB of memory, and HP emulation. Table 12.1 lists the features of these Apple lasers.

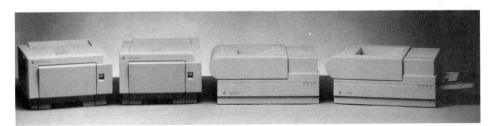

FIGURE 12.6: Apple's "older" lasers. Left to right, Personal LaserWriter LS, Personal LaserWriter NT, LaserWriter II NT, and LaserWriter II NTX (photo courtesy of Apple Computer)

PRINTER	RESOLUTION	CONTROLLER	ENGINE	SPEED	POSTSCRIPT	RESOLUTION ENHANCEMENT	MEMORY
Personal LaserWriter LS	300 dpi		Canon LBP-LX	4 ppm	No	No	512K, Compression
Personal LaserWriter NT	300 dpi	12MHz 68000	Canon LBP-LX	4 ppm	Level 1	No	2 to 8MB
LaserWriter IIf	Enhanced 300 dpi	20MHz 68030	Canon SX-8	8 ppm	Level 2	PhotoGrade, FinePrint	2 to 32MB
LaserWriter IIg	Enhanced 300 dpi	25MHz 68030	Canon SX-8	8 ppm	Level 2	PhotoGrade, FinePrint	5 to 32MB
LaserWriter NTR	300 dpi	16MHz Am29005 RISC	Canon LBP-LX	4 ppm	Level 2	No	1 to 4MB

TABLE 12.1:   Features of Current Apple Laser Printers

A number of companies provide high-speed, Apple-compatible Post-Script laser printers that are often significantly cheaper than Apple lasers. These include QMS, Texas Instruments with their upgradable TurboLaser series, NEC with the SilentWriter, and Hewlett-Packard's LaserJet IIIsi.

Laser Motherboard Upgrades

The main way to upgrade a laser printer is by swapping the laser logic board. Xante makes the Accel-a-Writer II replacement board with the Phoenix Page PostScript clone, 600×600 dpi resolution, and a RISC processor. The Accel-a-Writer II replaces the logic board in Apple's old LaserWriter II. Xante also makes upgrade boards for the LaserWriter, LaserWriter Plus, and Personal LaserWriter LS and NT. The downside of this process is the economics of the upgrade, specifically how much life remains in the old laser engine. CE Software's DiskTop will allow you to determine how many pages have been generated by a printer engine and how much "life" remains. It may be a good acquisition if you're evaluating an old laser printer for an upgrade.

Thermal Printers

Thermal printers use a high-resolution printhead with electrically headed pads instead of pins in conjunction with a wax-based ribbon. Thermal printers are usually used for PostScript color separations, and come with a high price tag.

Dye-Sublimation Printers

Dye-sublimation, like thermal printers, are normally used these days for producing color separations and come with PostScript interpreters. In dye-sublimation, dry dye is transformed to gas which is fused to paper to produce a continuous layer of color.

Color Prepress

Color prepress is the process by which computer print files are transformed into publishable color separations. Initially, a file is built in a publishing program using high-quality graphics from scanned images processed with a program such as Adobe Photoshop, or graphics created with a draw program such as Aldus Freehand. The files created are modified to create some overlap between colors—a technique known as trapping, which allows for irregularities in the print process. Before any print files are produced, the color files are calibrated, using RGB (red-green-blue), CMYK (cyan-magenta-yellow-black) values, or the newer international CIE color values used by Adobe in PostScript Level 2. This ensures that the ink mixtures used for printed finals will accurately match computer screen graphics. A variety of Mac color hardware calibrators are available, along with tables showing RGB, CMYK, and CIE color combinations. A number of Mac programs use Pantone color calibration for separations, but these are not considered particularly consistent.

When the color output is ready, it can be sent to a PostScript color device for proofing. If the file is adequate at this point, a service bureau can prepare color separations for printing.

If you're considering getting seriously involved in color prepress, you'll need a fast 68030 or 68040 Mac with a numeric coprocessor. You'll also need Aldus PageMaker, QuarkXPress, or Frame Technology's FrameMaker, depending on the size of the job. A PostScript draw program, such as Aldus FreeHand, and an image-preparation program, such as Adobe Photoshop, are essential, as is a PostScript color output device for preliminary proof output.

EVERYTHING YOU EVER WANTED TO KNOW ABOUT PLOTTERS

Plotters are used to output engineering and scientific plans, schematics, blueprints, and maps. They are more precise than printers and can produce graphics of the size required for the above uses.

Plotters are available in pen or electrostatic models and in flatbed, rollerbed, or continuous-roll formats. Pen plotters use a pen controller that gets plotter pens from a carousel and "draws" an image on the plotter. Pen plotters come in flatbed models, generally for small paper sizes in a desktop format, and in rollerbed models. Rollerbed plotters use a large-sized paper draped over a roller and move it back and forth, drawing on it with a pen moving from left to right.

Electrostatic plotters plot faster, have fewer moving parts, and commonly come in continuous-roll models for use as network plotters.

Plotters are designed to handle paper sizes A to E, $8^{1}/2$" to 36×48". Plotter speeds vary from 8–32 inches per second and accuracies vary from .4–.1%.

Common plotters are designed to work with the Hewlett-Packard Graphics Language (HPGL).

When you are selecting a plotter for your Mac, have a look at plotter driver packages that are available for your preferred plotter. You may want to look into Plottergeist, a full-featured plotter driver package for Macs.

PRINTER INTERFACES

There are three commonly used printer interfaces for Mac printers—serial, parallel, or SCSI. The most common is serial, which is found on both the printer and the AppleTalk ports. If you use a PC printer on a Mac, you usually need a serial-to-parallel interface such as the Grappler or Paralink.

Serial Interfaces

The Mac serial port is fast and "intelligent." It can communicate with the Mac, communicating print progress and interruptions, such as out-of-paper problems. In AppleTalk mode, the port can transmit data at up to 57,600 baud.

Serial ports transmit data one bit at a time. Because of this, they require fewer data wires and thinner cables. And, because there is less possibility of interference, cables can be longer than parallel cables.

Parallel Interfaces

The PC parallel port is not "intelligent" and does not communicate with the host computer. However, it is often the fastest data port on a PC (PC serial ports are commonly limited to 19,200 baud).

Parallel ports transmit data eight bits at a time over eight data lines. There is also a strobe line that tells a printer to look for data, an "ack" line that acknowledges receipt of data, and a ground line.

SCSI Interfaces

A number of Mac printers use the SCSI interface. They are subject to the same numbering and termination constraints as any other SCSI devices.

PRINT SPOOLERS—A BIG TIMESAVER

I've mentioned print spoolers and their advantages previously in this book, but it's time to bring them up again. If you have a large file to be sent to a printer, spoolers will send it to memory and then to a printer while you do something else. The downside of printer spoolers is the memory they use and the CPU slowdown they cause. But the increase in work time is worth it.

Spoolers available to Mac users include the Grappler Spooler, included with Grappler printer drivers, SuperLaserSpool from Fifth Generation Systems, compatible with the GDT drivers, and Apple's PrintMonitor and the System 7 spooler, used with Apple lasers. An upcoming version of GDT's PowerPrint will have a built-in spooler.

PRINTER PAPER AND YOU

The type of printer you buy will influence your paper requirements, and the paper you use will determine the quality of your printouts. Table 12.2 lists the common printer paper sizes. The quality of paper is commonly expressed as weight; heavier and thicker denotes higher quality. Rag content is an important measure of paper quality. Higher is generally better. Special clay-coated paper is available for the best print quality on lasers or inkjets. Be sure to note the arrow on paper packages. This is the "good side," the side you should print on.

Tractor-feed paper is available with a number of perforation types, including "razor cut" for a clean edge without tractor feed appearance.

NAME	SIZE
Executive	$7\frac{1}{4}" \times 10\frac{1}{2}"$
Letter	$8\frac{1}{2}" \times 11"$
Legal	$8\frac{1}{2}" \times 14"$
A4	210×297 mm
Monarch	$3.875" \times 7\frac{1}{2}"$
Business	$4.125" \times 9\frac{1}{2}"$
DL	110×220 mm
C5	162×229 mm
Computer	$11" \times 14"$

TABLE 12.2: Common Printer Paper Sizes

CHOOSING YOUR PRINTER OR PLOTTER

When you're evaluating a printer, first decide how you'll be using it. Do you need a continuous data record, or plan to print multipart forms or do mass mailings? If so, a dot-matrix printer may be a good choice.

- Do you want laser-quality output at a low price in a relatively quiet printer? In that case an inkjet printer may be your best choice.
- Do you need high-quality print, fast output, and low price, but not PostScript? Then opt for a QuickDraw laser.
- Do you need speed, high-quality output, and PostScript? Then go for one of the PostScript lasers.
- Finally, if you need color, you can opt for the PostScript thermal or dye-sublimation color printers, or the less expensive QuickDraw color inkjets.

Table 12.3 is a printer comparison table to help you with your choices.

WORKGROUP PRINTERS, HOW TO CHOOSE AND USE 'EM

Deciding which network printers to buy is no different than choosing an individual printer—you should begin by considering how they'll be used. QuickDraw printers are suitable as single station devices, whereas fast, high-output PostScript printers can be used by large workgroups. Slower lasers, plotters, or thermal printers can be used locally by smaller workgroups. Plotters can be used most effectively by a drafting, engineering, or mapping department. Thermal printers might be the ticket for a marketing, advertising, or graphics department.

PRINTER TYPE	RESOLUTION	CPI	PPM	LIFE SPAN	SUPPLY COST/REAM	PRINTER COST/REAM
9-Pin Dot-Matrix	160 dpi	28–150	.5–2.7	30,000 pages	$3.58–7.36	$2.92
24-Pin Dot-Matrix	360 dpi	90–150	1.9–2.7	30,000 pages	$3.58–7.36	$2.92
Inkjet	300 to 360 dpi	28–112	.5–2	100,000 pages	$25.08–32.10	$3.38
Laser	300 to 1200 dpi	220–440	4–8	160,000–600,000 pages	$12.50–18.00	$2.75

TABLE 12.3:   Comparing Printers

IN SUMMARY

Tailor your printer choices to your anticipated budget and requirements, remembering that you don't have to pay through the nose for high-quality output any more. The prices of QuickDraw and PostScript lasers are coming down daily. While dot-matrix printers have moved into the low end of the printer spectrum, they are still important for companies with point-of-sale systems that print to multipart forms. Inkjet printers are becoming popular as high-quality individual workstation and home QuickDraw printers. Color prepress and color devices continue to receive more attention and will continue to rise in popularity with more powerful Macs available to handle them.

TROUBLESHOOTING

Problem	Cause	Solution
File set to printer, but no output	Printer not selected in Chooser	Go to Chooser and select the printer
Font output on printer is not what you selected	Font substitution may be occurring	Make sure correct fonts are available
Print output is slow	Not using optimum printer setup	Consider faster printer drivers or Paralink cable if possible
Can't print a PostScript graphic	Running out of page-compilation memory	Install more printer memory
Jamming problems on a dot-matrix printer	Paper path skewed or tractors incorrectly set	Adjust tractors and rollers; leave one tractor loose
Print on dot-matrix printer too light	Incorrect paper thickness	Adjust paper thickness
No Apple LaserWriter test page; test LED is blinking or stays on	Possible problem with logic board	Take printer in for repair

CHAPTER THIRTEEN

Telecommunications

What's the point of hooking your Mac up to the phone lines? My experience since I started telecommunicating suggests all kinds of reasons.

I've used my modem to download shareware and freeware programs that would have cost me thousands of dollars to buy as commercial software. I've downloaded Apple software upgrades shortly after they were released and patches written by Mac users that solve a multitude of system problems. I've found text files and HyperCard stacks that cover all kinds of interesting topics, computer-related and otherwise. I've helped my kids with schoolwork by getting information online that they couldn't find elsewhere. I've solved hardware and software problems by consulting with users who'd been through them already and had solutions. I've contacted software and hardware manufacturers for product and upgrade information. I've made a long-distance call via a local gateway for the cost of a local call. I've sent data files across the city without having to jump in my car. Finally, I've had a chance to exchange ideas and information with other users from across the city and the continent.

Sound interesting?

PC TELECOM HISTORY

One of the earliest recorded uses of digital devices to "get online" is the illicit "blue box" business run by Steve Wozniak, the infamous telecom pirate Captain Crunch, and marketer Steve Jobs. The blue box produced the numeric tones used by telephones and allowed the user to make long-distance calls without paying. This may be where PC telecommunications got an early unsavory reputation.

The earliest 300-baud modems used a telephone adapter, two rubber cups that a telephone headset fit into. You may still be able to find a few of these in some collection of archaeological relics. If you do, bury them again. These devices were better than nothing, but not much. The phone always picked up a lot of room noise because the cups never sealed properly. This could cause problems when logging on to a remote computer, or cause loss of the signal once you logged on. At this point, most modems were used to access mainframe computers.

Racal-Vadic introduced the first 1200-baud modem in the early 70's, followed by the introduction by Bell Labs of a device using the internally developed 201A standard. Hayes pioneered the use of intelligent modems with built-in commands, called the AT command set. This was gradually adopted by all manufacturers, some of whom added their own extensions. Old modems, supposedly AT-compatible, may have some problems with modern telecommunications programs that use a full implementation of the AT command set.

By this time a number of programmers had written bulletin board software for microcomputers, and local computer bulletin board systems (BBSs) were begining to spring up. Many were run by local computer clubs. Methods of transferring programs by modem were developed using *transfer protocols*. The first popular transfer protocol was the *Christiansen Protocol*, or *Xmodem*.

When the 2400-baud modem became widely accepted, it implemented a standard developed by a group known as the (are you ready for this?) Comité Consultatif International Télégraphique et Téléphonique, or CCITT. That standard is known as V.22bis ("bis" stands in French for second, as opposed to "ter," for third). By now, the basic AT command set is also standard and built into any modem.

Newer modems operate at 9600 and 14,400 baud using "hardware compression and error correction" schemes. Fax modems, modems which can also send faxes, are also becoming quite popular.

Where will it end? Modems are approaching the limits of normal telephone line speeds and for maximum reliability must use special clean data lines. Even these are being tested to their limits. Widespread use of fiber optic cable and other high-speed data technologies will allow modems to step up to the next level of performance.

HOW MODEMS DO WHAT THEY DO

Modem, as you may have heard, stands for MOdulator-DEModulator. A telephone uses a transducer to convert a human voice into an analog signal. A modem performs much the same function for digital data. The modem generates a continuous, fixed-frequency, audible tone called a *carrier signal* which is detected by another modem. Digital data from your computer is converted to an analog signal by the modem and added to the carrier, in a process called modulation. The demodulation part, naturally, involves stripping the analog signal from the carrier and converting it to digits for the receiving computer.

HOW FAST ARE MODEMS?

Modem speeds in common use today are 1200, 2400, 9600, and 14,400 baud (*baud* refers to *bits per second*, or *bps*). But even if you know that a modem can pump 14,400 bits per second over the telephone lines, determining how much data it's actually sending is a little more complicated.

Modems send data as seven- or eight-bit *characters*. All basic ASCII data can be described in seven bits. To these seven bits a modem adds a start bit and one or two stop bits. The modem can also add a parity bit. The start bit and stop bits mark the beginning and end of a character. The parity bit is for a simple form of error checking. If a character sent has an odd number of bits, a parity bit will be added to make it even. When you do a little telecommunicating, you'll hear a lot about data bits, stop bits, and parity. Most bulletin board systems use eight data bits, one stop bit and no parity. Older mainframes often use seven data bits, one or two stop bits, and a parity bit.

The result of all this is that modem character transmission rates are roughly equal to the baud rate divided by nine or ten (the average bits per word). If you are sending files using hardware or software error checking, something called a checksum is added to the total, slowing things down further. With a "dirty" phone line, data losses and resends slow the data transmission speed even more.

LET'S SHAKE HANDS

Before two modems can transfer data, they have to establish contact, or "shake hands." Computer handshaking is a way of sending control and acknowledgment signals between two Macs connected by modem. Macs typically use one of two handshaking protocols—*software* and *hardware handshaking*. In the past, Macs have used a software handshaking protocol called *XON/XOFF*. XON/XOFF flow control matches the speed of one modem to another by padding the data stream with the characters "DC1" and "DC3," or send and pause. Modems up to 2400 baud should work fine with the standard Mac modem cable and software handshaking.

Newer modems pass data faster than software handshaking can handle. They require a cable that supports hardware handshaking. Hardware handshaking uses a special cable with CTS (Clear To Send) and RTS (Request To Send) pins connected. An RTS signal tells a remote modem to stop sending data. A CTS signal tells the modem to resume sending.

THE RS-232C "STANDARD"

The RS-232C serial standard, like SCSI, is nonstandard. Different versions of the serial plug can have different pins present or connected. RS-232C defines 25 data lines, though this many are rarely needed.

Apple's two Mac serial ports are compatible with RS-232 and RS-422. The "standard" serial plug on an external modem is a DB-25, or 25-pin plug connector. A Mac-to-generic modem cable has a mini-DIN 8 plug on one end, for the Mac's serial port, and a DB-25 plug on the other (see Figure 13.1).

SOFTWARE COMPRESSION AND ERROR CHECKING

By the time Mac users had begun sending files by computer, Apple II and PC users were experienced telecommunicators. They routinely compressed files with software utilities before transmitting them, and used software error-checking protocols to ensure that the files were received intact and error-free. Mac programmers soon developed their own software for file compression and adopted standard error-checking protocols.

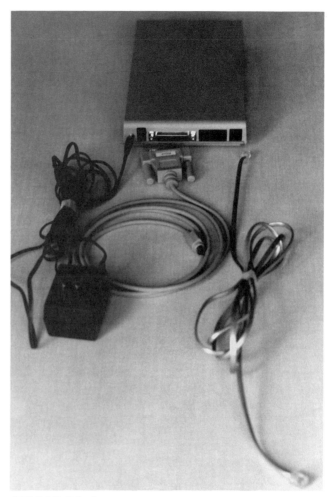

FIGURE 13.1:   A Mac modem cable, power supply, and phone line

File compression works its magic by removing redundancy from files. Often-repeated bytes, for example the words "and" and "it," are replaced by one byte and a code. Text files and graphics with large single-color areas benefit most from file compression.

Two of the most commonly used shareware utilities for telecommunications file compression on Macs are Compact Pro by Bill Goodman and Stuffit Classic by Raymond Lau. Stuffit is also available in an enhanced commercial version. DiskDoubler can also be used for archiving. All three programs can produce self-extracting archives for users who don't have the software.

A file-transfer protocol is a set of file transfer rules obeyed by sender and receiver. It consists of error-detection and error-correction protocols.

Error-detection protocols break data into packets, do computations on the packets, then send the data and computation bytes. The receiving modem does its own computation and compares it with computation bytes sent. If the two are not equal, it requests a resend. The computation done by a transfer protocol is called a *checksum*. The comparison of checksums by transmitting and receiving computers is called a Cyclical Redundancy Check, or CRC.

Error-correction protocols implemented by transfer protocols monitor checksums. If the comparisons fail, the receiving computer requests retransmission of data until the checksum is correct. A count of CRC errors is generally made and displayed. On a "dirty" telephone line a number of retransmissions may be required for every data packet sent. This will slow data transmission down considerably.

Fault-tolerant transfer protocols can recover from disconnects and dirty phone lines. These protocols will resume transmission from the point that a file transmission or reception was interrupted. Zmodem is an example of a fault-tolerant protocol.

There are a number of software transfer protocols in common use today. Different bulletin board systems support some or all of them. The more protocols a Mac telecommunications package supports, the more useful it is to you. A telecommunications package with a wide variety of protocols has a greater chance of being able to download software from older and non-Mac boards. Modems with hardware compression and error correction are becoming more common and may eventually supplant some software compression (and all error detection/correction) schemes.

Xmodem was the first, the most popular, and the most widely implemented transfer protocol. The Xmodem protocol standard:

■ requires an 8-bit serial port

■ sends data in 128-byte packets

■ prefixes each data packet by a 2-byte packet number

■ follows each data packet by a 1-byte checksum

■ defines receiver responses in simple 1-byte control characters

■ is receiver driven

■ avoids deadlock through a simple timing scheme

Xmodem does not send file names, so it originally couldn't do "batch" transfers. This was remedied by the development of Xmodem Batch and MODEM7.

The Xmodem 1-byte checksum allowed errors. To eliminate them, CRC-16 was introduced. With 128-byte block sizes, transmission was very slow, so Xmodem-1K was introduced. This uses a 1024-byte (1K) data-packet size.

Ymodem is one of the best extensions to Xmodem. It cleaned up batch mode and added special file information. Ymodem is basically a combination of Xmodem and CRC, with 128-byte and 1K packet sizes and an initial data packet with filename, exact length, and modification date. Ymodem is faster and more reliable than Xmodem.

Ymodem-G operates in "streaming mode." It divides a file into packets and sends error detection information, but does no handshaking with the remote modem. The protocol is incredibly fast. If errors are detected, the entire file is resent. Ymodem-G is normally only used with error-correcting modems.

Kermit is a file transfer protocol designed for use with mainframes. Kermit is the most flexible of file transfer protocols and is usable on a wide variety of systems. But Kermit is much slower than Xmodem or Ymodem. Like Xmodem, there is no provision for sending machine-specific data such as file type.

Frank Da Cruz and Bill Catchings of Columbia University developed Kermit for use on systems in character mode. Unlike Xmodem and Ymodem "binary" protocols (where data is unchanged after transfer), Kermit also supports a "text" mode (machine-dependent).

Zmodem, developed by Chuck Forsberg, does not "handshake" after each packet. Zmodem sends packets without waiting for an immediate response from the receiver. If the receiver detects an error, it transmits the position back to the sender, and the sender begins retransmission. Zmodem supports text and binary transfers. It is somewhat slow at error recovery but it responds very well when used with error-correcting modems.

HARDWARE COMPRESSION AND ERROR CHECKING

At the speed of modern modem hardware, software error checking just gets in the way. To let 9600-baud and faster modems operate at peak efficiency, compression and error checking must be done with hardware.

Figure 13.2 shows the maximum operating speed of various modem hardware protocols. The Bell 103J and 201A standards are modulation schemes for 300- and 1200-baud modems, respectively. The CCITT international V.22bis and V.32 high-performance modulation schemes are used for 2400- and 9600-baud modems, and the newest V.32bis modulation scheme starts at support for 14,400 baud.

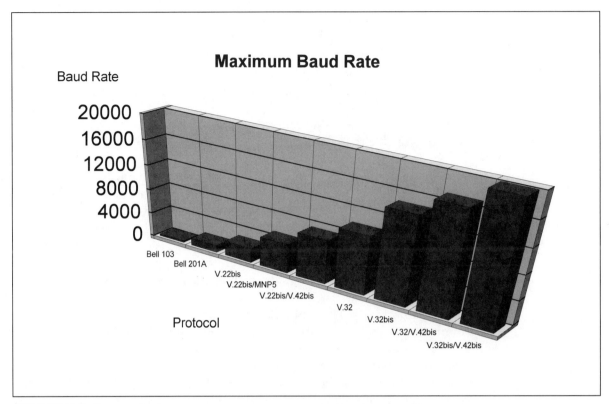

FIGURE 13.2: Maximum operating speed for modem hardware protocols

MNP 4 and 5 are error correction and data compression schemes, respectively, developed by Microcom and quite popular on new modems and commercial information systems. The most recent data-compression protocol added to modems is the CCITT V.42bis data-compression standard. Adding V.42bis compression to V.32 modulation will support throughput of 30,000 bps. V.42bis and V.32bis support a throughput of 38,400 bps. Using a hardware compression scheme like V.42bis with software-compressed files results in speeds slower than the rated modem speed. Obviously, hardware compression schemes work only if both sending and receiving modems implement the same scheme. V.42bis doesn't work with MNP 5, for instance, and vice-versa.

Some manufacturers use a proprietary compression scheme like US Robotic's HST compression, which is used on Courier Dual Standard and Hayes V-series modems. A number of bulletin boards use HST standard modems.

THE HAYES AT COMMAND SET

The AT command set is used to set up or change modem settings. The commands are called "AT" commands because they are always preceded by the letters AT. Commands used to set up a modem are called *modem initialization strings*. An initialization string lets you set the modem speed, local echo, or other modem features. The following is an example:

ATE1M1V1

The letters AT tells the modem that a command is coming. The E1 puts the modem on local echo. This means that characters typed on your keyboard while online will be "echoed" on screen (this is only necessary when communicating with remote modems that do not echo back typed characters). M1 turns the modem speaker on until the modem establishes a carrier. V1 tells the modem to return word status codes. The following string will dial a number from a touch-tone phone:

ATDT9,256-7890

The AT readies the modem for a command, DT sets touch-tone dialing, 9 dials out, the comma pauses, and the modem dials the number.

Following are some basic AT commands:

AT	Attention code. Start of command line. This is used to start almost all modem commands. It tells the modem that a command is coming. Example: AT H0.
+++	Escape code. Changes modem from online to command state. Sending this code gets the modem ready to receive a local command.
Ds	This command tells the modem to dial a number. ATDP9,403-268-6729 tells the modem to pulse (rotary) dial 9 (to get out of the local phone system), pause, then dial an area code and telephone number. The "*s*" can equal:
P	Pulse dial
R	Dial an "originate-only" modem (reverse-only) and wait for response.
T	Touch-tone dial

DP, DR, and DT can be followed and modified by: 9 (dial out); , (pause); # and * (keys on touch-tone telephone; () (for including area code); and – (used in phone numbers).

;   Return to command state after dialing.

A/   Repeat command, redial. Used without an AT or carriage return. This command is used to repeat a command line for things like redialing a number. It's used without an "AT."

A   Answer call immediately. This tells the modem to answer the phone and wait for a carrier. Example: ATA.

En Where n=0 or 1, and 0=no echo, 1=echo. The command tells the modem whether or not to "echo" characters to the computer screen. Example: ATE1 tells the modem to echo.

Fn Where n=0 or 1, and 0=half-duplex, 1=full-duplex. Some bulletin boards echo characters back to the sending system. In that case, you would select full-duplex: ATF1.

Mn Where n=0, 1, or 2, and 0=speaker off, 1=speaker on until carrier detected, 2=always on. Turns the modem internal speaker on or off. Off is a good idea, and is coded ATM0.

o   Return modem to online status. Could be used, for example, after +++. Example: ATo.

Qn Where n=0, 1, and 0=result code sent, 1=result codes not sent. Quiet command. You can choose whether to have the modem communicate with you in codes like "ready."

Sr?   Where r=0...27. Read register r. These lines are the modem's internal registers. You can use them to set a number of parameters for the modem. Example: ATS0=2 would answer the phone after two rings.

Sr=n Where r=0...27 and n=0...255. Sets register r to value n.

     S6   Wait time for dial tone

     S8   Length of pause

     S11   Duration and spacing of dial tones

	S0	Number of rings on which modem answers
	S1	Number of rings occurred
	S7	Wait time for carrier
	S9	Carrier detect response time in tenths of a second
	S10	Time between loss of carrier and hang up in tenths of a second
V*n*		Where *n*=0, 1, and 0=digit result codes, 1=word result codes. This lets you choose whether the modem will communicate with you in words or number codes.
X*n*		Where *n*=0, 1, and 0=basic result code sent, 1=extended result code sent. Enables extended result code, lets you display different combinations of result codes. ATX0 would enable okay, connect, ring, or no carrier.
z		Reset. This resets your modem to its default values.
C*n*		Where *n*=0, 1, and 0=transmitter off, 1=transmitter on. This command sets the modem carrier signal on or off. Example: ATC1 turns the carrier on immediately.
H*n*		Where *n*=0...2, and 0=on hook (hang up), 1=off hook, 2=special off hook. This is the "hang-up" command, which you use to pick up or hang up the phone. Example: ATH1 picks up the phone.
I*n*		Where *n*=0, 1, and 0=request identification code, 1=request checksum. This is the interrogate command. It tests modem ROM or reads a product code or manufacturer's number.

CHOOSING AND USING A MAC MODEM

Modems come in two forms, external and internal. External modems have their own case and power supply. Internal modems plug into a Mac's NuBus or PDS slot and draw power from the machine. These modems unclutter your desk, and are less likely to lose transmitted data at high speeds while multitasking with System 7, because you are directly connected to the Mac system bus.

Still, there are a lot more reasons to use external modems. These include adding portability, freeing up an expansion slot, unloading a computer's power supply, and keeping status lights in plain view. I prefer external modems, and I have one more reason—resale value.

Mac users have a *huge* selection of external modems to choose from. Thanks to modern standards, you can use almost any external modem with your Mac. Your choice of internal modems and fax modems is more limited. Internal modems, of course, are Mac hardware specific and fax modems require Mac-specific software to make the fax features useful to Mac users. Some general features that you should look for when evaluating a modem are:

Case size and shape	Make sure it's convenient. "Designer modems" are generally a pain in the desk.
A volume control	Have you ever heard a modem establishing a carrier? Enough said.
A power switch	Although I've never used a modem without one, I don't want to.
Status lights	They let you know what's going on and allow you to diagnose modem problems (see Figure 13.3).
Built-in RAM	Stores phone numbers and/or settings.
Bundled software	If it's *good* telecom software that you would buy anyway.

Generally, avoid 1200-baud modems unless you want to use them with local boards to get used to telecommunicating. In this case, don't spend more than $25–30. Better yet, find someone who's giving his old modem away. Get as much modem and as many features as you can comfortably afford. Modems, like computers, are on the fast track these days and will become obsolete quickly. Consider, however, that commercial bulletin board services charge more for the use of fast modem lines. If you're just browsing, you may want to set your modem back to 2400 baud. When you're downloading, boost the modem to whatever speed it will handle and that the service will support. If you're buying a 2400-baud modem, get a price in the $90–$150 range. The modem should support MNP 5 or V.42bis hardware compression if possible. 9600-baud modems should support V.32 or V.32bis modulation and V.42, V.42bis, or MNP 5 data compression/error correction.

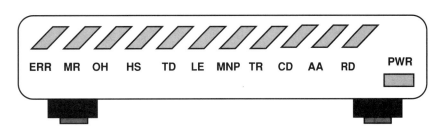

MODEM STATUS LIGHTS

ERR   Transmission or Reception errors. The modem is
      getting errors while using hardware error checking.

MR   The Modem Ready light. Lit when modem is ready
      to communicate with computer.

OH   Off Hook. Lights up when modem is connected to
      the phone line.

HS   High Speed. With some modems, indicates when
      high speed operation is in effect.

TD   Transmitting Data. The computer is sending data to
      the modem.

LE   Line Engaged. The telephone line is in use, and not
      available to the modem.

MNP   MNP active. For modems equipped with MNP 4 error
      checking and correction.

TR   Terminal Ready. The computer is ready to communicate
      with the modem.

CD   Carrier Detect. The modem has established a carrier
      with a remote modem.

AA   Auto Answer. The modem is set to automatically "pick
      up" the phone when it rings.

RD   Receiving Data. The computer is receiving data from
      the modem.

FIGURE 13.3:   Modem status lights

Remember that if you buy a high-speed, high-performance modem, you'll need a special cable that supports hardware handshaking. Supra (see Figure 13.4), Zoom Telephonics, Prometheus, and Practical Peripherals all have reputations for good-quality modems at a reasonable price. Hayes and Microcom generally sell at a premium.

FIGURE 13.4: A SupraFaxModem 14400 (photo courtesy of Supra Corporation)

TELECOMMUNICATIONS SOFTWARE

To make your modem fly, you're going to have to get it off the ground. For that you'll need some telecommunications software.

The best deal around is ZTerm, a shareware telecommunications program written by David Alverson and available from user groups and bulletin boards. Now in version 0.9, ZTerm supports a variety of advanced features, including Zmodem file transfers. The current version includes a scripting language.

The best commercial telecommunications program is probably White Knight, formerly (many moons ago) the shareware program Red Ryder. White Knight has a variety of advanced features including advanced file transfer protocols and a scripting language.

Finally, consider MicroPhone II. MicroPhone II is a very capable telecom program and deserves a look when you're shopping for software.

FAX MODEMS

The hot new idea for modems is fax modem capability. I have a few problems with the concept. Since many businesses use fax machines to transmit paper documents or records, a dedicated fax is probably a better choice for an office. However, fax modem capability is becoming so cheap that it's probably worth buying if you can get it at a good price. Because so many businesses have fax numbers these days, a fax modem is a good way to transfer a letter produced on your machine quickly at any time of the day or night.

Low-priced fax modems generally are of the 24/96 variety, meaning that they telecommunicate at 2400 baud but fax data at 9600 baud. Low-priced fax modems often only have send-fax capability. This may be satisfactory for your needs but send-receive fax capability is so cheap these days that you should probably try for it.

Group III fax machines transmit data at 9600 baud, and support 98×198 dpi standard and 198×198 dpi high resolution. Fax modems support these standards.

Good low-priced fax machines are available from MacProducts USA, Zoom Telephonics, Supra, Global Village Communication, and Prometheus. Supra's SupraModem (Figure 13.5) transmits at 14,400 baud, supports the new 14,400 baud send/receive fax speed, and is quite reasonably priced.

HOW TO USE YOUR MODEM

I've mentioned some of the uses of a modem, but here are some more details. You can access local bulletin boards for public domain software, Apple upgrades, and hints and tips. You should virus check *all* downloaded software, however. You can dial in to the local library or university computer, if it allows, and do a title search. If your university work requires computer access, most campuses let you do it by modem from home.

FIGURE 13.5: A SupraModem with Microphone II (photo courtesy of Supra corporation)

 Using the Auto-answer feature of your modem, you and a friend can exchange files with telecom programs. Using ZTerm, for instance, you can set your modem to auto-answer after two rings with ATS0=2. When your friend calls, the modem will answer after two rings. You can talk with him by typing in your ZTerm window. When your friend does a Zmodem send, your copy of ZTerm will automatically receive the file to a selected directory.

You can download software upgrade patches from software company BBSs or from commercial services. You can also get some fast commercial software troubleshooting the same way.

You also can access large commercial information services and all of their features.

INFORMATION SERVICES

The three largest online information services are America Online, Compu-Serve, and GEnie. These services feature major hardware and software manu-facturer upgrades and support, including special offers only available online. There are discount hardware and software stores, travel offers, online en-cyclopedias, round tables (online conferences), international E-mail, and other goodies. America Online and CompuServe have nifty Mac graphics "front-end" software. GEnie uses a text interface, but is sometimes cheaper.

Some services have basic areas that are covered by your subscription fee, but many of the "goodies" cost extra.

American Online, CompuServe, and GEnie cost, respectively, $4, $8, and $6 per non-prime hour at 2400 baud. However, remember that using high-speed modems can cost *considerably* more per hour.

If you have a local "gateway" for one of these services in your area, you can access it for the cost of a local call, an outstanding deal. If you have to use long distance and a "clean" data line like the Tymnet or DataPac packet-switching networks, your costs will go up *very* quickly and online services start to look a lot less attractive.

Online services can get expensive very quickly, so I recommend that you budget the time you spend online carefully. Use macros with your telecom program or program your "front-end" software to do exactly what you want and log off quickly. Call at night in non-prime hours (the reason a lot of us have bags under our eyes). Remember, unless you're calling from a local gateway and using a basic service, *the meter's running.*

ONLINE LINGO

Some of the expressions and shorthand you'll see online may seem like gib-berish when you first encounter them. In order to help you out, here are explanations of a number of common BBS expressions:

OLM	Online message
OIC	Oh, I see!
BTW	By the way
ROTF	Rolling on the floor
LMTO	Laughing my tush off
LOL	Laughing out loud
BCNU	Be seeing you
FWIW	For what it's worth
LTNT	Long time no type
LTNS	Long time no see
IMHO	In my humble opinion
PITA	Pain in the anatomy
RE	Again
OTW	On the way
H	HUH???
WLCM	Welcome
BRB	Be right back
BBL	Be back later
OTB	Off to bed
L8R	Later
ODM	On de move
TTFN	Ta ta for now
:-)	Smile/humor
:c	Pout
:-(	Frown
;-)	Wink
:-O	Shout
:X	Not talking
:#	Grimace/frustrated
:/	Disfavor/baffled

:-8	Talking out of both sides of your mouth
(:-$	Person is ill
(:-&	Person is angry
(:-(	Person is *very* sad
:-}	Message from a female
:)	Smile/happy
:D	Big smile or laugh
:/)	Not funny
:(	Frown/sad
'-)	Wink
:-(	Unhappy
:P	Sticking out tongue
;>	Sly wink

Telecommunicating is getting more popular every day and genuine celebrities often show up for online conferences on the major information services. Try it out! With a little care and attention, telecommunicating can be useful and a lot of fun.

TROUBLESHOOTING

Problem	Cause	Solution
You get onto an online system, but get a screen full of garbage	Data bits, stop bits, and/or parity probably set incorrectly	Reset and try again
You're getting a lot of errors trying to send a file, and transmission is very slow	You've got a dirty phone line	Call back and try again

Problem	Cause	Solution
You can't get a file transfer to work	Your version of a protocol may be incompatible with the BBS	Try other transfer protocols
Your modem won't work at top speed and your hardware compression doesn't work	You aren't in communication with a modem of similar speed that supports hardware files compression	Use the best speed and hardware transfer protocol available

CHAPTER FOURTEEN

Networking

The hot computer topic of the 90s is networking. With the continuing demise of mainframes, corporate MIS (Management Information Systems) departments are moving to *Local Area Networks* (LANs). LANs are also more popular than ever in schools, universities, and small businesses.

WHAT IS A LAN?

A LAN is a collection of computers linked together to share information and resources. The linked computers can share information and peripherals over a limited distance—hence the term "local area." The linked computers are managed by a *file server*, a computer that handles the storage of files and programs, including the network software.

Early LANs were primitive and used a technique called *file locking* to restrict program access to only one person at a time. Modern LAN programs support multiple users and protect data using a more flexible approach called *record locking*.

ADVANTAGES AND DISADVANTAGES OF LANS

All is not rosy in the land of LANs. You should balance the advantages and disadvantages of taking your school, company, or department down the LAN path.

Advantages of LANs

- Peripherals such as printers and modems can be shared by all of the users on the LAN.

- Users can share data files and keep them up to date.

- You can add more workstations and peripherals to the network, and link it to other networks at any time.

- LAN users can access mainframes or minicomputers.

- Network message systems and "groupware" programs allow an entire department to stay informed and work together on projects.

- Managers have rapid access to vital data.

- Users can share access to specialized workstations for uses like graphics or data analysis.

- Networks can easily be kept up to date with new software.

- Network security can prevent unauthorized access to files.

Disadvantages of LANs

- Cost! Networking still requires an expensive investment in a fast file server, cabling and installation, compatible software, and the salary or time of a network administrator.

- The network adds memory overhead to individual Macs, and CPU overhead to their processors.

- Users have another level of complexity to absorb. Although the learning curve for a basic Mac network use is not steep, learning to use the network *effectively* may take a little longer.

- Users lose *some* control over their machines.

- If data privacy is necessary, some form of data security has to be implemented.

- Programs used must be network-compatible or small enough to work with network software overhead.

DESIGNING A LAN AND LANDING A DESIGN

- The cost of a LAN is critical. If your budget won't support the installation and operating costs, maybe you should consider something simpler for the short term, like printer and modem sharing.

- The reliability of a LAN, once you've made the decision, is paramount. LANs should not be susceptible to crashes, and data has to be secure.

- The speed of the LAN is the next most critical concern. A pokey network will slow all of your projects and tie up your computer. Apple's LocalTalk networks are convenient and useful in some cases, such as primary schools, but they are *not* fast.

- Compatibility is important. Does your network support Mac hardware and software standards and is it compatible with the equipment and software you'll be using?

- Your network setups should be flexible and easily extended and linked to other LANs. You should be able to connect to the equipment you regularly use or plan to use.

- Be sure your network is easy to set up and use. This is critical because you'll probably be adding workstations and diagnosing network problems later.

- Are your network hardware and software standard and widely used? Will they be supported and upgraded? Network hardware and software are expensive and you don't want to sink money into something that won't be around in a few years.

- What type of cabling do you plan to use? Will it support current *and* future plans? Will it handle the data throughput your system will throw at it? The choice of cable should not *just* be based on price.

- Does the network you're planning have the levels of security you need?

ALTERNATIVES TO LANS

As I mentioned, all workgroups may not need a LAN. The entry level in data sharing is disk-swapping, also known as SneakerNet—because your sneakers do the networking. SneakerNet may be adequate for a small workgroup of three or four Macs, at least for a while.

If you're going to be swapping disks with PCs, you'll want a utility such as Insignia Solutions Access PC or Dayna's DOS Mounter. If you'll be sharing files with Apple IIs, you can use Xtend file translators for compatible Mac programs or Apple File Exchange translators. Both are available from DataViz. DataViz also provides a large variety of translators for MS-DOS programs.

If you need more than SneakerNet, but only to share peripherals like modems or printers, you may want to consider a multiline buffer. This device lets a number of Macs share one device, such as a printer, and dumps jobs to the device one at a time. It also frees up individual Macs after the jobs have been sent.

NETWORK STRUCTURE AND THE OSI MODEL

In order to provide some uniformity between different LAN models, the International Standards Organization (ISO) developed a model for networks called the Open Systems Interconnection (OSI) standards. Because PC networks follow these standards, Apple, in a drive for compatibility and connectivity, has implemented them as well.

The OSI model consists of seven layers:

- The application layer

- The presentation layer

- The session layer

- The transport layer

- The network layer

- The data link layer

- The physical layer

The application layer is where the Mac user operates and Mac software is run. The user at the application level can run ordinary Mac software without worrying about how the rest of the process operates.

The presentation layer is a standard interface under which Mac programs can run. It works by supporting network functions for these application programs. AppleTalk's presentation layer consists of the AppleTalk Filing Protocol (AFP), which supports AppleShare and Novell NetWare, and the PostScript Protocol. AFP handles network volumes, directories, files, and network logins, access to local and remote file servers, and translation from different types of file servers. PostScript Protocol handles communications between an AppleTalk network and PostScript devices.

The AppleTalk session layer handles the establishment and control of a communications session, including the construction, transmission, and routing of data packets. (*Data packets*, coded "packets" of information, are the way data is transmitted on networks.) Network software is responsible for detecting and preventing "collisions" between the packets. The session layer also manages AppleTalk zones and printer sessions.

The transport layer handles the preparation and identification of network data packets for transmission within and between networks.

The network layer handles physical delivery of data packets. Apple uses a Datagram Delivery Protocol (DDP) to handle the movement of data with different networks.

The data link layer provides access from AppleTalk to AppleTalk, Ethernet, and Token Ring hardware.

The AppleTalk physical layer is where network hardware is actually connected to a Mac. Macs all come equipped with LocalTalk circuitry and just have to be connected through one of the serial ports with AppleTalk active. AppleTalk will transfer data at speeds of up to 230 kilobits per second (Kbps).

To obtain better network performance, Macs can use Ethernet, capable of 10Mb/s (10 megabits per second), or IBM's Token Ring, capable of 16Mb/s. Macs using these protocols need appropriate interface cards connected via a NuBus or PDS slot, or a SCSI interface box for compact Macs.

NETWORK TOPOLOGY

In designing a network, you can choose from a number of *logical structures*. "Logical structures" refers to the way network wiring is organized and not the way it looks when wiring is complete (at which point the logical structure of a network is anything but obvious). Logical structures are also called network "topologies."

The most common topologies are daisy-chains, buses, rings, and stars (see Figure 14.1). Daisy-chain topology is the simple Mac-to-Mac network you can construct using Apple LocalTalk connectors, or Farallon PhoneNET or NuvoTech TurboNet ST connectors (Figure 14.2) with twisted two-pair phone

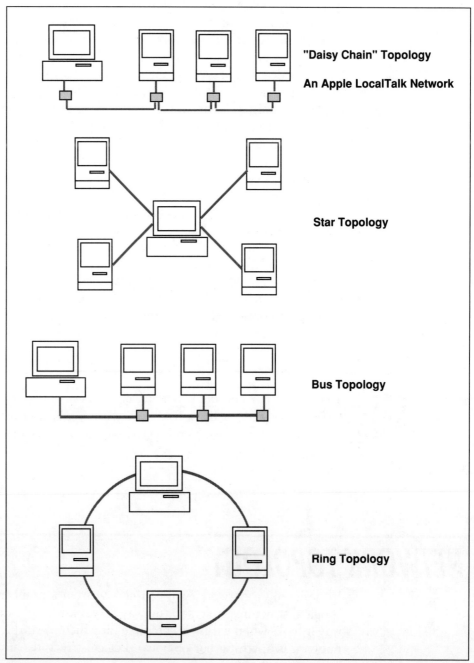

FIGURE 14.1: Network topologies

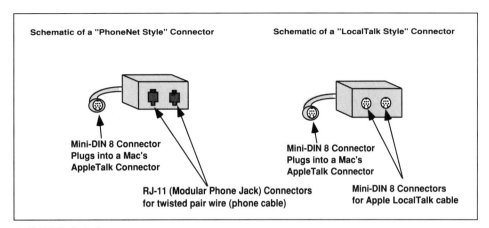

Schematic of a "PhoneNet Style" Connector   Schematic of a "LocalTalk Style" Connector

Mini-DIN 8 Connector
Plugs into a Mac's
AppleTalk Connector

Mini-DIN 8 Connector
Plugs into a Mac's
AppleTalk Connector

RJ-11 (Modular Phone Jack) Connectors
for twisted pair wire (phone cable)

Mini-DIN 8 Connectors
for Apple LocalTalk cable

FIGURE 14.2:   PhoneNET and LocalTalk connectors

wire. This system is cheap and easy to set up, but can create a wire snarl in a hurry. One computer going down can take out the rest of the network "down stream." Daisy-chain networks are often used by schools.

Star topology is the oldest system used by LANs. This organization will not be affected by the loss of one of the lines, and makes it easy to diagnose problems. However, because the entire network is dependent on a central server, this organization is less reliable than others.

Ordinary star topology is known as a *passive star*. Because all arms of the star are active, the number of devices the star can handle is usually severely limited. *Active star* technology puts a controller box such as Farallon's PhoneNET StarController or Nuvotech's Turbostar at the hub. The active controller actively links two computers, isolating machines that aren't active. This control, combined with signal amplification, improves the performance of this topology. It also lets you add more computers to the network at any time, up to the limit the controller box can handle—which is usually at least twice as many as on a passive star.

Bus topology uses a single connecting line, or "bus," with Macs connected along it at *nodes*. The bus cable is generally wired into the walls of an office or lab with plugs at the nodes. Bus topology is reliable and fairly straightforward when there are no cable problems (but when problems arise, they can be hard to diagnose). Losing an individual Mac doesn't mean losing the whole network.

Ring topology consists of a number of Macs connected point-to-point in a circular configuration. IBM's Token Ring is an example. Each node on the ring acts as an active repeater, retransmitting messages for other nodes. In this topology's simplest form, failure of any node results in the failure of the LAN.

THE COMPONENTS OF A LAN

A local area network needs a file server, server software, cabling, network adapter boards, and connector boxes.

The File Server

The computer selected for a file server should be the fastest you can afford, have enough memory to handle network software and print spooling if desired, and have enough fast disk space to take care of network requirements.

A server for a school Apple II, IIgs, or Mac Classic network should be a Mac LC or better. A small office LAN can use a Mac IIsi or Mac IIci. A large network will require a Quadra with multiple high-capacity disks or a disk array.

A Mac network can also use a fast PC or RISC server, or Macs can be connected to networks that use these servers.

Some Mac networking software uses a process called distributed networking, in which every Mac in the network shares in the file server chores. Unfortunately, this software requires more memory and processor overhead from your Mac.

Network Software

AppleShare, Apple's file server software, provides folder, not file, security. Its administrative software, ADMIN, is used to set up network users and workgroups, and provide reports for network users. Security includes login passwords and the ability to make a folder invisible to anyone but the user. The software also allows "superusers" that can handle multifile administration, without *full* administrative privileges.

Apple IIgs computers, and Apple IIe computers with Apple II workstation cards, can act as AppleShare workstations. PC file commands are converted to Server Message Blocks (SMBs) which are later changed into AppleTalk Filing Profile calls that AppleShare can understand.

AppleShare 3.0 allows up to 120 simultaneous users, and provides CD-ROM file exchange as well as System 7 publish and subscribe. Other features include new data security options, background printing, print spooling for up to five AppleTalk printers, and a log that will handle up to 1100 jobs.

Novell's NetWare 3.11 for the Macintosh runs on a PC server. A Mac workstation using NetWare 2.15 or later can recognize and use Mac and PC files on the NetWare server. NetWare supports print spooling. Because NetWare can distinguish its own IPX format from AppleShare format, AppleShare servers can be accessed from a Novell network. A NetWare utility converts Mac file names to MS-DOS names and vice-versa. This can cause some interesting naming problems if you're not careful. NetWare volumes appear on your Mac as file folders. NetWare has high-level security options for Mac data.

Sitka (formerly part of Sun Microsystems) makes TOPS for the Mac. TOPS is *distributed* networking software—that is, a copy resides on each Mac on the network. TOPS runs on Macs networked with LocalTalk or Ethernet cabling. Used with a TOPS Flashbox and FlashTalk, the software transmits data three times faster than AppleTalk. TOPSpool permits spooling to an Apple LaserWriter, TOPS NetPrint lets an MS-DOS machine use an Apple Image-Writer II or LaserWriter, and TOPS Translators inter-converts common MS-DOS and Mac programs.

Network Cabling

The simplest network cable is twisted two-pair (or telephone) wire with modular phone jacks (RJ-11 connectors). This is used with PhoneNET connectors on LocalTalk networks (see Figure 14.3). Ethernet supports this type of cable as 10BaseT. Recommended twisted two-pair wire gauge is 22 or 24 AWG (higher number is smaller).

Coaxial cable is also used for networks. Ethernet supports "thick" and "thin" coaxials. Thick coaxial cable is RG-8 50 ohm coax and is called 10Base5. It supports cable runs up to 3280 feet. Thin coaxial cable is RG-58 50 ohm coax and is called 10Base2. It supports runs up to 1000 feet.

Network Adapters and Connectors

I've mentioned Farallon's PhoneNET and Nuvotech's TurboNet connectors for LocalTalk Networks. These adapters are a lot cheaper than Apple's LocalTalk cables, and allow you to use cheap twisted two-pair phone cable to interconnect your networked Macs.

If you want to connect to a PC Token Ring network and get the benefit of the 16Mbps data transfer speed, you'll need Apple's TokenTalk card or a third-party equivalent.

If you want the fastest Mac-Specific network hardware now available for Macs, upgrade to Ethernet and its 10Mb/s data transfer speed (Figure 14.4). A variety of PDS and NuBus boards are available for modular Macs, and SCSI Ethernet adapters are available for compact Macs. Apple, Dayna, Dove, and Farallon Computing make Apple Ethernet adapters.

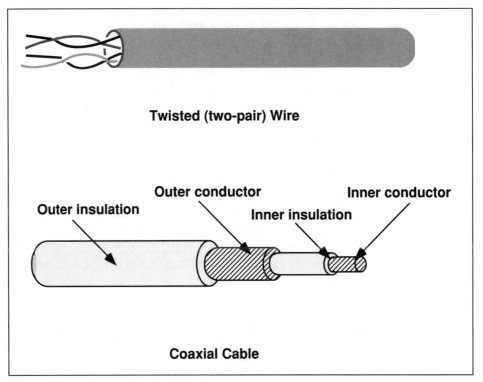

Twisted (two-pair) Wire

Outer conductor

Inner conductor

Outer insulation

Inner insulation

Coaxial Cable

FIGURE 14.3:   Twisted two-pair and coaxial cable

Individual LANs can be connected with *bridges* to form a large composite network. Using a dedicated Mac with a modem and Apple Remote Access software, a network can have a *remote bridge*. *Routers* are more sophisticated than bridges, and can analyze traffic conditions to determine the best way to send data on a network. Some good AppleTalk routers are Farallon's PhoneNET Liaison and Shiva's NetBridge. A couple of good EtherTalk routers are Shiva's FastPath5 and Cayman's GatorBox. *Gateways* are points at which a network connects to a dissimilar network or a mainframe. An example is Dayna's EtherPrint, which lets you use LocalTalk printers on an EtherTalk network.

MANAGING A NETWORK

Every network has its own potential glitches. It is up to the network administrator to keep it running smoothly. Technology Works GraceLAN or Apple's InterPoll Network Administrators Utility will help him or her identify problems with the system. Users can help a file server somewhat by using direct file transfer software such as Mac to Mac, SendExpress, or Flash.

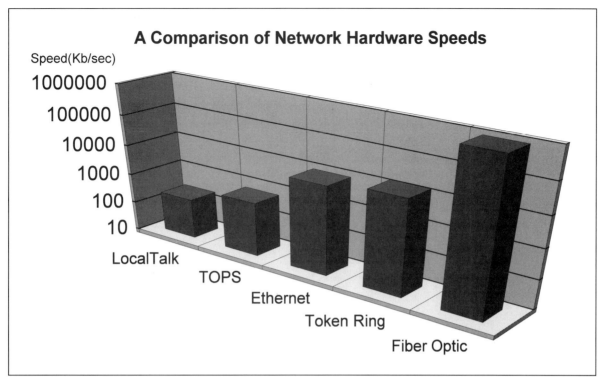

FIGURE 14.4:   Comparison of network hardware speeds

TROUBLESHOOTING

Problem	Cause	Solution
Part of your AppleTalk network works, part is "dead"	You may have loose or dead connectors	Try checking connectors or using a network *poller* program like Net-Atlas
Your network is slowing down	Overloaded file server and cabling	Split up the network and/or create separate print servers. Try faster hardware

Problem	**Cause**	**Solution**
Font and software incompatibility problems are common in the network	Incompatible software versions and incomplete font sets on different machines	Update software and add network-compatible version of Suitcase to set up a common font file

CHAPTER FIFTEEN

Graphics, Sound, and Multimedia

The Mac has been a *great* graphics and sound machine from the beginning. The machine's graphical operating system, four-voice sound chip, and high-resolution (at the time) monochrome monitor put it far ahead of any of its peers. Now, however, the Mac's built-in toolbox, graphics, and sound are starting to show their age. It's clear that *QuickDraw*, the set of ROM routines that handle Mac graphics, is due for an overhaul, as are the Mac video and sound hardware.

In response, Apple has extended the Mac's graphics capability, though it hasn't tampered with the sound chip (possibly to avoid infringing on an agreement with the Beatles' Apple records not to produce musical equipment). Apple provided an exciting software tuneup with the introduction of the QuickTime extension for System 7. QuickTime adds a set of powerful multimedia tools to the Mac's normal routines. Apple appears to be working on a QuickDraw upgrade as well. Obviously, the company is concerned with keeping the Mac up to date, and will continue to provide hardware and software tools to bring the machine into the multimedia age.

In the meantime, Mac music, sound, and video upgrades let you put together your own multimedia system. In this chapter, I'll discuss multimedia hardware and software for low- to high-end Mac systems and how they can be used with Apple's QuickTime extension. I'll also discuss methods for capturing high-quality graphics and sound for multimedia presentations, using hardware such as scanners and video digitizers.

THE SOUNDS OF MACINTOSH

The compact Mac sound chip has four *voices*—four separate registers that can be used to store music or sound samples, creating complex music, sound effects, or synthetic speech. The sound chip can record and play back 8-bit audio at sampling rates of up to 22kHz on at least two channels. Macs since the Mac II have a sound chip that will play four-channel 8-bit sound. The software to handle this chip is included with System 6.07 as the Sound Manager. The Mac sound chip is more than adequate for reasonable sound reproduction but not for high fidelity.

Mac sound files are stored as Sound documents, "SND" resources within documents, or 8-bit AIFF (Audio Interchange File Format) files. AIFF is an Apple standard for Mac mono or stereo sound at any resolution or sampling rate.

Mac sounds take up a lot of space—22K for one second of 22kHz 8-bit sampled sound and 5MB for one minute of 16-bit 44kHz sampled sound. The higher the sound-sampling resolution, the larger the file. You can reduce file sizes by reducing the sampling rate, but doing so reduces the sound quality. You have to decide whether the trade-off is worth it.

Recording Hardware

Up until now, the main source of low-to-medium quality sound for a Macintosh was Paracomp's (formerly Farallon's) MacRecorder. MacRecorder consists of a microphone, digitizer hardware box, and a serial cable that plugs into the Mac's modem or printer port. MacRecorder comes with SoundEdit software.

SoundEdit can be purchased separately for use with built-in sound recording hardware in the newer Macs. The software lets you view sonic waveforms and cut and paste for editing and special effects. There is a four-channel mix option to combine several files into one track. The software has four sampling rates, four compression rates, and a variety of special effects. Sound files can be saved as AIFF, instrument, or SoundEdit files.

Articulate Systems produces two 8-bit sound recording and editing tools—Voice Record and Voice Impact. Voice Record is a software voice recording and editing package. Voice Impact is a basic digitizer with volume control and Voice Record software.

The Mac's 8-bit sound chip is adequate for basic sounds and music, but does not have the CD quality of 16-bit sampled sound. 16-bit sampling can handle sampling rates up to 44.1kHz.

If you're going to be using 16-bit sampling, you'll probably be hearing more about *DSPs*, or Digital Signal Processors. These chips can quickly analyze, break up, and recombine complex analog data as 16-bit digital files. They can input and output CD-quality digital sound.

Articulate Systems Voice Impact Pro includes an advanced digitizer with an onboard DSP, compression, and additional audio input jacks. The system includes Voice Record editing software.

SoundEdit Pro from Paracomp is included with the MacRecorder System Pro. SoundEditPro supports multiple tracks, virtual memory, input from any Mac Sound Manager device, 8- or 16-bit sampling with MacRecorder and a sampling rate up to 48kHz. The software supports compression and can output SoundEdit Pro, Sound Designer II, System 7 sound, and AIFF-C sound files.

Apple Built-in Hardware

Since the introduction of Apple's low-cost modular Mac LC and IIsi, Macs have been available with built-in microphones and recording software.

Apple's AudioPalette HyperCard stack controls sound recording and playback, but better editing and control is available with Paracomp's SoundEdit and SoundEdit Pro. Apple's built-in recording hardware supports only 8-bit monophonic digital audio. To get 16-bit capability and/or stereo, you have to add extra hardware.

How You Play It

To add sound to your system, you can use sound inits or HyperCard stacks. If you're building multimedia presentation software packages, try dedicated QuickTime presentation packages.

If you want to enhance your system with some neat public domain sounds, or add a few of your own, try Bruce Tomlin's SoundMaster shareware cdev (Figure 15.1). It's available by itself, and also in a package with a great set of Star Trek digitized sounds licensed and sold by the Sound Source.

The Apple AudioPalette (Figure 15.2) HyperCard stack lets you play compatible sounds on any Mac with 2MB of memory or more.

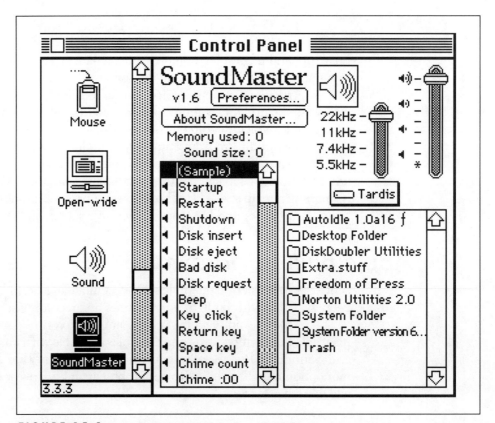

FIGURE 15.1:   The SoundMaster Control Panel

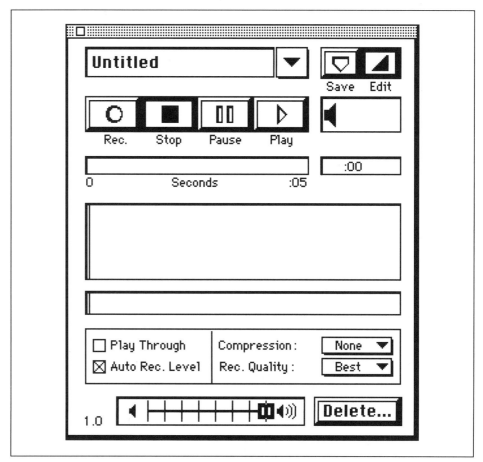

FIGURE 15.2: Apple's AudioPalette HyperCard stack.

Paracomp's MacRecorder sound system includes HyperSound, a system allowing you to record directly into HyperCard. The system allows you to create buttons to play sounds in any stack. The system includes XCMDs and XFCNs—commands and functions programmed in Assembler or a higher-level language—to allow you to add sounds to your HyperCard stack easily. The HyperCard *play* and *sound* commands allow you to add sound to HyperCard scripts.

Digital sounds can also be added to, and mixed with, video using multimedia authoring systems.

MAKING MAC MUSIC

Mac music hardware and software generally follow the MIDI (Musical Instrument Digital Interface) standard. The MIDI standard defines MIDI In, MIDI Out, and MIDI Thru connectors, with 16 channels per data line, and defines how MIDI devices communicate with each other.

Mac Music and MIDI

MIDI has become the standard of the music industry, supported by most high-end computer and digitizing equipment, as well as new digital music devices, such as sampling keyboards and drum machines.

Mac high-end MIDI digitizing equipment is available from Passport Designs, Opcode Systems, and Digidesign. To be compatible with television and recording industry sound standards, high-end sound boards must be capable of synchronization to SMPTE (Society of Motion Picture and Television Engineers) time code and digital input and output.

Recording with MIDI

MIDI recording and playback capability on the Mac doesn't necessarily require that you second mortgage the farm, but it isn't available for pocket change, either. At a minimum, you'll need an Apple MIDI interface box, a MIDI instrument, and control software. The MIDI interface box plugs into your Mac's printer or modem port. Control software like Passport Designs Sound Exciter is a good choice for this.

Digidesign, Passport Designs, and Opcode Systems provide intermediate to high-end MIDI recording and playback hardware and software. Digidesign produces the Audiomedia card and Deck software. The Audiomedia NuBus card has a Motorola 56001 DSP chip with real-time audio compression/expansion, a frequency response of 20–20,000Hz, and a sampling rate of 44.1kHz. The Deck software supports Sound Designer, AIFF, and "SND" resource formats, 4-track recording and playback, and a great variety of editing functions.

Audiomedia, which comes with Sound Access, is a set of HyperCard XCMDs and XFCNs that can play 16-bit sound from a HyperCard stack.

Many MIDI devices use sound *samples*, or *patches*, as waveforms to create custom instruments or as sound effects. Alchemy from Passport or Sound Designer from Digidesign can be used to grab digital sound samples.

Playing Back MIDI Sound

MIDI files recorded into high-end Mac *sequencer* programs can be used to create a professional recording, played back directly, or used to create a soundtrack in a multimedia presentation.

Sequencers are the control software for MIDI boards and adapters mentioned above. A sequencer does not record actual digital music data, but records characteristics of the music such as volume, relation between channels, waveform effects, and so forth.

MIDI recorded music can be incorporated into HyperCard stacks using custom XCMDs and XFCNs. In a multimedia program, a digital sound file can be added as a track and timed to coincide with animation and special effects.

Attached directly to a MIDI device, a sequencer can play back a composition complete with special effects. You'll have to load or build specific patches for the synthesizer, however.

The final output from a MIDI sequencer after mixing and studio editing can be used for a final recording.

CAPTURING MAC GRAPHICS

A number of suppliers provide Mac multimedia applications and graphics. These include selections of graphics on CD-ROM, scanners, digital cameras, and video digitizers.

CD-ROMs

NEC, Image Club, and other sources offer collections of graphics and images. These are good fodder for a multimedia project, but you'll have to establish the copyright status of the graphics you use.

Scanners

Scanners have obvious application to desktop publishing and graphic design as sources of high-quality images. Mac scanners are available in hand-held or desktop (*flatbed*) models.

A scanner shines an LED array or other light source across a page and captures *slices* of an image in a *CCD*, or charge-coupled device. The CCD is a light amplifier and digitizer (see Figure 15.3). The gray level of each portion of the slice is digitized by the CCD. A variety of *bit depths* are available in Mac scanners from 4 and 8 bits, reading 16 and 256 grays respectively, to 24-bit color. For processing images, scanner users need *image processing software*, such as

Adobe Photo Shop or Ofoto. These programs can be used to crop and resize images, as well as sharpening, lightening, or darkening scanned graphic images. Scanners can be used to capture textures and backgrounds for multimedia projects.

Hewlett-Packard and LaCie have good reputations for the quality, reliability, and features of their flatbed scanners. Logitech produces the high-quality ScanMan hand scanner.

Digital Cameras

We've been waiting for a while, but it appears that Canon has finally done it—produced a useful and reliable still camera that saves digital images to a floppy disk. The Canon RC-570 still video camera saves 25 color electronic photos to a reusable 2" diameter floppy with 450-line frame video resolution.

The RC-570 can be cabled directly to your Mac to download images with the aid of a software utility. The RC-570 give a new source of graphics to multimedia moguls.

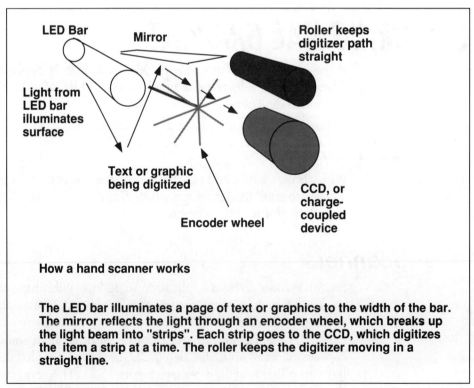

FIGURE 15.3:   Schematic diagram of a scanner

Video Digitizers

Framegrabbers, or *video digitizers*, are prime sources of multimedia graphics. These devices convert video signals from devices such as camcorders, VCRs, and laser disk players to single frame graphics or digital "movies." A video digitizer synchronizes with the video source's scanning and frame speed (about 30 frames per second for TV-quality video) and grabs a frame at a time. This is called *genlocking*. Depending on where these devices are sold, they will have to support NTSC (National Television System Committee—North America), PAL (Europe), or SECAM (France) video standards.

The Video Spigot Pro NuBus board from SuperMac (Figure 15.4) can capture up to 30 frames per second with 24-bit color in a 160 by 120 pixel window (Figure 15.5). The card is an integrated digital video framegrabber and 8/24-bit accelerated graphics card. The card supports QuickTime and the NTSC and PAL video standards.

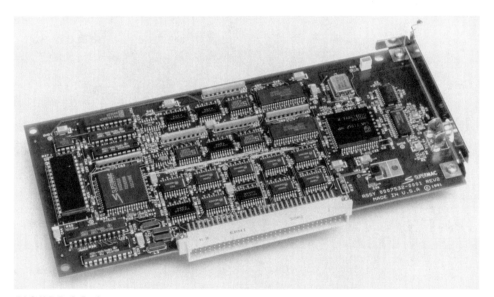

FIGURE 15.4:   The SuperMac VideoSpigot NuBus card (photo courtesy of SuperMac Technology)

Video Spigot Pro can synchronize the Mac's 8-bit audio to a video capture sequence. The newly released Spigot and Sound board provide more accurate synchronization and editing of high-quality video and audio input.

FIGURE 15.5:   The VideoSpigot card and its output (photo courtesy of SuperMac Technology)

MULTIMEDIA—GETTING IT ALL TOGETHER

Once you've acquired digital video, sound effects, and music to fit your master plan, you'll need to put it all together, record the result, and play it back to wow your thousands of adoring fans—or at least your boss. A multimedia system requires audio and video recording hardware, recording software, display equipment and display software. Some multimedia software stands alone, while some requires QuickTime. Simple multimedia can run on moderately fast compact Macs using HyperCard, but more complex recording and presentation will require a Mac IIci. For a presentation using fast 3-D animation and stereo sound, you may need a Quadra 950.

Dedicated Multimedia
Programs and QuickTime

Macromind Director is a powerful stand-alone multimedia presentation program, incorporating graphics and sound import and editing capability, detailed video and audio sequencing, a scripting language (called *Lingo*), and the ability to treat separate animated objects as *sprites*, or individually animated characters.

Director supports medium or high-quality digitized or MIDI sound and 8-bit, 256-color, NTSC-compatible graphic images.

Macromind also produces MediaMaker, used for organizing, collecting and editing Director animations.

Apple introduced QuickTime in the fall of 1991 as an init and a series of packaged utility programs for System 7. Eventually QuickTime may become part of the Mac's operating system, or even incorporated into ROM. While the Mac's Quick*Draw* firmware controls all screen drawing functions, Quick*Time* software controls time-based functions like animation, music, and sound.

QuickTime consists of a series of modular system components—the Movie Toolbox, the Component Manager, and the Image Compression Manager—as well as a number of add-on compression/decompression components called *codecs*. These include the Photo Compressor, Video Compressor, Animation Compressor, and "hooks" for other components from Apple or third-party developers. The Photo Compressor is a JPEG-compatible (JPEG, in case you don't recall, is the Joint Photographic Experts Group) software compressor that supports photo compression ratios ranging from 5:1 to 100:1. Decompression of a 24-bit screen takes approximately four seconds on a IIfx.

The Video Compressor uses a proprietary Apple algorithm for compressing and decompressing digitized video movies. Compression ratios range from 5:1 to 25:1. A 24-bit screen, once again on a IIfx, compresses in one second and decompresses in a half-second.

The Animation Compressor uses an Apple *real-time* animation compression algorithm that operates on the fly, at any color depth, using *lossless* or *lossy* compression (lossless compression preserves *all* video data and is a little slower, whereas lossy compression loses a little data but is *much* faster.) QuickTime requires a minimum of a 68020 processor and will run only on the Classic II or SE/30.

Apple distributes a QuickTime starter kit for an introduction to the system. The starter kit contains the QuickTime init (the software that contains the QuickTime code), plus SimplePlayer (which opens, plays, copies, and pastes movies), Convert-to-movie (which turns PICS animations, scrapbook sequences, PICT, SND, and AIFF files into movies), and PICT compressor (which uses JPEG compression). Figures 15.6 and 15.7 show an animated mathematical waveform run in a QuickTime window.

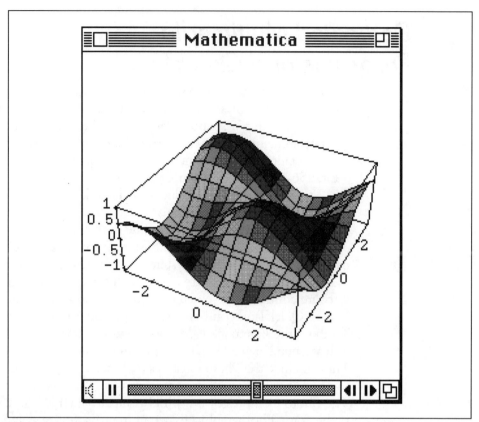

FIGURE 15.6:   A QuickTime animation—shot 1

QuickTime will support input from a variety of video and audio digitizing devices, including those mentioned above. Once again, to construct a complete screenplay, you'll need a video editing program such as Adobe's Premiere. Premiere can import movie clips, graphics, and animations and allow you to build a QuickTime movie. The project window in Premiere shows clips as picture icons, or *picons*. You can arrange movie clips by dragging the picons to an appropriate track. Premiere has two video tracks, which allow you to create transitions and special effects. The program includes special-effects filters.

Computer Friends packages a 24-bit color NuBus board called the MovieProducer with DiVA VideoShop QuickTime editing software (Figure 15.8). The board obviously requires a NuBus-capable Mac, and may require a Mac II or better (depending on the power draw). This setup allows you to:

- Digitize real-time video to your hard disk (plan on using a *large* hard disk).

- Use micons (which are like Premiere's picons) to assemble your movies.

- Edit individual movie frames.

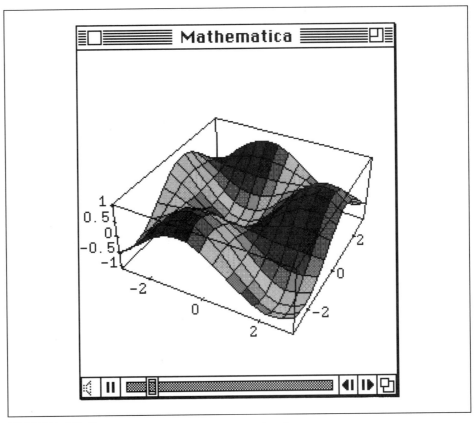

FIGURE 15.7:   A QuickTime animation—shot 2

- Add special effects.
- Organize movies and data.
- Include movies in any QuickTime-compatible program.

Picking a Multimedia System

The type of multimedia system you should choose depends on your requirements and your budget. A school probably won't need the fastest, highest-resolution system—it will need to be able to use common educational multimedia materials and build effective presentations. A business system will need high-resolution color and high-quality sound. A scientific presentation system will have to be sharp enough to present the details of a presentation clearly, and accurate enough to reproduce any important sound effects. Finally, a professional system for advertising and television special effects will need all the speed, power, and resolution that the owner can afford.

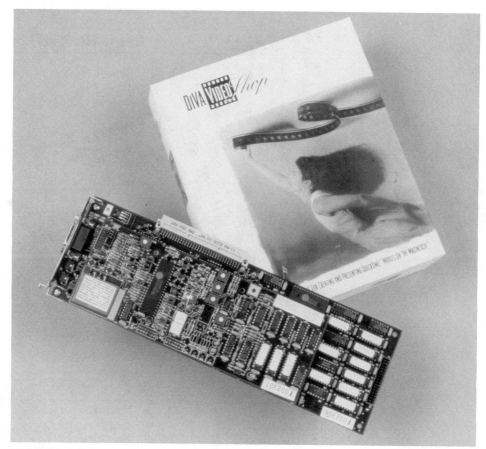

FIGURE 15.8:   Movie Producer NuBus board and DiVA VideoProducer software (photo courtesy of Computer Friends)

A Low-End Multimedia System

A low-end multimedia system (Figure 15.9) is good for a school or simple lab recording and presentations. It could consist of a video camera, laser disk, or CD-ROM as a source of graphics, a video framegrabber board, and control/editing software. Either QuickTime or stand-alone software will work well.

Your laserdisk player, if you use one, should support LANC or control L, a videotape control protocol from a consortium of manufacturers. When your presentation is built, it can be recorded and played on a VCR.

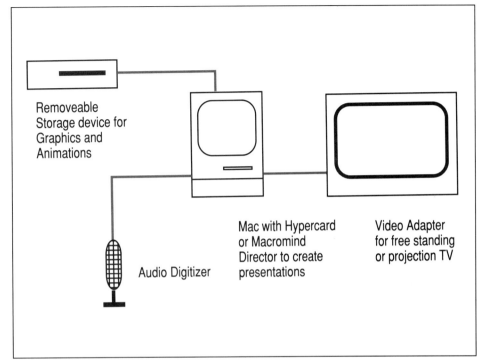

FIGURE 15.9:   Low-end multimedia system

An Intermediate Multimedia System

An intermediate system (Figure 15.10) might use a Mac IIsi with a NuBus adapter and a 24-bit framegrabber board. A TV and LANC VCR are required for reviewing the videos you build. You'll need an external 16-bit audio digitizer box for sound, and possibly additional audio and video sources such as a CD player.

A High-End Multimedia System

For you multimedia moguls, this may be the way to go. A high-end system (Figure 15.11) might include:

- Multimedia editing and control software.

- 3-D modeling software.

- Two ARTI ARM controllers—support for professional VTRs.

- Two professional editing VTRs and a TV for crossdubbing.

- High-quality 24-bit video capture, animation, and audiodubbing hardware.

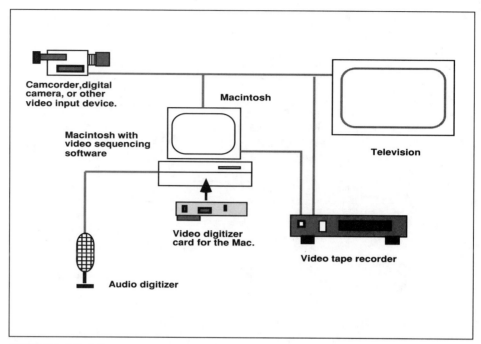

FIGURE 15.10: Intermediate multimedia system

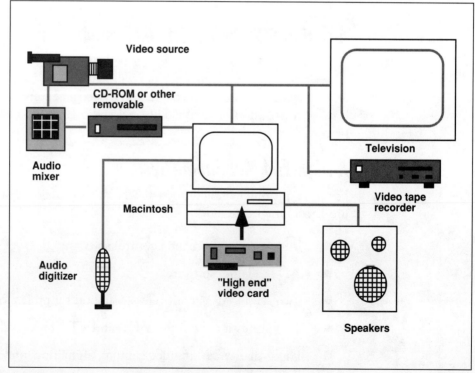

FIGURE 15.11: High-end multimedia system

MULTIMEDIA—IS IT FOR YOU?

Maybe you don't need a full-blown multimedia studio. Possibly you don't need anything close. Regardless of your situation, there is probably a way to incorporate multimedia into your workplace relatively painlessly.

I can think of all kinds of applications for multimedia. For example, a businessperson could demonstrate a manufacturing process that's still in the planning stage. A scientist could illustrate a complex organic molecule that's hard to visualize in 2D, but can be understood easily in 3D as a video clip. Teachers could use multimedia presentations to show the creation of a river valley or the formation of a geological fault without putting a classroom of students to sleep. With appropriate control hardware and software, a multimedia program could be used as a simple training simulator. These are just some ideas, and I'm sure you've got your own. If they sound like things you need to do, grit your teeth, grab your wallet, and go for it!

TROUBLESHOOTING

Problem	Cause	Solution
QuickTime movies won't play on the system	68000 Mac used	QuickTime requires a 68020 CPU or better
Slow performance of animations in HyperCard	Possible inefficient script used	Try to "streamline" animation script
Slow performance of MacroMind Director	Complex script	Try MacroMind Accelerator
Slow performance of QuickTime	Too much data being shuffled around	Reduce size of animation window
Grainy background or animations	Lower resolution data used	Use a higher resolution capture

CHAPTER SIXTEEN

Help! There's a PC in My Mac!

A whole chapter on viruses? Not exactly. The title's meant to suggest that this chapter is about software and hardware *emulators*. An emulator makes your Mac act like another, normally incompatible, system— able to display the system's graphics, read and write its files, and run its programs. Mac hardware and software emulators let it act like a PC, an Apple II, and a variety of mainframe terminals. One type of emulation, *virtual instruments*, even lets a Mac simulate measuring devices like oscilloscopes and gauges. It can be customized for any lab or industrial requirement.

I'll also be talking about file translation—using your Mac to read and write files compatible with non-Macintosh hardware.

EMULATING OTHER MACHINES WITH SOFTWARE

Software emulators are programs that let a computer run software written for a completely different, incompatible computer system. To do this, Mac emulators have to simulate the CPU and built-in instructions of an incompatible system, intercept and translate the signals that a foreign operating system and application program send to the foreign CPU and ROM, and emulate the foreign system's peripherals with a Mac's video, drives, and ports. Emulators have to do this quickly enough so that waiting for them isn't painful, and well enough that most applications for the system being emulated will run without problems.

Software emulators on the Mac and other machines have a long and checkered history. The first problem with software emulators is that many of the functions I mentioned above are not emulated perfectly enough to prevent application incompatibilities. "Well-behaved" application software that uses standard hardware codes will usually run fine, but software that uses non-standard hardware addresses and "tricks" to improve performance will generally cause problems.

The other difficulty, operating speed, is common to *all* software emulators. Even on a fast host Mac with an optimized emulator program, the emulator will not run quickly. Programs in RAM (like emulators) don't execute at nearly the speed of optimized operating system functions programmed into a computer's ROM firmware. Given the number of translations that have to take place for each foreign instruction to be executed, it's no wonder that software emulators are slow.

A general rule of thumb for emulators is that a successful program emulates a less powerful computer on a more powerful machine. A classic example was a program called "II in a Mac," which emulated an Apple IIe on a Mac. A 68000 Mac has speed and bus width advantages over a stock IIe. But apparently the program still ran somewhat slowly.

Insignia Solutions bucked the above trend slightly with SoftPC (Figure 16.1). Various flavors of SoftPC emulate different PC AT hardware on different Macs. More demanding PC AT emulation, including EGA video, requires a machine with a 68020 processor or better. The "power gap" between PC processors and the Mac's 68XXX processors is not as great as the one between the 68000 and the Apple IIe's 1MHz 65C02 processor, but SoftPC emulates the IBM PC successfully, if slowly.

SoftPC is *the* software emulator for the Mac. The program comes in three versions: Entry Level SoftPC, Universal SoftPC, and Soft AT. With Soft-Node, SoftPC can be used on a Novell network.

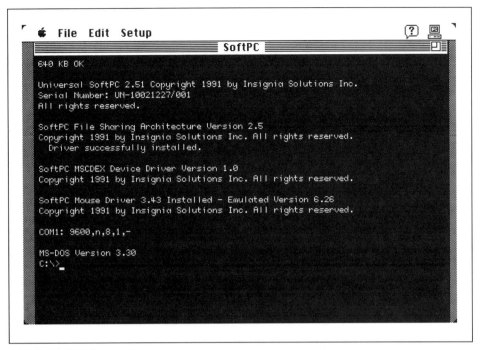

FIGURE 16.1:   SoftPC on the Mac

Entry Level SoftPC can be used with compact Macs including the Plus, SE, Classic, LC, original Portable, and PowerBook 100. To run SoftPC, a Mac needs hard drive space to use as a PC hard drive and a Mac SuperDrive (1.44MB or FDHD drive) to read PC files. You can add a third-party FDHD drive to a Mac Plus using external high-density drive kits from Dayna and Kennect.

SoftPC emulates a PC AT, and runs at PC XT speed, on the Mac Classic and LC. SoftPC needs a IIfx or better to exceed PC AT speeds. PC graphics-intensive programs like Windows, not surprisingly, don't run with acceptable speed on SoftPC. Even paging through documents will take you some time. Don't bother trying PC games.

SoftPC emulates IBM PC AT hardware, including the motherboard, controllers, ports and BIOS (Basic Input/Output System, the PC's ROM firmware) and remaps the BIOS and 80286 addresses to the Mac's 68XXX processor, as I described above. The program also maps all input and output to the Mac's I/O devices. Changing drives, video, serial ports, and adding an FPU, mouse, and expanded memory can be be done easily (anyone who has fiddled with DIP switches and configuration software in a PC will appreciate this). SoftPC supports two "hard drives"—Mac folders dedicated to DOS file storage up to 30MB—and treats Mac folders as network hard drives. Transfers between the two "worlds" are as simple as copying files (Figure 16.2). SoftPC ships with MS-DOS, GW BASIC, and a comprehensive manual.

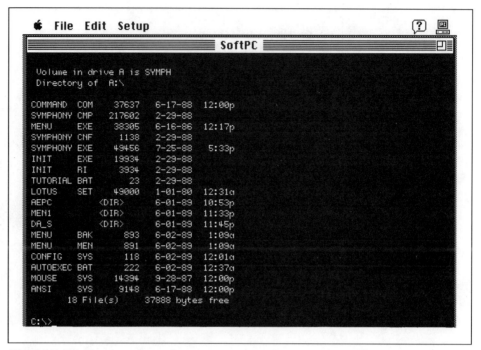

```
 File  Edit  Setup                                    ⑦ ▣

▓▓▓▓▓▓▓▓▓▓▓▓▓▓▓▓▓▓ SoftPC ▓▓▓▓▓▓▓▓▓▓▓▓▓▓▓▓▓▓

 Volume in drive A is SYMPH
 Directory of  A:\

COMMAND  COM    37637   6-17-88  12:00p
SYMPHONY CMP   217602   2-29-88
MENU     EXE    38305   6-16-86  12:17p
SYMPHONY CNF     1138   2-29-88
SYMPHONY EXE    49456   7-25-88   5:33p
INIT     EXE    19934   2-29-88
INIT     RI      3934   2-29-88
TUTORIAL BAT       23   2-29-88
LOTUS    SET    49000   1-01-80  12:31a
AEPC          <DIR>     6-01-89  10:53p
MEN1          <DIR>     6-01-89  11:33p
DA_S          <DIR>     6-01-89  11:45p
MENU     BAK      893   6-02-89   1:09a
MENU     MEN      891   6-02-89   1:09a
CONFIG   SYS      118   6-02-89  12:01a
AUTOEXEC BAT      222   6-02-89  12:37a
MOUSE    SYS    14394   9-28-87  12:00p
ANSI     SYS     9148   6-17-88  12:00p
     18 File(s)     37888 bytes free

C:\>
```

FIGURE 16.2:   PC files "mounted" on a Mac

Entry Level SoftPC is designed to work at acceptable speeds on low-end compact Macs and portables. Universal SoftPC works with all Macs, and like Entry Level uses CGA or low-resolution, PC graphics emulation (Figure 16.3). Universal SoftPC has been tested and works well with PC CD-ROMs and can be connected to a Novell network with SoftNode. SoftAT emulates a PC AT to the hilt, complete with EGA graphics as well as math coprocessor and expanded memory support. SoftAT requires 68020 or faster Macs. SoftNode PC lets SoftPC run Novell Network PC client software on any Mac.

So what can you do with a slow PC AT in your Mac? Well, for starters, with Universal SoftPC, you can get access to all of those other great CD-ROM disks which, up to now, were usable only on PCs.

If you want to connect your Mac to a network quickly and easily, you can use SoftPC with SoftNode. You can even use PC network software programs and utilities in a Mac window. With SoftAT installed on a Mac II or greater, you can easily view and edit PC graphics at EGA resolutions before exporting them to the Mac side.

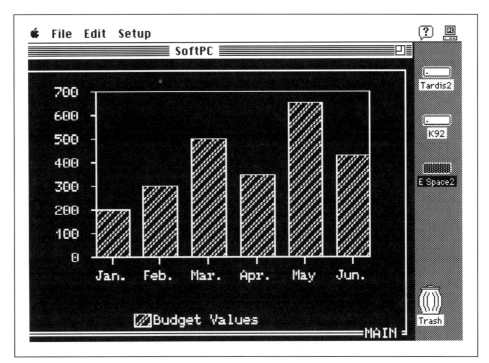

FIGURE 16.3: Universal SoftPC and CGA graphics

TRANSLATING AND TRANSFERRING

Another way to "emulate" other computer systems is by translating their files to a format usable on your Mac. Because Mac versions of a number of popular PC programs are now available, you can often create a file on the Mac and transfer it, complete with all formatting, to a PC. A number of Mac programs will read Apple II files, and a number of Apple II programs can do the same thing with files from the Mac.

If you want to transfer files to another system but your software doesn't have the translators you need, you can buy software translation utilities and format files that exchange your work with a huge variety of programs on other systems.

Finally, if you're tired of using the Apple File Exchange to transfer data to and from MS-DOS disks, you can get a utility that mounts these disks on your Mac's desktop. All you have to do is copy the files to the folder you want them in and read them with a compatible application.

Built-in File Exchange

The most common way to run files from incompatible computer systems on your Mac has been the built-in file translators provided with application software. If you expect to transfer a lot of files to a non-Mac environment and want to go this route, you should pick software that provides translation to the file types that the destination environment uses.

Because software vendors now realize that "no Mac is an island," most commercial software now includes at least some type of built-in file translation. WordPerfect for the Mac writes files that are compatible with PC versions of WordPerfect, although files with embedded graphics will be a problem. Microsoft builds a variety of translations into Word, including RTF (Rich Text Format—a Microsoft file exchange standard), and MS-DOS Word. Lotus 1-2-3 for the Mac saves files as MS-DOS pre-Lotus 1-2-3 version 3 spreadsheet files, as post-version 3 files, as text files, and as Microsoft Excel version 2.2 files.

If you have an Apple II and would like to transfer files to a Mac, a number of Mac programs will read Apple II formats directly. These include the integrated programs ClarisWorks and Symantec's Greatworks, which read AppleWorks Classic files, and BeagleWorks from Beagle Brothers which reads AppleWorks and AppleWorks GS files. Publish-It Easy, Timeworks' desktop publishing program, will also read AppleWorks and AppleWorks GS files.

If you're going to be exchanging Mac graphics you'll run into CGM, DXF, EPSF, IGES, and TIFF files (big-time alphabet soup!). CGM stands for Computer Graphics Metafile and is an ANSI (American National Standards Institute) standard vector graphics file format often used by plotters. DXF is the Data Exchange File format, created by AutoCAD, that is standard for PC CAD files. EPSF is an Encapsulated PostScript File. This is a binary or text file containing the PostScript graphics language code for creating a graphic. IGES is the Initial Graphics Exchange Specification, an ANSI graphics file format for 3-D wire-frame models.

TIFF is the Tagged Image File Format standard, created by Aldus and Microsoft. TIFF is a widely supported standard for exchanging bit-mapped graphics. TIFF 4.0 format has two levels, TIFF "B" and TIFF "R." TIFF "B" is used for black and white images, and TIFF "R" is for 2-, 4-, 8-, or 32-bit RGB color images. The newer TIFF 5.0 standard has three levels, TIFF "B," TIFF "P," and TIFF "R." In this case, TIFF "R" is used for 24-bit color files, and TIFF "P" is for 2–8 bit color files. All three file types, unlike TIFF 4, support compression.

If you want to read or write any of the above formats on a Mac, consider Canvas 3.0. It supports all of these formats.

Capture, a neat Mac DA, lets you capture Mac screens as TIFF 4 and 5 files (among others) using the ⌘–Shift-3 Mac "screen snapshot" sequence (Figure 16.4). Capture also lets you view all of the file types it supports with a software viewer utility.

CompuServe's popular graphics transfer format, GIFF (Graphics Interchange File Format), is accessible to Mac users thanks to GIFF Converter, a great shareware utility by Kevin A. Mitchell. Giff Converter will let you convert even large 32-bit color graphics files to a version that can be viewed on your Mac.

If you'd like to swap graphics between an Apple II and a Mac, you have a number of choices. Roger Wagner Publishing makes The Graphics Exchange, a utility that includes Apple II *and* Mac utility programs for transferring Mac-Paint files and Apple IIgs super Hi-Res screens between systems. The Mac utility in this package, Super Hi-Res Converter, includes a variety of "dithers" to convert a super Hi-Res graphic into a dithered monochrome image. The utility works well and the results look great.

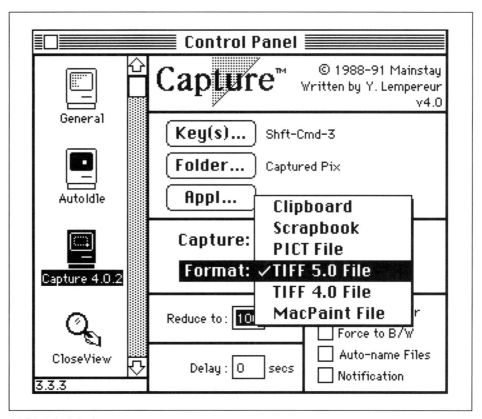

FIGURE 16.4:   Capture Control Panel

SuperConvert, an Apple IIgs utility by Jason Harper, supports a variety of graphics formats for Mac, PC, Atari, and Amiga computers, as well as common graphics interchange formats. Apple's System 6.0 for the IIgs will mount Mac disks on the gs desktop directly, without any file conversions. Text and MacPaint files should transfer with no problem, but files such as TrueType fonts, in which the bulk of the font is a resource, should be compacted on a Mac using StuffIT 1.5.1 format and unpacked on the IIgs using ShrinkIt, by Andy Nicholas.

Using Data Exchange Software

The two premier data exchange utilities for the Mac are the Apple File Exchange (often abbreviated as AFE) and Apple's XTND file exchange technology. AFE is a utility that can read and copy files from Apple II and PC disks to your Mac. XTND is an Apple system extension that allows compatible programs to add translators for a variety of different file systems at will. Apple and a number of third-party vendors produce XTND (Figure 16.5) file translators. Some translators should be provided with any XTND-compatible program you buy.

The software gurus at DataViz produce what are probably the best Mac file exchange programs, MacLinkPlus/PC and the MacLinkPlus/Translators.

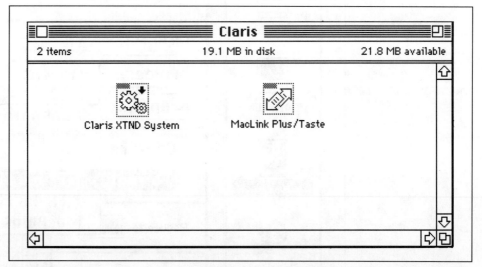

FIGURE 16.5: XTND and MacLinkPlus in the Taste word processor.

MacLinkPlus has over 350 Mac-to-PC translation combinations for spreadsheet, database, and graphics files. The program has both Mac and PC software, an RS-232 null-modem cable for a direct connection between machines, and Dayna's DOS Mounter, for mounting PC disks directly on a Mac desktop using an FDHD SuperDrive.

MacLinkPlus/Translators, like MacLinkPlus/PC, includes over 350 translators for word processing, spreadsheet, database, graphics, DOS Mounter, and Mac installation software.

The MacLinkPlus translator packages are compatible with System 7, DOS, and Windows, and can convert special European characters such as accents and umlauts.

A partial—and I mean *partial*—list of the available MacLinkPlus translators includes: Ami Pro, FrameMaker MIF 2.0 and 3.0, MacWrite 4.0, RTF, SunWrite, Microsoft Word Mac/PC, WordPerfect Mac/PC, DCA, WriteNow Mac and NeXT versions, AppleWorks WP, Excel, Lotus 1-2-3, AppleWorks SS, dBASE, Works Mac DB, the AppleWorks DB, AutoCAD.DXF, Lotus Freelance.CGM, PC Paintbrush .PCX, and PICT.

These file translators work with *both* AFE and XTND.

Mounting a "Foreign" File on Your Mac

I've already mentioned Dayna's DOS Mounter in conjunction with file translators. Another product with the same function is Access PC, produced by Insignia Solutions, the same folks that produce SoftPC. This mounting software lets you insert a DOS disk and, instead of offering to format it, shows it on the Mac desktop, or "mounts" it. You can just drag PC files off of the DOS disk and copy them onto your target Mac disk or file.

Dayna's DOS Mounter maps DOS file extensions to Mac applications; double-clicking on an MS-DOS file will automatically launch the appropriate Mac application. The program will also use "wild cards" to map two similar file extensions to one application. DOS Mounter will mount an unlimited number of MS-DOS volumes.

Dayna also makes DaynaFile II, an external 5¼" and 3½" drive that plugs into the Mac's SCSI port. The external 5¼" drive allows Mac users to read MS-DOS high-density floppies. The 3½" drive gives SuperDrive capability to a Mac Plus.

A similar product is available from Kennect Technology. The Drive 2.4 and Rapport are an external 3½" FDHD drive and plug-in controller for Macs without high-density capability. With a bundled copy of FastBack II, the drive can save up to 4MB of compressed data per disk. The Drive 2.4 works with Apple File Exchange.

PUTTING A COMPUTER IN A COMPUTER

If you want to run some serious applications for another computer system at a reasonable speed, you should consider installing a hardware emulator in your Mac. Hardware emulators are not without compatibility problems, but because they are using actual hardware compatible with non-Mac systems, software compatibility problems tend to be reduced. Problems occur when foreign application software accesses hardware locations for peripherals such as the keyboard or printer, or looks for ROM addresses that are not supported by the emulator board. This is a common occurrence with shareware and freeware application programs and games, and can cause the emulator to lock up or crash.

Currently available hardware emulators for the Macintosh include Orange Micro's Orange386 NuBus PC emulator board and Apple's Mac LC PDS-slot Apple IIe emulator board. A good secondhand buy, if you need PC XT compatibility and can find one, is AST's Mac86 emulator board for the Mac SE.

The Orange386

Orange Micro's Orange386 is a 16MHz Intel 386SX computer on a Mac NuBus board. Orange 386 comes with 1MB, expandable to 16MB, two PC AT slots, and an optional peripheral kit, for connecting external modems, printers, and floppy disk drives. Because the Orange386 is basically a 386SX on a board, you should be able to run almost all PC application software—even, God forbid, Windows. If you need to run high-end application software that's not available for the Mac, such as some mapping programs, this board may be a good choice for you.

Apple's Mac LC IIe Emulator Board

Apple produces an Apple IIe hardware emulator board for the Mac LC. The emulator board contains a 2MHz 65C02 processor, a 5¼"/3½" floppy drive port and a joystick/hand controller port, up to 256K of RAM, AppleTalk compatibility and standard Apple IIe display support. The card can use Mac hard drives, up to 1MB of Mac RAM, and Mac video as well as printer and modem ports. It provides a control panel to set "phantom slots" on the Mac LC, equivalent to the real slots on an Apple IIe. The card is started with a software utility installed on the Mac LC. Apparently the emulation produced by this card is quite good, although some graphics are a little strange due to a pixel mapping problem.

The IIe emulator board is a nice piece of work and certainly a remarkable achievement, but I wouldn't recommend it to IIe owners thinking of upgrading to an LC who want to keep their existing software. If you want to have IIe compatibility, keep your existing machine. The IIe has paid its dues, is reliable, and has *real* slots—no phantom slotting required. You can also use that single Mac LC PDS slot for something else like an accelerator, coprocessor, modem, or graphics card.

 One really good use for a Mac LC IIe emulator board is in a school Mac LC. The IIe emulator will let a teacher work on the LC or LC II as well as make up and mark assignments using IIe emulation.

A good secondhand buy for the Mac SE owner who can find one is the AST Mac86 PC XT emulator board. The board plugs into an SE's expansion slot and will run XT-compatible programs, allowing you to cut and paste between PC and Mac applications. Sun Remarketing sold these boards in the past and may be a good first place to look for one.

THE TERMINAL SOLUTION

Aaaahhhlll be baaack! No, we're not talking about Arnie here. Terminal emulators are Mac hardware and software packages that allow you to connect the machine to mainframes and configure it to perform like a dedicated terminal.

For example, DCA's MacIRMA workstation card and software (Figure 16.6) allows a Mac to act as an IBM 3270 mainframe terminal on an SNA network. The MacIRMA hardware/software combination can connect to a variety of IBM mainframes in a variety of other environments as well. The software fully supports an IBM terminal while allowing you to cut and paste between windows and sessions. Graphics emulation is available. The program supports System 7 publish-and-subscribe and Balloon Help.

The MacIrma combination can be used as a gateway on a variety of networks, including Token Ring.

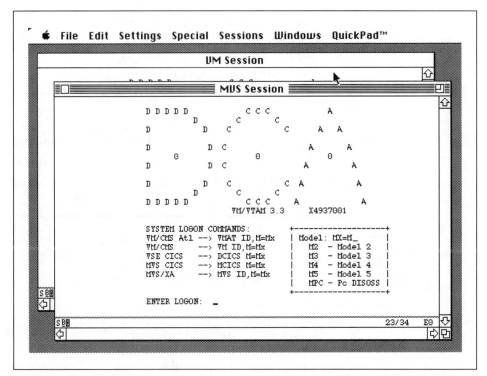

FIGURE 16.6:   The MacIRMA IBM workstation

Avatar/Tri-Data makes the MacMainFrame series of terminal emulator hardware/software for a variety of mainframe and PC network environments.

SOFT INSTRUMENTS?

National Instruments produces software that lets Macs do process measurement and control in labs. For slotted Macs, it offers LabView software and GPIB, VXI and RS-232 NuBus hardware interface cards; for compact Macs it offers SCSI boxes. GPIB and VXI are measurement standards for lab or factory data acquisition hardware. RS-232, of course, is the old serial "standard."

LabView 2 (Figure 16.7) is a graphical programming system that allows users to create software modules called virtual instruments (or VIs) instead of writing custom control programs for lab equipment. LabView 2 has a simple

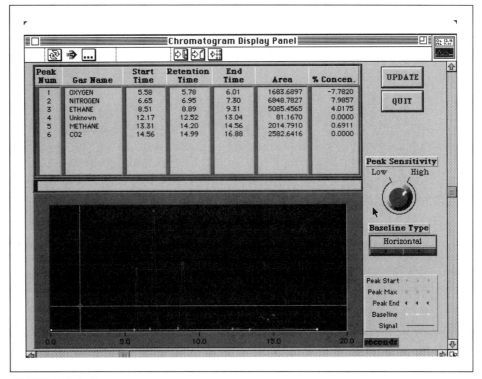

FIGURE 16.7:   LabView on the Mac

programming language for the creation of VIs. LabView 2 software "instruments" are interactive and take advantage of Mac multitasking. LabView lets users build custom instruments in addition to the standard ones provided, change their panel controls, and customize the flow and analysis of data from sensing instrument to the virtual panel.

TO EMULATE OR NOT TO EMULATE

As you see, there are a number of ways to make your Mac behave like another computer, trade files with a variety of different systems, or sit on a workbench and simulate a laboratory instrument. The only question now is what you want your Mac to do and whether or not emulation can help you.

TROUBLESHOOTING

Problem	Cause	Solution
Your Mac software will not translate a file it has translators for	Your software may not recognize newer versions of the datafile	Check the file type and resave in an older format or get newer file translators
You cannot access your hardware emulator card	You may not have the necessary hardware drivers loaded for the card	Make sure that the driver software is properly installed on your hard drive
Your lab measurement software is "dropping" data	Your machine may not be able to keep up with the amount of data it's being fed	Try a faster machine or a larger data buffer
Software used with the emulator locks, gives error messages, or crashes after starting to boot	Possible incompatibility with older operating system	Make sure that you have a compatible operating system installed
Screen graphics look odd with software run on a Mac LC Apple IIe emulator board	The difference between Mac and Apple pixels produces some strange effects, at least with older emulator boards	If this causes problems, you may want to try a newer board or an upgrade if one becomes available

CHAPTER SEVENTEEN

Summary

Now that you have some ideas for a Mac upgrade, you'll need to spend some time "sweating the small stuff." This chapter is meant to help. It shows how to do comparison shopping and where to look for bargains, gives some tips on setting up and looking after your machine and peripherals, and tells where to go for help.

BEFORE YOU GET SERIOUS—LOOKING AROUND

If you've finally decided to upgrade your Mac and know what you want, you're in a position to do some serious shopping. When you're in the market for a software upgrade, you can start checking Mac magazines, like *MacWorld* and *MacUser*, for software bargains. But wait a bit before you do.

Check the local tabloids first. It's not unusual to find ads from people selling the software still in the shrinkwrap.

Check your local software dealer's shelves for older versions of the program you're interested in. Older software will give you a lot of features for a substantial discount. The only caveat applies to people using, or thinking of upgrading to, newer operating systems like System 7. Be sure when you pick your bargain-basement software that it's compatible with your operating system.

If you can't find anything on the local software shelves and decide to go with mail-order, take your time and scan the ads for bargains. You can usually get an excellent price and, frequently, a software "bundle" containing a number of programs in addition to the one you're looking for.

If you're shopping for a hardware upgrade, especially a hard drive, don't forget to check the local computer hardware market. With the proper formatting software, cables, and mounting hardware, you can get locally supplied brand-name SCSI drives working with your Mac (don't forget that PC dealers carry SCSI drives too—but you'll have to know what you're looking for). When you buy hardware locally, you have a local dealer's warranty and repairs to fall back on, and you don't have to worry about shipping your drive out of town for repairs. If you order hardware by mail, try an established Mac hardware supplier, at least initially. It's important to find out as much about mail-order dealers as you can before spending a lot of money with them. If a mail-order house is a long-term, regular advertiser with a major Mac magazine, the odds are good that it's safe. However, you are well advised to try some minor purchases with a company to check their service and reliability.

Good Mac mail-order houses will be able to provide you with the correct hardware if you give them the correct information. Start with the type of Mac you have and type of peripherals you're looking for, the size of the peripherals, and how you'll be connecting them. With external SCSI devices, for instance, the company you're ordering from will need to know whether you need a Mac system cable (Mac to peripheral) or a Mac peripheral cable (50-pin SCSI to SCSI), and whether you need a terminator. If you're buying a Mac external SCSI device, ask the following questions:

- Does it have two 50-pin SCSI plugs on the back?
- Does it have a metal case (for more shielding/mechanical protection)?
- Does it have an external switch to set the SCSI ID?
- Does it include an external terminator?

- Will they supply the type of cable you need and will it cost extra?

- Do they supply formatting software?

- Does the device come pre-formatted with an operating system installed? (Which one? 6 or 7?)

- Is there any software bundled with the device?

If you're shopping for a Mac video upgrade, you have other things to consider. If you see a bargain price on a monitor, is it a true bargain? Another monitor may include a graphics card in the list price. However, if the card isn't one that you would normally choose, then this particular monitor and card bundle isn't a great deal for you. Consider what type of resolution you want and what sort of card will be necessary to handle it. Can you live with a monochrome monitor, or is grayscale a better choice? If you do a lot of desktop publishing, a two-page monochrome monitor might be the best investment for you. If you want a high-resolution monitor that will let you use QuickTime and view graphics in a sharp, photographic-quality format, while not blowing your budget, a good quality MultiSync grayscale monitor such as one of the NEC series may be your best choice.

A good variety of Macintosh printers is available from mail-order distributors, but you may want to check the local market for deals before going to a mail-order source. This reduces the risk inherent in shipping expensive, relatively delicate, hardware. However, you may find that a mail-order distributor's price is just too good to pass up.

Things to consider before buying a printer by mail-order include:

- What type of print quality, speed, noise level, and operating costs can you live with?

- Do you want to pay the premium for PostScript, or will a Quick-Draw printer "fit your pistol"?

- If you decide to go for a QuickDraw printer, can it be upgraded to PostScript later?

- Do you need a print spooler, and does spooler software come with the printer you're considering?

- Is the manufacturer of your printer known for reliability, service, and support?

- Is there a local repair depot for your brand and model of printer?

- Is there a local source for supplies like toner, cartridges, or ribbons for your printer?

- Docs the mail-order house handle specialized supplies for your printer and have they handled the brand for some time?

Mail-order is probably the best source of low-cost, high-performance, Mac-compatible modems. As I mentioned in the chapter on telecommunications, you should buy the fastest modem and the fastest hardware modulation and error checking you can afford. If you can get fax capability thrown in, so much the better. Try to get a fairly well-known brand such as Supra, Prometheus, US Robotics, or Hayes. This increases the chances of getting a modem repaired or replaced promptly, in case of problems. You can find some excellent deals on modems that are not made by major suppliers of telecom equipment, but don't expect much service and support.

Find out what is supplied with the modem. Will you get a cable, or should you tack that cost on to the price quote? Is any telecommunications software provided with the modem, and which package is it? If you see a *very* good deal on a fax modem, verify whether it is send-fax or send-recieve fax. Send-fax modems are much cheaper to build and lower-priced as a result. If you're getting fax capability with your modem, try to find out about the Mac fax software, how it works, and what Mac fax operations it supports.

Buying other types of hardware by mail-order will leave you with other important items to mention, and questions to ask the hardware vendor. Once again, know what you want and make sure that the mail-order dealer you're talking to knows what sort of hardware you're installing it on. Make a short list of things to ask and mention, and make sure they get said. This will ensure that you get the hardware you want and reduce the number of returns you have to make.

LOOKING TO NON-MAC DEALERS FOR BARGAINS

I've had a lot of luck with Mac hardware dealers and have been pleased with the service I've received. However, I can't deny that a lot of PC hardware discounters give phenomenal prices on high-quality, Mac-compatible peripherals. I mentioned above that when you buy from a non-Mac dealer, you should know *exactly* what you want. A PC hardware dealer is not going to be able to answer Mac hardware questions for you.

If you have formatting software and mounting hardware, you can buy Quantum LP or Connor (for instance) SCSI drives from a source such as Hard Drives International (HDI has advertised in Mac magazines, so they may have some folks who can answer Mac-specific questions). You can use *some* generic VGA monitors with your Mac LC and LC II. Not all VGA monitors are compatible with the LC, and you'll need the proper cable. A number of multiscanning monitors from NEC and Mitsubishi are compatible with *both* a Mac and a PC, and thus may be had from PC discounters. You'll need a Mac cable, but you may be able to get this from a local NEC or Mitsubishi dealer. PC QuickDraw lasers can be a good deal. They should be HP LaserJet compatible, so you can get Mac drivers for them. Okidata, in particular, produces a very low-priced 4 ppm non-PostScript laser printer.

To use a low-priced PC PostScript laser with a Mac, you'll need Mac drivers. It's hard to believe that the manufacturer of a PC PostScript laser printer would ignore the Mac market, so you should usually be able to get drivers directly from the manufacturer, if necessary. I *highly* recommend that you confirm this first.

The advice I gave you for dealing with Mac mail-order houses applies doubly to PC mail-order dealers. Make *sure* you know exactly what you need—model, size, type, power requirements, and other specs.

SHOPPING FOR BARGAINS

You can pick up some good Mac peripherals, and even CPUs, in the used equipment market. I repeat that "caveat emptor"—let the buyer beware—prevails. But used computers and monitors are often good secondhand buys.

A Mac has little in the way of moving parts except for the built-in $3\frac{1}{2}$" drive, and a used computer is well "burned in" (all the parts have been subjected to heat, and any inclined to fail have already done so). However, secondhand drives and printers are another matter. You don't know how much wear and tear they've been through.

For instance, was a hard drive used on a BBS (Bulletin Board System)? If so, the drive has been through hardware hell—continual operation and continual drive access.

If you're interested in a used drive or printer, you should at least ask for a demo, preferably a demo with the peripheral and/or Mac hooked up. If everything works properly and is reasonably quiet, you can assume as a first guess that the equipment is in reasonable shape (this is still a dangerous assumption for hard drives). If a secondhand peripheral looks a little banged up, chances are that it is.

You can look for used equipment at local user group sales (not a bad bet since this stuff is usually well looked after), in the local papers, at discount or closeout equipment sales from local dealers, or through private deals with Mac users who want to upgrade. Sun Remarketing is an authorized dealer of used Mac hardware and may be a good place to look.

GETTING IT HOME

When you've paid a lot of money for Mac hardware, you want to get it home in one piece. If you're ordering from a mail-order dealer, make sure that your purchase will be sent via a reliable shipper, and get a purchase order number so you can track the shipment if you have problems. Pay by credit card—you can cancel your charge if necessary and it gives you one more way to track an order. When your shipment arrives, check the packing for damage before you let the delivery company leave your order.

When you unpack, keep track of all pieces and make sure you received everything you ordered. As soon as possible, test your peripheral, computer, or software and make sure that it works properly. If there's a hardware problem, call the company you purchased from and let them know you'll be returning it. Find out if an RMA (return material authorization) number is required and *make sure* that you record it and note it on your return packaging. If your order is OK and includes some delicate hardware, keep the packing material. You'll be able to use it to ship the product if you have problems later.

If you're buying secondhand, try to keep old packing materials with the used equipment so you can transport it safely. Keep computers and monitors on the floor if you're moving them by car. It's wise to keep a floppy in the disk drive when you transport most computers. Exceptions are FDHD floppy drives, which park their heads when they're not in use, and removable drives, which retract the read-write heads.

Generally, expansion boards for modular machines are safer if they're left in the Mac for transport. Pack cables carefully so that they won't get stepped on. Make sure not to place heavy articles on connectors—that might result in warped plugs and bent pins. It may be safer to transport dot-matrix printers with a piece of paper on the platen roller to protect the printhead pins. If you're transporting a used laser printer, ask the owner if he has the original shipping plugs and insert them before moving the laser.

UNPACKING THE GOODIES

I mentioned that you should check your purchases when you receive them from a mail-order company. This check should cover these basic questions:

- Is everything I ordered included? If not, is there a back-order notice?
- Is there any damage to anything?

- Are all the parts I need included?

- Is everything in working order?

When you buy from a local dealer, be sure of what you're buying. What does his package deal include, and are all the pieces available immediately? If anything is missing or to be delivered, *make sure* that the dealer notes on your invoice what is to be supplied, when it will be shipped, and that shipping does *not* cost extra.

Make sure that you keep your invoice. It will be of use to you later. When you get the boxes home, open them up, make sure all of the parts are present, and compare the contents to your invoice. If anything is missing, notify the dealer *immediately*. If you have a lot of unresolved trouble with an Apple dealer, try writing him a letter and sending a copy to Apple. That may help get his attention.

As I said, when buying secondhand, caveat emptor applies. This also applies to unpacking and reassembling old equipment. If connectors have had a lot of use, they may start to loosen up. Treat them with TLC, and the equipment will last long enough to become someone else's secondhand Mac hardware.

SETTING 'EM UP

Set up a safe, well-ventilated place for your new, or newly upgraded, Mac equipment. Avoid cable "snakepits." Plan cable runs to keep cables safe and out of sight. Back up any installation software and never, never use originals for installations. At the very least, make sure that your installation disks are locked before you use them. If you're planning to partition a storage device, plan the size and number of partitions to make backing up and restoring your software (and organizing your device) easy for you.

ERGONOMICS—MAKING IT COMFORTABLE

When you set up new peripherals or rearrange your old ones, do it with your comfort in mind. Ergonomics is the study of how humans interact with devices and how the interaction can be made easier. You can set up your own ergonomic project with your computer room as the target.

Making your computer room more comfortable doesn't just involve moving peripherals—it involves changing some habits. The following rules for making a computer room more comfortable are often suggested by researchers into computer-related health problems:

- Don't stare at your computer screen for very long periods of time. Shift your vision and look into the distance periodically.

- Take breaks to do other things about once an hour.

- Your keyboard should be no higher than $2\frac{1}{2}$"($6\frac{1}{2}$ cm) above your desktop and should be as thin as possible.

- Your wrist and lower arm should be parallel to the floor, and you should move your keyboard from time to time.

- If your arms and wrists get tired, consider using a wrist rest.

- A thick book or phone book can be an effective foot rest. For a wrist rest, you can use a rolled slab of foam rubber or a rolled towel.

- Your monitor should have tilt and swivel adjustment if possible. The top of the screen should be at eye level and the screen tilted back 10°–20°.

- The distance between your eyes and the computer screen should be 18"–20" (45–50 cm).

- Printed documents you're typing from should be at the same level as your computer screen, to cut down on head and neck movements.

- Your chair should be adjustable with good support in the small of the back. You should set it so that your back and neck are straight and both feet are flat on the floor.

- Do periodic wrist and neck exercises, to "loosen things up."

- Place your CRT out of direct light and at least 50° to an overhead light.

KEEPIN' 'EM SAFE

When you've spent a (small) boatload of money on a Mac upgrade, you're going to want to safeguard your investment. This will require a little planning and regular maintenance on your part, as well as some additional hardware investment.

The first and most important safeguard for a Mac is a *good* surge protector with a phone plug. If you live in an area where lightning doesn't strike and power surges and sags are not a problem, you may not need one, but otherwise, don't take chances. Good surge protectors often use MOVs, or metal oxide varistors, to divert surges to ground. You want the *clamping voltage* (the voltage where the protector kicks in) as low as possible and a *response time* as quick as possible. Even small power spikes can injure your Mac. Their effect on the machine's ROMs is cumulative, and eventually will cause a system failure. A power surge through the phone lines can cook your modem *and* your computer.

If you live in the country and have a lot of power fluctuations, you may want to look at a UPS, or uninterruptible power supply. This type of system has battery power to smooth out power fluctuations (line power charges the battery, and the battery runs your computer). In the event of a power outage, you have time to save your work and shut down your Mac. A UPS also isolates your computer from powerline surges, sags, and spikes.

Keep your equipment clean. Dust can do strange and occasionally nasty things to computer equipment. You can use "canned air" to clean off a modular Mac logic board periodically. Clean your computer screen regularly with screen cleaner and clean your keyboard regularly. Keep hard drive and computer vents and fans clear. Clean your floppy drive heads about once a year. Clean and lubricate your printer according to the manufacturer's instructions.

USER GROUPS—THE BEST MAC UPGRADE NEVER SOLD

You've seen how you can improve your Mac's memory, speed, and video output, how you can enhance print quality, and how you can run software written for other computer systems. But an Apple users group is your ultimate upgrade—a large, real-time help file and diagnostic utility for your Mac that you'll never find on a software dealer's shelf.

Your friendly neighborhood user group is a source of system software upgrades and the latest public domain shareware and freeware programs. Apple-sanctioned user groups receive copies of Mac Technotes concerning Mac hardware and software details, hints, and tips.

If you're looking into a hardware or software upgrade, you can get an unbiased evaluation from people who use the products you're interested in. You can often pick up good deals on used equipment from the guy who wants to move up to the latest and greatest in Macdom.

It took some time, but apparently Apple now recognizes the importance of user groups for evangelizing their hardware and software, and consults user groups for ideas and suggestions. Apple's User Group Connection program is an attempt to maintain contact and keep ideas flowing.

Finally, user groups often get volume discounts and special presentations from software vendors that aren't available *anywhere* else.

If it sounds like I'm a fan of user groups, you're getting my message. I've been a member of a local user group for about twelve years now.

You can get information about your local Apple user group from local computer enthusiasts, Apple authorized dealers, local newspapers, or Apple bulletin board systems. You can also call the Apple User Group Connection toll-free at 1-800-538-9696 or write:

The Apple User Group Connection

Apple Computer, Inc.

20525 Mariani Avenue, M/S 48AA

Cupertino, CA 95014.

THAT'S ALL FOLKS!

Well, there you have it—any number of ways to improve and enhance your Mac. I hope you're a little bit more comfortable working "under the hood." But watch it, hardware hacking can be addictive. Be careful by all means, but, above all, have fun!

Hardware and Software Manufacturers and References

These addresses and phone numbers are correct as we go to press. Be aware that they may have changed by the time you read this.

HARDWARE AND SOFTWARE MANUFACTURERS

Adobe Systems
1585 Charleston Road
P.O. Box 7900
Mountain View, CA 94039-7900
(800) 833-6687
Adobe Type Manager, PostScript

Advanced Gravis Computer Technology
1602 Carolina Street, #D12
Bellingham, WA 98226
(800) 663-8558
Gravis Mousestick

Advent Computer Products
449 Santa Fe Drive, Suite 213
Encinitas, CA 92024
(619) 942-8456
Neotech Image Compressor board, other video processors

Aladdin Systems
165 Westridge Drive
Watsonville, CA 95076
(408) 761-6200
StuffIt Classic, Deluxe

Aldus
411 First Avenue S., Suite 200
Seattle, WA 98104
(800) 332-5387
PageMaker

Alsoft
Box 927
Spring, TX 77383
(800) 257-6381
DiskExpress II, Master Juggler

America Online
Quantum Computer Services
8619 Westwood Center Drive
Vienna, VA 22182
(800) 227-6364
Online information service

Apple Computer
20525 Mariani Avenue
Cupertino, CA 95014
(408) 996-1010
The Macintosh line, and many other software and hardware products

Applied Engineering
3210 Beltline Road
Dallas, TX 75234
(800) 554-6227
Accelerators, FPUs, modems, and a variety of hardware

Articulate Systems
600 W. Cummings Park, Suite 4500
Woburn, MA 01801
(800) 443-7077
Voice Navigator

Alliance Peripheral Systems (APS)
2900 S. 291 Highway
Independence, MO 64057
(800) 233-7550
Hard and Optical Drives

Alysis
1231 31st Avenue
San Francisco CA 94122
(800) 825-9747
More Disk Space compression utility

ATEC
Niedstrasse 22
D-1000
Berlin 41, Germany
011-49-30-8592958
FPU Classic

ATTO Technology
Baird Research Park
1576 Sweet Home Road
Amherst, NY 14228
(716) 688-4259
Fast disk controllers

Avatar
65 South Street
Hopkinton, MA 01748
(800) 235-3270
MacMainFrame

Aztech Micro Solutions
130 McCormick Avenue, Suite 103
Costa Mesa, CA 92626
(800) 524-3500
Merida upgrade kits, Galexa upgrades

Beagle Brothers
6215 Ferris Square, Suite 100
San Diego, CA 92121
(800) 345-1750
Flash, BeagleWorks

BMUG
(Berkeley Macintosh Users Group)
1442A Walnut Street, Suite 62
Berkeley, CA 94709-1496
(510) 549-2684
**Mac information; technical assistance
for members only**

Bootman 1.1
Bill Steinberg
CompuServe 76703,1027
AOL XO542
GEnie BillS
**Freeware, increases heap size under
System 6—similar to HeapFixer**

Broderbund Software
P.O. Box 6125
Novato, CA 94948-6125
(800) 521-6263
TypeStyler

CalComp
2411 W. LaPalma Avenue
Anaheim, CA 92801
(800) 225-2667
CalComp Plotters

CE Software
P.O. Box 65580
West Des Moines, IA 50265
(800) 523-7638
DiskTop, QuicKeys, HeapFixer

Central Point Software
15220 N.W. Greenbrier Parkway #200
Beaverton, OR 97006
(503) 690-8090
PC Tools Deluxe, PC Tools V.2.0 Mac

CH Products
970 Park Center Drive
Vista, CA 92083
(800) 624-5804
RollerMouse

Claris
5201 Patrick Henry Drive
Santa Clara, CA 95052
(800) 628-2100
ClarisWorks

CompuServe
5000 Arlington Center Boulevard
Columbus, OH 43220
(800) 848-8199
Online information service

Computer Friends
14250 N.W. Science Park Drive
Portland, OR 97229
(800) 547-3303
Movie Producer board & software

Connectix
2655 Campus Drive, Suite 100
San Mateo, CA 94403
(800) 950-5880
**Mode32, Virtual 3.0, MAXIMA, MC73
PMMUs**

Corel Systems
1600 Carling Avenue
Ottawa, Ontario
Canada K1Z 8R7
(613) 728-8200
WORM Drives

CoStar
22 Bridge Street
Greenwich, CT 06830
(800) 426-7827
Stingray trackball

Dantz Develop
1400 Shattuck Avenue
Berkeley, CA 94709
(510) 849-0293
Retrospect

DataViz
55 Corporate Drive
Trumbull, CT 06611
(800) 733-0030
**MacLink/Translators, MacLink/PC,
MacLinkPlus**

Dayna Communications
50 S. Main Street, Fifth Floor
Salt Lake City, Utah 84144
(800) 531-0600
DaynaFile

Daystar Digital
5556 Atlanta Highway
Flowery Branch, Georgia 30542
(800) 962-2077
Accelerators, cache cards

DCA
1000 Alderman Drive
Alpharetta, GA 30202
(404) 442-4000
MacIRMA workstation

Deneba Software
7400 S.W. 87th Avenue
Miami, FL 33173
(800) 6-CANVAS
Canvas

Digital Vision
270 Bridge Street
Dedham, MA 02026
(617) 329-5400
Video digitizer

E-Machines
9305 S.W. Gemini Drive
Beaverton, OR 97005
(800) 344-7274
Monitors

Eastman Kodak
901 Elmgrove Road
Rochester, NY 14653
(800) 344-0006
Diconix portable printer

Educorp Computer Services
7434 Trade Street
San Diego, CA 92121
(800) 843-9497
CD-ROMs

Envisio
510 First Avenue North, Suite 303
Minneapolis, MN 55403
(612) 339-1008
**VideoSIMM display adapters for Classic,
Classic II, and PowerBook display adapters**

Everex Systems
48431 Milmont Drive
Fremont, CA 94538
(800) 821-0806 Ext. 2222
EMAC drives

Farallon Computing
2000 Powell Street #600
Emeryville, CA 94608
(510) 596-9000
**PhoneNET Connectors, Timbuktu,
EtherMac and EtherTalk cards,
PhoneNET StarController**

Fifth Generation Systems
10049 N. Reiger Road
Baton Rouge, LA 70809
(800) 873-4384
**Suitcase, Fastback II, Public Utilities,
SuperLaserSpool**

FWB
2040 Polk Street, Suite 215
San Francisco, CA 94109
(415) 474-8055
Hard Disk Toolkit, HammerDrives

GCC Technologies
580 Winter Street
Waltham, MA 02154
(800) 422-7777
QuickDraw and PostScript laser printers

GDT Softworks
P.O. Box 1865
Point Roberts, WA 98281
(800) 663-6222
PowerPrint and BetterWriters print drivers

GEnie
401 N. Washington Street
Rockville, MD 20850
(800) 638-9636
Online information service

Golden Triangle Computers
4849 Ronson Court
San Diego, CA 92111
(800) 326-1858
Disk twinning hardware; continuous real-time backup

Grolier Electronic Publishing
Old Sherman Turnpike
Danbury, CT 06816
(203) 797-3500
New electronic encyclopedia, CD-ROM products

Hayes Microcomputer Products
P.O. Box 105203
Atlanta, GA 30348
(404) 441-1617
V Series SmartModem 9600, Smartcom II

Hewlett-Packard
19310 Pruneridge Avenue
Cupertino, CA 95014
(800) 752-0900
DeskWriter, DeskWriter C, DeskJet, DeskJet C, LaserJets

Image Club Graphics
1902 11th Street, S.E.
Calgary, Alberta
Canada T2G 3G2
(800) 661-9410
Fonts and digital graphics

Insight Development Corporation
2200 Powell Street, Suite 500
Emeryville, CA 94608
(510) 652-4115
MacPrint HP print drivers

Insignia Solutions
254 Geronimo Way
Sunnyvale, CA 94086
(800) 848-7677
Entry Level SoftPC, Universal SoftPC, SoftAT, SoftNode

Iomega Corporation
1821 W. 4000 South
Roy, UT 84067
(800) 456-5522
Bernoulli Box cartridge drives

Kennect Technology
120-A Albright Way
Los Gatos, CA 95030
(408) 370-2866
Rapport/Drive 2.4

Kensington Microware
2855 Campus Drive
San Mateo, CA 94403
(800) 535-4242
Turbo Mouse 4.0, NoteBook KeyPad, Expert Mouse

KeyTronic
P.O. Box 14687
Spokane, WA 99214
(800) 262-6006
MacPro Extended Keyboard

Kiwi Software
6546 Pardall Road
Santa Barbara, CA 93117
(800) 321-5494
Kiwi Power Windows

Kurta
3007 East Chambers Street
Phoenix, AZ 85040
(800) 445-8782
Kurta IS/ADB Graphics Tablet

La Cie
19552 S.W. 90th Court
Tualatin, OR 97062
(800) 999-0143
**Express Drive, DAT Drive, Optical
Drive, Pocket Drive, Silverscanner,
Silverlining**

Lapis Technologies
1100 Marina Village Parkway, Suite 100
Alameda, CA 94501
(800) 435-2744
**Compact and modular Mac displays and
adapters**

Laser Connection
P.O. Box 850296
Mobile, AL 36685
(800) 523-2696
QMS laser printers

MacLand
4685 S. Ash Avenue
Tempe, AZ 85282
(800) 333-3353
Monitors, hard drives, optical drives

Macromedia
600 Townsend Street, Suite 310
San Francisco, CA 94103
(800) 248-4477
**MacroMind Director, Three-D,
MediaMaker, FilmMaker, MacRecorder,
SoundEdit Pro, SwivelArt**

MicroMat Computer Systems
7075 Redwood Boulevard
Novato, CA 94945
(415) 898-6227
MacEKG diagnostic program

MicroNet Technology
20 Mason
Irvine, CA 92718
(714) 837-6033
MicroNet hard drives and disk arrays

MicroSeeds Publishing
7030-B W. Hillsborough Avenue
Tampa, FL 33634
(813) 882-8635
**Redux HD Backup and Restore, HAM
launcher**

Microsoft
One Microsoft Way
Redmond, WA 98052
(800) 426-5400
Word, Excel, Windows, Works, Write

Microtech International
158 Commerce Street
East Haven, CT 06512
(800) 626-4276
Hard drives and SIMMs

MicroTouch Systems
55 Jonspin Road
Wilmington, MA 01887
(508) 694-9900
The UnMouse

Mirror Technologies
2644 Patton Road
Roseville, MN 55113
(612) 633-4450
Monitors, hard drives

Mitsubishi International
701 Westchester Avenue
White Plains, NY
(914) 997-4999
Monitors

Mobius Technologies
5835 Doyle Street
Emeryville, CA 94608
(800) 669-0556
**Display adapters for compact and
modular Macs**

Mouse Systems
47505 Seabridge Drive
Fremont, CA 94538
(510) 656-1117
A+ Mouse and Trackball/ADB

National Instruments
6504 Bridgepoint Parkway
Austin, TX 78727
(800) 258-7017
**LabView software, IEEE-488, VXI bus,
and RS-232C data acquisition cards**

NEC Technologies USA
1414 Massachusetts Avenue
Boxborough, MA 01719
(800) 388-8888
Monitors, CD-ROM drives

Newer Technology
7803 E. Osie, Suite 105
Wichita, KS 67207
(316) 685-4904
**FPU-882 and Index Gold Mathmate
floating point boards (Classic II and
Classic II/LC)**

NewGen Systems
17580 Newhope Street
Fountain Valley, CA 92708
(800) 888-1689
NewGen Turbo PS/400, other lasers

NewLife Computer
603 March Road
Kanata, Ontario K2K 2M5
(800) 663-6395
**NewLife Accelerator/video boards for
compact Macs**

Nisus Software
107 S. Cedros Avenue
Solana Beach, CA 92075
(800) 922-2993
**Nisus and Compact Nisus word-processing
programs**

Northgate Computer Systems
P.O. Box 41000
Plymouth, MN 55441
(800) 548-1993
OmniMac Ultra Keyboard

Novy Systems/Systech
1860 Fern Palm Drive
Edgewater, FL 32141
(800) 553-2038
**Compact Mac accelerators; LC and
Classic II FPUs**

Omega Sane
AppleLink:SANE.Bugs
**Early version of a fast SANE patch for
FPU and non-FPU Macs**

Orange Micro
1400 N. Lakeview Avenue
Anaheim, CA 92807
(714) 779-2772
Grappler interface and printer drivers

Outbound Systems
4840 Pearl East Circle
Boulder, CO 80301
(800) 444-4607
Outbound laptop computers

Pinnacle Micro
19 Technology
Irvine, CA 92718
(800) 553-7070
Hard and optical drives

PLI
47421 Bayside Parkway
Fremont, CA 94538
(800) 288-8754
Optical and floptical drives

PowerR
1601 Dexter Avenue N.
Seattle, WA 98109
(206) 547-8000
VGA and LCD display adapters for compact Macs

Practical Solutions
1135 N. Jones Boulevard
Tucson, AZ 85716
(602) 322-6100
The Cordless Mouse

Pre-Owned Electronics
205 Burlington Road
Bedford, MA 01730
(800) 274-5343
New and used Apple parts and complete peripherals and CPUs

Prometheus Products
9524 S.W. Tualatin Sherwood Road
Tualatin, OR 97062
(800) 328-2337
Modems and fax modems

QMS
One Magnum Pass
Mobile, AL 36618
(800) 523-2696
QMS laser printers

Quantum Corporation
1804 Yosemite Drive
Milpitas, CA 95035
(800) 752-8894
ProDrive LPS series drives

Quantum Leap Systems
15875 Highland Court
Solana Beach, CA 92075
(619) 481-8427
Classic II C2FP fast FPU board

Qume
260 S. Milpitas Boulevard
Milpitas, CA 95035
(800) 457-4447
Qume Lasers

Radius
1710 Fortune Drive
San Jose, CA 95131
(800) 547-2677
Displays and display adaptors, accelerators

RAMDisk+
Roger D. Bates
10899 N.W. Valley Vista Road
Hillsboro, OR 97124
(503) 645-3930
Shareware init to create RAM disk, $35

RasterOps
2500 Walsh Avenue
Santa Clara, CA 95051
(800) 729-2656
Color video controller boards

Salient Software
124 University Avenue, Suite 300
Palo Alto, CA 94301
(415) 321-5375
AutoDoubler, DiskDoubler

SCSI Evaluator
William A. Long
Digital Microware
P.O. Box 3527
Mission Viejo, CA 92690
SCSI drive test utility; shareware, $20

SCSI Probe
Robert Polic
AppleLink POLIC
AOL POLIC
SCSI diagnostic and mounting utility; freeware

Seiko Epson
20770 Madrona Avenue
Torrance, CA 90505
(800) 289-3776
Epson dot-matrix and laser printers

Shiva
One Cambridge Center
Cambridge, MA 02141
(800) 458-3550
EtherGate, NetBridge, and NetModem

Shreve Systems
3804 Karen Lane
Bossier City, LA 71112
(800) 227-3971
Apple parts and complete CPUs and peripherals

Sigma Designs
47900 Bayside Parkway
Fremont, CA 94538
(510) 770-0100
DoubleUp hardware compressor, a variety of video boards

SoundMaster
Bruce Tomlin
15801 Chase Hill, #109
San Antonio, TX 78256
Shareware that attaches sounds to Mac system actions; $15

Spectral Innovations
1885 Lundy Avenue, Suite 208
San Jose, CA 95131
(408) 727-1314
MacDSP AP1M and other Mac digital signal processor cards

Speedometer 3.1
Scott Berfield
26043 Gushue Street
Hayward, CA 94544
Excellent hardware evaluation utility; shareware, $30

Storage Dimensions
1656 McCarthy Boulevard
Milpitas, CA 95035
(408) 954-0710
Hard disks and fast drive controllers

Storm Technology
1861 Landings Drive
Mountain View, CA 94043
(800) ASK-JPEG
Picture Press image-compression accelerator

Summagraphics
60 Silvermine Road
Seymour, CT 06483
(800) 221-9244
SummaSketch graphics tablets

Sun Remarketing
Box 4059
Logan, UT 84321
(800) 821-3221
Used and reconditioned Mac equipment

Super Mac Technologies
485 Potrero Avenue
Sunnyvale, CA 94086
(408) 245-2202
Spectrum monitors, interface cards, accelerators

Symantec
10201 Torre Avenue
Cupertino, CA 95014
(800) 441-7234
Norton Utilities for Macintosh (now includes SUM II, Symantec Utilities for Macintosh), GreatWorks

SyQuest
47071 Bayside Parkway
Fremont, CA 94538
(510) 226-4000
Removable hard disk cartridges

Tektronix
P.O. Box 500
Beaverton, OR 97077
(800) 426-2200
Lasers and PostScript color printers

Technology Works
4030 Braker Lane West, Suite 350
Austin, TX 78759
(800) 688-7466
SIMMs, GraceLAN

Telebit
1315 Chesapeake Terrace
Sunnyvale, CA 94089
(800) 835-3248
Trailblazer modems

The Software Toolworks
60 Leberoni Court
Novato, CA 94949
(415) 883-3000
The Software Toolworks World Atlas CD-ROM

Thunderware
21 Orinda Way
Orinda, CA 94563
(800) 628-0693
Thunderscan and Lightningscan scanners

TimeWorks
625 Academy Drive
Northbrook, IL 60062
(800) 535-9497
Publish It!

T/Maker
1390 Villa Street
Mountain View, CA 94041
(800) 688-2850 (ordering only)
ClickArt, WriteNow

Bruce Tomlin
15801 Chase Hill Boulevard, #108
San Antonio, TX 78256
SoundMaster

TOPS/Sitka
950 Marina Village Parkway
Alameda, CA 94501
(800) 445-8677
TOPS

Total Systems
1720 Willow Creek Circle
Eugene, OR 97402
(800) 874-2288
Accelerator cards

Tulin
2156H O'Toole Avenue
San Jose, CA 95131
(408) 432-9025
Hard, floptical, and tape units and kits

US Robotics
8100 N. McCormick Boulevard
Skokie, IL 60076
(800) 342-5877
Courier and Courier HST modems

Wacom
501 S.E. Columbia Shores Boulevard, Suite 300
Vancouver, WA 98661
(800) 922-6613
Wacom graphics tablets

Wetex International
1122 W. Washington Boulevard, Suite D
Montebello, CA 90640
(800) 759-3839
Computer and drive cases and cables

REFERENCE BOOKS AND MAGAZINES

A+/InCider
IDG Communications
80 Elm Street
Peterborough, NH 03458
(603) 924-0100
Apple II and Mac hard and software information

Computer Shopper
Coastal Associates Publishing
One Park Avenue
New York, NY 10016
A source of low-priced hardware that can be used for Mac upgrades

Macintosh Product Registry
Redgate Communications Corporation
660 Ranchland Boulevard
Vero Beach, FL 32963
Every Mac product you wanted to know about, and a few you didn't

MacWorld
MacWorld Communications
501 Second Street
San Francisco, CA 94107
Hardware upgrade information, advertising and tips

MacUser
950 Tower Lane
18th Floor
Foster City, CA 94404
Hardware upgrade information, advertising and tips

OTHER RECOMMENDED SYBEX TITLES

The following Sybex computer books are also available from your local bookstore on these selected topics:

Encyclopedia Macintosh
Craig Danuloff and Deke McClelland
The only Macintosh reference you'll ever need—with dozens of software tips and techniques.

The Macintosh Hard Disk Companion
J. Russell Roberts
An indispensible reference guide to hard disk maintenance on the Macintosh.

Macintosh System 7: Everything You Need to Know
Deke McClelland
Excellent coverage of System 7. The book includes a disk of useful utility programs.

The Audible Macintosh
David M. Rubin
An excellent resource guide to sound and music on your Mac—a wealth of hardware tips.

Anybody's Mac Book
Tom Cuthbertson
A plain-English guide for anybody new to computers and the Macintosh.

Totally Rad Mac Programs
Owen W. Linzmayer
A compendium of entertaining and useful programs for the Mac.

Software and Hardware Error Codes

When the Mac has a problem, it often tells you what's wrong through the use of error codes. These can be a big help when you do a home upgrade—if you have Mac trouble even after you've read this book (unlikely though it may seem...), the codes can help you troubleshoot. Below is a complete list of Mac error codes.

SOFTWARE ERROR CODES

System 6 reports system software errors as codes (System 7 "translates" these for human consumption).

Table B.1 lists the codes that tell why your system bombed. They appear in a box on your screen along with a bomb icon.

Table B.2 shows the codes for "general error alert" dialog boxes. For some errors, you can click "OK" in the box and return to your application, sadder but wiser. For others, the Mac will close your application and return you to the system.

ERROR	ERROR MESSAGE	MEANING
1	Bus Error	Either a software bug or a hardware problem.
2	Address Error	Unrecognized address used by program.
3	Illegal Instruction	Program gave instruction to computer that is not in the 680x0 instruction set.
4	Division by Zero	Mac applications can't process values divided by zero.
5	Range Check Error	Number exceeds allowable range.
6	Overflow	Integer data "overflow."
7	Privilege Violation	User mode set when supervisor mode should have been in use.
8	Trace Mode Error	Error while debugging.
9	Line 1010 Trap	Serious system error.
10	Line 1111 Trap	Used for debugging.
11	Hardware Exception Error	Application error or incompatibility.
12	Unimplemented Core Routine	Undefined code.
13	Uninstalled Interrupt	Unusual interrupt (i.e., pushed programmer's switch).
14	I/O Core	A low-level input/output error.
15	Segment Loader Error	Failure to read and load a program segment. Corrupted System file?
16	Floating Point Error	Error with a calculation. Corrupted System file?
17	List Manager Not Present	Program tools absent. Corrupted System file?
18	Bit Edit Not Present	Program tools absent. Corrupted System file?
19	Disk Initialization Package Not Present	Can't locate the disk initialization tools. Corrupted System file?

TABLE B.1:   System Bomb Errors

ERROR	ERROR MESSAGE	MEANING
20	Standard File Not Present	Program tools absent. Corrupted system file?
21	SANE Not Present	Can't find SANE tools. Corrupted system file?
22	SANE Transcendental Functions Not Present	Portion of SANE missing. Corrupted system file?
23	International Utilities Not Present	Missing international conversion utilities. Corrupted system file?
24	Binary-Decimal Conversion Package Not Present	Program tools absent. Corrupted system file?
25	Out of Memory	Memory has been filled or is highly fragmented.
26	Bad Program Launch	Could not find and launch a program. Segment loader error.
27	File System Map Trashed	Major damage to the disk's file system.
28	Stack Ran Into Heap	Ran out of heap memory.
29	AppleShare Error	Problem with an AppleShare server.
30	Disk Insertion Error	
31	No Disk Inserted	
32	Memory Manager Error	
33	Memory Manager Error	Unexpectedly ran out of memory.
34-50	Memory Manager Error	
41	The Finder Could Not Be Found on the Disk	
51	Unservicable Slot Interrupt	Mac malfunctioned or has a NuBus error.
52-53	Memory Manager Error	
81	Bad SANE Opcode	Error in a SANE call.

TABLE B.1: System Bomb Errors (continued)

ERROR	ERROR MESSAGE	MEANING
84	Menu Purged While in Use	The Menu contents were removed from memory while being used. Software error.
85	Couldn't Load MBDF	
86	Couldn't Load Hierarchical Menu's Parent	
87	Couldn't Load WDEF	
88	Couldn't Load CDEF	
90	Floating Point Coprocessor Not Installed	Program was looking for an FPU and couldn't find one.

TABLE B.1: System Bomb Errors (continued)

Input/Output Errors	
ERROR	**ERROR MESSAGE**
−17	Can't perform requested control procedure.
−18	Can't perform requested status procedure.
−19	Can't read.
−20	Can't write.
−21	Device or driver unknown.
−22	Device or driver unknown.
−23	Driver not opened for requested read or write.
−25	Attempt to open driver.
−26	Driver resource missing.
−27	Input or output request aborted.
−28	Driver not open.

TABLE B.2: General Error Alert Codes

File Errors	
ERROR	**ERROR MESSAGE**
−33	Directory full.
−34	Disk full.
−35	No such drive.
−36	I/O error.
−37	Bad name.
−38	File not open.
−39	End of file reached while reading.
−40	Attempted to position before start of file.
−41	Memory full.
−42	Too many files open.
−43	File not found.
−44	Volume physically locked.
−45	File locked.
−46	Volume locked by software flag.
−47	File busy: attempt to delete open file(s).
−48	Duplicate file name.
−49	File already open for writing.
−50	Error in file specification or disk drive information.
−51	Attempted to use improper file path.
−52	Error getting file position.
−53	Disk ejected or volume offline.
−54	Attempt to open locked file for writing.
−55	Volume already mounted and online.
−56	No such drive.
−57	Not a Macintosh disk.

TABLE B.2:   General Error Alert Codes (continued)

File Errors	
ERROR	**ERROR MESSAGE**
−58	External file system error.
−59	Problem during rename.
−60	Bad block on master directory: must reinitialize.
−61	Writing to read-only file.

Disk Errors	
ERROR	**ERROR MESSAGE**
−64	Drive disconnected.
−65	No disk inserted.
−66	Disk seems blank.
−67	Can't find address mark.
−68	Verification of read failed.
−69	Bad address mark.
−70	Bad address mark.
−71	Missing data mark.
−72	Bad data mark.
−73	Bad data mark.
−74	Write underrun occurred.
−75	Drive error.
−76	Can't find track 0.
−77	Can't initialize disk controller chip.
−78	Tried to read side 2 of disk in single-sided drive.
−79	Can't correctly adjust disk speed.
−80	Drive error.
−81	Can't find sector.

TABLE B.2:   General Error Alert Codes (continued)

Clock Chip Errors	
ERROR	**ERROR MESSAGE**
−85	Can't read clock.
−86	Verification of time changed failed.
−87	Verification of parameter RAM failed.
−88	Validity status not $A8.

AppleTalk Errors	
ERROR	**ERROR MESSAGE**
−91	Socket already active or not known.
−92	Data-size error.
−93	Bridge between two AppleTalk networks missing.
−94	Protocol error.
−95	Can't get clear signal to send.
−97	Can't open driver because port already in use.
−98	Can't open driver because port not set for connection.

Scrap Errors	
ERROR	**ERROR MESSAGE**
−100	Clipboard not initialized.
−102	Scrap Manager doesn't contain data of type requested.

Memory Errors	
ERROR	**ERROR MESSAGE**
−108	Not enough heap memory.
−109	NIL master pointer.
−111	Attempt to use free block.

TABLE B.2:   General Error Alert Codes (continued)

Memory Errors	
ERROR	**ERROR MESSAGE**
−112	Attempt to use purge locked block.
−117	Block is locked.

Resource Errors	
ERROR	**ERROR MESSAGE**
−192	Resource not found.
−193	Resource file not found.
−194	Unable to add resource.
−195	Unable to remove resource.

More AppleTalk Errors	
ERROR	**ERROR MESSAGE**
−1024 to −3109	AppleTalk Error Range.

TABLE B.2: General Error Alert Codes (continued)

HARDWARE ("SAD MAC") ERROR CODES

On the Mac Plus and earlier machines, hardware errors are characterized by a single line of six numbers under the Sad Mac icon, as shown in Table B.3.

On the SE and SE/30 computers, errors are characterized by two lines of eight numbers under the Sad Mac icon, as shown in Table B.4.

On the Mac II, startup chimes have diagnostic significance, as described in Table B.5.

NUMBERS	MEANING
010601	ROMs are mismatched.
014120	Analog board needs adjusting.
01FE01	Mismatched ROMs.
03002-030080	Logic board problem. SIMMs 1 and 3?
030100-03800	Logic board problem. SIMMs 2 and 4?
0F000A	Bad partition map on an external SCSI HD.
0F000D	Programmer's interrupt switch is contacting logic board switch.
0F0002	Logic board problem. Damaged traces?
0F0002&3	Problem with HD partition map.
0F0064	Incompatible system software.
000001-008000	Logic board problem. Soldered-on RAM.

TABLE B.3:   Error Codes on the Mac Plus and Earlier Models

FIRST ROW	SECOND ROW	MEANING
00000001-0000000E	00000000-08000800	Problem is on the logic board. Check SIMMs.
0000000F	00000003	Hard drive problems.
0_0_0_0_	0_F_0_F_ or F_0_F_0_	Problem is on the logic board. Check SIMMs.
0_0_0_	F_0_F_0_	Problem is on the logic board. Check SIMMs.

TABLE B.4:   Error Codes on the SE and SE/30

CHIMES	MEANING
Error chord, two sets of different tones.	Logic board or SCSI problem?
Two sets of different tones.	SCSI problem?
High note, then above four.	SIMM problem?
High note, higher note, above four.	SIMM problem?
Power light, but no chimes.	Problem with logic board.

TABLE B.5:   Mac II Startup Chimes and Their Meanings

Glossary

Sometimes computer jargon can confuse even an old hand, which is why it's hard to imagine a computer book without a glossary. One warning about the following and any other Macintosh glossary: some terms may have different meanings in other platforms. Mac glossaries are Mac-specific.

A/UX Apple/Unix. Apple's version of the Unix multitasking operating system. Unix has historically run on workstation-class computers. A fast 68030 or 68020 Mac and a PMMU is required.

Accelerators Add-on boards that replace a standard Mac processor with a faster CPU and fast memory.

Access time The time required for read-write heads to locate a sector on a disk. Usually expressed as average access time.

ADB The Apple Desktop Bus. The low-speed bus that handles the Mac keyboard and a variety of peripherals.

AppleTalk Apple's networking software. Usable with LocalTalk and Ethernet hardware.

ASCII   The American Standard Code for Information Interchange. Completely described with seven-bit binary code. $2^7=128$ characters. An extended ASCII code is in the works.

ASIC   Application-specific integrated circuit. An integrated circuit designed for a specific control application.

AT command set   The standard for modem commands. Developed by Hayes.

Auto-answer   Setting on a modem that has it answer the phone automatically.

Background printing   The System 7 process in which a print file is handled as a low-priority or "background" job.

Baud   Bits per second. A measure of modem speed, but not a complete evaluation of modem data transfer efficiency. Modems can require ten bits or more per character sent.

BBS   Bulletin board system. A remote computer system equipped with a modem, hard drive, and BBS software. With a computer and modem, you can access discussion groups, news, and public domain files.

Bidirectional printing   Many non-laser printers have the option of printing in both directions to eliminate carriage returns and increase print speed.

Bit   Smallest unit of computer information, conveying only "yes" or "no" (on or off).

Boot blocks   The area on a boot device that starts the Mac boot process, and loads additional boot code that continues the process.

Buffer   An area of memory used to hold data temporarily until it can be downloaded to the main computer or peripheral memory. Examples are modem and printer buffers.

Bus masters   Expansion cards that take control of the Mac system bus to initiate high-speed data transfers.

Byte   Eight bits.

Cache   An area of main memory used to store the last executed instructions, which increases the processor's speed by reducing its need to access the disk, or a fast memory area used to increase processor speed by reducing its need to access slower main memory.

Cartridge hard drives   Hard drives with the "platters," spindle, and sometimes, the heads in a removable metal or plastic cartridge. The most common Mac cartridge drive is the SyQuest drive, with a plastic disk cartridge.

CD-ROM Compact disk-read only memory—A data disk in audio CD format. Information is stored as "pits" in a metallic surface, and cannot be erased (which is why it's "read only"). Capacity is 600MB to 1GB.

cdev Control Panel device. A Macintosh application or utility that's accessed through the Macintosh Control Panel.

Checksum Sum of the value of a series of bytes. Can be compared to a previous checksum for error checking.

Clock speed Computer operations are timed by the system clock oscillator, and the faster the clock speed, the more operations executed per second. The system chip and clock have to be compatible to avoid damage.

CMYK A color reproduction process that uses cyan-magenta-yellow-black color separations.

Compact Macintosh Apple's original Macintosh design with everything, including monitor and drives, included in one case.

Compression The process of reducing the size of a file by removing redundancy (in the form of often-repeated bytes) and replacing it with codes.

Coprocessors Chips that "offload" tasks (such as video updates, mathematics, or control of the SCSI bus) from the CPU.

Copy back cache A caching method in which data is written to main memory only when necessary or requested.

Corona wire The positively charged wire in a laser printer that transfers its charge to copier paper passing under it. Negatively charged toner clings to the paper.

Corrupted Refers to an application, data file, or System file structure that contains a number of fatal errors.

CPS In printing, characters per second.

CPU Central processing unit. Depending on the usage, can refer to the main processor chip in a computer—in Macs, the 680x0 series—or the entire system "box."

CRC Cyclical redundancy check. During data transmission, data is sent with a checksum. If the receiving device doesn't get the same checksum, it requests a resend.

Cut-sheet feeder An attachment for dot-matrix printers. Used to feed single sheets.

DAT Digital audio tape. A high-density (up to 1.3GB/cartridge) 4 mm digital tape storage medium.

Data and resource forks Portions of a Mac file used to store data and program codes, respectively.

DIP Dual inline package. Refers to chips (like RAM chips) with two sets of vertical pins, one per side.

DIP SIMMs Dual inline package SIMMs, which are taller than SOJ SIMMs. The RAM chips have pins instead of surface-mount solder pads. Pins are inserted through the SIMM board and soldered.

DIP switches Sets of small switches used to configure some printers (generally printers made for PCs) or other devices. DIP stands for dual inline package, like the chips. DIPs are on-off "toggle" switches.

Disk arrays Redundant groups of hard drives that write the same data simultaneously, preventing data loss in the event of a single drive failure.

Disk fragmentation The breakup of data blocks on a disk drive, resulting from continual copying and deleting of files. Creates gradually increasing file access times.

DMA Direct memory access. The process by which a device controller accesses system memory directly, without requiring the intervention of the CPU.

Dot-matrix A printer that works by firing a pattern of pins at an ink ribbon and paper.

DPI Dots per inch. Used to measure printer, mouse, scanner, and other I/O device resolution.

Emulator A software or hardware device for simulating a computer or terminal.

Error-correction protocol A modem protocol for creating checksums and, if necessary, resending data.

Ethernet High-speed network hardware (up to 10 megabits/sec) that can use coaxial cable or twisted two-pair wire. A better solution than Apple LocalTalk hardware for high-speed data transfer.

Fax modem A modem that can transmit and receive text and data to and from a facsimile machine.

FDHD The Mac's high-density drive. Stands for floppy drive high density. An FDHD drive can read and write HFS (Mac), ProDos (Apple II), and MS-DOS disks and files. Also called a SuperDrive.

Floptical drives SCSI devices, with up to 20MB capacity, that use optical tracks on special media to control data storage. These devices have fast access times and can use ordinary floppy disks.

FPU Floating point unit. See "Numeric coprocessor."

Fuser rollers Heated rollers that fuse toner onto a laser printer page.

Gap bytes Used as "padding" between sector data.

Gateway A hardware and software combination used to link two different networks.

Gigabyte 1.073 billion bytes, or 1024 megabytes. Abbreviated GB.

GIS Geographic Information System. A mapping and database application specifically designed to handle the acquisition and display of geographical data.

Graphics tablets Input devices in which a sensing tablet with a wire grid detects the position of a graphics pen via radio frequency emissions from the pen.

Grayscale Monitor that displays up to 256 true shades of gray. This lets it display graphics with almost photographic quality.

Handshaking Refers to the process of establishing communication between two computers, or a computer and a peripheral.

HFS Hierarchical File System. The Mac disk "filing system."

init System initialization file. A utility or application that installs itself in memory at boot up.

Initialize On a hard drive, refers to the process of writing the HFS "filing system." On a floppy drive, refers to the process both of writing physical tracks and sectors *and* of writing the HFS filing system.

Inkjet printer Printer that operates by heating up ink and causing it to form a "bubble," jetting out of a nozzle and onto the printer paper.

Interleave Also called "skew." Recording patterns used to optimize hard drives of different speeds. A fast machine would use 1:1 interleave, or a pattern going straight through sectors 1-2-3-4. 2:1 interleave would move between sectors in a pattern like 1-11-2-12-3-13.

Interrupts Instructions telling a processor to stop operations while an external process is carried out.

Jumpers Small connector blocks that "short out" pins on a circuit board to set the board's configuration. They are found on hard drives and other devices like the "jumper" SE.

Kilobyte Abbreviated K. 1024 bytes.

Killy clip A plastic device with metal spring clips that fits over a CPU and is used to attach an expansion board in Macs without a slot.

Laser printer A printer that uses Xerographic (photocopier) technology in conjunction with a laser or LED to create an image.

LCD Liquid crystal display. Laptops commonly use LCD displays because they are moderately sharp and use little power.

LED Light-emitting diode. Small lights used by hard drives, some expansion cards, and some laser printers.

Local area networks (LANs) A number of computers cabled to each other and a file server in a relatively small area.

LocalTalk Apple's networking hardware. Consists of cable and LocalTalk boxes with two mini-Din 8 connectors each. Connection is in daisy-chain fashion via individual Mac AppleTalk ports. A somewhat slow protocol.

Logic board The main circuit board of a computer, containing the CPU, controller chips, ports, and slots, if any.

Low-level format The process that writes the physical tracks and sectors on a hard drive.

Megabit Abbreviated Mb. 1,048,576 bits.

Megabyte Abbreviated MB. 1,048,576 bytes (1024 kilobytes).

Memory fragmentation The "breakup" of disk memory blocks that occurs when a number of programs are copied to and deleted from memory. When fragmentation gets bad enough, "out of memory" errors will result.

Modem MOdulator-DEModulator. A modem translates digital data into the modulation of an audio carrier wave, to let computers communicate by telephone.

Modem registers The internal modem memory where settings are stored and changed.

Modular Macintosh Any one of Apple's "newer" Macs, starting with the Mac II, that consist of a modules—CPU, monitor, external drive, and so forth.

Molex connector A small modular connector, keyed to prevent incorrect insertion. Used for the Mac speaker connector.

Monochrome A monitor displaying only black and white. Each computer pixel is represented by a data bit with only two settings: 1 (on) and 0 (off). Sometimes called a 1-bit display.

Motherboard What everybody used to call a logic board before we went uptown.

Mounting The process of placing a device icon on the Mac desktop and having it recognized by the Mac file system.

Mousestick A joystick that plugs into the Mac's ADB port.

MTBF Mean time between failures. A statistical measure of peripheral reliability and life span. "Statistical" means there's no guarantee that the peripheral will survive to the MTBF hour value.

Multimedia The integration of still graphics, animation, and sound into a presentation.

MultiSync monitor A monitor that is able to adjust itself to a variety of input frequencies provided by a number of different graphics controller cards.

Multitasking A computer processing method in which the CPU switches rapidly between a number of programs, making it appear to be executing them simultaneously.

Nanosecond One billionth of a second. Used when measuring computer operation speed and the speed of memory chips.

NuBus A standard for expansion card and bus design developed by Texas Instruments and adopted by Apple for the Mac. The bus does not require any hardware or software configuration.

Numeric coprocessor, or floating point unit (FPU) Coprocessor chip specially designed to handle complex numeric calculations such as floating point arithmetic and transcendental functions.

Parallel communications Parallel interfaces send data eight bits at a time. The interface is relatively quick but not "intelligent." Commonly used by PC printers.

Parity checking A simple error-checking protocol frequently used in SIMMs destined for Mac government applications. The parity check helps to guarantee SIMM integrity.

Peripheral A device that plugs into a Mac to perform a function. Peripherals include monitors, keyboards, printers, and external storage devices.

PGA Pin grid array package. Multi-pin package chip typically used for advanced CPU and FPU applications.

PMMU   Paged memory management unit. The chip that handles transfer of memory "pages" to and from a storage device. Built into the 68030 chip.

PostScript   Adobe's page-description language, built into many laser printers.

PowerPC   A high-speed RISC (Reduced Instruction Set Computing) chip produced by Motorola, using IBM-licensed technology, for computers made by Apple and IBM.

PPM   Pages per minute. Generally used to time a laser or similar printer's print speed.

PRAM   Macintosh Parameter RAM. Battery-powered memory where settings made with the Control Panel or Chooser are kept. You can clear ("zap") the PRAM, by pressing Command-Option-Shift while choosing the Control Panel. On a Plus or earlier, unplug the machine and remove the battery.

Print spooler   Software that portions out, or spools, a print job to memory or disk and gradually feeds it to the printer during "free" CPU periods. This lets you continue to work on your computer even while you print.

Protocol   A hardware or software compression or modulation standard.

Public-domain software   Software that is released by its author to the public. Shareware is released on a trial basis. You pay the author if you like it. Freeware is released free of any charges.

QuickTime   Apple's multimedia operating system tools.

Qwerty   The standard typewriter keyboard, used by all computers. Refers to the letter keys just below the number row on the left side.

RAM   Random access memory. A computer's "short-term memory."

RAM disk   An area of RAM memory that's used as a fast disk drive. Anything stored in a RAM disk is volatile and disappears when power is turned off.

RFI   Radio frequency interference. Interference in the radio band resulting from computer electronics. Commonly guarded against with metal RFI shielding.

RGB   Red-green-blue. Color reproduction, on screen or in print, that creates color through combinations of red, green, and blue.

RJ-11 The "modular telephone jack" connector used for keyboards in the Mac Plus and earlier, and for modem phone line jacks.

ROM Read-only memory. A computer's "long-term memory."

SCSI Small computer systems interface. A fast parallel interface for connecting peripherals to a Mac.

Sectors Segments of a track where data is written. The smallest unit of data storage.

Seek time Another name for "access time" (defined above).

Send fax Type of modem that is capable only of compiling and sending a fax document. It can be built much more cheaply than a send/receive fax modem.

Serial communications Refers to the process of sending data a bit at a time, sequentially. Devices using serial communication are capable of "intelligent" interconnection.

SIMM Single in-line memory module. A memory expansion board for Macs with eight (or nine in the case of parity SIMMs) RAM chips soldered on. Common sizes are 1MB, 4MB, and 16MB.

SOJ SIMMs Surface-mounted SIMMs. Have a lower profile than DIP (dual inline package) SIMMs and are ideal for the tight areas in compact Mac cases.

Spooler See "Print spooler."

SQL Structured query language. A database access language that lets you build custom queries for a database.

SRAM (static RAM) Static RAM does not have to be periodically "refreshed" by an electrical current to preserve memory, like dynamic RAM. SRAM is fast and expensive.

SuperDrive See "FDHD."

SWIM chip Super Wozniak Integrated Machine. The chip that powers Apple's FDHD drive. Allows the drive to read and write ProDos, MS-DOS, and HFS disks.

Terminator Resistor pack used at the end of a SCSI chain to absorb signals and prevent bounce-back "noise" on the SCSI bus.

Thermal printer Specialized printer that uses a hot print head and wax-based ink. Many also come with the PostScript page-description language.

32-bit clean Applications and hardware that can work with Apple's latest 32-bit addressing scheme, for memory upgrades potentially up to 1GB.

Token Ring   IBM network hardware. Can be utilized by a Mac with an Apple TokenTalk card. Previous versions had a transfer speed of 4Mbs (megabits/second), newer versions transfer at 16Mbs.

Toner   Dry ink used by photocopiers and laser printers.

Touch screen   A touch-sensitive monitor cover that detects the position of your finger and moves the Mac cursor accordingly.

Touchpad   A device that uses the position of a finger on a capacitance-sensitive pad to control the Mac cursor.

Trackball   A stationary device with buttons and a ball in the top. The Mac cursor is controlled by moving the ball with a finger. A "drag button" is required to allow you to drag and drop icons.

Tracks   Concentric areas on a computer disk where data, organized in tracks and sectors, is written.

Tractor feed   A method of feeding paper to a dot-matrix printer, using rollers with pins and paper with perforated, removable edges.

Transcendental functions   Logarithmic and trigonometric functions. Generally, these benefit the most from an FPU.

Virtual memory   Areas of a hard disk that are treated as system RAM. Data is swapped to and from these areas as necessary.

Voice interface   A combination of microphone, interface, and software that allows you to control your computer with voice commands. The interface has to be trained.

VRAM (Video RAM)   Video memory. Adding additional VRAM allows a Mac to display higher graphic resolutions.

WORM   Write-once, read-many. A permanent recording mechanism. Lasers burn permanent recording pits into optical disk media. Capable of 600-1000MB of data storage.

Writethrough cache   A caching process in which data is written both to cache and to system memory to preserve data integrity.

WYSIWYG   "What you see is what you get." What you see on screen will be reproduced on your printout. One of the Mac's best features, and one of its best acronyms.

Troubleshooting

For easy reference, here's a collection of trouble-shooting tips for the upgrades described in this book.

MAC CRACKING

Problem	Cause	Solution
Cables can't be removed.	Tight connectors.	*Carefully* wiggle connectors until they can be removed.
Parts don't fit properly.	Inserted incorrectly.	Check again, replace carefully. Obviously, computer parts are not designed to be tight.
Bent pins on chips.	Inserting this way will damage them further.	Straighten pins with a pin straightener.

Problem	Cause	Solution
Video problems after opening case.	Probably a loose video connector.	Reopen and tighten up.
Sad Mac error codes.	If it occurs after a memory upgrade, improperly installed SIMMs.	Open the case and reinstall.
Floppy drive doesn't take disks correctly.	Misaligned drive.	Reinstall, realign with a floppy in the drive.
Hard drive won't spin up.	Loose power connector.	Open case and "snug up."

INSTALLING MEMORY

Problem	Cause	Solution
Sad Mac errors after memory installation.	Possibly incorrect memory, poor installation, or improper installation.	Check and reinstall memory.
Mac II startup chime followed by high note, four-note sound, screen blackout.	Possible SIMM problems.	Check and reinstall.
SIMM connectors smudged with oil from fingers.	SIMM connectors not handled carefully.	Remove with a *clean* eraser or a *small* amount of 99% isopropyl alcohol. Should be clean before inserting.

INSTALLING AN ACCELERATOR

Problem	Cause	Solution
Intermittent problems or "flaky" behavior.	Possible accelerator/System init, cdev conflict.	Selectively remove or deactivate.

No power and computer plugged in.	Accelerator not getting power.	If accelerator has separate power supply, check. Otherwise check logic board power.
Strange video, i.e., checkerboard or vertical lines, on boot.	Possible bent pins, poor video connection.	Reconnect video board.
Wavering vertical lines after powerup.	Accelerator power not connected properly.	If board has auxiliary power supply, not properly connected. Otherwise check main board supply.
Sad Mac on powerup.	Incorrect or incorrectly installed accelerator memory. Incorrect logic board memory.	Reinstall.
Intermittent Sad Mac or system bombs.	Software conflicts, poor connection with Killy clip, or intermittent power.	Check.

INSTALLING AN FPU OR CACHE CARD

Problem	Cause	Solution
Mac will not boot or locks up.	Cache or FPU card software conflicts with system extensions and control panels.	Selectively remove or disable.
Still having problems after above.	Possible corrupted System file.	Repair or replace.
Don't get a normal start sound, or get a different sound.	Possible defective or damaged board.	Return and replace.
Getting "flaky" software behavior with cache board or FPU turned on.	Incompatibility of cache or FPU with your software.	Turn the cache or FPU off, if possible.

INSTALLING MAC STORAGE

Problem	Cause	Solution
Happy Mac appears, then a floppy and question mark.	Corrupted boot blocks, System file, or disk logical structure.	Use disk recovery program, reinstall System and driver.
Flashing Happy Mac, drive does not boot.	Corrupted boot blocks or System files.	Use disk recovery or reinstall System.
Happy Mac, drive seeks constantly before boot.	Hard reset without proper exit, Mac reverifying data structures.	No problem. Run disk first aid.
Sad Mac.	0F or 000F software, else hardware.	Check for source of hard or software problems (see Appendix B, Table B.3).
No drive activity.	Blown fuse or power supply problem.	Replace fuse or power supply.
Partial drive mount followed by crash.	Virus, corrupted System, not enough System 6 heap space, multiple System files, corrupted logical structure.	Virus checker, disk repair utility, heap expander, remove one System file, disk repair utility, or restore from backup.
Device does not mount.	Potential connection, media, SCSI, or other problems.	Try each of the above.
"Do you want to initialize?" message.	Corrupted logical structures.	Run recovery program.
Drive mounts but cannot be used for startup.	Bad boot blocks or hardware problem.	Check startup Control Panel, hardware connections, system software.

INSTALLING AN I/O DEVICE

Problem	Cause	Solution
The device is plugged in, but doesn't work.	No apparent problems.	Check ADB connections, control software, settings.

The device is connected, but doesn't work.	ADB connector wiggles.	You may have a bad ADB connector.
The device is connected, but doesn't work.	You plugged it into the ADB with power on.	*Arrrghhh!!!* You may have blown an ADB fuse or cooked the controller.
Your mouse doesn't track well and the pointer moves erratically.	The mouse ball may be dirty.	Wash ball with warm, soapy water, dry with a lint-free cloth, replace.
Your optical mouse doesn't work.	The mouse got zapped with static electricity.	Unplug and replug. Hopefully, this will do the trick.
You spilled pop in your keyboard and it sticks.	The pop is sticking in the keys and may corrode contacts.	*Carefully* pry up keys and clean keyboard with iso-propyl alcohol (watch for reactions!).

INSTALLING A SOFTWARE UPGRADE

Problem	Cause	Solution
Unexpected application bombs.	Too little RAM allocated to application.	Check "About the Finder" for memory use. Close some applications. Eventually add memory.
Frequent "Out of Memory" errors with lots of system memory.	Too little RAM allocated to application.	Select application and choose "Get Info" from file menu. If application memory too small, increase.
Frequent bombs and unexplained quits on a loaded System 6.	Running out of system heap memory.	Use HeapFixer or BootMan to increase heap size.
Strange behavior of an application under System 7.	Program may not be 7-compatible.	Check and upgrade if possible.
Application bombs under 32-bit addressing.	Program may not be "32-bit clean."	Check and upgrade if possible.

"REPACKING" A MAC

Problem	Cause	Solution
You only have a checkerboard, lines, or garbage on the video screen.	Your video card or cable is loose.	Tighten up the card or cables.
Your drives won't power up.	You may have bad connections or power supply.	Check connections and the power supply.
You've got a Sad Mac error after adding memory.	You've installed the wrong memory, done it in the wrong order, or the SIMMs are loose.	Check SIMMs and reinstall.
"Flaky" behavior of some software.	May be accelerator or control software incompatibility.	Turn off accelerator or FPU patch, if installed.

INSTALLING A PRINTER

Problem	Cause	Solution
Print file sent, but no output.	Printer not selected in chooser.	Go to chooser and select the printer.
Font output on printer is not what you selected.	Font substitution may be occurring.	Make sure correct fonts are available.
Print output is slow.	Not using optimum printer setup.	Consider faster printer drivers or Paralink cable if possible.
Can't print a PostScript graphic.	Running out of page-compilation memory.	Install more printer memory.
Jamming problems on a dot-matrix printer.	Paper path skewed or tractors incorrectly set.	Adjust tractors and rollers, leave one tractor unlocked.
Print on dot-matrix printer too light.	Incorrect paper thickness setting.	Adjust paper thickness setting.

| No Apple LaserWriter test page, test LED is blinking or stays on. | Possible problem with logic board. | Take printer in for repair. |

INSTALLING MODEMS

Problem	**Cause**	**Solution**
Your telecom program logs in, then you get a screenful of garbage characters.	Problem with settings.	Reset data bits, stop bits, parity.
You can't use a high-speed modem with your Mac.	You've got the wrong cable.	Get a cable that supports hardware handshaking.
You can't use all your modem's features.	You don't have the right driver for your modem.	Get and install the correct driver.

INSTALLING A NETWORK

Problem	**Cause**	**Solution**
Computers or printers "not visible" to network.	Bad cables or connections.	Use a network *poller*, like NetAtlas or InterPoll, to diagnose cable integrity.
Network is slowing down.	Bad device causing spurious signals on network, or poor design and heavy traffic areas creating slowdowns.	Try using a traffic monitor like Farallon's TrafficWatch II or EtherPeek.
Network Printer access is slow.	Heavy printer load is causing a slowdown.	Dedicate a computer as a print server.
Network communication is slow.	LocalTalk hardware is too slow for you.	Try Ethernet or other fast hardware.

INSTALLING A MULTIMEDIA SYSTEM

Problem	Cause	Solution
QuickTime movies won't play on the system.	68000 Mac used.	QuickTime requires a 68020 CPU or better.
Slow performance of animations in HyperCard.	Possible inefficient script used.	Try to "streamline" animation script.
Slow performance of MacroMind Director.	Complex script.	Try MacroMind Accelerator.
Slow performance of QuickTime.	Too much data being shuffled around.	Reduce size of animation window.
Grainy background or animations.	Lower resolution data used.	Use a higher resolution capture.

INSTALLING A HARDWARE OR SOFTWARE EMULATOR

Problem	Cause	Solution
Your Mac software will not translate a file that it has translators for.	Your software may not recognize newer versions of the data file.	Check the file type and resave in an older format or get newer file translators.
You cannot access your hardware emulator card.	You may not have the necessary hardware drivers loaded for the card.	Make sure that the driver software is on your hard drive.
Your lab measurement software is "dropping" data.	Your machine may not be able to keep up with the amount of data that's being transferred.	Try a faster machine or a larger data buffer.
Software run with the emulator locks, gives error messages, or crashes after starting to boot.	Possible incompatibility with older operating system.	Make sure that you have a compatible operating system installed.

Problem

Screen graphics look odd with software run on a Mac LC Apple IIe emulator board.

Cause

The difference between Mac and Apple pixels produces some strange effects, at least with older emulator boards.

Solution

If this causes problems, you may want to try a newer board or an upgrade if one becomes available.

Index...

Q

Help Yourself with
Another Quality Sybex Book

Macintosh System 7 at Your Fingertips
Nancy B. Dannenberg

This quick-reference guide is a must for System 7 users. It offers fast access to concise information on every feature of the system, with reference entries organized alphabetically by topic. Perfect for experienced users seeking brief explanations of new features or for anyone who sometimes needs a quick answer on the job. Includes an overview of new features.

235pp; 4 3/4" x 8"
ISBN: 0-7821-1001-0

Available
at Better
Bookstores
Everywhere

Sybex Inc.
2021 Challenger Drive
Alameda, CA 94501
Telephone (800) 227-2346
Fax (510) 523-2373

SYBEX

Sybex. Help Yourself.

SYBEX

FREE BROCHURE!

Complete this form today, and we'll send you a full-color brochure of Sybex bestsellers.

Please supply the name of the Sybex book purchased.

_____

How would you rate it?

_____ Excellent   _____ Very Good   _____ Average   _____ Poor

Why did you select this particular book?

_____ Recommended to me by a friend

_____ Recommended to me by store personnel

_____ Saw an advertisement in _____

_____ Author's reputation

_____ Saw in Sybex catalog

_____ Required textbook

_____ Sybex reputation

_____ Read book review in _____

_____ In-store display

_____ Other _____

Where did you buy it?

_____ Bookstore

_____ Computer Store or Software Store

_____ Catalog (name: _____)

_____ Direct from Sybex

_____ Other: _____

Did you buy this book with your personal funds?

_____ Yes   _____ No

About how many computer books do you buy each year?

_____ 1-3   _____ 3-5   _____ 5-7   _____ 7-9   _____ 10+

About how many Sybex books do you own?

_____ 1-3   _____ 3-5   _____ 5-7   _____ 7-9   _____ 10+

Please indicate your level of experience with the software covered in this book:

_____ Beginner   _____ Intermediate   _____ Advanced

Which types of software packages do you use regularly?

_____ Accounting   _____ Databases   _____ Networks

_____ Amiga   _____ Desktop Publishing   _____ Operating Systems

_____ Apple/Mac   _____ File Utilities   _____ Spreadsheets

_____ CAD   _____ Money Management   _____ Word Processing

_____ Communications   _____ Languages   _____ Other _____
                                                                    (please specify)

Which of the following best describes your job title?

_____ Administrative/Secretarial   _____ President/CEO

_____ Director   _____ Manager/Supervisor

_____ Engineer/Technician   _____ Other _____
                                         (please specify)

Comments on the weaknesses/strengths of this book: _____

_____

_____

_____

_____

Name _____

Street _____

City/State/Zip _____

Phone _____

PLEASE FOLD, SEAL, AND MAIL TO SYBEX

SYBEX, INC.
Department M
2021 CHALLENGER DR.
ALAMEDA, CALIFORNIA USA
94501

SYBEX

SEAL

THE MAC UPGRADE TOOLKIT (ALL MACS)

- An antistatic wrist strap
- A pair of needle-nose pliers for a variety of jobs, including holding and inserting small screws
- A medium-size Phillips screwdriver to use when dismantling your Mac
- A small electronic or jeweler's screwdriver

FOR COMPACT MACS ONLY

- A 1" spring clamp for "cracking" the compact Mac case
- A soft pad to set the Mac upon when cracking the case
- A long flat-bladed, insulated screwdriver to drain residual charge from a compact Mac CRT
- A grounding wire to discharge a compact Mac CRT anode
- A Torx screwdriver, at least 9" (22.86 cm) long
- For the PowerBook 140/170, #8 and #10 Torx screwdrivers